# Human Rights in India: Theory and Practice

# Human Rights in India
## Theory and Practice

Satnam Singh Deol

SERIALS PUBLICATIONS
NEW DELHI (INDIA)

First Published – 2011

ISBN: 978-81-8387-464-9



*Published by*

**SERIALS PUBLICATIONS**
4830/24, 1st Floor, Ansari Road
Darya Ganj, New Delhi-110002 (India)
Phone : 23245225. Fax : 91-11-23272135
E-mail : serials@sify.com
serialspublications.india@gmail.com
Website: www.serialspublications.com

## *Dedicated to*

The violators who do not know
what the word HUMAN means
&
The victimized who do not know
what the word RIGHTS means

## Contents

## Foreword

It is with great pleasure that I write a foreword to this unique exposition and analysis of theory and practice of human rights in India. India's acknowledgement and commitment to human rights has been explicit since time immemorial. India percepts its own theory of human rights that is totally unique to the Western perspective and all other third world countries. Indian perspective of human rights glows from its great social, religious and political historical developments that took place during different eras. Especially since Independence, all required and expected provisions are commenced in its Constitution and Law for the promotion and protection of human rights. But in spite of a well designed theory of human rights, the actual state of human rights in India is totally dissatisfactory. Violation of various categories of human rights of Indian people is a depressing reality of Indian scenario.

There can be a few researchers better equipped to reveal the real and systematic picture of theory and practice of human rights than Dr. S.S. Deol. His specialization and research expertise in the field of human rights supplement and complement to make him write in the field of human rights. Although, he is still much younger and has been recently awarded Ph.D degree by the P.U. Patiala for his research in human rights, he has authored several research papers on human rights which have got published in various national and international journals. He has been consistently active in participating and presenting papers in various conferences, seminars and lectures.

Present work is a distinctive scholarly manuscript that observes and analyses the established theory and actual practice of human rights in India. The book, in its forefront chapters, discusses the meaning, nature, characteristics, classification and different theories of human rights along with the historical development and the western viewpoint of human rights. Discourses on the theory of human rights especially in Indian context is the lime-light of the part one of the book. The second part of the book deals with the actual practice of human rights in India. In this part author has observed, under different chapters, various forms of human rights violations taking lace in India including custodial violence, unlawful killings, violence against women, violation of child rights, and violation of the rights of the SCs and STs. Scientific methodology, empirical observation and critical analysis establishes the book as a significant and valuable text manifesting theory and practice of human rights in India.

This book is an exceptional document for those who want to be acquainted with the detailed theory and actual practice of human rights in India. The scholars, teachers, researchers and students of the subject of human rights must read this book that shall definitely comprehend their knowledge as far as their enthusiasm to be familiar with the theory and practice of human rights is concerned.

**Dr. Jagroop Kaur**
Professor & Head,
Department of Political Science,
Punjabi University, Patiala.

## Acknowledgement

I take this opportunity to express my deepest sense of gratitude to all those who enabled me to author this book. I really feel indebted towards my parents who facilitated, appreciated and supported me much more than my needs and expectations. Undoubtedly, bursting credit goes to my wife also for being so patient, supportive for getting my book completed. I convey my apology to my little innocent kid for not spending much time to play with him while authoring this book.

Writing a book on such a vast subject like human rights is impossible without constant help and valuable suggestions from the eminent scholars. It is my cherished privilege to gratefully acknowledge my sincere gratitude to Dr. Jagroop Kaur, Professor & Head, Department of Political Science, Punjabi University, Patiala. Her prompt help, perceptive observations and insight suggestions motivated me to dedicate myself heart and soul to this book. I express my deepest regards and sincere thanks to Dr. Narinder Kumar Dogra (Professor), Dr. Manju Verma (Professor), Dr. Satish Kumar Sharma (Professor), Dr. Surinder Kaur Guraya (Professor), Dr. Dalbir Kaur Bajwa (Reader) at the Department of Political Science of Punjabi University, Patiala for their scholarly suggestions. I owe my sincere thanks to Dr. Jamsheed Ali Khan, Professor of Political Science at the Department of Distance Education of Punjabi University, Patiala for his valuable suggestions and prompt help.

The human rights NGOs such as Human Rights Watch, Asian Centre for Human Rights, Amnesty International and PUCL deserve a gratitude for their relevant and precious reports, papers and other literature related to the theme of the book. My cordial thanks are due to all office bearers of the governmental and non-governmental human rights organisations, the lawyers, police personnel and human rights activists, who helped me in comprehending the real picture of the status of human rights in India. I will be failing in my duty if I do not acknowledge the victims of human rights violations and their relatives, who discussed frankly but truly during their interviews, the agony of their human rights violations.

I extend my thanks to my sister Mrs. Rajwinder Kaur Gill for the cooperation, generous help and good wishes provided to me during this work. I am grateful to all my friends especially Sahil Gandhi, Balwinder Singh Brar, Gurpreet Singh Brar, Khushpreet Singh Brar, whose motivation and enthusiasm helped me to complete the book.

## Abbreviations

| | | |
|---|---|---|
| **ACHR** | : | Asian Centre for Human Rights |
| **APDP** | : | Association of the Parents of Disappeared Persons |
| **APHC** | : | All Party Hurriyat Conference |
| **ASI** | : | Assistant Sub Inspector |
| **BJP** | : | Bahujan Samaj Party |
| **BSF** | : | Border Security Force |
| **CAT** | : | Convention Against Torture |
| **CBAWG** | : | Community Based Anti-Trafficking Watch Group |
| **CBI** | : | Central Bureau of Investigation |
| **CCDP** | : | Committee for Coordination on Disappearances in Punjab |
| **CIIP** | : | Committee for Information and Initiative on Punjab |
| **CIS** | : | Commonwealth of Independent States |
| **CRPF** | : | Central Reserve Police Force |
| **DGP** | : | Director General of Police |
| **DSP** | : | Deputy Superintendent of Police |
| **FGM** | : | Female Genital Mutilation |
| **FIR** | : | First Information Report |
| **HRW** | : | Human Rights Watch |
| **IG** | : | Inspector General of Police |
| **IMR** | : | Infant Mortality Rate |

| | | |
|---|---|---|
| **JC** | : | Judicial Custody |
| **KCP** | : | Kangleipak Communist Party |
| **MLA** | : | Member of Legislative Assembly |
| **NCDHR** | : | National Campaign on Dalit Human Rights |
| **NCRB** | : | National Crime Record Bureau |
| **NCRB** | : | National Crime Records Bureau of India |
| **NCW** | : | National Commission for Women |
| **NGOs** | : | Non Governmental Organisations |
| **NHRC** | : | National Human Rights Commission |
| **NPPW** | : | National Perspective Plan for Women |
| **OAU** | : | Organisation of African Unity |
| **PC** | : | Police Custody |
| **PCPNDT** | : | Pre-Conception and Pre-Natal Diagnostic Techniques |
| **PLA** | : | The People's Liberation Army |
| **PREPAK** | : | People's Revolutionary Party of Kangleipak |
| **PUCL** | : | People's Union for Civil Liberties |
| **PWG** | : | Peoples War Group |
| **RR** | : | Rashtriya Rifles |
| **SCs** | : | Scheduled Castes |
| **SGPC** | : | Shiromini Gurudwara Parbhandak Committee |
| **SHRC** | : | State Human Rights Commission |
| **SSP** | : | Senior Superintendent of Police |
| **STs** | : | Schedule Tribes |
| **U5MR** | : | Under 5 Mortality Rate |
| **UDHR** | : | Universal Declaration of Human Rights |
| **ULFA** | : | United Liberation Front of Assam |
| **UN** | : | United Nations |

| | | |
|---|---|---|
| **UNCRC** | : | United Nations Convention on Rights of the Child |
| **UNESCO** | : | United Nations Educational Scientific and Cultural Organisation |
| **UNICEF** | : | United Nations Children's Fund |
| **UNIFEM** | : | United Nations Development Fund for Women |
| **UNLF** | : | United National Liberation Front |
| **US** | : | United Nations |
| **UT** | : | Union Territory |
| **WHO** | : | World Health Orgnisation |

# Introduction

Man is a social animal. Welfare and development of human personality are the ultimate ends of all organized societies. All activities, associations and relationships in the society are initiated by the human beings for existence, survival and development of their lives. Human beings need certain type of milieu in which they can ensure the proper growth of their physical, social, economic, political and cultural life. Rights are those conditions which are essential for the all-round development of human beings.

Human rights inherit in every human being. These rights are acknowledged as being inherent, absolute, inalienable and universal privileges, which every individual must hold by virtue of his being a member of the humankind. Human rights are basic civil, political, economic, social and cultural conditions to which all individuals are entitled as human beings, equally by virtue of their humanity, irrespective of race, nationality, or membership of any particular social group.

The western perspective considers human rights as an inborn virtue of all individuals and believes that human rights are an inherent factor in all human beings. In western world, the dogma of human rights is found be originated on religion, humanitarian traditions and the resistance of human beings for liberty and equality. The Western standpoint thus establishes a modest and liberal theory of rights which assumes the man possessing certain inherent and inalienable rights since birth, and by nature. So, it is obligatory for the State to protect these natural rights of the individuals, without which the individuals cannot survive and positively expand all their innate potential abilities and capabilities.

Third World countries have not characteristically experienced the natural and individual rights of the liberals or the social and economic rights of the socialists. Diverse character of their societies has compelled them to stress on the rights of the minorities along with the whole society. That is why they prefer to provide some privileges to the marginalized sections of the society. The third world societies have comprehended that the attainment and enjoyment of the individual rights is vested in providing all rights and privileges to all groups of the society and especially the minority or marginal groups.

Although India, being a Third World country, shares similar perception of human rights which generates from the sole blender of liberal and socialist school of thought. But it possesses its own different and unique perception of human rights that emanates from its ancient culture and civilization. The Indian conception of human rights does not vision the man as an isolated individual, but the individual is a unit of a society, whose interdependent rights and duties are determined by his/her position within a hierarchical network of relationships within the society. In India, human rights movement does not develop as unrest against the political authority, but there are several social, cultural and religious circumstances which have played prominent role in the formation and practice of human rights in India. Humanistic vision of ancient scriptures, impact of religious philosophies, reform movements, British colonialism and the nationalist movement for independence influenced the perception of human rights in India and characterized the Indian human rights conception with a perspective, which is different and unique to the Western and Third World perspectives.

The Constitution adopted by the People of India in January 1950 is a mile-stone as well as a turning point in the history of the development of the notion of human rights in India. The Preamble, Fundamental Rights and the Directive Principles of State Policy together provide the basic human rights for the people of India. Democratic socialism spelt out in the Preamble and the Directive Principles is meant to provide the context in which the fulfillment of Fundamental Rights has to be achieved. While Fundamental Rights stress on individual and the existing rights, Directive Principles provide the dynamic movement towards the goal of providing collective human rights for all.

India, keeping in line with the obligation of a mature and responsible democracy, is committed to provide and protect all reasonable rights and liberties of the people. India has established different ways of protecting human rights. A written Constitution incorporating fundamental rights, an accountable parliament, an executive who is ultimately subject to the authority of elected representatives and an independent, impartial judiciary are the features of Indian polity which work to protect and enhance the human rights of people. Despite the existence of several provisions for the protection of human rights incorporated in the Indian Constitution and in the law, violation of human rights now has been taking place in almost every part of the country.

Since Independence, India has experienced terrorism and insurgency and brutal violence in its one or the other region. Religious terrorism in Punjab (1984-1995) cross-border terrorism in Jammu and Kashmir, and ethno-nationalist terrorism/ethno-linguistic terrorism in North-Eastern parts have further aggravated problem of human rights violation in India, besides other tribulations. The security forces deployed in these conflict-effected regions have reportedly deliberately or allegedly under constraint or compulsion, have lethally violated the international as well as domestic laws and norms of human rights. The police and security forces positioned in these areas have been largely involved unlawful and extra-judicial killings of the insurgents, terrorists, suspected-terrorists and even the relatives and the supporters of the terrorists. Innumerable persons are allegedly killed by the police and security forces in Punjab and Jammu & Kashmir unlawfully after arresting, detaining and torturing them in the illegal custody. These murdered persons, allegedly the terrorists or insurgents, have been exposed as disappeared from the custody of police or security forces. Besides that, torture, brutality, rape and sexual harassment of women by the security forces have also been common in these states.

The rights of women in India are in jeopardy. The existence and the survival of women in the country are at the stake as the vicious practices of 'foeticide' and 'infanticide have been frequently practiced to murder them respectively before their birth, and after their birth. Women are physically abused, sexually harassed, socially sidelined, culturally victimized, economically exploited, and politically underestimated in India. The graph of different crimes against women such as murder, rape, sale, buying, trafficking, sexual harassment, dowry demands, dowry deaths is on a consistent rise throughout the country.

The SCs (Schedule Castes) in India, known as Dalits also, are severely deprived of all physical, economic, social, cultural and political conditions which are prerequisite for their upliftment and development. The evil practice of untouchability and discrimination against SCs has still been practiced in several parts of India. Similarly the STs (Schedule Tribes) are also disadvantaged of the rights and liberties, preconditioned for their existence, survival and development. The constitutional safeguards, a number of legislative provisions along with the Protection of Civil Rights Act and the SC/ST Prevention of Atrocities Act are not yet able to promote and protect the inherent and inalienable human rights of the SCs and the STs.

As far as the state of child rights is concerned, India does not possess a satisfactory and acceptable reputation regarding the promotion and protection of child rights. The number of street children, abandoned children, unhealthy children, illiterate children, child labourers, child beggars, chiid prostitutes has been constantly increasing all over the country. The poor execution of the constitutional provisions for child rights and the disappointing implementation of the legislations privileging children have resulted in an immense violation of human rights.

In the complex circumstances when the severe violation of human rights takes place in a country in several forms, and the people belonging to all regions, genders, age-groups and social-groups become vulnerable to the lethal violation, it becomes a paramount prerequisite to obtain an in-depth and holistic study of the violation of human rights transpiring in that country. In the modern scenario, there establishes a uniform universalisation and internationalization of human rights. Therefore, human rights have come to be acknowledged nationally and internationally as a major concern and essential condition in the development not only of the individual but also of the nation and ultimately of the whole international community. Although, human rights have been acknowledged internationally and nationally from legal, theoretical and historical viewpoint, yet the practical and actual observance of the same is found to be insufficient world over. Keeping this fact in mind, it becomes imperative that while assessing human rights situation, consideration should be given to the areas in which human rights are being violated at national. Hence, the present book entitled "Human Rights in India: Theory and Practice" gains a persuasive significance due to its imperative subject-matter, thorough analysis, scientific approach and a conclusive output regarding the established theory and actual practice of human rights in India.

Although, the primary purpose of the book is to be acquainted with the 'established theory' and 'actual practice' of human rights in India. To fulfill the primary objective, the other purposes of the book are to introduce and enhance the uniform and universally accepted meaning, nature, characteristics and theories of the human rights. Moreover, the book concentrates on understanding the doctrine of human rights from historical perspective. Furthermore, the book is an attempt to understand the western perspective of human rights. Besides these objectives, the prime focus of the book is to understand the theory of human rights from Indian perspective and to be acquainted with the historical, theoretical and legal aspects of the Indian perspective of human rights. Among these, the book also focuses on recognizing the nature and areas of the violation of civil and political rights by the State in India including custodial violence, extra-judicial killings and enforced disappearances. In addition to that, the purpose of the book is to recognize the nature and areas of the violation of social, cultural and economic rights in India which preferably include the violation of the rights of women, Children, SCs and STs.

To achieve the aforesaid objectives, the book has been divided into two parts. The first part deals with the theoretical aspects of human rights developed at international as well as national level. The first part studies the universally accepted meaning, nature, features, historical development and various theories of human rights along with western perspective of human rights. However, the prime focus of that part is to study the Indian perspective of human rights from historical, theoretical and legal point of view. The second part of the book deals with the various kinds of violation of human rights taking place in India. The violation of human rights by the State agencies including custodial violence, extra-judicial killings and unlawful killings and enforced disappearances has been studied under different chapter titles. Further, different forms of violation of the rights of women, children, and SCs/STs have been studied under separate chapter titles. As far as the chapter scheme of the book is concerned, it has been divided into eleven chapters; four chapters in the first part and the remaining seven chapters in the second part of the book.

The first chapter of the book entitled as "Human Rights: A Theoretical Perspective", deals with the meaning, definition and nature of the phenomenon of human rights. All prerequisite characteristics, classifications and various theories of human rights are also discussed in the chapter along with the contemporary philosophical debates related to various aspects of human rights.

The second chapter, "Development of Human Rights: A Historical Perspective", studies the phenomenon of human rights from historical viewpoint. The recognition, acknowledgement and nature of human rights during ancient, medieval and modern periods have been discussed precisely. All noticeable events, landmark steps and developmental proceedings related to human rights occurred in various eras of human history are probably observed in the chapter. The special emphasis of the chapter is also on highlighting the role of UN (United Nations) in internationalizing and universalizing the doctrine of human rights. Besides that, the human rights developments which have taken place in various parts and poles of the world in recent history such as development of human rights in Europe, Africa, Middle-East, Asia and developments within commonwealth etc. are also taken into consideration briefly. A precise historical retrospection of human rights has also been mentioned at the end of the chapter.

The third chapter of the book entitled as "Western Perspective of Human Rights" is an analytical attempt to study the historical as well as theoretical development of human rights in the Western world. The ancient Greco-Roman traditions acknowledging the human rights explicitly or implicitly, the theory of natural law emerged during medieval period; the theory of positivism developed in early modern phase and contemporary liberal theory of human rights are discussed in the chapter.

The fourth chapter "Human Rights in India: A Theoretical Perspective" deals with the recognition, nature and predominant sources of human rights in India during the ancient, medieval and modern period of history. The religious rituals, cultural traditions and political conventions of ancient as well as medieval era, along with the proceedings of modern era such as political awakening, social reformation and nationalist movement for Independence are highlighted as the basic foundation of the Indian perspective of human rights in the chapter.

The fifth chapter of the book has been entitled as "Custodial Torture and Deaths in India: A Lethal Violation of Human Rights". The chapter is an analytical approach to understand the nature, types and causes of custodial violence in India. The chapter, at the beginning, discusses the measures taken at international as well as domestic level to define and mitigate brutal acts of custodial torture and deaths. The chapter further studies the methods and most vulnerable targets of the custodial violence. The statistical data of the total complaints of custodial deaths by NHRC (National Human Rights Commission) during 14 years of its working, and the statistical data of recent 10 years (1999-2008) displayed by NCRB (National Crime Record Bureau) regarding total number of reported cases of custodial torture and deaths throughout India has been critically analysed in the chapter with the help of appropriate figures and diagrams. The chapter also analyses the causes of custodial violence and suggests a number of recommendations to minimize the incidents of custodial violence in India.

The sixth chapter entitled as "Extra-Judicial Killings in India: A Brutal Violation of Human Rights by State" exposes the unlawful killings in the States of Punjab (during terrorism and counter-terrorism era) Jammu and Kashmir and North-Eastern States under different sub-headings. The chapter is an empirical as well as observational study to examine the nature and different forms of extra-judicial killings in these States. Case study method has been taken into consideration for being acquainted with the causes and characters of unlawful killings in different terrorism/insurgency ridden parts of the country.

The seventh chapter named "Enforced Disappearances in India: Atrocious Violation of human Rights" brings into light the vicious practice of 'enforced disappearances' executed by the Indian Police and security forces. The chapter, equipped with the case study method reveals the individual cases in which the police or security forces had first arrested the alleged persons into their custody and later those persons were shown as disappeared from the custody or even denied to ever contain them in the custody. The most-highlighted illustrative cases of enforced disappearances occurred in Punjab during counter-terrorism era (1992-1995) and the cases still occurring in Kashmir are taken into consideration. The chapter concludes that the practice of enforced disappearances has been practiced by the police and security forces as an integral part of counter-terrorism policy of the Indian state.

Earlier it was practiced in Punjab during counter-terrorism era and now it has been practiced in Kashmir frequently in spite of a strong agitation of local public, Indian civil society and international community. At the last of the chapter, a variety of suggestions are given to the Central as well as the State governments along with the police and security forces to totally prohibit the crime of enforced disappearances throughout India.

The eighth chapter has been entitled as "Violation of Women Rights in India". The chapter critically analyses various forms of violations and crimes committed against women in India. The chapter highlights the lethal crimes against women such as torture, molestation, sexual harassment, indecent behavior to women, rape, kidnapping and abduction of women, women trafficking, importation of women, dowry demands, dowry deaths, female foeticide, and female infanticide. The statistical data of NCRB of recent thirteen years (1996-2008) has been critically analyzed to be acquainted with the exact number, ratio and growth of the incidents of crimes against women India. The statistical analysis further highlights average number of various crimes reported to be committed against women in ten years, in a year, month, week, day, hour or even a minute in India. All forms of violations and crimes against women are systematically and statistically undertaken with the help of appropriate figures and diagrams. A number of suggestions for the promotion and protection of the rights of the women are presented to conclude the chapter.

The ninth chapter entitled as "Violation of Child Rights in India" focuses on the various forms of violations of human rights take place against the children in India. The problem of child labour, child abuse and its types including physical abuse, sexual abuse, emotional abuse; and all major categories of crime against children including murder, infanticide, rape, kidnapping and abduction, abetment to suicide, abandonment and exposure, procuration of minor girls, child marriage and buying and selling of girls have been spotlighted in the chapter. To obtain a scientific, accurate and statistical data regarding various categories of crime against children, the statistical data displayed by the NCRB of recent ten years (1999 to 2008) regarding various categories of crime against children has been presented in appropriate figures, tables and diagrams. The average number of various crimes reported to be committed against the children in India in ten years, in a year, in a month, in a week, in a day, in an hour or even in a minute are revealed in the chapter. Some suggestions are imparted at the end of the chapter as the possible solutions to curtail the number, intensity and area of violation of the rights of the children.

The tenth chapter of the book has been entitled as "The violation of Human Rights of SCs and STs in India". The chapter has been further partitioned into two parts; 'The Violation of the Rights of SCs' and 'The Violation of the Rights of STs'. In the first part, various categories of violations of human rights and crimes committed against SCs such as untouchability, discrimination, murder, rape, kidnapping and abduction, arson, hurt, violation of the Protection of Civil Rights Act 1955 (Prohibiting Untouchability), violation of SC/ST Prevention of Atrocities Act 1989 are taken into consideration. The statistical data of total reported cases of the crimes of various types against SCs in ten years (1999 to 2008) given by NCRB has been analyzed to identify the exact number, average, ratio and growth of various categories of crimes against the SCs. The statistical data displayed with the help of appropriate figures and diagrams, asserts the average number of various categories of crimes reported to be committed against SCs in ten years, in one year, in a month, in a week, in a day, in an hour or even in a minute. In the second part of the chapter, all major categories of violations and crimes against STs such as murder, rape, kidnapping and abduction, arson, hurt, violation of the Protection of Civil Rights Act 1955 (Prohibiting Untouchability), violation of SC/ST Prevention of Atrocities Act 1989 are discussed comprehensively. Again, the statistical data given by the NCRB regarding total number of reported cases of various types of crimes against STs in ten years (1999 to 2008) has been critically analyzed. The analysis of the figures and diagrams containing the statistical data reveals in detail the average number of the reported cases of various categories of crimes against STs in ten years, in a year, in a month, in a week, in a day, in an hour, or even in a minute. At the end of the chapter, a number of suggestions are given to minimize the violation of human rights of the SCs and STs.

The eleventh chapter of the book entitled as "Concluding Remarks" wraps up various aspects of the book under one title. The chapter principally describes the gap between the theory and practice of human rights prevailing in India.

The book is based on both primary as well as secondary sources. The primary sources include United Nations (UN) covenants, conventions, declarations and periodic reports regarding human rights; NHRC reports; NCRB's reports and statistical data; and reports of the Trans-national, national and regional NGOs working in the field of human rights. The secondary sources comprise the information obtained from books, journals, newspapers and research articles. The present work has been studied through historical-analytical approach. The case study method has been applied while studying and analyzing the nature and forms of the violation of civil and political human rights in India including extra-judicial killings and forced disappearances. Individual cases of human rights violations, expressing the nature, causes and forms of custodial violence, extra-judicial killings and enforced disappearances from all over India have been critically analyzed. The same method has been employed to study the violation of the rights of women, children, SCs, and STs. Besides the aforesaid method, year-wise statistical data of complaints received and admitted by the NHRC, and the year-wise statistical data of custodial violence, extra-judicial killings, various crimes against women, children, SCs and STs, displayed by the NCRB has been analyzed to study the accurate number, intensity and growth of various categories human rights violations throughout India. Furthermore, information has been supplemented through interview techniques. Interviews of the victims of human rights, the relatives of the deceased and the office-bearers of the human rights organizations and human rights activists have been conducted to obtain a first hand, reliable and empirical information and facts relevant to the study.

# PART–1

# PART-1

# 1

## Human Rights: A Theoretical Perspective

Human rights are those rights which are preconditions for the continued existence of human beings and enlargement of all dimensions of human personality. These are based on mankind's increasing demand for a decent, civilized life in which the inherent dignity of each human being is well respected and protected. Human rights are fundamental to the very existence of mankind, without which people cannot live as human beings.[1] In the true sense, human rights are those minimal rights which every individual must contain by virtue of his being as a member of human society.[2]

Generally, human rights can be termed as a special sort of inalienable moral entitlement. These are attached to all persons equally by virtue of their humanity, irrespective of race, nationality, or membership of any particular social group. Human rights uphold the dignity and status of the person. Human rights assure the affirmation of a satisfactory and dignified life to each individual.[3] These are basic civil, political, economic and social conditions to which every individual is entitled as a human being.

The concept of human rights is as old as the ancient doctrine of natural rights founded on natural law, the expression human is of recent origin. Human rights are a dynamic concept and endeavors to adopt itself to the need of the day. Human rights constitute those very rights which one has precisely because of being human. They are not earned, bought or inherited nor does any contractual authority create them. Difference of sex, race, language and colour do not change these rights. Human rights are essential for full development of human personality and for human happiness. They are indispensable for physical and mental upliftment of the human race. These rights are expression of what is a life minimally worth living, about primary necessities of life. But still some rights must be regarded as fundamental like right to life with dignity, right to freedom of conscience and of course right to minimal means of subsistence. All human rights are basic rights in the fundamental sense that systematic violation of any human rights precludes realizing a life full of human dignity[4]. Hence, human rights are based on mankind's increasingly demand for a decent and civilized life in which the inherent dignity of each human being will receive respect and protection.

The concept of human rights describes a detailed story of the attempts, made to define basic dignity and worth of the human beings and their most fundamental entitlement. The denial of human rights and fundamental freedoms, is not only an individual and personal tragedy but also creates conditions of social and political unrest, sowing the seeds of violence and conflict within and between societies and nations.[5]

## Meaning and Definition

As a concept, human rights are complex and contradictory. The most striking feature of the concept of human rights is that they may be difficult to define but impossible to ignore. Hence, it is necessary to go through some of the standard definitions given by different scholars from time to time to get familiar with the meaning and nature of the human rights.

Accoring to Aristotle, "Rights are two dimensional: They should help in the development of individual's own powers and should help in creating conditions for the development of powers of action of others also."[6]

According to Harold J. Laski, "Rights, in fact, are those conditions of social life without which no man can seek, in general, to be himself at his best".[7]

In the words of President Jefferson, human rights are "inherent and inalienable rights of man," and hence a state that violates them in its laws and its actions, actually breaches one of the very prerequisites of civil co-existence between states and may be legitimately brought to account.[8]

Justice V.R Krishna Iyer has described that "Human Rights and Fundamental Freedom are indivisible. Full realization of civil and political rights and cultural rights, is impossible. This process of realization calls for legal postivisation, not political polemics nor diplomatic claptrap but normative formulation. But what are human rights? Religion of man is located in the Vedas, Buddhist Texts, Bible, The Quran or the holy literature or other authentic teachers to uphold human dignity. Every human being is a divine being and has a little to dignity, liberty, equality and other basic rights. We cannot understand or evaluate human rights divorced from the historical and social context. Idle ideals and empty assertions cut no ice. The status of human rights has taken us to the lifestyle of a society, which is why the Indian constitutional approach is soaked in the social milieu and human conditions. India is plural society and the concept of the human rights in such society has a different and a unique position".[9]

The United Nations has described Human Rights and Fundamental Freedoms, "as the conditions which allow us to fully develop and use our human quality, our intelligence, our talents and our conscience and to satisfy our spiritual and other needs. They are based on mankind's increasing demand for a life in which the inherent dignity and worth of each human being will receive respect and protection"[10].

The New Encyclopedia Britannica defines human rights as "the rights that belong to an individual as a consequence of being human. They refer to a wide continuum of values that are universal in character and in some sense equally claimed for all human beings. Human rights are understood to represent individual and group demands for the shaping and sharing of respect, tolerance, and forbearance in the pursuit of other values."[11]

According to Britannica Concise Encyclopedia, "rights that belong to an individual as a consequence of being human are called human rights. As understood today human rights refer to a wide variety of values and capabilities reflecting the diversity of human circumstances and history. They are conceived of as universal applying to all human beings everywhere and as fundamental, referring to essential or basic human needs".[12]

Columbia Encyclopedia defines human rights, "as universal rights which belong to individuals by virtue of their being human, encompassing civil, political, economic, social and cultural rights and freedoms, and based on the notion of personal human dignity and worth."[13]

Law Encyclopedia attaches human rights with the "personal liberties that protect individuals and groups against individual or state conduct prohibited by international law or custom". It further says that, "human rights are freedoms established by custom or international agreement that impose standards of conduct on all nations. Human rights are distinct civil liberties, which are freedoms established by the law of a particular state and applied by that state in its own jurisdiction."[14]

The Lexicon Universal Encyclopedia describes the dogma of human rights as, "basic political and social conditions – variously defined – to which every individual is entitled as a human being. Originally they were called natural rights or the rights of man, and included the rights to life, liberty, and the pursuit of happiness cited in the U.S. Declaration of Independence over the years of concept of human rights has been broadened to include rights to social benefits such as social security, rest, leisure and education."[15]

Thus human rights are those minimal conditions which every individual must have by the virtue of his being a 'member of the human family' irrespective of any other consideration. Human rights have been identified as those rights which are important, moral and universal.

It is a manifest reality that the doctrine of human rights is as old as the human civilization. In every phase of the history and every part of the world, people had demanded similar type of rights which were necessary for the existence, survival and development. That is why the history of human rights highlights the universality and indivisibility of human rights. But such type of universality and indivisibility is seldom found in defining the human rights. The definition of human rights differs from time to time, place to place and even from person to person. There is hardly any consensus among the scholars about the universal definition of human rights.

## Nature of Human Rights

Despite the lack of consensus, a number of widely accepted and interrelated postulates can assist in the task of defining the nature of human rights. Broadly, there are five postulates which explicit the nature of human rights in the in most established and wider perspective.

First, regardless of their ultimate origin or justification, human rights are understood to represent individual and group demands for political power, economic prosperity and social dignity. Second, human rights are commonly assumed as the "fundamental" claims and are distinct from "nonessential" claims or the "privileges". The tendency is to emphasize "basic needs" and to rule out "mere wants". Third, reflecting the changeable environmental circumstances, and responding to the continuous change in the surrounding conditions, human rights refer to a wide range of claims, ranging from the most justifiable to the most ambitious also. Human rights share both the legal and the moral orders. They are representatives of both the "is" and the "ought" in human affairs. Fourth, the rights of individuals or groups, in particular circumstances are restricted as much as is necessary to secure the comparable rights of others and the aggregate common interest. This limitation connects rights to duties. Human rights are sometimes designated *prima facie* rights, hence, there is no sense to think or talk of them in absolutist terms. Finally, if a right is determined to be a human right, it is understood to be essentially general or universal in character. Human rights are equally possessed by all human beings everywhere, without discriminations irrelevant to merit or need, simply for being human."[16]

As generally used today, the term human rights covers the series of those universally accepted rights and liberties which are essential requirements for the people to enjoy their life with a sense of human dignity. Human rights, in the views of the exponents, are regarded as being inherent, inalienable and universal rights. Human rights are *inherent* in the sense that these rights inhere in all human beings exactly since their birth. People enjoy these rights simply by virtue of their human existence. People do not depend on any superior or sovereign authority to be granted these rights to them. *Inalienability* is another paramount feature of the human rights which depicts that these rights cannot be aliened or disaffected by the human beings. People cannot agree to give them up or have them taken away from them. Human rights are *universal* in nature. These are not privileges arranged for some individuals, citizens or groups. Human rights apply on all persons regardless of their group identities.[17]

## The Specific Characteristics of Human Rights

When human rights are defined as those rights that stem from human dignity, it becomes apparent that they have some peculiar characteristic. The following are some of these characteristics.

### *Internationalism*

The whole international community, in spite of the differences and distinctions regarding the nature and form of the governments, has expressed their consent, consensus and concerns for almost similar type of human rights. The guarantee of the respect for human dignity, the right to pursuit of happiness and all other civil, political, economic and social rights stated in the United Nations (UN) Charters, the Universal Declaration of Human Rights, the Vienna Declaration of Human Rights and other important international conventions are taken into consideration by whole international community. Following a trend of internationlisation of human rights, it was agreed by a majority of the states to observe these rights equally and with sincerity. Consequently, the guarantee of human rights, not only by the individual states but by the international community as a whole, is a vital and ever-ascendant issue. Human rights have become the common ideology of the whole international community, going beyond state borders.

### *Universality*

All human rights, in equal proportion, should be recognized universally without any discrimination, distinction, and without any exception. While distributing the rights, nobody should be discriminated because of his race, colour, sex language, religion, political opinion, nation, social position, property or other circumstances. Everybody should e endowed with all rights and freedoms. Moreover, nobody can be discriminated because of membership in a particular self-governed or dependent state, his rights because of political, legislative or international position.

### *Inheritance*

Human rights cannot be said to have been granted in accordance with any state or any law but are instead recognized as natural and inherent rights. Human beings inherit these rights by their birth as being the humans and hence do not need the approval or command of any authority to enjoy theses rights. These are the birth-rights of all human beings just because they are the members of human family.

### *Inalienability*

Human rights are inherent rights of human beings. Thus human beings can never alien these rights at any cost under any circumstances. Nobody can exist and survive satisfactorily by giving up his/her human rights. Human beings cannot transfer their own rights to another individual. These cannot be aliened or given up.

### *Absolute*

As human rights are inalienable rights recognized universally, these are actually absolute rights. The essence of human personality, human dignity and worth, confirms the inviolability of human rights and carries the responsibility of guaranteeing such inviolability. As such the state must guarantee the people's civil, political, legal, social, economic, cultural rights by preventing any law which would do otherwise.

### *Unavoidability*

As human rights are considered inherent, inalienable and absolute rights of all individuals, none of the state can avoid the availability of these rights to its people. None of the state can ignore or avoid its responsibility to make adequate constitutional and legal provisions to make these rights equally available to al its citizens. Irrespective of the differences of form and nature of the governments, all states should recognize and protect these rights.

### *Inviolability*

As human rights are inherent and absolute rights which are universally recognized and internationally enforced, these rights cannot be violated. The violation of these rights will really hinder the proper development of the personality of the people and may even cause threats to their existence and survival. In addition to this, it is the foremost duty of the state to make appropriate constitutional and legal provisions to prevent the violation of these rights. The state itself may not alienate these rights. The state cannot even limit or violate these rights.

### *Permanence*

The parameters and dimensions of development, dignity and worth of human beings do not change over time by the situation. Human rights must be guaranteed regardless of time and place, because they possess the absoluteness of being guaranteed. Hence, human rights should not be guarantees temporarily for a fixed period of time but should be permanently guarantees rights of which nobody can be deprived. The history o guaranteeing human rights actually leaves traces along with the history of human beings.

### *Individuality*

All people are independent individuals. Every individual has its own necessities which are more or less different to others. Each individual possesses the right to be independent which cannot be taken away by any other individual, group or authority. Every person has a right to determine his/her destiny, which is a prerequisite of individual rights. Fundamentally, the subject of human rights is neither of a nation nor of a collective body, but is the subject of the individual.

### *Self-Determination*

All people have the right to self-determination on the basis of inherent human dignity. Based on this right, all people freely determine their own economic, social and cultural development. In addition to this, it can be said that in every nation, the nature, type and scope of human rights is determined by the people themselves and not these are not imposed by the governments or any other authorities.

### *Fundamental*

Human rights are internationally recognized as the prerequisite for the existence, survival and development with dignity, worth and happiness. Consequently, being a value norm included in fundamental norm, it produces a basic principle which has become a standard for analyzing the essence of effectiveness of laws and ordinances. Thus it should be considered a standard of human dignity and worth as far as it is included both in establishing the laws and analyzing them.

## Classification of Human Rights

Human rights can be classified broadly into two different perspectives: firstly from the perspective of various aspects of human life- social, economic, political, moral and civil; and secondly, from the perspective of the methods securing them. On the second basis, they are constitutional or legal. These classifications can be discussed under the following headings:

### *Natural Rights*

Natural rights are those rights which are considered to be inherent and integral to human nature. In fact, every individual by nature is given an individual property of his own natural rights which cannot be taken away by any other authority. Such rights include intellectual rights, right to mind and also rights of acting as an individual for his on comfort and happiness, provided they are not injurious to the natural rights of others. These rights belong to people simply because they are human. These rights do not have to be earned, bought or inherited. People are equally entitled to these rights regardless of their sex, race, colour, language, national origin, age, class, religious or political beliefs.

### *Moral Rights*

These rights are based on the general principle of fairness and justice. These are simply aspirations and ideals of the people who claim for it. Sometimes, people justify these rights on the ground of the role they perform or the position they occupy in society. For example, the mother of a family might complain that she has the right to be consulted about what is going on in her family. In this case, she is applying the principle that parents are entitled to be consulted when family decisions affect the members. So, it is the moral duty of other members to the same.

### *Fundamental Rights*

There are certain rights which are more important and basic than the others. For example, right to life is the most basic of all rights upon which the enjoyment of other rights depends. These rights can never be restricted or taken away by any authority. That is why every society has a fundamental duty to protect it all times. Among other basic rights are the right to be recognized as a person before the law, the right to equal protection under law, and freedom from illegal arrest and detention. Recognising the fundamental and prerequisite nature of these most important rights, most of the countries incorporate these rights in their constitutions as fundamental rights.

### *Legal Rights*

Legal rights are otherwise known as positive rights. These rights are laid down in law. They are also guaranteed and protected by the law of the state. Thus, legal rights are uniform and open to all irrespective of the caste, colour, race or culture. These are rights that are laid down in law and can be defended in a country's court of law. Most, but not all, legal rights are written down and are codified. Large number of people in a country does not regard sometimes legal rights as moral rights. This happens for example hen the law allows some people to discriminate against others because of their sex, race, colour, language or religion. These rights are based on general principles of fairness and justice. These are often, though not always, based on religious beliefs. A moral right may or may not be a legal right. A moral right, which is not a legal right sometimes, cannot be defended in the court of law.

### *Civil and Political Rights*

Rights that are granted by government or civil society are called civil and political rights. These rights provide the bases for the fulfillment of elementary conditions of the social life. Without them, civilized life is not possible and they are, therefore considered very essential for the free and progressive life of man. Civil and political rights, however, include the right to freedom of speech, of assembly, right to move freely, to hold property and practice trade or profession, and right to take part in the government of one's country. Part III of the Indian Constitution has resemblances with these rights.

These rights include:

- Right to live, freedom and safety.
- Right to rule of law i.e. (equality before the law)
- Right to freedom of expression and communication
- Right to be considered innocent until proven guilty

- Right to freedom from torture and cruel and degrading punishment
- Right to freedom from interference in your home
- Right to freedom of association and assembly
- Right of people to form their government.
- Right to leave your country and return.

*Economic, Social and Cultural Rights*

These are entitlements of the individual *vis-à-vis* the state, in order to eradicate social inequality, economic imbalances and to limit disadvantages caused by nature, age and so on. These rights, however, are bestowed by the State. The State is not bound to meet these entitlements all at once. It depends upon the economic resources of the society. Most of the socialist States recognize these rights as fundamental rights of the people. Right to equality, right to work, right to have family, right to privacy, right to information, right to public assistance during old age and sickness, right to health care, right to special care during childhood and during motherhood are some of the examples of these rights. Such rights have been incorporated in Part IV of the Indian Constitution as Directive Principles of Sate Policy.

- These rights include:
- Right to employment
- Right to equal pay for equal work
- Right to work and choose your kind of work.
- Right to earn enough pay to support your family
- Right to a decent home, good food and shelter.
- Right to adequate health care.
- Right to own property and not be deprived of it without good reason.
- Right to an education without fees
- Right to choose how and what your children will be taught.

- Right to form and join a trade union.
- Right to be protected in illness and in your old aye.

*Environmental and Development Rights*

These rights include:

- Right to a clean and healthy environment.
- Right to a safe environment.
- Right to freedom from pollution or other activities which harm the environment.
- Right to live in a country which is able to develop its economy without interference from other countries.
- Right to enjoy the cultural and recreational life of one's community.

*Some Overlapping Rights*

These rights include:

- Though often listed as a political right, freedom from discrimination frequently involves social and economic affairs as well. Freedom of religion and freedom of association are seen by some as political rights but by others as social rights.
- Though usually classified as a social or economic right, the right to join and form a trade union might be seen as a political right because the unions have been so active in politics.

**Theories of Human Rights**

In order to gain the basic understanding of human rights, one should look at certain theories of the subject so that the shifting priorities of rights during different phases of history could be observed. The function of theory, however, is to provide an analytical tool by which it is possible to determine the precise subject matter of the concept upon which there might be an agreement. A precise insight into the major theories of rights is as follows:

### *The Theory of Natural Rights*

This is the earliest theory of rights and its origin can be traced back to the ancient Greeks. This theory propounds that rights belong to man by nature and thus are self-evident truths. They were considered as inborn, absolute, pre-civil and even pre-social. They can be asserted anywhere and everywhere. Thomas Paine, Grotius, Tom Paine and John Locke are the main exponents of this theory.

However, the critics of the natural rights theory argue that rights are not abstract, absolute or unidentified phenomena. They argue that Liberty lives within restraints. So restraints upon rights create social conditions where everyone has a share to develop his personality and correspondingly has his obligations to others. Rights and obligations, in fact are the two sides of the same coin. Despite the above shortcomings, the theory of natural rights inspired the idea that any kind of unjust, arbitrary or oppressive treatment to human beings is an assault upon humanity itself. Apart from this, it also provided the basis of English, French and American revolutions, thereby resulting in the Bill of Rights.

### *The Legal Theory of Rights*

The legal rights theory has emerged as a reaction against the theory of natural rights. Exponents of this theory have opposed the natural rights theory by giving the argument that the ideas of natural law and natural rights are abstract and thus a ridiculous phenomenon. Hence, the existence and enjoyment of fundamental rights of an individual could e better maintained and practiced by the State rather than by the individual himself. Thomas Hobbes, John Austin and Jeremy Bentham are main pronouncers of this theory. According to them, rights are purely utilitarian concepts and thus the rule and regulations are necessary for the identification and protection of the rights. Towards this end, every individual has to sacrifice certain rights and freedoms for the general welfare of the whole society.

Bentham held that the notion of moral rights was "nonsense upon stilts" because rights require social recognition and moral rights have none. The issue of whether rights require social recognition can be illustrated with an example from Martin. Martin holds that, because there was no social recognition of their rights, the victims of Aztec human sacrifice rituals did not have a right not to be killed. While it was wrong for the priests to kill their victims, they did not violate any rights. Others hold that, while social recognition is a necessary feature of legal rights, it is not a necessary feature of moral rights. These scholars hold that the victims of Aztec human sacrifice rituals had moral rights which the priests violated.

This theory has been sturdily criticized on the ground that law alone does not create rights. Rather, it recognizes and protects them. Custom, tradition and morality also have a strong basis for rights. However, the truth in this theory lies in the fact that it enables individuals to demand certain specific and recognized rights as granted and guaranteed by the Sate.

### *The Anti-Utilitarian Theory of Rights*

There is another category of theorists who strongly argue that the priority of the well-being of the majority as stated by the utilitarians is not the prime objective of the State. Amongst them Dowrkin, Nozic and John Rawls are the leading ones. They hold the view that the welfare of majority might lead to detrimental consequences as far as the welfare of a particular person or a group of persons is concerned. So, there has to be proper reconciliation between the well-being of the majority and the well-being of the individuals. Above all there should be a better enjoyment of social and individual rights. Today, the demand for right to development on international is perhaps the manifestation of this theory.

### *The Legal Realist Theory of Rights*

The Legal-Realist theory of rights is of recent origin. It was mainly originated in USA with the expansion of regulatory activities followed by President Roosevelt's 'New Deal Policy'. A group of jurists such as Karl Llewellyn, Roscoe Pound and others discussed the point as to what law does, rather than what law is, in a highly complex and industrialized societies.

These theorists did not propound a common theory of rights. Rather, they considered rights as the end product of both the interaction of prevailing moral values of the society as well as the broad-based onternational sharing of values. So, human rights, as they argue, are nothing but a manifestation of an on going process rather than a theoretical debate. This kind of a new approach to the concept of rights does away with the problems relating to the abstract nature of the concept. However, this theory goes about questioning the existing laws, their values and the actions, so far enacted upon the society. In other words, it questions the shortcomings and ineffectiveness of the existing laws but does not prescribe any solution in the form of super-value of a human being.

*The Marxist Theory of Rights*

According to Marxism, the rights are simply a bourgeois concept and a product of bourgeois capitalist society basically designed to maintain and reinforce the predominant position of the ruling class.[18] This theory of rights is very simple and to a certain extent convincing too. He regards the Sate a coercive agency to uphold the particular type of social organization and law is a tool of the Sate that perpetuates and safeguards the interest of the dominant group in the society.

Marx and Engles stated that the recognition of the rights of man by the modern state has no other meaning than the recognition of slavery by the ancient state. The ancient state had slavery as its natural basis, the modem state has as its natural basis, the civil society; and that is the individual man linked with other men only by the ties of private interest and unconscious natural necessity, the slave of labour for gain and of his own as well as other men's selfish needs.[19] The very notion of human rights, according to Marx and Engles is linked to the competitive struggle that is the hallmark of the bourgeois society and is based on vision of society and the individuals as inheriting separate and antagonistic units.

Human rights are thus viewed as instruments for carrying out adversary relations between competing primary atomistic individuals. Central to Marxism in its concerns for human beings and the idea that man, stripped of 'his human essence' when he first fell into the class of the exploited, confronts the destruction of all humanity in him in a bourgeois society. The process of bourgeois exploitation, with its naturally 'corollary greed and the war between the greedy competition' holds the entire society at the mercy of the market forces. It 'estranges man from nature from himself, his own active functioning, from his universal, essence. It makes his essence into a mere means for his existence. It estranges his spiritual, his human essence. It results in the alienation of man from man.[20] Such kind of alienating, depersonalizing and dehumanizing impact of bourgeois system makes the whole context that Marx stated about communism that it is the actual phase necessary for the next stage of historical development in the process of human emancipation and recovery. Thus in a communist society, Marx argued in the critique of the Gotha program in which working class would enjoy the right to compensation for labour.

Karl Marx firmly believes that rights can exist and flourish only in a classless society where all are equal and no one is exploiter. Social and economic rights are thus the main concerns of this theory. However, the contribution of Marxist thought to the development of international concern on economic, social and cultural righhts has been found in the International Covenant on Economic, Social and Cultural Rights (ICESCR) in 1966. However, this theory does not include religion, customs, tradition and morality as integral components of human rights.

### *The Interest Theory of Rights*

The Interest theory of rights was first proposed by Bentham and has been defended by the scholars such as Lyons MacCormick and Joseph Raz. Defenders of Interest theory argue that a person has a right when others have duties which protect one of that person's interests. Main strength of Interest theories is that they can account for the relational aspect of rights. There is an important difference between failing to respect someone's rights and failing to fulfill an obligation which is not part of the rights. Consider the difference between failing to pay a debt and failing to give to charity. In failing to pay the debt, one wrongs the debt-holder. In failing to give to charity one does something wrong, but one does not wrong anyone. Rights are relational in the sense that the obligations implied by rights are owed *to* someone. According to interest theories, the obligation implied by a right is an obligation *to* the right-holder because it is the right-holder's interest which is protected by the right.

Perhaps the central objection to interest theories is that there seem to be rights which are not in the interest of the right-holder. One might inherit some property which is literally more trouble than it is worth. Suppose that the property in question is bound up in complex legal proceedings which prevent its sale but require a great deal of time and attention. The rights of public officials also pose a difficulty for interest theorists. A judge's right to impose sentence seems to be justified by the public's interest in a well-functioning criminal justice system, not by a judge's personal interests. In a particular case, it might well be in a judge's interest not to impose the sentence. The judge might even have the threat to be the target of an angry mob of the accused's defenders.

### *The Choice Theory of Rights*

The choice theory was first proposed by Hart (1982 and 1983) and has been defended by scholars such as Montague (1980) and Steiner (1994). Defenders of choice theories argue that a person has a right when others have duties which protect one of that person's choices. Choice theories have no problem accounting for the relational nature of rights. According to choice theories, the obligation implied by a right is an obligation *to* the right-holder because it is the right-holder's choice which is protected by the right.

A central problem for choice theories is that there seem to be rights which do not protect the right-holder's choices. Suppose that a police officer is ordered by a judge to arrest an individual. The police officer clearly has a right to arrest the individual. But she has no choice because she has a duty to perform the arrest. The rights of beings which cannot choose (e.g., animals and human newborns) pose another problem for choice theories. If rights necessarily protect an individual's choices then individuals who cannot choose cannot have rights.

## Three Generations of Human Rights

The doctrine of human rights and its development is always controversial because of differing views about definitions and concepts, on the one hand, and about political connotations and consequences, on the other. There are different opinions about the areas to which the concept of human rights applies. It is a common feature today to distinguish three generations of human rights.

### *First Generation of Human Rights*

Traditional conceptions of basic human rights are based on the political philosophy of liberal individualism and the economic and social doctrine of laissez-faire. Therefore, they propose that a state's responsibility lies in guaranteeing the freedom from interference of its citizens' basic human rights, and moreover, an active effort to realize these rights.[21] The embodying of these human rights consists of various types of negative liberties afforded as basic civil and political rights, such as the right to vote, right to own property, freedom of speech.[22] The human rights thinking that originated in the 17th and 18th centuries with the advent of enlightenment movement is represented by the Declaration of Independence of the United States of America, and the French Declaration of the Rights of Man and the Citizen.[23] In the historical contexts, discussions of basic human rights are considered domestic legal issues in nation-states.

First-generation human rights deal essentially with liberty. It fundamentally advocates the rights, civil and political in nature and bound to protect the individual from excesses of the state. The expression of First Generation of Human Rights can be seen in Articles 3 to 21 of the Universal Declaration of Human Rights (UDHR) by the United Nations, and the International Covenant on Civil and Political Rights. First-generation rights include, *inter alia*:

- Right to vote
- Right to assemble
- Right to free speech
- Right to a fair trial
- Right to freedom from torture, abuse
- Right to protection of the law

***Second Generation of Human Rights***

Liberal democratic theory of human rights had not been accepted both by the socialist countries as well as the developing countries. The socialist theory, whose roots are essentially traced back to Marx, argued against the individualism of traditional human rights theory. Marxism, which was adopted by several developing countries at the beginning of 20th century as the solution of their social and political barbarities believed that the so-called rights of men were nothing but the rights of egoistic man separated from other man and from the community.[24] Karl Marx went on to extend his basic postulate by emphasizing the necessary connection between bourgeois society and the notion of human rights.[25]

Marxism considers that liberal-individualist rights have inevitably become a legal tool of the bourgeoisie, by dominating the proletariat class to protect their own class interests. Therefore, socialists emphasize the state's role in actively guaranteeing the economic, social, and cultural position of its citizens[26]—in particular, workers, women, minorities, and all other disadvantaged individuals. Weimar Constitution in Germany and Declaration of Rights of the Working and Exploited People in Russia best represent the results of the socialist revolution. As for capitalist states, their roles changed from watchman states to welfare states, and conceptions of human rights shifted from first-generation of negative rights of protection against state intervention to second-generation positive rights for demanding state welfares. Hence, the second generation of human rights developed favouring the provisions for various types of economic and social rights like right to work right to social security and right to existence[27]. Like first generation rights, they are also acknowledged by the Universal Declaration of Human Rights. Articles 22 to 27 of the UDHR, and the International Covenant on Economic, Social, and Cultural Rights deal with he Second Generation of Rights. The Second Generation of Rights includes the rights *inter-alia*:

- Right to education
- Right to housing
- Right to health
- Right to employment
- Right to an adequate income
- Right to social security

***Third Generation of Human Rights***

In view of the ineffectuality of the established international system for protecting human rights against various violations during the Second World War, The President of the United States of America Franklin D. Roosevelt and British Prime Minister Winston Churchill were the first to link the objectives of their two countries' war of resistance to international human rights demands, producing the Atlantic Charter in August 1941.[28] This document called for restoration of national sovereign rights and self-government, as well as the realization of a free life for the entire world's people. In forming the United Nations, each of the Allies gave special thought to how to achieve international co-operation in promoting and encouraging respect for human rights and for fundamental freedoms for all.[29] A provision from Paragraph 3 in Article 1 of the United Nations Charter foresaw the trend towards internationalization of the human rights emerging after the Second World War. The United Nations, and its subordinated organizations of human rights protection, played an active role in international oversight and support work.

In 1950s and 1960s, there was rise of more complex international relations. It made difficult for a single country to fulfill its obligations to protect human rights on its own. Moreover, the international community started getting concerned with any individual country's human rights violations. The internationalization of human rights made the issue of human rights violations an international concern rather than restricting it to remain as a supranational matter.

However, Senegalese jurist Keba M'Baye was the first to point out this trend in contemporary human rights in 1972 through his monograph on the rights to development "*Le Droit du Developpement comme un Droit de l'Homme*". But it was Karl Vasak who properly prescribed the Third Generation of Human Rights.[30] In November 1977 at UNESCO, in a speech commemorating the thirtieth anniversary of the passing of the Universal Declaration of Human Rights, he asserted that "third generation rights are those born to the obvious brotherhood of men and their indispensable solidarity, and provide that 'everyone is entitled to a social and international order in which the rights set forth in this Declaration can be fully realized."[31]

The greatest distinction between third-generation human rights and the two earlier generations is that third-generation human rights superseded the scope of national constitutions. Third-generation human rights are no longer a matter of the relationship of people to their respective states, focusing only the individuals or minority groups. Rather, the subject of third-generation human rights is people taken as a whole, with their social solidarity—typically, the people of a country. Therefore, third-generation human rights are not traditional human rights of the individual, but a type of collective internationalization of rights.[32]

The third generation of human rights encompasses collective rights, such as the right to peace, right to development, or to a social and international order in which the rights and freedoms proclaimed in the Universal Declaration can be fully realized. This generation of rights remains the most debated one and is least covered by legal or political means. The Third Generation of Human Rights includes the rights *inter-alia*:

- Right to self-determination
- Right to economic development
- Right to natural resources
- Right to communicate
- Right to participation in mankind's heritage
- Right to prosperity
- Right to benefit from economic growth
- Right to social harmony
- Right to a healthy environment, clean air and water, etc.

## Philosophical Analysis of the Concept of Human Rights

Human rights are rights that attach to human beings and function as moral guarantees in support of their claims towards the enjoyment of a minimal good life. In conceptual terms, human rights themselves are derived from the concept of the 'right'. Therefore, it is worthy to focus upon the philosophical analysis of the concept of 'right' in order to clearly reveal the various elements of the concept from which human rights emerge. In order to gain a full understanding of both the philosophical foundations of the doctrine of human rights and the different ways in which different kinds human rights function, a detailed analysis is required.

### *Moral vs. Legal Rights*

The distinction drawn between moral rights and legal rights as two separate categories of rights is of fundamental importance to understand the basis and potential application of human rights. Legal rights refer to all those rights found within existing legal codes. A legal right is a right that enjoys the recognition and protection of the law. Questions as to its existence can be resolved by simply locating the relevant legal instrument or piece of legislation. A legal right cannot be said to exist prior to its passing into law and the limits of its validity are set by the jurisdiction of the body which passed the relevant legislation. Legal positivists argue that the only rights that can be said to legitimately exist are legal rights, rights that originate within a legal system.

It propounds that moral rights are not rights in the strict sense, but are better thought of as moral claims, which may or may not eventually be assimilated within national or international law. For a legal positivist, such as the 19th Century legal philosopher Jeremy Bentham, there can be no such thing as human rights existing prior to, or independently from legal codification. For a legal positivist determining the existence of rights is no more complicated than locating the relevant stature or precedent. In stark contrast, moral rights are rights that are claimed to be existing prior to, and independently from, legal counterparts. The existence and validity of a moral right is not deemed to be dependent upon actions of jurists and legislators.[33]

It might, therefore, appear tempting to draw the conclusion that human rights are best identified as moral rights. Human rights certainly share an essential quality of moral rights, namely, that their valid existence is not deemed to be conditional upon their being legally recognized. Human rights are meant to apply to all human beings everywhere, regardless of whether they have received legal recognition by all countries everywhere. Clearly, there remain numerous countries that wholly or partially exclude formal legal recognition to fundamental human rights. Supporters of human rights in these countries insist that the rights remain valid regardless, as fundamental moral rights. The universality of human rights positively entails such claims. The universality of human rights as moral rights clearly lends greater moral force to human rights. However, for their part, legal rights are not subject to disputes as to their existence and validity in quite the way moral rights are. It would be a mistake to exclusively identify human rights with moral rights. Human rights are better thought of as both moral rights and legal rights. Human rights originate as moral rights and their legitimacy is necessarily dependent upon the legitimacy of the concept of moral rights.[34]

### *Universalist vs. Relativist Conceptions of Human Rights*

This overview leads directly to the dominant contemporary intellectual debate on human rights; the Universalist vs. the Relativist controversy. This debate is also relevant to the theory of development. Essentially, the universalist-relativist controversy is about the question whether human rights are universally comprehensible, binding and applicable or whether they are essentially a Western concept. From the latter argument it would follow that he interpretation of what human rights are and how they can be implemented is always relative to the cultural traditions and conditions of specific societies. From this point of view it is often argued that the West centric concept and connotation of human rights is yet another form of Western imperialism or neo-colonialism. This argument is especially forwarded by Asian scholars and politicians; it is at the core of the so-called 'Asian value debate'. At the same time, it is an important element in the intellectual discourse between the Islamic world and the West.[35]

To a certain degree, the debate about the universal or relative significance of human rights is artificial. Although, the Universal Declaration of Human Rights (UDHR) by the UN in 1948 was a positive step in developing a universal approach regarding the recognition, promotion and protection of human rights. But still there was a lack of an international consent and consensus regarding the issue. Formally, at least since the UN World Conference on Human Rights adopted its Declaration at Vienna in 1993, this question has been solved. The Vienna document, signed by an overwhelming majority of all countries, proclaims unmistakably that human rights are of universal nature. There are also many other UN documents which explicitly or implicitly refer to the universal nature and the indivisibility of human rights in one way or another, beginning with the Charter of the United Nations, the Universal Declaration of Human Rights, and the Covenants of Political and Social Rights of 1966.[36]

To answer these questions there are four different view points. The first point of view as explained by Hundrick

Kaptein is works. He revealed that concept of human rights presupposes that the state has a duty to advance to protect these basic rights. Human rights also do with relationships of citizens among themselves. Human rights are more absolute than rights in general. This leads to a fundamental point of view concerning human rights.[37]

The second is the normative-ethical point of view, which stresses that human rights are based upon ethical necessity of life worth for everyone. Equality is the basis of human rights and must be given in any conception of normative ethic.[38] Normative ethics must at least provide a principle of equality concerning the conduct of human beings to each other. All normative ethics pre-suppose the recognition of person quo human beings. Such a minimal ethics already is recognition of Human Rights.

The third is the legal point of view which concerns legal recognition, and protection of human rights asserts that these arts are given a legal coverage by the state under constitution and fundamental laws. Moreover, human rights that are recognized by international treaties and conventions, criminal law are also legal protection of the fundamental arts to life, physical integrity and property. Administration law ensures possibility for citizens to receive redress when theirs human right are infringed upon by the state. It should be noted that human rights not only define relationship between citizen and the State, but also determine rights, duties and obligations of citizens themselves.

The fourth point of view relates to the factual, empirical anthropological, sociological, and historical point of view. It reflects on the historical, geographical and cultural background of human rights. It is the duty of the state, regardless of their political, economic and cultural backgrounds, to promote and protect all human rights and fundamental freedom.

## References

1. A.S. Anand, "Protecting Human Rights", *The Tribune*, November 17, 2003.
2. J. Shivananda (ed.), *Human Rights–Origin and Development*, Alfa Publications, New Delhi, 2006, p. 32.

3. M. Stephen, *Human Rights: Concepts and Perspectives*, Concept Publishing Company, New Delhi, 2002, p. 9.
4. Jack Donnelly. "*Universal Human Rights in Theory and Practice*" Ithaca New York: Cornell University Press, 1989, p. 41.
5. Gukulesh Sharma, *Human Rights and Legal Remedies*, Deep & Deep Publications, New Delhi, 2000. p. 3.
6. S.C. Saxena, *Political Science for Civil Service Examination*, Macmillan, Delhi, p. 70.
7. Harold J. Laski, *The Grammar of Politics*, George Allen & Unwin Ltd., London, 1938, p. 91.
8. J. Vadackumuchery, *Human Rights and Police in India*, A.P.H. Publishers, New Delhi, 1998, pp. 1-2.
9. V.R Krishna Iyer, *Human Rights and the Law*, Vedpal Law House, Indore, 1986, p. 88.
10. United Nations, *Human Rights: Questions and Answers*, United Nations Publications, New York, 1987, p. 4.
11. *The New Encyclopedia Britannica*, Vol. 6, Fifteenth Edition, 1994, Chicago, p. 137.
12. Human Rights: Definition and Much More, http://www.answers.com/topic/human-rights.
13. *Ibid.*
14. *Ibid.*
15. *Lexican Universal Encyclopedia*, Lexican Publications INC, New York, pp. 297-298.
16. Richard Pierre Claude, *et al.* (ed.), *Human Rights in World Community: Issues and Actions*, University of Pennsylvania Press, 2006, p. 20.
17. Arun Ray Mohapatra, *National Human Rights Commission of India*, Radha Publications, New Delhi, 2001, p. 10.
18. Scott Davidson, *Human Rights*, Philadelphia Open University Press, 1993, p. 37.
19. Pramod Mishra, *Human Rights: Global Issues*, Kalpaz Publications, New Delhi, 2000, p. 13.
20. *Ibid.*, pp. 14-15.
21. Andrew Fagan, *Human Rights*, The Internet Encyclopedia of Philosophy, http://www.iep.utm.edu/h/hum-rts.htm.
22. *Ibid.*
23. Darren Jo' Byrne, *Human Rights-An Introduction*, Pearson Education, Singapore, Indian Branch, Partapganj, Delhi, 2004, pp. 37-44.
24. *Ibid.*
25. Hendrick Kaptein, "Morals of Post-Modern Human Rights", *Indian Socio-Legal Journal*, Vol. XIX. No. 2, 1993, p. 34.
26. *Ibid.*, p. 35.

# 2

## Development of Human Rights: A Historical Perspective

Through out the history, every society has sought to define the concept of human dignity, in the sense of seeking to ascertain the qualities and inherent values of each person and his relationship to society. These questions have been answered in various ways, whether on the basis of the social obligations and duties owed by individuals, in terms of a social hierarchy based on birth or sex, through submission to the will of royal or divine forces, or on the basis of the over-riding importance attached to the maintenance of social harmony. Invariably, the ethical, religious or political bases by which each society has premised its answers to these questions have been reflected, to a large extent, in the values and systems by which that society has in turn been governed. It is in this context that the concept of human rights, a concept which tends to emphasize the worth of the individual and to recognize his or her rights against their society, arises. The basic ingredients of human rights, as proposed by the proponents *inter alia* pose certain fundamental questions regarding the very ethics of the subject because of the fact that the question of human rights has always been an important, interesting and acute one within the discourse of social science, particularly in recent times.[1] In this context, many researchers have been prompted to explore the basis, nature and scope of human rights. So an historical enquiry may help to understand its growth and development in different phases of human history.

Man's universal character is evident from the commonalities that the man shares his fellow beings. Human beings in the societies have been observed, since the remote past, as being able to express joy and pains, desires, and appreciations of law of nature that have given rise to the cultivation of literary propositions, cultural and moral principles and legal provisions observed in human societies. The concern for human rights became popular particularly in the twentieth century, though it had its roots in different forms since the time immemorial.

**Human Rights during Ancient Period**

In the Western world, human rights in fact, have its origin back in the ancient Greece and Rome, closely tied up to the pre-modern natural doctrines of *Greek Stoicism* and *Hellenistic Stoicism*.[2] In *Greeco-Roman* and medieval times, natural law doctrines taught mainly the duties, as distinguished from the right of 'Man'. Moreover, as evident in the writing of Aristotle and St. Thomas Aquinas, these doctrines recognized the legitimacy of slavery and serfdom and in doing so, excluded perhaps the central most idea of human rights as they are understood today.

A myth talks about the people of *Yourba,* that even the crippled and the handicapped such as the blind, the humpbacked, the deaf the dumb and the maimed are to be considered sacred and deserving of praise and respect because all are the creatures and children of the one God (Myth 64-65)[3] *Kono* mythology stresses that whites and the blacks are all brothers, descendents of a single father and mother. (Myth 26)[4]

The philosopher Cicero (106 BC-43 BC) confirms that the rights are not based on imagining and guessing, but the natural, fixed and necessary justice is based on human conscience.[5] The Stoics philosophers in the 4th century BC led by Zenon laid down the basis of their thoughts about man as: "The principal and most excellent aspect of Stoic ethics and politics concerns its feelings of participation and cooperation which could be carried out only regarding fellow countrymen and the country but also regarding the entire people believing in the cosmopolitan. This belief in the unity of human species is one of the main sources of Roman law "(concerning the right of the individuals) which is regarded as the law of nations and nature."[6]

The philosophers led by Aristotle and Diogenes were of the opinion that "it is due to their tendency towards evil, carnal passion and intense greed that people have been forced to lay down civil laws in mundane life, adding them to the natural laws.[7] There are evidences to indicate that this important discussion prevailed among the fifth century BC people of Athens who held such discussion in front of their convention site.

### *Human Rights in Ancient India*

The ideas of human rights could be found in Vedic Scriptures of Hinduism. The Vedas, the metrical religious works of the ancient Hindus, offer guidance, *inter alia,* on religious and social obligations. These constituted the base on which the Hindu Law was built[8] Hence, the ancient Indian law was founded on social and sociological concepts and was an admixture of religion and ethics with legal precepts.

Some of the sources of humanitarian law in ancient India were:

1. The four Vedas (verses of wisdom) - Rig, Yajur, Sama and Atharva- and their respective appendices, the Brahmans which were revelations of the sacred law to the Hindu sages of the Vedic period, approximately 4,000 to 1,000 BC. Rig- Veda cites three Civil Rights, that of *Tana* (Body), *Skridhi* (Dwelling place) and *Jibhasi* (life)'" The '*Shantiparva*', one of the books of the Indian epic, *Mahabharatha,* sets out in great detail the rules governing the conduct of rulers. This work contains a systematic body of political ideas and embodies a comprehensive theory of kinship and government. It also tells about the importance of the freedoms of the individual (civil liberties) in a State. 'The concept of Dharma - rights and duties of individuals, classes,

communities and castes- has been delineated in our scriptures. It has been all pervading, governing, ordering, regulating and directing human beings in their earthly and spiritual pursuits. It has been a liberating force helping man to attain freedom from bondage, indiscretion and exploitation"'.[9]

2. The *Smritis*, namely *Dhārmasustras*, which deal with the duties of men in their various relations and *Dharamashastras* which are rules for religious observance and expiation;
3. Manu Smriti, compiled around 200 BC has 2,694 verses which expounded a code of conduct covering a wide range of situations and relationships a man could find himself in. Even *Arthasastra*, the best known ancient Indian Treatise, authorized by Kautilya, based on the principle of law and government, treats of the 'duties' of a king towards his subjects rather than of divine 'prerogatives'. It says, 'in their happiness lies his happiness, in their welfare, his welfare'.[10]
4. *Narada Smriti*: which emphasis's that custom overrides any text of law.
5. *Puranas* compendium of legends and religious instructions.
6. *Upnishads*: 112 speculative and mystical scriptures which are best known for their doctrine of Brahman, the ultimate reality of pure being and consciousness.

### *Human Rights in Persian Empire*

The Achaemenid Persian Empire of ancient Iran established unprecedented principles of human rights in 6th century BC Under Cyrus the Great. After his conquest of Babylon in539 BC, the king issued the Cyrus Cylinder which was discovered in 1879 and recognized by many as the first human rights document.[23] The cylinder declared that citizens of the empire would be allowed to practice their religious belief freely. It also abolished slavery, so all the palaces of the Kings Persia were built by paid workers in an era where slaves typically did such work.[24] These two reforms were reflected in the biblical books of chronicles and Ezra, which state that Cyrus released the followers of Judaism from slavery and allowed them to migrate back to their land. The cylinder now lies in the British Museum, and a replica is kept at the United Nations headquarters.

### Human Rights during Medieval Period

In the medieval period which roughly ranges from 13th century to the Treaty of Westphalia (1648), absorbing the period of Renaissance and the decline of feudalism, certain basic changes in the beliefs and practices of society were seen because people felt the idea of human rights as a general social need. The teachings of Aquinas and Hugo Grotius in the European continent and the Magna Carta (1215), the Petition of Rights (1628) and the English Bill of Rights (1689) in England were proof of this change.[11] All testified to the increasingly popular view that human beings are endowed with eternal and inalienable rights, never renounced even when human kind contracted to enter the society from the primitive state and never diminished by the claim of the '*Divine Rights of Kings*'.[12] Because the idea of human rights was to take hold as a general social need and reality, it was found necessary that the basic changes in the beliefs and practices of society should take place and the changes as evolved from about the 13th century, during the Renaissance and the decline of feudalism be effected. The resistance to religious intolerance and political economic bondage began changing into the long transition of liberal nations, talking in terms of freedom and equality particularly in relation to the use of ownership of property came in to force. That was the time when the foundations for what are today called truly as human rights were laid.

It was primarily in the 17th and 18th centuries that the scientific and intellectual achievements provided the strong basis to the transition of natural rights to the more explicit and broader concept of human rights. The discoveries of Galileo and Sir Isaac Newton, the materialism of Thomas Hobbes, the rationalism of Rene Descartes and Gottfried Wilhelm Heibniz, the pantheism of Benedict de Spinoza, the empiricism of Francis Bacon and John Locke, encouraged the belief that natural law had in the content of Universal order. With this impetus, during the 18$^{th}$ century, known as the 'Age of Enlightenment', a growing confidence in human reason and in the perfectibility of human affairs consolidated its hold and became a more comprehensive expression of this period. Further, during 17$^{th}$ century English philosopher John Locke arguably the most important natural law theorist of modern time, being in complete agreement mainly with the writings associated with (Glorious Revolution) the Revolution of 1688 agreed to the fact that certain rights self-evidently pertain to individuals as human beings. He further asserted that the chief among them were the rights to life, liberty (freedom from arbitrary rule) and property. He argued that upon entering the civil society (pursuant to a social contract), human kind surrendered to the state only the rights to enforce these natural rights and not the rights themselves. However, the state's failure to secure these reserved natural rights (the state itself being under contract to safeguard the interests of its members) gives rise to a right to popular revolution. These philosophers who postulated their theories building on the argument of Locke's thoughts, had all argued to the fact that they all had supreme faith on reason and vigorously attacked religious and scientific dogmatism, targeting even intolerance, censorship and socio-economic restraints. They sought to discover and act upon universally valid principles harmoniously governing nature, humanity and society including the theory of the inalienable 'rights ethical and social gospel'.

It is in the works of John Locke that the doctrine of Natural Rights finds full expression. He asserts that right to life is coupled with two other rights, namely, liberty and property. In fact, what is life to Hobbes is property to Locke. In Locke's philosophy, right to property includes life and liberty as well. In this way the derivation of Natural Rights from Natural Law is completed in Locke's 'Two Treaties on Civil Government'[13]. The ideas of Locke about life, liberty and property are Natural

Rights and are fundamental rights, appealed to Revolutionaries and freedom fighters both in Europe and across the Atlantic. Those ideas found expression in the American Declaration of Independence, 1776 and in the French Declaration of the Rights of Man and Citizen, 1789. These two Declarations are of great historic importance. In fact, they are the prelude to the contemporary movement of human rights in the world.[14]

Human rights have a long history but it was in the eighteenth century that the law of nature had begun to assert itself to protect the individual against the power of state. This culminated in the great Declaration of the Rights of Man and Citizen in France in 1789 and in the United States Constitutional Amendment of 1791.[15]

### *Declaration of the Rights of Man and Citizen*[16]

The representatives of the French people, organized as a National Assembly, believing that the ignorance, neglect, or contempt of the rights of man were the sole cause of public calamities and of the corruption of governments. It had determined to set forth in a solemn declaration of the natural, unalienable, and sacred rights of man and citizen in order that this declaration, being constantly before all the members of the social body, shall remind them continually of their rights and duties; in order that the acts of the legislative power, as well as those of the executive power, may be compared at any moment with the objects and purpose of all political institutions and may thus be more respected, and lastly, in order that the grievances of the citizens, based hereafter upon simple and incontestable principles, shall tend to maintenance of the constitution and redound to the happiness of all. Therefore the National Assembly recognized and proclaimed, in the presence and under the auspices of the Supreme Being, the following rights of man and of the citizen;[17]

*Articles of the Declaration of the Rights of Man and Citizens:*

1. Men are born and remain free and equal in rights, social distinctions may be found only upon the general good.

2. The aim of all political associations is the preservation of the natural and imperceptible rights of man. These rights are liberty, property, security, and resistance to oppression.
3. The principle of all sovereignty resides essentially in the nation. No body or individual may exercise any authority which does not proceed directly from the nation.
4. Liberty consists in the freedom to do everything which injures no one else; hence the exercise of the natural rights of each man has no limits except those which assure to the other members of the society to enjoyment of the same rights. These limits can only be determined by law.
5. Law can only prohibit such actions as are hurtful to society. Nothing may be prevented which is not forbidden by law, and no one may be forced to do anything not provided for by law.
6. Law is the expression of the general will. Every citizen has a right to participate personally, or through his representative, in its foundation. It must be the same for all, whether it protects or punishes. All citizens being equal in the eyes of law, are equally eligible to all dignities and to all public positions and occupations, according to their abilities, and without distinction except that of their virtues and talents.
7. No person shall be accused, arrested, or imprisoned except in the cases and according to the forms prescribed by law. Any one soliciting, transmitting, executing, or causing to be executed, any arbitrary order, shall be punished. But any citizen summoned or arrested in virtue of the law shall submit without delay, as resistance constitutes an offense.
8. The law shall provide for such punishments only as are strictly and obviously necessary, and no one shall suffer punishment except it be legally inflicted in

virtue of a law passed and promulgated before the commission of the offense.

9. As all persons are held innocent until they shall have been declared guilty, if arrest shall be deemed indispensable, all harshness not essential to the securing of the prisoner's person shall be severely repressed by law.

10. No one shall be disquieted on account of his opinions, including his religious views, provided their manifestation does not disturb the public order established by law.

11. The free communication of ideas and opinions is one of the most precious of the rights of man. Every citizen may, accordingly, speak, write, and print with the freedom, but shall be responsible for such abuses of this freedom as shall be defined of law.

12. The security of the rights of man and of the citizen requires public military forces. These forces are, therefore, established for the good of all and not for the personal advantage of those to whom they shall be entrusted.

13. A common contribution is essential for the maintenance of the public forces and for the cost of administration. This should be equitably distributed among all the citizens in proportion to their means.

14. All the citizens have a right to decide, either personally or by their representatives, as to necessity of the public contribution; to grant this freely, to know to what uses it is put, and to fix the proportion, the mode of assessment and of collection and the duration of the taxes.

15. Society has a right to require of every public agent on account of his administration.

16. A society in which the observance of the law is not assured, nor the separation of powers defined, has no constitution at all.

17. Since property is a sacred and inviolable right, no one may be deprived of it unless a legally established public necessity obviously requires it, and upon condition of a just and previous indemnity.

Similarly the Declaration of American Independence framed in 1791, is the most important of all American historical documents. It is essentially a partisan document, a justification of the American Revolution presented to the world. The Declaration asserts the fundamental American ideal of government, based on the theory of natural rights, which had based on the theory of natural rights, which had been held by among others, John Locke, Emerich de Vattel, and Jean Jacques Rousseau.

The Declaration of American Independence further states that all men are created equal, that they are endowed by their creator with certain inalienable Rights, that among these are Life, Liberty and the pursuit of Happiness- that to secure these rights, Governments are instituted among Men, deriving their just powers from the consent of the governed – that whenever any form of government becomes destructive of these ends, it is the Right to the people to alter or to abolish it.[18]

The main individual rights and freedoms guaranteed under the first constitutional amendment of the USA are as follows:

- Freedom of expression, press, religion and opinion.
- Enjoyment of equal rights and privilages.
- Right to ownership and use of blessing of life.
- Right to any convict to be aware of the subject of the charge brought against him/her witnesses.
- No freeman shall be convicted except upon a verdict issued unanimously by a jury, members of which are to be selected from among upright and righteous people.
- The excessive bail bond shall not be demanded from an accused.
- No freeman shall be put into prison or deprived of using his/her own property of the gift of life and

liberty or be subjected to banishment unless upon a conviction of law and by virtue of a decree issued by a court of competent jurisdiction.

- Penal laws shall have no retroactive effect in cases where more intense punishments are deemed impossible.

All this liberal intellectual ferment had, not surprisingly, great influence on the Western world of the late 18th and early 19th centuries. With practical example of English Revolution of 1688 and the Bill of Rights which provided the rationale for the wave of revolutionary agitation. It had swept the West most notably in the North America and France, with these revolutions and the idea of human rights, which played a key role in the 18th and 19th century's struggles against political absolutism. It was indeed, seen as the failure of rules to respect the principles of freedom and equality, which had been central to the philosophy of the natural law, which was from the beginning responsible for the overall development of societies. In the words of Maurice Cranston, a leading student of Human Rights, "absolutism prompted man to claim (human or natural) rights precisely because it denied them".[19]

Despite these thoughts, the idea of human rights as natural rights was not without its detractors. Even at this receptive time, with states frequently associates themselves with religious orthodoxy, the doctrine of natural rights became less and less acceptable to philosophical and political liberals. Additionally, because they were conceived as essentially absolutist 'inalienable', 'unalterable', eternal terms, natural rights found themselves coming to conflict increasingly with one another. Most importantly, the doctrines of natural rights came under powerful philosophical and political attack from both the right and the left. In England, for example, conservatives Edmund Burke and David Hume united with liberal thinker Jeremy Bentham in condemning the doctrine. These assaults upon natural law and natural rights, which began during the late 19th and early 20th centuries once again met their savior, John Stuart Mill, who despite his vigorous defense of liberty, proclaimed that rights ultimately are founded on utility. The German jurist Friedrich Karl Von Sauigny, England's Sir Henry Maine and others, placing similar arguments, emphasized that right are a function of cultural and environment variables unique to particular communities. Opposing such thinking once again it was the jurist Austin and the philosopher Ludwig Willgenstein respectively who insisted, that the only law is 'the command of the sovereign' and that it is the only truth which can be established by verifiable experience. By the time of First World War there were scarcely any theorists who would or could defend the 'Rights of Man' along the lines of natural law. Indeed, under the influence of 19th century German idealism and parallel expressions of rising European nationalism, there were some like Marxists, for example who, although not rejecting individual rights altogether, maintained that rights from whatever source derived, belong to communities or to the whole of the societies and; nations pre-eminently. Yet, despite having its heyday the natural rights proved short to completely strengthen the idea of human rights, nonetheless, endured in one form to another. The abolition of slavery, factory legislation, popular education, trade unionism, the universal suffrage movement etc. of 19th century's reformist impulse afford ample evidence that the idea was not being extinguished even if its trans-empirical derivation had become a matter of general skepticism.

## Twentieth Century – A New Era of Human Rights

The promotion and protection of human rights and fundamental freedom of individual in the present form, stormed directly from the realization by the international community that the recognition of the inherent, equal and inalienable rights of all members of human family is the foundation of freedom, justice and peace in the contemporary world.[20] The pathetic incidents during World War First also pointed the need for an expansion of the rights guaranteed to minorities particularly because of the growth of nationalistic sentiments and the very real danger of suppression and oppression, faced by racial, ethic, linguistic as well as religious minorities. As a consequence, the principal allied and associated states including Austria, Greece, Bulgaria, Hungary, Poland, Turkey, Romania and Yugoslavia started taking initiative. These states promised just and equal treatment of their minority groups.[21] Later on, similar guarantees were given by Albania, Estonia, Iraq, Laliva and Lithania as pre- conditions of their admission to the League of Nations.

At the end of World War First, the reassertion of the tradition for the suitable treatment of individuals, in the form of Minor Treaties concluded between the Principal Allied and Associated Powers. Several enlarged States which emerged after the War, did arise in the context of a general international principle of promoting human rights.[22] At the end of World War First, international concern for human dignity and rights had also found expression in the Covenant of the League of Nations.[23]

The League of Nations is remembered in the international history as the child of War. The League of Nations was the first effort in human history to furnish the international political institution.[24] Article 22 of the Covenant of League of Nations Established the Mandates System which proclaimed the principal that the well being and development of the people in mandated territories formed a sacred trust of civilization. Mandatory powers were supposed to administer these territories under the conditions which will guarantee freedom of conscience and religion and the prohibition of abuses such as slave trade. The mandatory powers also undertook to provide the League of Nations, annual reports regarding the discharge of their responsibilities in this regard. These reports were reviewed by the Mandate Commission of the League.[25]

Member states accepted the obligation to secure and maintain fair and human condition of labour for men, women and children and also to ensure just treatment for inhabitants of their colonies.[26] Even under the Mandates system, established by the Covenant of the League of Nations, certain powers accepted as a sacred trust took the responsibility for the well being and advancement of the people placed under their mandate.

Moreover, in 1919 the International Labour Organization was established in the realization that Universal peace could be achieved only if it was based on social justice.[27] The organization was established with a guiding principle that all human beings, irrespective of race, creed, or sex had the right to pursue their material, well being and spiritual development in conditions of freedom and dignity of economic security and equal opportunity.[28]

In 1929, Institute of International Law, New York, United States (US) prepared a Declaration of Human Rights and Duties.[29] The Institute submitted the declaration of human rights and duties to Inter American Legal Committee. In Article 1, it proclaimed that it is a duty of every State to recognize equal rights of an individual to life, freedom and property and to fully grant and protect these rights on its entire territory regardless of nationality, sex, race, language or religion[30] and Article 2 reveals that it is a duty of every State to recognise the equal rights of an individual to the free execution, whether in public or in private, of any faith, religion or worship, the practice of which is not in violation of public order and good manners.[31]

On August 14, 1941, Atlantic Charter, (an agreement between Wintson Churchill, the Prime Minister of Britain and President Franklin Roosevelt of America in a ship in the Atlantic Ocean) emphasized the importance of defending life, liberty, independence and religious freedoms and preserving human rights and justice at every land.[32] During the inter war periods (1919-39), there was systematic persecution of the Jews in Nazi Germany especially 1933 onwards. This mass persecution of the Jews shocked the conscience of mankind and inevitably raised the question whether State sovereignty permitted a government to treat the nationals as it would like or there are limits to its authority imposed by any higher order.[33]

The Nazis in Germany committed atrocities on the Jews, their own nationals, which surpassed in brutality and barbarity even the monstrosities of Chengiz Khan, Nadir Shah and other similar devils. It is estimated that 12 million Jews were done to death in a cold and calculated manner to satisfy the crazy theories of German bigotry. The Nazi persecutions of the Jews and their acts of vandalism, loot and plunder in occupied lands gave birth to a new concept in international criminal code, that of Crime against Humanity.[34]

The systematic elimination of Jews in Germany during the Nazi rule (1933-45) gave yet another word to the criminal code, namely, the 'crime of genocide'. These two words sum up the holocaust let loose upon humanity by the Nazis. The subjection and the various kinds of oppression and persecution of the innocent people in mid 20th century further accelerated the movement to uphold the inalienable rights of human beings all over the world. Even during World War Second, the necessity of promoting and preserving human freedoms and rights was affirmed in various statements, declarations such as the Declaration by the War time United Nations (Jan. 1, 1942) and the Tehran Declaration (Dec. 1, 1943) and the Dum Parton Oaks Conventions (Aug. 21 and Sep. 29, 1944).[35]

After the war was over and humanity was freed of its traumatic consequences, there was widespread feeling that never again should mankind be put to such barbarity. There were two demands in particular which voiced Universally: (1) that world peace should never be disturbed and war among nations should be banned strictly and for ever (2) that there should be identified and codified body of rights and freedoms which should be respected by all nations irrespective of the stipulations of their individual national constitutions and these should be upheld in all circumstances, in times of peace as well as war, and treated as sacred and inviolable.[36]

The history of human rights covers thousands of years and draws upon religious, cultural, philosophical and legal developments throughout recorded history. But prior to the 1940s, the term 'human rights' was rarely used. There was no sustained international movement in its name. There were no non-governmental organizations (NGOs) with a global reach to defend its principles.

## Role of United Nations

The dogma of human rights still prevailed as an ambiguous ans sidelined national/domestic matter till 1940s. The was absence of a uniform and universal definition of human rights to be acceptable to international community. There was no consent or consensus on the nature, scope and jurisdiction of human rights at international level. Above all, human rights were still, more or less, an academic concern, and not a reality. It was the advent of United Nations (UN), which provided uniformity, universality, a precise definition, and a drafted jurisdiction to human rights. There was no international law crafted to protect human rights prior to UN.[37] The first documentary use of the expression 'human rights' is to be found in the Charter of the United Nations, which was adopted after the World War II, at San Francisco on June 25, 1945 and ratified by a majority of its signatories in October that year.[38]

### *Charter of United Nations*

The preamble of this Charter, which was drawn up to prevent recurrence of the destruction and suffering caused by the second World War, by setting up the international organization reveals that United Nations shall constantly advance, *inter alia* to reaffirm faith in the fundamental human rights. Thereafter, Charter of the United Nations stated that the purpose of the United Nations shall be, among others, to achieve international co-operation in promoting and encouraging respect for human rights and for fundamental freedoms for all without distinction as to race, sex and language, or religion.[39] The UN Charter, however, was not a binding instrument and merely stated the ideal which was to be later developed by different agencies and organs of UN itself. The first major and concrete step towards formulating the various human rights was taken by the UN General Assembly in December, 1948, by adopting the Universal Declaration of Human Rights (UDHR).[40]

U.N. Charter today imposes a duty to all the nations to respect the human rights of their citizens.[41] The Preamble states: "We the people of United Nations"... not merely the Member states ... reaffirm their "faith in fundamental human rights and in the dignity and worth of the human persons, in the equal rights of men and women of nations large and small ..." Article 1(3) includes among stated purposes, the achievement of "International Cooperation in solving international problems ... And in promoting and encouraging respect for human rights and for fundamental freedom for all without distinction as to race, sex, language, or religion ..." The General Assembly shall initiate studies and make recommendations for the purpose of "assisting in the realization of human rights and fundamental freedoms for all."[42] The important provisions are probably those contained in Article 55 and 56 of the Charter. Art 55 provides that UN shall promote inter-alia, "Universal respect for all and observance of human rights and fundamental freedom for all without distinction as to race, sex, language, religion. While in Article 56, all members pledge themselves to take joint and separate action in cooperation with the organization for the achievement of purpose set forth in Art 55. Article 62 (2) authorizes Economic and Social Council to "make recommendations for the purpose of promoting respect for observance of human rights and fundamental freedom for all."[43] Further, it is provided that, the Economic and Social Council shall set up commissions for the "Protection of Human rights".[44] Provisions are also made under Art 76(c) as the basic objective of the trusteeship system, "to encourage respect for all distinction as to race, sex, religion, language."[45]

### *Preamble of Universal Declaration of Human Rights (UDHR)*

Universal Declaration of Human Rights is a pledge for all nations to secure all basic human rights of all human beings without any discrimination of caste, colour, creed, gender etc. UDHR, in its preamble believes that the recognition of the inherent dignity and of the equal and inalienable rights of all members of the human family is the foundation of freedom, justice and peace in the world. All nations and all people belonging to those nations should reaffirm their faith in fundamental human rights.[46] The General Assembly called upon all member countries to publicize the text of the UDHR and to cause it to be disseminated, displayed, read and expounded principally in schools and other educational institutions, without distinction based on the political status of countries or territories.

***Article 1.*** *Right to Equality*

All human beings are born free and equal in dignity and rights.They are endowed with reason and conscience and should act towards one another in a spirit of brotherhood.

***Article 2.*** *Freedom from Discrimination*

Everyone is entitled to all the rights and freedoms set forth in this Declaration, without distinction of any kind, such as race, colour, sex, language, religion, political or other opinion, national or social origin, property, birth or other status. Furthermore, no distinction shall be made on the basis of the political, jurisdictional or international status of the country or territory to which a person belongs, whether it be independent, trust, non-self-governing or under any other limitation of sovereignty.

***Article 3.*** *Right to Life, Liberty, Personal Security*

Everyone has the right to life, liberty and security of person.

***Article 4.*** *Freedom from Slavery*

No one shall be held in slavery or servitude; slavery and the slave trade shall be prohibited in all their forms.

***Article 5.*** *Freedom from Torture, Degrading Treatment*

No one shall be subjected to torture or to cruel, inhuman or degrading treatment or punishment.

***Article 6.*** *Right to Recognition as a Person before the Law*

Everyone has the right to recognition everywhere as a person before the law.

***Article 7.*** *Right to Equality before the Law*

All are equal before the law and are entitled without any discrimination to equal protection of the law. All are entitled to equal protection against any discrimination in violation of this Declaration and against any incitement to such discrimination.

***Article 8.*** *Right to Remedy by a Competent Tribunal*

Everyone has the right to an effective remedy by the competent national tribunals for acts violating the fundamental rights granted him by the constitution or by law.

***Article 9.*** *Freedom from Arbitrary Arrest, Imprisonment, Exile*

No one shall be subjected to arbitrary arrest, detention or exile.

***Article 10.*** *Right to fair Public Hearing*

Everyone is entitled in full equality to a fair and public hearing by an independent and impartial tribunal, in the determination of his rights and obligations and of any criminal charge against him.

***Article 11.*** *Right to be Considered Innocent until Proven Guilty*

(1) Everyone charged with a penal offence has the right to be presumed innocent until proved guilty according to law in a public trial at which he has had all the guarantees necessary for his defense.

(2) No one shall be held guilty of any penal offence on account of any act or omission which did not constitute a penal offence, under national or international law, at the time when it was committed. Nor shall a heavier penalty be imposed than the one that was applicable at the time the penal offence was committed.

***Article 12.*** *Freedom from Interference with Privacy, Family, Home or Correspondence*

No one shall be subjected to arbitrary interference with his privacy, family, home or correspondence, nor to attacks upon his honour and reputation. Everyone has the right to the protection of the law against such interference or attacks.

***Article 13.*** *Right to Free Movement in and out of any Country*

(1) Everyone has the right to freedom of movement and residence within the borders of each state.

(2) Everyone has the right to leave any country, including his own, and to return to his country.

***Article 14.*** *Right to Asylum in Other Countries from Persecution*

(1) Everyone has the right to seek and to enjoy in other countries asylum from persecution.

(2) This right may not be invoked in the case of prosecutions genuinely arising from non-political crimes or from acts contrary to the purposes and principles of the United Nations.

***Article 15.*** *Right to Nationality and Freedom to Change it*

(1) Everyone has the right to a nationality.

(2) No one shall be arbitrarily deprived of his nationality nor denied the right to change his nationality.

***Article 16.*** *Right to Marriage and Family*

(1) Men and women of full age, without any limitation due to race, nationality or religion, have the right to marry and to found a family. They are entitled to equal rights as to marriage, during marriage and at its dissolution.

(2) Marriage shall be entered into only with the free and full consent of the intending spouses.

(3) The family is the natural and fundamental group unit of society and is entitled to protection by society and the State.

***Article 17.*** *Right to Own Property*

(1) Everyone has the right to own property alone as well as in association with others.

(2) No one shall be arbitrarily deprived of his property.

***Article 18.*** *Freedom of Belief and Religion*

Everyone has the right to freedom of thought, conscience and religion; this right includes freedom to change his religion or belief, and freedom, either alone or in community with others and in public or private, to manifest his religion or belief in teaching, practice, worship and observance.

***Article 19.*** *Freedom of Opinion and Information*

Everyone has the right to freedom of opinion and expression; this right includes freedom to hold opinions without interference and to seek, receive and impart information and ideas through any media and regardless of frontiers.

***Article 20.*** *Right to Peaceful Assembly and Association*

(1) Everyone has the right to freedom of peaceful assembly and association.

(2) No one may be compelled to belong to an association.

***Article 21.*** *Right to Participate in Government and in Free Elections*

(1) Everyone has the right to take part in the government of his country, directly or through freely chosen representatives.

(2) Everyone has the right of equal access to public service in his country.

(3) The will of the people shall be the basis of the authority of government; this will shall be expressed in periodic and genuine elections which shall be by universal and equal suffrage and shall be held by secret vote or by equivalent free voting procedures.

***Article 22.*** *Right to Social Security*

Everyone, as a member of society, has the right to social security and is entitled to realization, through national effort and international co-operation and in accordance with the organization and resources of each State, of the economic, social and cultural rights indispensable for his dignity and the free development of his personality.

***Article 23.*** *Right to Desirable Work and to Join a Trade Union*

(1) Everyone has the right to work, to free choice of employment, to just and favourable conditions of work and to protection against unemployment.

(2) Everyone, without any discrimination, has the right to equal pay for equal work.

(3) Everyone who works has the right to just and favourable remuneration ensuring for himself and his family an existence worthy of human dignity, and supplemented, if necessary, by other means of social protection.

(4) Everyone has the right to form and to join trade unions for the protection of his interests.

*Article 24. Right to Rest and Leisure*

Everyone has the right to rest and leisure, including reasonable limitation of working hours and periodic holidays with pay.

*Article 25. Right to Adequate Living Standards*

(1) Everyone has the right to a standard of living adequate for the health and well-being of himself and of his family, including food, clothing, housing and medical care and necessary social services, and the right to security in the event of unemployment, sickness, disability, widowhood, old age or other lack of livelihood in circumstances beyond his control.

(2) Motherhood and childhood are entitled to special care and assistance. All children, whether born in or out of wedlock, shall enjoy the same social protection.

*Article 26. Right to Education*

(1) Everyone has the right to education. Education shall be free, at least in the elementary and fundamental stages. Elementary education shall be compulsory. Technical and professional education shall be made generally available and higher education shall be equally accessible to all on the basis of merit.

(2) Education shall be directed to the full development of the human personality and to the strengthening of respect for human rights and fundamental freedoms. It shall promote understanding, tolerance and friendship among all nations, racial or religious groups, and shall further the activities of the United Nations for the maintenance of peace.

(3) Parents have a prior right to choose the kind of education that shall be given to their children.

*Article 27. Right to Participate in the Cultural Life of a Community.*

(1) Everyone has the right freely to participate in the cultural life of the community, to enjoy the arts and to share in scientific advancement and its benefits.

(2) Everyone has the right to the protection of the moral and material interests resulting from any scientific, literary or artistic production of which he is the author.

***Article 28.*** *Right to Social Orders assuring to Human Rights*

Everyone is entitled to a social and international order in which the rights and freedoms set forth in this Declaration can be fully realized.

***Article 29.*** *Community Duties Essential to Free and full Development*

(1) Everyone has duties to the community in which alone the free and full development of his personality is possible.

(2) In the exercise of his rights and freedoms, everyone shall be subject only to such limitations as are determined by law solely for the purpose of securing due recognition and respect for the rights and freedoms of others and of meeting the just requirements of morality, public order and the general welfare in a democratic society.

(3) These rights and freedoms may in no case be exercised contrary to the purposes and principles of the United Nations.

***Article 30.*** *Freedom from State or Personal Interference in the Above Rights*

Nothing in this Declaration may be interpreted as implying for any State, group or person any right to engage in any activity or to perform any act aimed at the destruction of any of the rights and freedoms set forth herein.

Eleanor Roosevelt had said in 1948 while commending the UDHR to the General Assembly of the United Nations that it might well become the international Magna Carta of all mankind.[47] That statement must have sounded as an exaggeration. The experience of the World shows, that in the first post-war decade, many countries used the UN Declaration of Human Rights for the political reconstruction, embodying the provisions of the Declaration in their own national constitutions.

Thus, for the first time in history, responsibility for the protection and pursuit of human rights was assumed by the international community and was accepted as a permanent obligation. The General Assembly also proclaimed the UDHR as a common standard of achievement for all people to promote and secure the effective recognition and observance of the rights and freedoms. Following a resolution to this effect adopted by the General Assembly on December 10, 1950, the 10th December of each year is declared to be celebrated as Human Rights Day all over the world.

A careful reading of the Preamble to the Universal Declaration of Human rights shows that the Preamble contains the ideals and aspirations of the world community to promote and establish human rights to all. It declares the highest aspirations of the common man- his rights and freedoms which he desires to secure for him for others- for all in the world.

The UDHR (adopted and proclaimed by General Assembly resolution 217 A (III) of 10th December 1948) states the basic hopes and wishes that are common to all humanity. The UDHR records the wishes not only of people from countries which had already reached a certain economic standard of living, but it also sets out the rights of people in countries where hundreds of millions of human beings were weighed down by oppression, poverty and lack of adequate education. The UDHR is not a treaty, not even a legal agreement between countries, or a binding legal document. It is rather a declaration, a statement of intent or principle. In its 30 Articles, the Universal Declaration of Human Rights sets forth the basic rights and freedom to which all men and women are entitled, without any discrimination.

However, United Nations and human rights was devoid of any legal sanctions to compel states to meet the obligations of ensuring observance and implementing of human rights enriched in it. So to transform the principles into provision casting binding legal obligations on the part of ratifying state, the General Assembly promulgated in December 1966, International Covenant on Civil and Political Rights, and Optional Protocol to the Covenant on Civil and Political Rights.

### *International Covenants*

To develop the UN Charter into an international code of human rights law, the international community created a number of multilateral human rights treaties. The two most significant of these were the international Covenant on Civil and Political Rights and Covenant on Economic, Social and Cultural Rights.[48] Both were put into effect in 1976. Those treaties forbid discrimination on the basis of race, color, sex, language, religion, political or other opinion, national or social origin, property, birth or other status. The two covenants, alongwith the UN Charter, the Universal Declaration of Human Rights, and an accord called the Optional Protocol to the Covenant on Civil and Political Rights (1976), constitute a body of law that has been called the International Bill of Human Rights. The two Covenants came into force in December, 1976, after the Requisite number of member states (35) ratified them. Many other states ratified the Covenants subsequently. These Covenants are therefore, legally binding on the ratifying states.[49]In this growing body of human rights the International Covenant on Civil and Political Rights is easily the first milestone. They constitute the first generation of rights. Then the Economic, Social and Cultural Rights were also added which were passed by the United Nations General Assembly in 1966. These were the second generation of human rights.

Unlike the first generation of human rights, which are prohibitive to the states, the second generation of human rights empower the state towards achieving the basic social and economic rights of its citizens The first generation of human rights would not remain safe without making grounds for a healthy, viable, and a just set of second generation of human rights. There is today an expanding of human rights and mention needs particularly be made of the International Convention on the Elimination of all forms or Social Discrimination (1969), Convention against Torture and other 'Treatment and Punishment (1984) and the Convention of Children (1990). There constitutes the third generation of human rights.

The status of the fourth generation of human rights like right to environment, right to common heritage of mankind among others, as endorsed by the respective bodies of United Nations in the new world order; is found to be the utmost important to the third world countries. It has not been fully crystallized and it has to be adequately developed in the 21st century.

## Major International Conventions

The International Bill of Human Rights served as the inspiration for more than 150 conventions on human rights instruments that have been concluded within the United Nations a wide range of issues. Some of them are:[50]

- *Convention on the Prevention and Punishment of the Crime of Genocide (1948)* - It is a crime under international law. Those guilty of genocide, in wartime or peace can be tried in the countries where the crime was committed.
- *Convention relating to the status of Refugee (1951)* defines the right and makes provision for various aspects of their right to work, education, public assistance and so on.
- *Convention on the Elimination of all forms of Racial Discrimination (1965)* is one of the most widely ratified treaties, with 143 state parties as of June 1995. It finds any policy of racial superiority based on racial difference, totally unjustifiable, scientifically false and morally and legally and condemnable.
- *Convention on the Elimination of all forms of Discrimination against Women (1979)* - State parties shall take all appropriate measures to eliminate discrimination against women in the field of employment in order to ensure, on a basis of equality of men and women, the same right shall accord to women equally with men before law and shall take appropriate measures to eliminate discrimination against women in all matters relating to marriage and family relations.

- *Convention against Torture and other Inhumane or Degrading Treatment (1984)* - Torture is one of the most alarming human rights abuses. It is used as punishment, to obtain information or force confessions, but even more so to spread fear and induce shock and passivity in individuals and in entire communities. It is as an international crime and holds state parties accountable for preventing and punishing torture.
- *Convention on the Rights of the Child (1989)*- It recognizes the particular vulnerability of children and brings together in one comprehensive code benefits and protections for children who are refugees, disabled or members of minorities.
- *Declaration on the Rights of Persons belonging to National or Ethnic, Religious and Linguistic Minorities (1992)*- It proclaims the rights of minorities to enjoy their own culture; to profess and practice their own religion; to establish and maintain contacts with other members of their groups.

Hence, in the language of United Nations Charter of Human Rights- human rights could be generally defined as those rights which are inherent in our nature and without which people cannot live as human beings. It was a yardstick of international standards and a path finding instrument. It defines specific rights- civil, political as well as social economic and cultural with equality and freedom. The United Nation Charter reflects a new approach to the protection of human liberty and freedom, both of experience of World War 11 and the years immediately preceding it, when the flagrance violations of human rights and denial of basic dignity of man were the hallmarks of regimes challenging and violating international peace and society.

The 20th anniversary of the adoption of the Universal Declaration of Human Rights was commemorated in 1968 as the International Year for Human Rights. The major event of the year was the International Conference on Human Rights. The International Conference on Human Right held in Teheran

(Iran) was the first worldwide governmental reviewed progress made since the adoption of the Universal Declaration. It evaluated the effectiveness of the human rights activities and adoption of a program of action and a proclamation. The conference called for measures to ensure the better protection of civilians, prisoners and combatants in all armed conflicts. The World Conference on Human Rights (Vienna 14-25 June 1993)[51] was the first global review of human rights since the International Conference on Human Rights in Teheran in 1968. The Conference demonstrated a growing determination among member states and human rights NGO'S and other activities that the existing body of law be backed up by vigorous operational activities undertaken by the United Nations. It should be ensured that these laws be carried out by the governments. Human rights, in the words of Vienna Declaration, adopted at the World Conference had become the legitimate concern of the international community. It proclaims that "democracy, development and respect for human rights and independent and mutually reinforcing." Secretary General Boutros Ghali called the Vienna Declaration a program of action and a new vision for global action for human rights into the next century.

The Declaration adopted by historic new steps to promote and protect human rights particularly those of women, children and indigenous people by:

- Supposing the establishment of a special Rapport's on violence against women.
- Calling for the universal ratification by I995 of the convention of the rights of the child.
- Recommending that the General Assembly proclaims an international decade for the world's indigenous people and a decade for human rights education.

The fiftieth session of the United Nations Commission of Human Rights placed between January 31 and March 11, 1994, adopted 109 resolutions and took other actions addressing human rights violations in thirty countries.[52] The resolution condemned violence and human rights violations directed against women. The commission also sought to implement the Vienna conference's call for the identifications of gender-specific abuses as human rights and the integration of women's human rights throughout the United Nations.

The conference's achievements include:

- Recommending the establishment of a High Commissioner for Human Rights.
- Reinforcement of universality of human rights.
- Recognition for the first time, by consensus, that the right to development is an inalienable right.
- Recognition of democracy as a human right, thus opening the way to the strengthening and promotion of democracy, democratization and the rule of law.
- Recognition that the acts, methods and practices of terrorism aim at the destruction of human rights.
- Reinforcement of policies and programs to eliminate racism and racial discrimination, xenophobia and intolerance.

Addressing the World Conference on Human Rights at the Vienna on 14th June, 1993, His Excellency Boutros Boutros Ghali expressed his views in the importance of human rights as follows: "One thing is certain that there can be no sustainable development without promoting democracy and, thus, without respect for human rights. Only by heightening the International Community's awareness of human rights in this way and involving everyone in this effort can we present future violations that our conscience, and the law, will condemn." [53] He further stated "May human rights create a special climate of solidarity and responsibility. May Human Rights become the common language of humanity."[54]

Since the passage of the UDHR in 1948 there have been political, economic, social and cultural changes which have unquestionably made impression on the concept of human rights. It has also put an impact on the effectiveness and on the actual respect held for them in today's world. It is difficult to find a period in the history of mankind when the question of human rights has had a greater significance in theory and practice than during the period from 1948 to the present. There have been times when the mater held great importance in a given State of region, but never has the question of human rights been the object of such wide general attention as nowadays. Furthermore, this matter has never held such interest for the masses and the people of practically the whole world as it has during these years. Even recently, the Student Protest Movement in China and the fall of Communism, have demonstrated the tremendous cries for representation and personal freedoms, as well as the success and failures in regard to human rights.

The universalization of the question of human rights, a characteristic phenomenon of our era never seen in its present form, has been associated with the legal and political internationalization of the issue, as seen initially in the UDHR. Now human rights are no longer a question, which attracts the attention of mankind solely from a historical, philosophical and doctrinal point of view, but have become, both politically and legally, a matter of interest to the international community as a whole. This has been the success of the efforts to promote human rights. But it should be recommended that international acceptance of the question of human rights is an unending process whose future is always open to all possibilities.

There is a considerable body of human rights law and standards which currently supplement the International Bill of Human Rights in areas dealing with diverse issues, such as the right to self-determination, the prevention of discrimination, war crimes and crimes against humanity, slavery, forced labour, rights refugees, freedom of information, freedom of association, political rights of women, social welfare and international cultural development and co-operation. The most notable instruments adopted in the past two decades have been, The International Convention on the Suppression and Punishment of the Crime of Apartheid, the Declaration on the Prohibition of Torture and the Declaration on the Rights of Handicapped Persons, all stemming from the initial promise of human rights in 1948.

The methods employed by the UN for setting and urging the application of standards in human rights thus far have unclouded the making of recommendations, the adoption of declarations o bodies of principles and the preparation and adoption of international treaties. Methods utilized in more recent times have included the standards suggested in studies prepared by UN human rights officials, standards suggested by the Secretariat, standards suggested by working groups of human rights organs, drafts submitted by NGOs and standards proposed by governments. The UN has not lacked for instruments upholding the rights of individuals to live freely and experience all the human rights that are afforded to them. However, the main difficulty has been implementing these agreements and the scope of the UN as an implementing body. The 30 articles of the Declaration together form a comprehensive statement covering economic, social, cultural, political and civil rights. The document is both universal and indivisible. A declaration, however, is not a treaty and lacks any enforcement provisions. Rather it is a statement of intent, a set of principles to which United Nations member states commit themselves in an effort to provide all people a life of human dignity.

### *European Convention*

In between the Universal Declaration and the two International Covenants of 1966, a collective implementation of the Universal Declaration was made by a group of states who were members of the Council of Europe, by adopting it in 1950, a European Convention is legally binding on those states who had ratified it, i.e. 18 states. After such ratification, it came into force in 1953. Though people outside Europe are not directly interested in the working of the European Convention, it has an important role for the entire World interested, in the constitutional protection of human rights, because the convention had set up a European Court of Human Rights in 1959.[55]

This court has the function of determining disputes arising from the enforcement of the convention, and its decisions are propounded in the form of legal judgments. These decisions involve the interpretation of the text of the convention, and are valuable guides, in the interpretation of any national constitution which embodies identical or similar guarantees of fundamental rights.[56]

In December 1965, the General Assembly adopted and opened for signature the international convention on the Elimination of all forms of Racial Discrimination. It called for an end to racial discrimination in all its forms and established international machinery for that purpose. A Committee on Racial Discrimination was formed to achieve that aim. The committee composed of 18 experts. The convention, however, entered into force on 4 January 1969 and the committee began meeting early in 1970.[57] The International Conference on Human Rights, which met at Tehran from April 22 to May 31, 1968 to review the progress made in the past twenty years, emphasized the obligation of members of international community to promote and encourage human rights for all. This conference went on to affirm its faith in the principles set out in the International Bill of Human Rights and other relevant international instruments and to urge all people and governments to decide themselves to those principles and to redouble their efforts to provide for all dignity and conducive to physical, mental, social and spiritual welfare.[58]

## Development within the Commonwealth

The adoption of the covenants at the international level inspired the members of commonwealth for the development and protection of human rights. It was felt that the ideals of the Commonwealth could be converted into reality only if racial discrimination was altogether banned by the member countries within their respective territories.

Inspired by this object, the Heads of the Governments of the Commonwealth countries meet at Singapore in January 1971 and declared *inter alia*:

(a) We recognize racial prejudice as a dangerous sickness threatening the healthy development of the human race. Each of us will vigorously combat this evil within our own nation.

(b) We oppose all forms of colonial domination and racial oppression and are committed to the principles of human dignity and equality.

(c) We will therefore use all our efforts to foster human equality and dignity every where.

The meeting of Commonwealth Head of Governments at Lusaka in August 1979 pointed out the practice of apartheid in South Africa and declared *inter alia* –

We reject as inhuman all policies designed to perpetuate apartheid based on theories that racial groups are or may be inherently superior or inferior.

It was also emphasized in particular that the Commonwealth should enhance the co-ordination of its activities with those of other organizations similarly committed to the promotion and protection of human rights and fundamental freedoms.[59]

### *The Helsinki Conference*

The Helsinki Conference of 1975 gave the UN Declaration a new momentum and a new direction. 35 countries participated in the Helsinki meeting promising to encourage the effective exercise of civil, political, economic, social, cultural and other rights and freedoms. The conference had its principal purpose, a mutually satisfactory definition of peace and stability between East and West, previously made impossible by the Cold War.

The Final Act of the Conference also known as the Helsinki Accords, begins with a Declaration on Principles Guiding Relations between participating states, in which the participating states solemnly declare their determination to respect and put into practice, alongside other guiding principles, respect for human rights and fundamental freedoms, including the freedom of thought, conscience, religion or belief and respect for the equal rights of the people and their right to self-determination. It was hoped that this declaration, the importance of which is reflected in its having been signed by almost all of the principal governmental leaders of the day, wouid mark the beginning of liberalization of authoritarian regimes.[60]

## African Charter and Development in Africa

In 1979 the Organisation of African Unity (OAU) began the process of establishing a regional commission on human rights. Two years later, in 1981, the OAU Assembly adopted the African Charter. The African Charter was a reflection of discussion held at conferences in the 1960s and 1970s. These discussions reflected the frustration felt by many Africans about the OAU, which loudly condemned human rights violations by white ruled governments in Africa but was virtually silent about similar abuses committed in other parts of the continent.

This frustration was expressed by Uganda's President Yoweri Museveni at an OAU summit meeting in the 1980s. He said that lack of reaction by African states to human rights violations by other African states tends to undermine our moral authority to condemn the excess of others, especially South Africa's racist regime Tyranny is colour-blind and should be no less reprehensible because it is perpetrated by one of our kind.[61] The African Charter has developed certain rights that reflect the needs of Africa. It aims to combine the specific needs and values of African cultures with standards that have been universally accepted. So far example, it recognizes the right to national self-determination and the right to development.

## Development in the Middle East and Asia

Action for the international promotion and protection of human rights has proceeded at the regional level in the Middle East and Asia also. These regions, however, are still on the path to create the enforcement mechanisms within the framework of a human rights charter. The Permanent Arab Commission on Human Rights, founded by the Council of the League of Arab States in September 1968, has been preoccupied primarily with the rights of Arabs living in Israeli-occupied territories. Functioning more to promote than to protect human rights, at the end of 1990s it had yet to bring a proposed Arab Convention on Human Rights to a successful conclusion.[62]

Nevertheless, work by other intergovernmental and non-governmental bodies manifested a continuing desire to establish human rights protection mechanisms in the Middle East. Building the Universal Islamic Declaration on Human Rights (1981) and the Cairo Declaration on Human Rights in Isma (1990) are the solid initiatives taken in the Middle East. Besides that, the League of Arab States approved an Arab Charter of Human Rights in September 1994. The charter provides for periodic reports to the League's Human Rights Committee by state parties and for an independent committee of experts apparently empowered to request and study reports and submit its own findings to the Human Rights Committee. More so than in most of the other regions of the world (except Asia), the states of the Middle East were greatly divided over the need to enforce human rights law and the desirability of achieving as true regional system for the promotion and protection of human rights.[63]

In Asia, despite efforts by NGOs and the United Nations, the states of the region have been at best ambivalent and at worst hostile to human rights concerns, thus precluding agreement on almost all regional human rights initiatives. In early 1993, anticipating the Vienna World Conference on Human Rights later the year, a conference on Asia-Pacific NGOs adopted on Asia-Pacific Declaration of Human Rights, and in 1997 another meeting of NGOs adopted an Asian Human Rights Charter. Both of these initiates supported the universality and indivisibility of human rights. However, whereas the first initiative called for the creation of a regional human rights regime, the second-seemingly in deference to the cultural diversity and vastness of the region-urged instead the establishment of national human rights commissions and so-called "people's Tribunals", which would be based more on moral and spiritual foundations rather than on legal ones.[64]

### Human Rights Developments in Asia

The states of Asia were slow to respond to the recommendations. Their positions were indicated at an UN sponsored workshop in 1996, where the 30 participating states concluded that it was premature to discuss specific arrangements relating to the setting up a formal human rights mechanism in the Asian and Pacific region. The same states agreed, however, to explore the options available and the process necessary for establishing a regional mechanism. It remains to be seen whether the economic and political crisis that beset Asia at the end of the 20th century will stimulate efforts en ensure greater respect for human rights through regional cooperation.

Beside these major international treaties, conventions and conferences at international as well as regional level, international community has also adopted several other human rights treaties. These include the Convention on the Prevention and Punishment of the Crime of Genocide (1948); the Convention to Suppress of Women (1953); the Convention to Suppress the Slave Trade and Slavery (revised 1953); the Convention against Torture and other Cruel, Inhuman or Degrading Treatment (1987); and the Convention on the Rights of the Child (1990). Similarly American convention on Human Rights, 1969, Singapore Declaration, 1971 and Cuaska Declaration, 1979 can be recognized as those regional efforts which have done a lot for the establishment of better human rights mechanism in their respective areas.

## References

1. Arun Ray Mohapatra, *National Human Rights Commission of India*, Radha Publications, New Delhi, 2001, pp. 10-11.
2. Human Rights, *The New Encyclopedia Britannica*, London, 1768, p. 713.
3. Youli Bayer, *Africa: The Fables of Creation*, Routledge, New York 1993, p. 299.
4. *Ibid.*
5. Muhammad Ali Tashkiri, *Human Rights*, Department of Translation and Publication, Islamic Cultural and Cultural Relations Organisation, Tehran, 2001, p. 33.
6. Mohammad Yaqi Jafri, *Universal Human Rights*, Al Hoda International Publishers, Tehran, 1999, p. xv.
7. *Ibid.*, p. xi.
8. V.T. Thamilmaran, *Human Rights in the Third World Perspective*, HarAnand Publications, 1992, p. 52.
9. Kanta Mitra, "Human Rights in Hinduism", in Arelene Swidler (ed.), *Human Rights in Religious Tradition*, Sage Publishers, New York, 1982, p. 48.
10. C.G. Weeramanty, *The Law in Crisis*, Capemoss Publications, London, 1975, p. 258.

11. Richard Pierre Claude & H. Weston Burns, *Human Rights in the World Community: Issues and Actions*, University of Philadelphia Press, Philadelphia, 1989, p. 31.
12. Vasak Karl (ed.), *The International Dimensions of Human Rights*, UNESCO Press, Paris, 1982, p. 27.
13. D.Jack, *Universal Human Rights in Theory and Practice*, Cornell University Press, New York, 2003, pp.47-48.
14. Nilanjana Jain, *op. cit.*, p.144.
15. J. Shivananda, (ed.) *Human Rights: Concepts and Issues*, Alfa Publications, New Delhi, 2006. pp 17-21.
16. Declaration of the Rights of Man and Citizen, http://history.binghamton.Medu/hist/30/hist130.htm.s
17. Lynn Hunt, (ed.), *The French Revolution and Human Rights: A Brief Documentary History*, Brill Academic Publishers, Boston, 1996, pp 76-78.
18. The Columbia Encyclopedia, Sixth Edition, 2001-07, *Declaration of Indpendence*, http://www.bartle by.com/65/de/Declar Ind.html.
19. The New Encyclopedia Britannica, *op.cit.*, pp. 714-715.
20. *Ibid.*, p. 43.
21. Stephen and Harley Susan, *On Human Rights: The Oxford Amnesty Lecturers*, Oxford University Press, London, 1993, pp. 77-79.
22. J. Shivananda (ed.), *Human Rights: Concepts and Issues*, Alpha Publications, New Delhi, 2006, P. 25.
23. S.K. Kapoor, *International Law*, Central Law Agency, Allahabad, 1992, p. 483.
24. Michael Duffy, *Primary Documents: Covenant of the League of Nations, 1919-24*, firstworldwar.com http://www.firstworld war.com/source/league of nations. Html.
25. Anghie Antony, "Colonialism and the Birth of International Institutions: Sovereignty, Economy and the Mandate Systems of the League of Nations", *New York University Journal of International Law and Politics*, Vol. III, 2002, p. 34.
26. D.Jack, *op. cit.*, p.103.
27. Zdzislaw Kedzia, *United Nations Mechanism to Promote and Protect Human Rights*, University of Warsaw, Poland, 2003, pp. 91-92.
28. P.S. Jaswal, *op. cit.*, pp. 8-9.
29. S.Subramanian, *op. cit.*, p. 4.
30. Frank Newman and David Weissbradt, *International Human Rights: Law, Policy and Process*, Anderson Publishers, Cincinnati, 1990, p. 76.
31. *Ibid.*, p. 78.
32. James Vadackumchery, *Human Rights and the Police in India*, A.P.H. Publishing Corporation, New Delhi, p. 9.
33. Kenneth Cmiel, "The Recent History of Human Rights", *The American Historical Review*, Vol. 109, February 2004, No.1, pp. 117-118.

34. M.Cherif Bassiouni, *Crimes Against Humanity, Crimes of War,* http://www.crimesofwar,org/Thebook/crimes-against humanity.Html.
35. Nilanjana Jain, *op. cit.*, p. 144.
36. *Ibid.*, p. XVII,
37. Kenneth Cmiel, "The Recent History of Human Rights", *The American Historical Review,* Vol. 109, No. I, February 2004, p. 117.
38. "Reference Material on the United Nations", *The New York Times,* February 3, 2008.
39. S. Subramanian, *op. cit.*, pp. 13-18.
40. Johannes Marsink, *The Universal Declaration of Human Rights: Origin, Drafting & Intent,* University of Pennsylvania, Philadelphia, 1999, p. 1023.
41. Quincy Write, "National Courts and Human Rights", *Journal of International Law,* 1951, p. 83-84.
42. Charter of United Nations (UN Charter), Article 13-(1) (b).
43. *Ibid.*, Article 62.
44. *Ibid.*, Article 68.
45. *Ibid.*, The UN Charter refers generally to Fundamental Rights in Articles 1(3), 55(c ), 62(1), 68 and 76 (c ).
46. *Ibid.*
47. Eleanar Roosevelt, "Address to the United Nations General Assembly on the Adoption of the Universal Declaration of Human Rights", in America Rhetoric, *Top 100 Speeches,* http://www.americanhetoric.com/speeches/ eleanaroo-sevelt-declaration-humanrights.htm.
48. J. Shivananda (ed.), *op. cit.*, p. 9.
49. *Ibid.*, p. 34.
50. F.E. Dowrick (ed.), *Human Rights: Problems, Perspectives,* Alderson Publications, Gower, 1984, pp. 139-143& 159-172.
51. The Conference was the Largest Gathering of its Kind in History. The Ambassadors from 171 Nations had Attended United Nations Center in Vienna.
52. John R. Crook, "The Fiftieth Session on the U.N. Commission on Human Rights", *American Journal of International Law,* October, 1994, Vol. 88, No. 4, pp. 806-821.
53. The Opening Address Boutros Boutros Ghali, UN Secretary General, at the World Conference on Human Rights on 14th June 1993, Published in *Human Rights: The New Consensus,* Regency Press (Humanity Ltd.) London, 1994, p. 42-43.
54. *Ibid.*, p. 43.
55. J.A. Andrews and W.D. Hines, *International Protection of human Rights,* Manshell Publications Limited, London, 1987, p.15.
56. *Ibid.*, p.16.
57. Gokulesh Sharma, *op cit,* p.49.
58. *Ibid.*, p.49.
59. J. Shivananda, *op. cit.*, p.35.

60. *Helsinki Conference,* The free Dictionary by FARLEX, http://encyclopedia.Farlex.com/Helsinki/conference.
61. *Human Rights and Governance in Africa,* African studies, Columbia university libraries, http://www.columbia.edu/cu/web/indiv/africa/cuvl/iorights.html
62. Reza Afshari, "On historiography of Human Rights Reflections on Paul Gordan Lauren's, The Evaluation of International Human rights: Vision Seen", *Human Rights Quarterly,* vol. 29, no.1, February 2007, pp.1-15.
63. Nazila Ghanea Hercock, "Human Rights of Religious Minorities and of Women in the Middle East", *Human Rights Quarterly,* Vol. 26, No.4, August 2004, pp.705-729.
64. Danial A. bell, "The East Asian Challenge to Human Rights: Reflection on East West Dialogue", *Human Rights Quarterly* Vol. 18, No.3, pp. 641-645.

# 3

## Western Perspective of Human Rights

The concept of human rights is as old as human civilization.[1] But evolution and Crystallization of the Concept took a long time.[2] To understand human rights one must look through history of mankind, which puts light on the fact that the demands for the rights emerged from the day when man first started living in groups. The nature has bestowed man with two related characteristics – first as an individual and then as a social being. Living in a group or organized community is natural to him. While living in an organised society, it was natural that many instances might have prevailed over what could be claimed as right of the individuals. There was not any consent and consensus among the individuals over the nature and scope of rights. Thus, those who held power, dominated the weaker and mistreated their claims to attain the required conditions. The claims for rights gave birth to the conflicts in society over the fairness of rights. To avoid any confrontation between the dominant and weaker and particularly to provide safeguards to the weaker, certain type of understandings in shape of customs and values were established.[3]

With the passage of time, these rights or established customs or understandings including the relationship between the rulers and ruled were brought together in different forms in various parts of the world. They found expression in the concept of natural law and became the symbol of people's movement against absolute despotism, and the corner-stone of constitutional democracy everywhere.[4] In recorded history and ancient scriptures, there have been references on the basic human rights, though they were not referred to by that name. The modern concept of human rights, which is believed to take origin during medieval period and formally developed during the modern era, actually has its roots, deeply attached with the ancient period. The roots of the concern for human rights may be traced to ancient cultures, societies and civilizations in all parts of the world.

Although, the manifest and formal references regarding the term 'human rights' are not found as such in ancient historical sources. Nevertheless, the literary sources and theological scriptures belonging to various ancient civilizations, present the basis for a human rights theory stemming from the religion as well as the polity. The sources expounding or referring human rights can be found in all societies and civilistions developed in all parts of the world. But the Western world possesses a great deal of endeavour towards human rights since ancient period.

## Human Rights in Western Perspective

According to western political and philosophical thinking, human rights are innate in individuals and are an inherent factor in the human persons. In western world, the root of the concern for human rights may be traced to religion, humanitarian traditions and to the unleashing struggle for freedom and equality in all parts of the world. The term 'Human Rights' as such is not found in traditional religions. Nevertheless, theology presents the basis for a human rights theory stemming from a law higher than the state and whose source is the Supreme Being.[5]

### *The Law of the gods and Greek Ideas of Justice*

A deep study of the classical literature of ancient Greece gives a striking expression of the belief in the power exercised by the gods in a human society based on law. The gods establish a law which stands above the obligations imposed by the rulers of the community. The Greek thinkers developed the idea of 'natural law' and laid down its essential features. According to Socrates man possesses *insight* and this insight reveals to him the goodness and badness of things and makes him know the absolute and eternal moral rules. This human *insight* is the basis to judge the law. Citizens of certain Greek city-states enjoyed such rights as '*isonomic*' (equality before law) '*isotonic*' (equal respect for all) and '*isogoric*' (equal freedom of speech).[6] These can be said as the *de facto* valid norms established by the 'natural law', which is now more than two thousand years old.[7]

The ancient Greeks made two basic distinctions that started the long tradition in the Western world about the human being as a person. They distinguished between men and the Gods on the one hand and between men and beast on the other.[8] The main characteristic they saw that distinguishes man from the gods is the latter's immorality. On the distinction between men and animals they saw the presence of rationality in man and its absence in the beast as the decisive factor. With the latter distinction the Greeks simultaneously separated man from the brute and also established the basis for the theory of natural law, the oneness of the human race and the equality of all men based on the concept of justice, the human possession of reason and language.

The idea of justice, at an early stage in Greek philosophy, was a guiding principle not only for the behavior of the individual, but also for the organization of society. According to Plato, an idealistic political philosopher of ancient Greece, justice is the bond which holds a society together, a harmonious union of individuals, each of whom has found his life work in accordance with his natural fitness and his training.[9] The most outstanding among the Greek philosophers who speculated on the concept of justice was Aristotle (384-322BC). As we know, one of the main ideas of Aristotle's ethics is that like shall be treated as like, and unlike as unlike. But what does this likeness or unlikeness consist of? Here, Aristotle gives two guidelines, '*Arithmetic*', justice, i.e. equality is the rule according to which a balance between contribution and counter contributions is to be set with. However, when the question arises of sharing goods of various kinds between persons of various qualifications, then the distribution must be proportional, based on the difference in qualifications. Again Aristotle calls this distribution of justice 'geometrical' justice. Positions and power, honours and resources should be distributed according to the degree of effort or qualities that should be decisive. Should power in society be distributed according to each individual's wealth, wisdom, and strength? On this point Aristotle makes it clear that the criterion should be based on expedience without giving any unambiguous solution.[10]

Aristotle describes the nature of man as both 'rational' and 'political'. The point Aristotle was making is twofold. First, he was pointing to the fact that man is the type of animal whose habitat is the state or polis, such that we can say it is the nature of man 'to live, in a polis (state). Man is 'political' in that sense. Secondly, for man to be an inhabitant of a state, he has to be equipped by nature with the necessary instruments namely, "the power of speech" which is "different from voice" or sounder because it is the "capacity for rational communication.[11]

The school of philosophy, which emerged a few generations after Aristotle and known as '*stoics*', is the most significant in the history of the development of natural law. The doctrine of the stoics was characterized by the similarity it established between the regularity of nature and the general regularity which is incumbent for human existence. The stoics were subsequently to influence several jurists and statesmen in ancient Rome, more particularly to Marcus Tullius Cicero.[12]

Stoicism believed not only in the oneness of human nature but in oneness of nature in general. Stoicism held that man's rationality, capacity for speech and moral awareness equip him for life in a society that is truly human. This complex structure of relationship is summarized by Sabine in this manner. He revealed that Right reason is the law of nature, the standard everywhere of what is just and right, unchangeable in its principles, binding on all men whether ruler or subjects, the law of God[13]. Hence Natural Law was generally seen as a fundamental law or law of nature, lying behind the civil law of every nation and binding, because of its intrinsic justice, upon all peoples and upon subjects and rulers alike.[14]

### *The Roman Jus Naturale*

Roman lawyers followed the stoics closely in stressing the fundamental similarity and equality of men stemming from their common possession of reason and from their capacity to develop, and to attain virtue, in spite of differences in learning and ability. The influence of 'Natural law' was also found in the institutes, where justice was defined as the constant perpetual desire of giving to every man what was due to him.[15]

It has been observed that the great Roman jurists were legal technicians rather than legal philosophers. Here, a distinction is made between the fundamental concepts and the technicality employed by the Roman jurists. In Roman Law, a clear emphasis is made on the difference between Roman national law (jus Civile) and the law which is actually common to all nations (jus gentium).[16]

It must be pointed out that the expression *jus gentium* develops in more recent times into the concept for the rule of law regulating relationships between States, i.e. international law, of which developed the branch of the law of human rights. *Jus Naturale,* on the other hand, is the law which Nature herself has established, Slavery exists among all people, and in this respect, is part of *jus gentium*; but slavery conflicts with *jus naturale,* since all people are originally born free.[17]

### *The Catholic Doctrine of Natural Law*

The idea of advocating a law, higher than any human authority, governing the affairs of men and directing them as to what was lawful and what was not, continued to dominate the Middle Ages. In the middle ages, this law was the divine law which was identical with natural law. In the words of Ernest Barker, "The natural law was the law which did not proceed from human legislator. So far as it was revealed, it was the stern daughter of the voice of God; so far as it was natural, it was the inevitable outcome of the reason in man".[18]

Great philosopher Thomas Aquinas reaffirmed that the '*natural law*' is higher than the positive laws and it should be obeyed by all. According to him, any order or authority which contravened the natural law, could be disobeyed, for unjust law has no moral validity.[19] Simultaneously, St. Thomas Aquinas had revealed that the legal rules of society only possess the quality of law if they conform to right reason; their validity is then derived from eternal principles of law. If a law deviates from the injunctions of reason, we are dealing with violence and not with law. But even an unjust law borrows the validity of eternal law when it exists as a law by virtue of the authority of the law giver. This probably means that according to Thomas Aquinas positive law loses its validity only if it grossly and unquestionably violates the demands of reason.[20]

Church philosophy continuously emphasized Christianity's message of the never-ending value of the human personality. Man was brought to the centre of stage of world affairs by Greek philosophers. Likewise, the early scholars of the church engrafted on this and developed the concept of man by establishing the ideas that man is crated in God's image and represents the supreme value in the universe.[21]

### *Natural Law and Human Rights*

The search for a law, which was higher than positive law, carried out by philosophers and jurists developed the theory of natural law. They emphasized that natural law embodied these elementary principles of justice which were right reason, i.e. in accordance with nature, permanent and eternal.[26 Ibid, p.31] Hugo Grotius, one of the great figures in history of international law and father of natural law, writes in his *De Jure Belliac Pacis* that the law of nature, again is unchangeable– even in the sense that it cannot be changed by God.[22] He further added that natural law is as measureless as is the power of God. It can be said that these are certain rights over which even the power of God does not extend. Because even God cannot cause that two times two should not make four and God cannot cause that, which is intrinsically evil be not evil.[23]

Despite all the polemics of philosophers, the condition of man remained unchanged. However, the situation changed materially with renaissance, as it opened new vistas. The most important event of this period was the signing of Magna Carta by the king of England which is said to be the first milestone on the road of liberties of the people of England in 1215 AD. The Magna Carta, which is known as 'the great charter of liberty' provided that no person should be captured or imprisoned or ill-treated or outlawed or exiled or in any way destroyed, except by the lawful judgment only under the law of the land.[24] The doctrine of natural rights passed into the sphere of practical reality when an absolute monarch named king John himself was made to acknowledge that there were certain rights of the subject which could not be violated even by a sovereign in whom all powers were legally vested.[25] The later development led to the presenting of Petition of Rights, 1628 which was enacted as a statute by parliament and it became a part of the positive law of England.[26]

It is notable that the belief in natural law did not suggest the theory of Natural Rights until the seventeenth century. In the *Leviathan*, Hobbes assumes that every man has a 'right to life' and the 'right to its preservation' so much so that the social contract in which every man surrenders all of his rights to a man or body of men does not deprive the individual of his right to life. Hobbes writes that the social contract is dissolved automatically and man returns to the state of nature in case the Sovereign fails to protect the life of the individual.[27]

Hobbes had indicated that humans had an innate right to security from the State. Grotius based his beliefs on a moral commitment to international justice.[28] Actually it was John Locke (1632-1704), who first suggested that there are such things as natural rights; rights which belong to human beings by virtue of the fact that they are human. According to Locke, these rights are shared by all people. Moreover, these rights are inalienable, and cannot be removed by any political authority.[29] He claimed that the State emerges, solely out of the occasional need for an independent arbiter in any disputes which may arise over the trade or property. Clearly, much of

Locke's philosophy was provoked by the influence of the Judaeo-Christian tradition, which maintains that the responsibility to protect our rights and those of others, and for the better of ourselves, fell on us as individuals. He thus uses the idea of rights as an attack on the idea of strong State. Locke's natural rights were threefold" Life, Liberty and Property; he is thus considered to be the founder of modern liberalism.[30]

It is in the works of John Locke that the doctrine of Natural Rights finds full expression. According to him the right to life is coupled with two other rights, namely, liberty and property. In fact, what is life to Hobbes is property to Locke. In Locke's philosophy, right to property includes life and liberty as well. In this way the derivation of Natural Rights from Natural Law is completed in Locke's 'Two Treaties on Civil Government.[31]

John Locke, one of the modern liberalist argued in detail, that certain rights like right to life, liberty and property self-evidently pertain to individuals as human beings because they even existed in the "state of nature" before humankind entered into civil society. He further argued that while entering into civil society through contract humankind surrendered to the state only the right to enforce these natural rights and not the rights themselves. He also cautioned that, if the state fails to protect these rights people also have a right to revolt against state[32]. The liberal philosophers though belonged to varied current of thoughts had a common supreme faith in reason and vigorously attacked religious and scientific dogmatism, censorship and socio- economic restraints. Despite the apparent universalism of natural rights, liberties and right to estate etc, his philosophy provided justification for these rights and freedom only for upper class males, women, wage-labourers, menial workers of either sex and non- Europeans were not entitled to be right holders.

The ideas of Locke about life, liberty and property are Natural Rights and are fundamental rights, which appealed to revolutionaries and freedom fighters both in Europe and across the Atlantic. These ideas found expression in the American Declaration of Independence, 1776 and in the French

Declaration of the Rights of Man and Citizen, 1789. These two declarations are of great historic importance. In fact, they are the preface to the contemporary movement of human rights in the world.[33]

Human rights have a long history but it was in the eighteenth century that the law of nature had begun to assert itself to protect the individual against the power of State. This culminated in the great Declaration of the Rights of Man and Citizen in France in 1789 and in the United States Constitutional Amendment of 1791.[34]

The Declaration of American Independence is the most important of all American historical documents. It is essentially a partisan document, a justification of the American Revolution presented to the world. The Declaration asserts the fundamental American ideal of government, based on the theory of natural rights, which had based on the theory of natural rights, held by among others, John Locke, Emerich de Vattel, and Jean Jacques Rousseau.

Similarly, Declaration of the Rights of Man and Citizen was an initiative of the representatives of the French people, organized as a National Assembly. The Declaration was based on the faith that the ignorance, neglect, or contempt of the rights of man was the sole cause of public calamities and of the corruption of governments. It had determined to set forth in a solemn declaration of the natural, unalienable, and sacred rights of man and citizen in order that this declaration shall remind them continually of their rights and duties; Therefore the National Assembly recognized and proclaimed, the rights of man and of the citizen.[35]

The Declaration of American Independence further states that all men are created equal, that they are endowed by their creator with certain inalienable Rights, that among these are Life, Liberty and the pursuit of Happiness- that to secure these rights, Governments are instituted among Men, deriving their just powers from the consent of the governed – that whenever any form of government becomes destructive of these ends, it is the Right to the people to alter or to abolish it.[36]

The English writer, Paine (1737-1809), a most enthusiastic campaigner of natural rights, retains the notion of a contract, although in his view, it is a contract between equals for the creation of executive officials. The contract is not, therefore, a contract to guarantee rights. His book entitled *The Rights of Man* contains a declaration which begins with the announcement that all men are free and equal in respect of their rights. The declaration proceeds to the assertion that the end of the political associations is the preservation of the natural and imprescriptible rights of man. These rights are liberty, property, security and resistance of oppression.

The idea of human rights, however called by another name, played a key role in the late 18th and early 19th century's struggles against political absolutism. It was, indeed, the failure of rulers to respect the principles of freedom and equality, which had been central to natural law philosophy almost from the beginning that was responsible for this development of the doctrine of human rights.

### *Positivism and Human Rights*

The doctrine of natural rights came under powerful philosophical and political attack. In England for example, Conservatives like Edmund Burke and David Hume united with Jeremy Bentham, one of the founders of utilitarianism, started condemning the doctrine. The former out of fear that public affirmation of natural rights would lead to social ambiguity and upheaval; the latter proclaimed that the declarations and proclamations of natural rights cannot be acknowledged as substitute for effective legislation.[37] They held the view we can never know the nature of man, and thus we can never identify human rights. For if human nature is impossible to identify or if no such idea as the nature of something can be meaningful so that human nature does not exist such that we could know it -then the rights that people have because they are human beings, that is, by virtue of the humanity, human nature cannot be identified. They further condemned the doctrine out of fear that public affirmation of natural rights would lead to upheaval. Despite belief in natural law they expressed doubts that the rights of man could be derived from it. They criticized the Declaration of Rights of Man as "Monstrous Fiction" of human equality.

Bentham one of the founders of utilitarianism was more critical. He asserted that 'right is the child of law, from real law come real rights but from imaginary laws, come imaginary rights'.[38] He goes on to the extent of calling it (natural rights) as 'simply nonsense, natural and imprescriptible rights, rhetorical nonsense, upon stilts'[39]. This assault upon natural law and natural rights for the intensified and broadens during 19th and early 20th century by J.S.Mill and John Austin.

Immunal Kant, J.G. Merills, and Roscoe Pound strongly maintain that legal orders recognizing and protecting rights, and human rights in particular. are rather historical and social phenomena the struggle for which has been as old as human history itself for the reason that it concerns and needs to protects the individuals against the abuse of power by the tyrant. They emphasized that human rights are rights of individuals and ought to protect individuals, against other individuals and the State. In real life he finds himself constantly at odds with other individuals and the State. There are many unwanted separations and conflicts between individuals in their relations to one another and to the State. In these circumstances human rights imply protection of individuals against each other and against State as well. Thus, human rights are not superfluous at all".

Jeremy Bentham was no less scornful. He possessed the view that the term 'Rights' is the child of law. In his book *Principles of Legislation*, Bentham declared that real rights come from the real law, and from imaginary laws or from law of nature, there come only imaginary rights. He condemned the theory of natural rights by proclaiming that natural right is a simple nonsense.[40]

John Stuart Mill, the successor of Jeremy Bentham's utilitarianism was also a critic of the theory of natural rights. Despite his vigorous defense of liberty, he proclaimed that rights ultimately are founded on utility.[41] The German jurist Friedrich Karl Von Savigny and England's Sir Henry Maine emphasized that rights are a function of cultural and environmental variables unique to particular communities. However, the critical analysis of natural human rights as mischievous nonsense, anarchical fallacies continued throughout the nineteenth century and well into twentieth century.[42]

### *Human Rights and Positive Liberalism*

T. H. Green held the view that the rights of a man were derived not from what he had been, but from what he had it in him to become; to become by virtue of his pursuit of ideal ends. Green further reveals that every moral person is capable of rights. In other words, rights come from the moral character of man himself. To say that a person is capable of rights is to say that he ought to have them. Green believes that rights depend on recognition, but their recognition is granted by the moral consciousness of the community and not by the State. Green ultimately transfers the concept of natural rights to the idealist theory of rights.

Harold J. Laski criticizes both the natural rights theory and the legal rights theory. He argues that rights are not grant of some historic conditions possessed in the childhood of the race, and lost in the process of time. He feels that few theories have done greater harm to philosophy, or more violence to the facts they seek to summarize, than the notion that they represent as the recovery of the lost inheritance.[43] Laski rejects the legal theory of rights. He holds the view that so purely legalistic a view has nothing to contribute to an adequate political philosophy. Rights are prior to the State in the sense, that recognized or not, they are that from which its validity derives. He further adds that rights are not historical in the sense that they have at some time won their recognition. They are not natural, in the sense that a permanent and unchanging catalogue of them can be compiled. They are historical in the sense that at some given period and place, they are demanded by the character of its civilization. The rights are natural in the sense that under those same limitations, the facts demand their recognition.[44] Rights have a content which changes with time and place. They are rights because they are useful to the end, the State seeks to serve.

Laski also emphasizes social and economic rights including right to work and right to equal wages and right to education. He also gives stress on right to hold political power. This right contains three derivative rights: the right to franchise, the right to be chosen as a governor, and freedom of speech, of association and of public meeting. Laski further advocates the right to property also for all, which is necessarily to be subordinated to the maintenance of common welfare.

Thus classical liberalism, which lies at the heart of natural rights tradition, cannot be acceptable to modern liberal democracies as it rested on the sanctification of bourgeois self-interest. Although these natural rights were supposed to express the human essence, and were claimed in the name of human freedom, they are not now regarded as a sufficient statement of human essence or freedom, even in the countries where they originated.[45]

### *Marxism and Human Rights*

Liberal democratic theory of human rights had not been accepted both by the socialist countries as well as the developing countries. The socialist theory, whose roots are essentially traced back to Marx, argued against the individualism of traditional human rights theory. Making a scathing attack on natural rights' concept, Marx considered it as the ideological expression of bourgeois egoism and social atomization. Marxism, which was adopted by several developing countries at the beginning of 20$^{th}$ century as the solution of their social and political barbarities believed that the so-called rights of men were nothing but the rights of egoistic man separated from other man and from the community. Karl Marx went on to extend his basic postulate by emphasizing the necessary connection between bourgeois society and the notion of human rights.[46]

Concepts such as law, justice, morality, democracy, freedom, etc, are considered historical categories, whose content is always determined by the materiality of the life of people and by their social circumstances. Therefore, if the conditions of life be changed, so the content of notions and ideas may be changed. In fact, rights and freedoms of individuals are materially stipulated and depend on socio-economic, political and other conditions of society. Getting affected by those factors, doctrine of human rights changed its definition, nature and scope from time to time, place to place, and society to society. Although at the beginning of 20th century, the idea of human rights had got mature enough to start curving towards a universally accepted definition and nature of human rights.

The Western perspective develops liberal theory of rights which believes that man by nature possesses certain inherent and inalienable rights. So, it is the duty of the State to protect these natural rights of the individuals, without which the individuals cannot grow and express and elaborate all their abilities and capabilities. In addition to this autonomy of human nature, further elaborations were made in the context of his private property. Man's consumeristic attitude, passions and drives motivated him to acquire possession of property through competition and conflict with other individuals. [47] Individual self-aggrandisement defined in terms of ownership of material objects was then added to the nature of man. Thus private property becomes the central point of a free enterprise economic system.[48]

## References

1. Gokulesh Sharma, Human *Rights and Legal Remedies*, Deep & Deep Publications, New Delhi, 2000, p. IX.
2. S Subramanian, *Human Rights: International Challenges*, Vol. I, Manas Publications, New Delhi, 1997, p. 3.
3. South Asia Human Rights Documentation Centre, *Human Rights*, Oxford University Press, New Delhi, 2006, p. 2.
4. Karel Vasak (ed.), *The International Dimensions of Human Rights*, Vol. I, Green Wood Press, West Port, Connecticut, 2001, p. 21.
5. Jerome J. Shestak, "The Jurisprudence of Human Rights", in Theodar Meron (ed.), *Human Rights in International Law : Legal and Policy Issues*, Oxford Publications, New Delhi, 1984, pp. 75-76.
6. Erica and Irece A. Daes, *Freedom of the Individual Under Law– A Study on the Individual's Duties to the Community and the Limitations on Human Rights and Freedom Under Article 29 of the UDHR*, UN Press, 1990, p.137.

7. V.T. Thamilmaran, *Human Rights in Third World Perspective,* Har- Anand Publishers, New Delhi, 1992, p. 27.
8. H. Charles Kahn, *The Art and Thought of Heraclitus: An Addition of the Fragments with Translation and Commentary,* Cambridge University Press, 1983, p. 10.
9. George H. Sabine and Thomas L. Thorson, *A History of Political Theory,* (Fourth Edition), Oxford and IBH Publishing, New Delhi, 1973, p. 64.
10. D'Entreves, *Natural Law,* Penguin Publications, New York, 1970, pp. 15-16.
11. A.H. Armstrong, *An Introduction to Ancient Philosophy,* Brill Academic Publishers, Boston, 1966, p. 150.
12. P. S. Jaswal, *Human Rights and the Law,* A.P.H. Publications, New Delhi, 1996, p. 5.
13. George H. Sabine, *A History of Political Theory,* New York, 1962, p. 150.
14. *Ibid.,* p. 442.
15. V.T. Thamilmaran, *op. cit.,* p. 28.
16. D'Entreves, *op. cit.,* p. 26.
17. V.T. Thamilmaran, *op. cit.,* P. 28.
18. Ernest Barker, *Greek Political Theory: Plato and His Predecessors,* (Fifth Edition), Methuen & Strand, 1960, pp. 342-343.
19. P.S. Jaswal, *op. cit.,* p. 5.
20. V.T. Thamilmaran, *op. cit.,* p. 30.
21. *Ibid.,* p. 31.
22. Sheiner J. and Alston Philip, *International Human Rights in Contact: Law, Politics, Morals,* Oxford Press, London, 1996, pp. 37-41.
23. Hugo Grotius, *De Jure Belle ac Pacis,* Whewell Edition, Cambridge University Press, Cambridge, 1933, p.105.
24. P.S. Jaswal, *op. cit.,* p. 596.
25. D.D. Basu, *Human Rights in Constitutional Law,* Printence, New Delhi, 1994, p. 41.
26. P.S. Jaswal, *op. cit.,* p. 6.
27. Darren Jo' Byrne, *op. cit.,* pp. 29-30.
28. E. Knud Hakonssen, *Natural Law and Moral Philosophy from Grotius to the Scottish Enlightenment,* Cambridge University Press, Cambridge, 1996. pp. 326-328.
29. Darren Jo" Byrne, *op. cit.* p. 30.
30. *Ibid.,* p.30.
31. D.Jack, *Universal Human Rights in Theory and Practice,* Cornell University Press, New York, 2003, pp. 47-48.
32. Ernest Barker (ed.), *Social Contract: Locke, Hume, Rousseau,* Oxford University Press, 1948, 77.
33. Nilanjana Jain, "Human Rights Under Democracy", *The Indian Journal of Political Science,* Vol. LXVII, No. 1, Jan-March, 2006, p.144.

34. J. Shivananda (ed.), *Human Rights: Concepts and Issues*, Alfa Publications, New Delhi, 2006. pp 17-21.
35. Lynn Hunt (ed.), *The French Revolution and Human Rights: A Brief Documentary History*, Boston, 1996, pp 76-78.
36. The Columbia Encyclopedia, *Declaration of Independence*, Sixth Edition, 2001-07, http://www.bartle by.com/65/de/Declar Ind.html.
37. Koechler Hans, *The Principles of International Law and Human Rights*, http:/hanskoechler.com/Filoso/ia-del-derecho.htm.
38. Jeremy Bentham, *An Introduction to the Principles of Morals and Legislation*, Hafner Publications, New York, 1948, p. 47.
39. Jermy Waldron, *Nonsense Upon Stilts: Bentham and Marx on Rights of Man*, Oxford University Press, 1981, pp. 101-144.
40. N. Kinsella. "Tomorrow's Rights in the Mirror of History", in G. Gall, (ed.), *Civil Liberties in Canada*, Butterworth's Publications, Toronto, 1982, p.17.
41. *Ibid.*, pp. 711-738.
42. Stig Toft Madson, *State, Society, and Human Rights in South Asia*, A.P.H. Publishing, New Delhi, 1996, p. 7.
43. Harold J. Laski, *Grammar of Politics*, George Allen & Unwin, London, 1938, p. 89.
44. *Ibid.* p. 91.
45. Gokulesh Sharma, *op. cit.*, p.25.
46. *Ibid.*, p. 27.
47. Jim Powell, "John Locke Natural Rights to Life, Liberty, and Property", in Foundation for Economic Education, *The Freeman: Ideas on Liberty*, August 1996, Vol. 46, No. 8, p. 453.
48. Micheline Ishay, *The History of Human Rights: From Ancient Times to the Globalization Era*, University of California Press, 2004, p. 63.

# 4

## Human Rights in India: A Theoretical Perspective

Most of the Third World countries, freed from the cluster of colonial rule, have the common goals to achieve. All Third World countries desperately need to accelerate the economic development through industrialization. These countries possess the characteristics of multi-ethnicity and multi-religious societies. So the nation-building is another goal which these countries want to achieve. In due course of time, one of the most important as well as pertinent question that has made the process of development all the more difficult is the question of the rights and freedoms of the man vis-à-vis State in these countries. The Third World countries are characterized by their traditional cultural patterns and ethnic social set up. They do not fully share either the intellectual heritage of the West or that of the socialist interpretation of the rights. However, the contemporary nationalist elite, having been influenced by concepts and ideologies of the West, have developed a new kind of approach to the theory and practice of human rights.[1]

Third World countries have not typically practiced the natural and individual rights of the liberals or the social and economic rights of the socialists. Heterogeneous character of their societies has compelled them to give emphasis on the group rights or the rights of the minorities. They realize that the enjoyment of the individual rights is vested in providing all rights and privileges to all groups of the society and especially the minority or marginal groups.[2] In these countries,

State is viewed as an organic whole which is not the product of class conflict as propounded by the socialists and not just a necessary evil as viewed by the early liberals. State is an embodiment of different castes, creeds, racial groups and ethnic communities. The government works as the representative or the trustee of the State for promotion, protections and maintenance of the rights and liberties.[3]

Third World countries witnessed huge changes as far as the nation-building is concerned amidst all kinds of social upheavals. Due to these continuously changing socio-economic circumstances, the Third World countries in Africa, Asia, Middle East and the Latin America have given priority to the social and economic rights over the civil and political rights. It is the prerequisite for the Third World countries to have solidarity of these two categories of rights, as their ultimate objective is to attain economic development, running parallel with preservation and growth of their diverse religious and cultural heritage.[4] Most of the times, these countries are ambiguous, uncertain and strange while behaving in the field of human rights. Sometimes, they behave in a manner more socialistic than the socialist countries, and on the other occasions become more capitalists than the capitalist countries. It appears that the Third World countries are hanging in between the two worlds—the capitalist and the socialist.[5]

Although India, being a Third World country, shares similar perception of human rights which generates from the two mentioned school of thought, *i.e.*, liberal and socialist. But it possesses its own different and unique perception of human rights that emanates from its ancient culture and civilization.

## The Indian Perspective of Human Rights

The rights of man have been the concern of all civilizations since time immemorial. The historical overview and a deep survey of the history of civilizations of different countries establish it beyond doubt that the people of earlier age were also familiar with human rights. The same has been the case with Indian civilization. The Indian society is warranted by the fact that human rights jurisprudence has always progressed through historical path in smooth manner and never lost its link with the past. The history of Indian civilization shows that the basic rights of human beings were in existence even during ancient period. It is quite evident from the survey of ancient Indian scriptures that human rights jurisprudence has always occupied a place of prime importance in India's rich legacy of historical tradition and culture.

## Human Rights in Ancient India

It is a matter of great national pride for all Indians that the concept of human rights prevailed in its highest stage in the Indian scriptures and religious books.[6] The doctrine of human rights is very old and some references pertaining to human rights can be found in ancient Indian scriptures. In the long history of the Indian civilization, the freedom of thought and speech, freedom of one's own life in the light of one's beliefs, freedom of association and freedom of public debate between the contending philosophical schools were taken to be natural foundations of human relationships. Since ancient period, there is a bulk of literature available on the ideas of rights. The word *Adhikar* was used to convey a similar sense as rights; however, it always had much deeper meaning. From the morphological point of view, the morpheme, *"krre"* is the stem or the root of the Sanskrit word *adhikar*, which means 'to do' or 'to perform a duty'.[7] Thus the ancient Indian jurisprudence advocates the inter-relation and inter-dependence of rights and duties and totally denies the enjoyment of right without performing duties.

The quest for equilibrium, harmony, knowledge and truth inspired to ancient Indian minds more than their counterparts, the Greeks and Romans. About 5000 years ago, ancient Indian philosophers and thinkers expounded a theory of higher moral law over and above positive law embodying certain values of universal validity like Dharma (Righteousness) *Artha* (Wealth) *Kama* (Desires) and Moksha (Salvation), with a view to establish a harmonious social order by striking a balance between inner and outer, spiritual and material aspects of life. The ancient Indian legal philosophers were universalistic, humanistic, rationalists and above all, moralists who evolved a system of legal theory which was based on higher values and ideals, i.e. on their conception of *Dharma*, which governed in an integrative manner all civil, religious and other actions of men in society, be it king or his subjects. Above all, every aspect of life was regulated by *Dharma*, the supreme law in ancient India.

An observation of the ancient Indian jurisprudence shows that it had established a duty-based society. Its postulate was not only the duty of individual towards the society but also the duty of rulers towards the individuals and the society. The concept of absolutist monarchies had always been rejected by the supremacy of *Dharma* (Law) and spirit. *Dharmashastras* impressed upon the kings to look upon the people as God (*Praja Vishnu*) and serve them with love and reverence. The basic philosophy that for the good of the greater number, the interests of the individuals and the smaller groups should be subordinated and sacrificed to the extent necessary, was deeply embodied in, the foundation of Dharma.

This aspect is evident from the verse in *Udyogaparva* of *Virduraniti* (Ch. 37-17) which reads:[8]

> Sacrifies the interest of individual for the sake of the family.
> Sacrifies the interest of the family, for the sake of the village.
> Sacrifies the interest of the village, for the sake of the country.
> And lastly for the sake of securing Moksha (eternal bliss) of the Atma, reject the world.

### *Human Rights and Indian Dharma*

The concept of *Dharma* has been eternal spring of Hindus' ethic and has been all-pervading, governing and regulating conduct of human beings. The five *Yamas* – ahimsa (non-violence) truth, non-theft, total self-denial and non possession and five *Niyamas*–purity, contentment, penance, study of scriptures and surrender to God were enunciated by great saint Patanjali to attain self-discipline and to establish equilibrium in society, so that all can enjoy the required conditions essential for the holistic deveolment.[9] The foundations of human rights may be established in two different frameworks of perceiving man and world; one is that of the modern Western political thought and philosophy and of law; and the other of *Dharma* and its method that characterizes the saga of Indian civilization. Keeping this in the view, the Western philosophy had its own way of perceiving man, society and their relationship from which it propounded the foundation of human rights. But nevertheless, the Indian philosophy characterizes the foundation in the ancient conception of *Dharma* and *Danda* which regulated the governance of State and its citizens. The concept of *Sanatan Dharma* which laid down these foundations in ancient civilization is more than 2,000 years older than Western Christianity with a central theoretic doctrine. It laid down the foundation of a society in ancient Indian civilization which was based on the moral code, righteousness and responsibilities. It was certainly wider and broader than the concept of religion, as used in Western historiography. It is basically founded on the principle that the detailed rules were laid down for the guidance of the King. It was his duty to uphold the law and he was as much subject to law as any other person. Equality before law and equal protection of law can be noticed from that practice. One of the paramount duties of the King was implementation of the justice according to the law of religious texts, local customs, usages and written codes. This was actually the human rights enforcement mechanism in its rudimentary stage.[10]

The king was bound by the *dharmashastra* to decide cases according to rules of *Shastras*. In the absence of a provision in the texts, he should follow the usages. The king was hardly restricted to act according to his own personal wish. There was a notion that such an action on the part of the King causes danger to him and brings ruins to the people. The Hindu conception of kingship was that it would be seen as the arm of *Dharma*, the unchanging law, the upholder of social order and a limb of the social organism.[11] The King had not the right of changing the laws. The *shruti*, the *Smriti*, the *Puranas* and customs or usages were the principal source of law. Three persons, each one of whom knows one of three principal Vedas, a logician; one who knows the *Nirukta*, one who recites the institutes of the sacred law, and three men belonging to the first three order shall constitute a *parishad* (assembly) consisting in all of the least 10 members competent to lay down a new provision of law.[12]

### *Human Rights during Vedic Period*

The ideas of human rights could be found in Vedic Scriptures of Hinduism. The Vedas, the religious works of the ancient Hindus, offered guidance, *inter alia,* on religious and social obligations. The Vedas were written in archaic Sanskrit, important source language of the *Indo-Europeans* language group. Many modern words relating to law and justice are thought to go back to Sanskrit roots as, for example, 'justice', which is traceable through Roman *jus* to the Sanskrit *Vu* meaning 'to join' or alternatively to the Sanskrit *yos,* a word of religious connotation.[13] The charter of equality has been incorporated in the Vedas, the first and the highest authority among the sources of law. In *Rigveda* (5-60-5), the most ancient of the Vedas, equality of all was declared in the following words:[14]

> No one is superior or inferior. All should strive for the interest of all and should progress collectively.

Again in *Atharvaveda, samjaanaskuta,* the right of each individual in respect of collective natural resources was declared thus:

"All have equal rights on articles of food and water. The yoke of the chariot of life is placed equally on the shoulders of all. All live together with harmony supporting another like spokes of the chariot connecting its rim and hub." (Manu IX 311) It further states that the King should protect and support all his subjects without any discrimination in the same manner as the earth supports all living beings. [15]Besides that, the entire concept of welfare state is brilliantly summed up by Kautilya. He says that King's happiness lies in the happiness of the subject; in the welfare of common masses, lies the welfare of king. Whatever pleases the King himself, shall not consider as good; whatever pleases his subject, the King shall consider as good.[16] This is the eternal *Dharma* beacon light, which shows the right path to the rulers under any set up of the government, to be a welfare state for the welfare of people.

### *Human Rights in Ramayana and Mahabharata*

In Valmiki's *Ramayana* also, there are certain fundamental human rights enumerated. In Ramayana Lord *Rama* forbade *Lakshman* to use a weapon of war which could destroy entire humanity. The *'Shantiparva'*, one of the books of the Indian epic, *Mahabharata*, depicts the rules and principles governing the conduct and obligations of the rulers. These can be seen in the discourses of the saga *Bhisma*, in response to King Yudhisthira. Mahabharata also highlights the fact that without ethical and moral principles, there is no true happiness and the society cannot hold together. *Bhagvat Gita*, being a part of *Mahabharata* disseminates the preaching to meet the responsibilities and duties of life, always keeping in view the spiritual background of human existence which is the manifestation of an ultimate and the infinite. In other chapter of *Mahabhararta*, Arjun observing the laws of war refrained from using *Pashupatastra*, a hyper destruction weapon, because human rights of civilians could be violated by using that dangerously destructive weapon.[17]

A period of Hindu law marked by the movement from remembered law to written law is 100-400 A.D. These written laws had come into existence due to the appearance of two pioneer and outstanding law books of the ancient world. These books were- the *Yajnavalkya Smriti* and the *Narada Smriti*. The influence of these books in the field of law can be witnessed from the fact that these two are still authoritative source books of Hindu law, specifying *inter alia*, rules of drafting, pleading, procedure and judicial conduct.[18]

### *Human Rights during Post-Vedic Period*

During post-Vedic period, villagers, traders and guilds had their own judicial system which composed of their own men and the presiding officer of the court held the office either by elections or by inheritance to local customs. Such courts settled the cases of grave crimes also. When the condemned party refused to obey the judgment of the local courts, the court presided over by the King gave the final verdict in such a case. Thus in ancient India, the King along with members of *sabha* constituted the judicial tribunal. The King with the help of *sabhayas* (members of the court) used to conduct the enquiry of law suits, without violating the rules of *Dharmashastra* and the *Arthashastra*. The *sabhayas* were well-versed in these scriptures.[19] The main prerequisite characteristic of the early Hindu judicial system was that justice was never administrated by a single individual. That characteristic of the judicial system is similar to the later theme of Aristotle which propounds that it is almost impossible to find or discover a supremely wise person as arbiter. Hence several ordinary men are better than one to disseminate the justice.[20]

During the rule of Chandra Gupta Mourya, Kautalya authored *Arthashastra* which revealed the political, social and economic code of conduct. *Arthashastra* depicted certain principles of law of punishment as the foundation of social existence. These principles then became the basis of law against, *inter alia*, illegal arrests, and detentions, custodial deaths, ill treatment of women such as rape, inequality of gender, corrupt judicial system, etc.[21]

However, the violation of human rights cannot be ignored in ancient India which had emerged from the then social stratification. Social life in India in ancient times was divided into four major categories: the *Brahmans* (priestly class); the *Kshatriyas* (rulers and warriors class) the *Vaishyas* (trading class) and the *Shudras* (labourer and unskilled workers). The rights and duties of the aforesaid classes were determined according to their assigned duty. The Brahmans, due to their hegemony over the caste system, denied the rights to lower caste, the untouchables, and other deprived sections of the society. As a result, there was a severe violation of the human rights of the lower sections of Indian society. But in general the Indian society was peaceful within moral code of conduct of the society provided by religion, which in due course of time hegemonised all sections of the society within its rules and principles.[22]

### *Human Rights and Budhism*

Buddhism, another paramount religion existent in India since ancient times, realized the deeper significance of humanism and human rights. Theory of humanism propounded by Buddhism is concerned with the ways which would be helpful in the elimination of human sufferings. Through the recognition of theory and practice, Buddhism discovered the way of humanization of man and the regeneration of man as a strictly human being. All this projects Buddhism as an ardent supporter of humanism and thereupon a champion of human rights. Buddhism views all human beings as equal; therefore Buddhism is committed to the principle of human equality. Buddhism attacked the caste system which had divided the society in upper and lower castes thereby depriving the lower castes of certain rights such as the study of Vedas, Repudiating the superiority by birth, Buddhism declared that:

> No Brahman is such by birth
> Not outcaste is such by birth
> An outcaste is such by his deeds
> A Brahman is such by his deeds.[23]

Mahatma Buddha, the founder of Buddhism, criticised slavery in every form. Buddha may be declared as the pioneer of abolition of slavery. He suggests five ways in which a master should serve his employees. These are 1.work should be assigned in proportion to the employee's health; 2.due food and wages be given to him; 3.proper care should be taken in his sickness; 4 specially tasty luxuries should be shared with him; 5.holidays should be given to employees at due intervals.[24]

Buddhism is deeply rooted in the concept of religious freedom, respect and tolerance. Sidharatha Gautama urged that his followers not bear ill-will toward anyone who speak ill of him. Rather Gautama declared that, "if anyone were to speak ill to me or my doctrine or my order, do not bear ill-will toward him, do not upset or perturbed at heart; for if you were to be so, it will cause you harm"[25]

Buddhism may be honoured as the campaigner of political justice also. The Buddhist political justice enjoins special responsibility to the King. As the head of State he must adhere to specific code of conduct as he is at the helm of affairs of the State. Buddha felt that the personal moral conduct of the king, along with his officials would be expressed in the political affairs of the State. Thus, the righteous character of the State would help prevailing universal righteousness on earth. Hence deliverance through peaceful coexistence would become easily attainable for all.[26]

### *Human Rights and Jainism*

However at individual level, there were some other significant contributions by other religious prophets with regard to the basis of human rights in India. Mahavir, the greatest prophet of Jainism said that the foundation of human freedom in its deepest sense is truth, known as *Ankantaved*. Jainism preaches the message of tolerance, non-violence and universal fraternity. The unique and an admirable aspect of the philosophy of Jainism is that it does not acknowledge the right only of the human beings to survive till the attainment of salvation, but it also advocates the right to survive and of life to all other species including the birds, animals, insects etc.

### *Human Rights and Islam in India*

The principles of *Dharma* as enunciated by ancient legal system remained in force substantially in the medieval period of history also. All the Hindu kings and Mughal emperors adopted these principles for the welfare of society. The disputes and controversies were decided according the *Dharma*. In this period, the *Mohammaden* culture made inroads in Indian culture and system, and also affected the justice distribution system. But subsequently, there was no change, because under *Mohammaden* system, the justice was delivered according to principles of *Koranic* and Muslim law.[27] Substantially, there was no change in the Hindu concept of *Dharma* and Muslim concept of *Koranic* law barring few exceptions with regard to law of marriage and divorce succession and other principles of law, effecting personal life of man. The principles of all kinds of public and other laws other than personal remained one and the same.

Islam became the paramount determinant in the Indian religion, society and culture after the Muslim conquest during the tenth century A.D. Thus in the medieval period, however, the basic elements of ancient Indian tradition, 'universalism' and 'humanism' in its philosophical thought remained so alive and the struggle against caste system and religious tolerance received a fresh relevance and impetus from Islam.

Islam disseminates almost similar notions about human rights as were propounded by the ancient Indian religions. Human rights in Islam mean the rights granted by God. These rights have not been given by any King or Legislative Assembly. Kings or legislative assemblies can withdraw human rights only if they are the source of these rights. But since in Islam, human rights are conferred by God, none of the Kings, governments or legislative assemblies have any right to change, cancel or violate these human rights conferred by God. No one has the right to abrogate or withdraw these rights.[28] In Islam, human rights are concerned with the dignity and prestige of the individual, the level of self respect that secures personal identity and promotes the human community. Islam advocates establishing such type of society in which freedom and justice can prevail and grow. It develops an idea that perfectibility of human beings should be preferred, respected and given the opportunity. But parallel to that, the overall social, political and economic development of the whole society should also be recognised.

The Qur'an also shows equal concern for human beings as well as their rights. The following message of Islam to the humanity highlights its concerns:

> "The organized society must live under law, that would guide their everyday life-Based on external principles of righteousness and fair dealings, cleanliness and sobriety, honesty and helpfulness. One to another - yet shaped into concrete forms, times and circumstances. And the varying needs of average men and women be fulfilled; the food to be clean and wholesome, blood feuds to abolish. The rights and duties of heirs to be recognized after death;... Check all selfish wrongdoings; the courage to fight in defense of right to be defined. The pilgrimage to be sanctified... Charity and help to the poor to be organized;..."[29]

The practical implementation of the Islamic human rights norms can be witnessed from the Mughal history of India. No doubt, the Mughal Government could be typically characterized as centralized despotism, but its judicial administration was characterized with all basic features and components of modern doctrine of due process of law, fair trial and independent judiciary.[30] Akbar's great regard for rights, justice and secularism could be cited as an example in this regard. Besides other achievements, he is remembered as the founder of a new religious policy *Din-e-Ilahi* (divine religion). By persuading his religious policy, he tried to preach the ideas of religious tolerance and secularism (respect for all religion).The social, political, and economic status of the Hindus were quite equal to the Muslims during the reign of Akbar.[31] Similarly, parallel to Akbar's exquisite religious reform policies, his son Jehangir adopted the policy of universal reconciliation and tolerance. He was also concerned and committed with the welfare of his subjects without any discrimination of religion or caste.

The Mughal period attempted to bring the Hindus and Muslims together to evolve a common way of living. Complete fusion between class conscious Hindus and the ruling class Muslims was a tremendous emblem of social equality in India, which is a paramount feature of the doctrine of human rights. The liberal secular policies of the government acted as catalyst and synthesis between the two great religions and cultures. Further the integration of a greater part of India into a single unit subject to uniform system of administration and the consequent elimination of barriers opened out fresh vistas for reorientation of religion, art, literature and culture. This was an era of growing harmony and Indianisation.[32]

The success of the movement of secularism and religious tolerance provided a healthy environment for the growth of religious movements like *Bhakti* (Hindu) and *Sufi* (Muslim). The *Bhakti* and *Sufi* movements made remarkable contributions towards eliminating the irreligious practices of the contemporary society. These movements tried to receive the ancient humanist tradition and preached the sacred principles of humanism and universalism. These movements denounced the narrow sectarianism prevalent in both the religions-Hindu and Muslim.[33] The great saints like Shankara, Ramanya, Madhara, Tulsidas, Kabir, Guru Nanak and others reinterpreted the ancient Dharma with a fresh fervour. The main intention was to re-establish the notion of equality, religious tolerance, humanism, and universalism. The philosophy of these socio-religious reformers and leaders was nothing but a reinstatement of natural law with religious fervour to enthuse people towards the path of *Dharma.*

Bhagat Kabir, a great social and religious reformer and a distinguished figure of Bhagti movement hits hard the useless and condemnable rituals prevailing in the contemporary socio-religious sphere of India. He criticizes the caste system and religious bigotry which had divided the people on the social and religious grounds. He is a great champion of equality of the mankind and universal brotherhood. His couplets convey the message of egalitarianism and the brotherhood of whole mankind, and are used as the slogans of equality even today. He preaches the mankind the message of universal fraternity as:

> First, God produced his sacred creative glow.
> By his sacred creative power, nature has created all humans equal.
> From one sacred glow, the entire universe welled up.
> Hence, no one is good, no one is bad?[34]

Bhagat Kabir disseminated the significance of non-violence, peace and solidarity. He advised the Kings, his subordinates and the dominants not to repress the poor and weaker.

He criticized explicitly the use of force by a dominant over the weaker as:

> Kabir, they repress living beings and kill them,
> And call it justified. When the Lord calls for their account,
> What will their condition be?
> Kabir, it is brutal to use force,
> The Lord shall call you for account.[35]

### *Human Rights and Sikhism*

The champion of Bhakti movement, Guru Nanak Dev, founded the most advanced, scientific, humanistic religion of the world, the Sikhism. The teachings and even history of the Sikh religion is the great saga of human rights. The history of Sikhism during medieval period is the history of human rights violations. Guru Nanak, the first Sikh Guru was imprisoned, along with thousands of other innocent Indian civilians, by Babar, the first Mughal to invade India. Guru Nanak wrote about the barbarity of the invasion in which innocent civilians were tortured, women were raped and disgraced, their hair were cut off, whole families were starved and their homes were razed to the grounds.

> (There was such terror and countless cruel beatings.
> Did you feel no pain O' Lord?
> If some powerful man strikes out against another man,
> then no one feels any grief in their mind.
> But if a powerful tiger attacks a flock of sheep and kills them,
> its master must answer for it.
> The priceless lives have been laid waste and defiled by dogs,
> and no one pays any attention to the dead.[36]

Guru Nanak had sketched the brutal nature of the government and the barbaric activities of their officials, who tortured the masses. He had openly criticized the tyrannical, repressive and exploitive activities of the cruel government and the administration of his contemporary times. The Babarbani, written by Guru Nanak Dev is an expression of human rights.

> The Kings are tigers, and their officials are dogs;
> They go out and awaken the sleeping people to harass them.
> The public servants inflict wounds with their nails.
> The dogs lick up the blood that is spilled.[37]

Guru Amar Dass, the third Guru of Sikhs had also raised his voice in favour of social equality. He opposed the inequalities established by the *Verna Pratha* (Caste System) and challenged the dominance of Brahmin class over social and religious deeds as:

(No one should be proud of his social class and status.
So much sin and corruption comes from this pride.
Everyone says that there are four castes.
They all emanate from the drop of God's seed.
The entire universe is made of the same clay
The Potter has shaped it into all sorts of vessels.[38]

He further suggests the preconditions and the prerequisites for the existence of a true and righteous justice.

He who himself is True,
And true is his throne.
Seated upon it,
He administers True justice.[39]

The fifth Guru, Arjan Dev and ninth Guru, Teg Bahadur were subjected to grievous violation of their human rights when they tried to safeguard the religious freedom of their own and that of others. The ninth Guru had sacrificed to protect the interest of Hindu religion and had disseminated the spirit of secularism.[40]

## Human Rights during British Era

The modern version of human rights jurisprudence may be said to have taken birth in India during modern era, and especially during the time of British Rule. The British brought India under one uniform government. They practiced more or less uniform law in India. They promoted western, scientific and modern education in India. No doubt, they had introduced all these policies and programmes just to promote their selfish interests, but these steps happened to be highly fruitful in the advancement of modern doctrine of human rights in India. People came to know about the barbaric attitude of British through out the nation. It promoted the sense to fight with collective efforts among Indians against inequalities, subjugation and brutality forced by the British. With the dissemination of western education, Indians became familiar with the western ideas of liberty, equality and self-rule. They grasped thoroughly the French Declaration of Rights of Men and Citizen, England's Glorious Revolution and Declaration of American Independence.

### *Human Rights and Indian Reform Movements*

Some Indian leaders, being influenced by English education, western ideas and liberal principles started a movement for Renaissance and Reformation. Raja Ram Mohan Roy, called the Father of Modern India due to his campaign for social reforms in India, demanded the abolition of Sati system, female infanticide and caste system and also initiated a movement for widow remarriage and female education.[41] Similarly, Swami Vivekanand probed deep into India's needs. He found the nation exhausted of liveliness, not through the faults of Hindu religion as westernized reformers were maintaining, but because of those who did not know how to grow and those who knew but had failed to share with the others. He further added that one of the main causes of the downfall of the nation was the neglect of masses. He suggested that the solution of India's misery and degradation was not to bring down the higher but to raise the lower. Swami Vivekanand was of the view that it was only possible through the implementation of social justice and human rights for establishing a welfare State in true sense so that individuals and society can obtain all the needed rights and liberties.[42]

Besides these mass movements, there were several other social reform movements at local as well as regional level which aroused the voice to protect the rights of minorities, women and other neglected sections of Indian society. Prominent among them was Satyashodhak Samaj, a reform movement founded by Jyotirao Gobindrao Phule in Maharashtra during nineteenth century. He was a prominent thinker, activist and reformer who was also famous by the name of Mahatma Jyotiba Phule due to his efforts in bringing positive renovations in the fields of education, agriculture, caste system and social position of women. Jyotaba Phule's life was a struggle for providing equal rights to farmers, women and lower section of the society. To promote the equal right of education for girls, he opened first school for girls in India in 1848. Phule vehemently advocated widow-remarriage and got a home built for housing the upper class widows in 1854.[43]

*Dalit* community's struggle for cultural independence and separate identity was actually a struggle to enhance the social, cultural, religious, economic, and political rights of *Dalit* community in India. The word *Dalit* was used to replace the word of untouchable, backward or depressed classes and *harijans*. The word *Dalits* identified those whose culture had been deliberately broken, crushed to pieces by the Varna Hindu culture. The adoption of this new identity as *Dalits* was an affirmation of the *Dalit* community's struggle for cultural independence and separate cultural identity. At the dusk of nineteenth century and the dawn of twentieth century, these early *Dalit* communities came to articulate an emergent *Dalit* cultural identity through the construction of syncretic form of Hindu Bhakti culture. Through this syncretic form of Bhakti Hinduism, it is argued, that the early *Dalit* community sought to establish themselves as an independent panthic community within Hinduism and began to provide a *Dalit* perspective of Indian society which challenged Varna Hindu cultural values and practices.[44] It provided a foundation for the later *Dalit* movement under the leadership of Dr. B. R. Ambedkar.

### *Measures taken by the British in India*

These social reform movements had a great impact on Indian society as well as British government in India. The British officials in India took several initiatives which were initiated to eradicate the backwardness, useless orthodoxy and unnecessary bigotry from Indian society, but these initiatives proved to be the mile stones in the advancement of modern saga of human rights in India. In 1789, Lord Cornwallis stopped the sale and purchase of slaves, and 22 years later, in 1811, the importing of slaves was declared illegal. Warren Hastings (1772-1785) campaigned against many of the then existed human rights violations that were found prevalent in India. The practice of Sati was formally abolished by Governor General William Bentick. To stop the practice of child marriage, Child Marriage Restraint Act, prohibiting marriage of minors was passed in 1929.

During 1818, it has been estimated that there were as many as 839 self-immolations. Lord Bentnik by regulation xvii of 1829 legally prohibited the burning and burial of widows alive there and declared them to culpable homicide. As certain classes of Rajputs practiced infanticide; in 1870, an Act was passed for the registration of births and verification of the survival of girl children. The Khands of Orissa had the horrible practice of human sacrifice and it was stamped out in 1854 by the efforts of Major General John Campbell. Lord Ellenberough prohibited the legal recognition of slavery in India by Act V of 1843. Earlier, the widows were not allowed to remarry. It was Lord Dolhousie(1848-1856) who permitted the widows to remarry. Lord Rippon (1880-1884) passed the Factory Act by virtue of which working hours of women and children were reduced. Children below seven years of age were not allowed to be employed in factories. The Factory Act, 1891 passed by Lord-Lands Journal (1888-1894) provided protection for children, adults and women by granting to them weekly holidays and rest for half an hour in the afternoon.[45]

### *Theory of Swaraj- a Mile-stone of Civil and Political Rights*

Although, British had launched several social reforms in Indian society to make the rights of minor, weaker and vulnerable sections a reality, but over all British Rule in India was illegal, immoral, selfish, discriminatory and repressive. It was, therefore necessary to agitate for the change in the government for the introduction of representative system, for the transfer of political power from British to Indian hands. Thus very soon after the establishment of British Rule in India, resistance to foreign rule was manifested in the form of demand for fundamental freedoms and civil and political rights for the people.[46] The Indian National Congress, founded in 1885, was the vanguard of the freedom struggle, took the lead in this matter. The main objective to be achieved by the Indian National Congress was *Swaraj*, which is Self-Rule. The Indian desire for civil rights was implicit in its formation. Indians wanted the same rights and privileges that British enjoyed, in India and that they enjoyed among themselves in England. In the early years of its formation, it asked for increasing Indian participation in the political affairs of the country.[47] The earliest demand for recognition of fundamental rights commenced with the Constitution of India Bill, 1895 was probably issued under the inspiration of Lokmanya Bal Gangadhar Tilak and described as the Home Rule Bill by Annie Besant. The Bill talked about a constitution guaranteeing every one of the citizens' basic human rights like freedom of expression, inviolability of one's own home, right to property, equality before law, etc. A glimpse of the human rights in the form of the human rights and directive principles may be found in the Bill itself. The Bill also had provisions guaranteeing free state education and compulsory primary education.[48] In August 1918, Indian National Congress demanded incorporation of a Declaration of the Rights of the People of India as British citizens. It demanded, *inter alia*, guarantees of Equality before Law, protection in respect of Liberty, Life and Property, Freedom of Speech and Press and the Right of Association. In the Delhi Session of December 1918, Indian National Congress included the Principles of Self Determination as one of the basic rights.[49]

Constitution of the Irish Free State 1921 included a list of Fundamental Rights. This had certainly influenced the thinking of the Indian National Congress, which prepared a draft of 'Commonwealth of India Bill' embodying a Declaration of Rights.

Madrass Congress of the Indian National Congress agitated in 1927 that a Declaration of Fundamental Rights should be incorporated in any future constitutional framework. A committee under Moti Lal Nehru was appointed. Reporting in 1928, this committee declared that the first concern of the people of India is to secure fundamental rights.

The Rights emphasized by the Moti Lal Committee were:[50]

- Personal Liberty, Inviolability of dwelling place and property;
- Freedom of conscience and of profession and practice of religion subject to public order and morality;

- Right to free expression of opinion and to assemble peacefully and without arms and to form association and unions subject to public order and morality;
- Right to free elementary education and in the matter of admission into any educational institution maintained and aided by states without distinction of caste or creed;
- Equality for all citizens before the law and in civil rights;
- Right to every citizen to the writ of Habeas Corpus;
- Protection of respect of punishment under *ex-post facto* law;
- Non-discrimination against any person on grounds of religion, caste or creed in the matter of public appointment, office or power or honour and in the exercise of any trade or calling;
- Equality of Right to all citizens in the matter of access to, and use of public roads, wells and other places of public resort;
- Freedom of combination and association for the maintenance and implementation of labour and economic conditions;
- Right to keep and bear arms in accordance with Regulations; and
- Equality of Rights to men and women as citizens.

Lahore Congress of 1930 declared Freedom from Foreign Rule as a political Right. Karachi Congress passed a resolution in 1931 on 'Fundamental Rights and Social Change.' The resolution was in three parts;(A) Fundamental Rights and Duties; (B) Labour and (C) Economic and Social Programme.[51]

The in-depth analysis of the modified Karachi resolutions makes it clear that they reflected totally which is today called as Fundamental Rights and Directive Principles of State Policy. At that time there was no separation between these two. It might have thought that all these had to constitute an integral whole to bring about a social revolution in India. Similarly, the Government of India Act, 1935 also incorporated certain fundamental rights which characterized political, economic and social rights. Section 297-300 of the Government of India Act, 1935 incorporated certain type of rights.[52]

In the broader spectrum of human rights, the subject of fundamental rights and its incorporation in the future constitution of India was discussed at length by Sapru Committee in 1945 with Tej Bahadur Sapru as its chairman. Various associations, groups, individuals sent their views on the desirability of India with right of writ remedy in case of violation of these rights and the machinery that could be suggested for the enforcement of these fundamental rights which were not justifiable. It was the time when the separation of rights started in India first of all. The Sapru Committee considered the suggestions received from various quarters on the subject of fundamental rights and reached the following conclusion. First, protection of the minority rights was really necessary. Second, there was a need for legislative and administrative actions and the courts. Third, that the justiciable and non-justiciabe fundamental rights be discussed and pleaded for incorporation in the future constitution. It, however, did not suggest how best the division could be made. It left the whole matter to be decided by the constitution making body. The Indian Constitution (1949) was drafted even before the Universal Declaration of Human Rights (1950) but it was adopted at the time when the discussions for the Universal Declaration were in the air, so framers of the Indian Constitution were influenced by the concept of human rights, and always guaranteed most of the human rights which later came to be embodied in the International Covenants in 1966.[53]

Even prior to the framing of the constitution for India, Mahatma Gandhi had announced before the Second Round Table Conference that the aim was to establish a political society in India in which there would be no distinction between high class and low class people; that women should enjoy the same rights as men; and dignity and justice, social, economic and political be ensured to the millions of India.[54] This was the main objective which inspired Jawahar Lal Nehru in drafting the historic 'Objectives Resolution' in the Constituent Assembly and which was adopted on January 22, 1947. Clause 5 of the Resolution stated that this Constituent Assembly declares its firm and solemn resolve to proclaim India as an Independent, Sovereign Republic and to draw up for her future governance a Constitution.[55]

The Constituent Assembly, on January 24, 1947 voted to form the Advisory Committee. The duty of this Committee was to report to the Assembly on the list of Fundamental Rights and the clauses for the protection of the minorities etc. Advisory Committee in turn set up five sub-committees, out of which one was the Sub-Committee on Fundamental Rights. Acharya Kripalani became the chairman of that sub-committee. The members of the Sub-Committee quickly decided that the Fundamental Rights should be justiciable, they should be included in the Constitution, and they decided form these rights should take.[56] Finally, Constituent Assembly drafted the constitution including Fundamental Rights and Directive Principles of State Policy as justiciable and non-justiciable rights respectively for the purposes of enforcing human rights.[57]

### Post-Independence Era

Promulgation of the Constitution by the People of India in January 1950 is a watershed in the history of the development of the concept of human rights in India. The Preamble, Fundamental Rights and the Directive Principles of State Policy together provide the basic human rights for the people of India. Democratic socialism spelt out in the Preamble and the Directive Principles is meant to provide the context in which the fulfillment of Fundamental Rights has to be achieved. While Fundamental Rights stress on individual and the existing rights, Directive Principles provide the dynamic movement towards the goal of providing collective human rights for all.

The makers of Indian Constitution were fully aware about need and necessity of the Indians regarding human rights. Due to that sense of responsibility towards human rights, the Indian Constitution begins with by mentioning varieties of rights for all Indians in its Preamble.

The Preamble of the Constitution of India declares that the People of India have solemnly resolved to constitute India into a Sovereign, Socialist, Secular, Democratic, Republic and secure all its citizens:

| | | |
|---|---|---|
| JUSTICE | : | Social, Economic and Political; |
| LIBERTY | : | of thought, expression, belief, faith and worship; |
| EQUALITY | : | of status and opportunity; and to promote among them all; |
| FRATERNITY | : | assuring the dignity of the individual and the unity and integrity of the nation. |

## Fundamental Rights and Directive Principles of State Policy

Fundamental rights incorporated in the Part III of the Indian Constitution are those prerequisite principles which forbade the government to violate the civil and political rights of the people. The fundamental rights incorporated in the India Constitution express the civil and political rights. These are the unique compilation of all those rights and liberties which are necessary of the Indian citizens for the fullest development of their civil and political life exceedingly expected in a democracy. Fundamental Rights are the bindings on the State which actually restrict the Indian State to constitute any law, or execute any function which hinders, minimizes or mitigates the civil, legal and political rights and liberties of the Indian citizens. To make the government committed to guarantee the social and economic rights of the people of India, Directive Principles of the State Policy are introduced in the Indian Constitution. These Directive Principles given place in the Part IV (Articles 37 to 51) contain what may be described as the active obligations of the State. The State shall secure a social order in which social, economic and political justice shall inform all the institutions of national life. Wealth and its resources of production shall not be concentrated in the hands of the few but shall be distributed so as to subserve the common good. There shall be adequate means of livelihood for all and equal pay for equal work. The State shall endeavour to secure the health and conditions of work and proper wage for workers, a uniform civil code, and free and compulsory education for children should be secured by the State. The State shall take steps to organize village panchayats, promote the educational and economic interests of the weaker sections of people, raise the level of nutrition and standard of living, improve public health, organize agricultural and animal husbandry, separate the judiciary from the executive and promote international peace and security.[58]

Basically the Directive Principles of State Policy possess two characteristics. Firstly, they are not enforceable in any court and therefore, if a directive is not obeyed or implemented by the State, its obedience or implementation cannot be secured through judicial proceedings. This characteristic has been diluted in practice by court decisions which have enforced some of the directive principles in support of the fundamental rights. Secondly, they are fundamental in governance of the country and it shall be the duty of the State to apply these principles in making laws. The expression 'laws' must be construed in a generic sense and should include all normative exercise of power including the decision making.[59]

Even though, the Indian nationalist leaders and the makers of Indian constitution adopted the Western framework of political rights, but they rejected the Lockean theory of *a priori* or natural rights. They considered rights as the gifts from the state hence are not absolute and their enjoyment is considered by a number of factors-social, economic and political. The rights of different groups and society are counter balanced by the rights of the State and its obligation to the weaker sections of the society. The Indian intellectuals generally accepted the view that rights are not over and above the State, rather they are gift from the State itself. To them, rights of the individual must be balanced with the interest of society as a whole.

As far as the constitutional history of human rights in India is concerned, the Constitution of India which came into force in 1950 is an eloquent testimony of the nation's deep commitment to human rights. It proclaims basic human rights and fundamental freedoms and guarantees their enjoyment by all, irrespective of caste, colour, sex or religion. It has also created legal institutions to enforce the fundamental rights comprising liberty, equality, and social justice. India has been steadfast in its convictions that democracy is the best guarantor of human rights and it also provides an optimal political framework for development. The institutions India has fashioned to sustain as plural, multi-ethnic, multi-religious, multi-linguistic and a secular polity, had the over-reaching objectives of consolidating the norms and principles of our democracy.[60]

India has elected parliamentary institutions and conducts free and fair elections at Local, State and Centre. It has built mechanism for peaceful and elderly changes of government in response to popular will. The governmental mechanism such as police, security forces are also working to safeguard the life, liberty and security of people. India's independent judiciary which is the custodian of the rights of people has also been acting zealously to protect them. Public Interest Litigation (PIL) an additional system of Indian judiciary has also been instituted for this cause. A free and vibrant press, existence of various interest groups, strong public opinion, an assertive NGO community and above all, the Rule of Law fortify India's democratic system and its legal safeguards. India is also a signatory to the UDHR and party to various international covenants, conventions and treaties. Furthermore, greater access to the statesman of various countries and international human rights agencies has facilitated. It is to reaffirm the atmosphere of freedom and India's commitment to its own catalogue of rights.[61]

India has ratified the International Covenant on Civil and Political Rights (CCPR) and International Covenant on Economic, Social and Cultural Rights (CESCR) on March 27, 1979. By ratification, it has established on the international plane its consent to be bound by them. It has an obligation to provide the individuals the rights contained in the two covenants.

Many rights enshrined in the Covenant on Civil and Political Rights have been recognized specifically in the Fundamental Rights. The following table shows the different Articles of the Covenant and the Constitution wherein identical rights are stipulated:[62]

| *Rights* | *Covenant on Civil & Political Rights* | *Indian Constitution* |
|---|---|---|
| Forced Labour | Article 8(3) | Article 23 |
| Equality before Law | Article 14(1) | Article 14 |
| Prohibition of discrimination | Article 26 | Article 15 |
| Equality of opportunity to public service | Article 25(c) | Article 16(1) |
| Freedom of speech and expression | Article 19(1),(2) | Article 19(1)(a) |
| Right for peaceful assembly | Article 21 | Article 19(1)(b) |
| Right of freedom of association | Article 22(1) | Article 19(c) |
| Right to move freely withinthe territory of State | Article 22(1) | Article 19(1) (d),and (e) |
| Protection in respect of conviction for offences | Article 15(1) | Article 20(1) |
| Protection from prosecutionand punishment | Article 14(7) | Article 20(2) |
| Not to be compelled to testify against himself | Article 14(3)(g) | Article 20(3) |
| Right to life and liberty | Article 6(1),9(1) | Article 21 |
| Protection against arrest and detention in certain cases | Article 9(2)(3)(4) | Article 22 |
| Freedom of conscience and religion | Article 18(1) | Article 25 |

The 'Directive Principles' which broadly incorporate the economic and social rights are as much a part of human rights. Many human rights enshrined in the Covenant on Economic, Social and Cultural Rights (CESCR) are incorporated in the directive principles is evident from the following table:

| *Rights* | *Covenant on Economic, Social & Cultural Rights* | *Indian Constitution* |
|---|---|---|
| Equal pay for equal work | Article 7(a)(i) | Article 39(d) |
| humane condition of work | Article 7(b) | Article 42 |
| Maternity relief | Article 10(2) | Article 42 |
| Right to work | Article 6(1) | Article 41 |
| Opportunities to children | Article 10(3) | Article 39(f) |
| Compulsory education to children | Article 13(2)(a) | Article 45 |
| Living wages | Article 7(a)(ii) | Article 43 |
| Conditions of work | Article 7(d) | Article 43 |
| Adequate standard of living | Article 11 | Article 47 |
| Right to child education | Article 13(1) 21-A | Article 45 |

Besides these International Covenants on Human Rights, India has become party to other international Conventions on Human Rights. The list of these Conventions to which India is a Party, is given below:[63]

- International Convention on the Elimination of All Forms of Discrimination (1965) was signed on March 2, 1961 and ratified by India on December 3, 1968.
- International Convention on the Suppression and Punishment of the Crime of Apartheid (1973, was ratified by India on September 22, 1977. Further, International Convention against Apartheid in Sports (1985) has been ratified on September 12, 1990.
- Convention on the Prevention and Punishment of the Crimes of Genocide (1951) was ratified on August 27, 1959.
- Convention on the Rights of the Child (1989) was ratified on December 11, 1992.
- Convention on the Elimination of All Forms of Discrimination Against Women (1979) was ratified on July 9, 1993.
- Protocol of 1953, amending The International Slave Convention (1926) was ratified on March 12, 1954 and the Supplementary Convention on the Abolition of Slavery, the Slave Trade and Institutions and Practices Similar to Slaves was ratified on June 23, 1960.
- Convention for the Suppression of the Traffic in Persons and of the Exploitation of the Prohibition of the others (1949) was ratified on January 9, 1953.
- Convention on the Prevention and Punishment of the Crimes of Genocide (August 27, 1959).
- Convention on the Rights of the Child (December 11, 1992).
- Convention for the Suppression of the Traffic in the Person and of the Exploitation of the Prostitution of others (January 9, 1953).
- Convention against Torture and other Cruel, inhuman or Degrading Treatment of Punishment (October 14, 1997).

- Convention on the Non-Applicability of Statutory Limitations to War Crimes and Crimes Against Humanity.
- Convention on the Nationality of Married Women.

Earlier, it was realized that constitutional provisions, along with international treaty obligations and ratified Covenants and Conventions, are sufficient to meet the growing need of human rights and their enforcement. It was also felt that apart from courts, the sole enforcing agency of constitutional human rights provisions, some other agency should also be created for the enforcement of human rights. It would really release the burden of the courts also. At the same time western human rights activists also raised the problem at international level that Indian human rights performance was not up to the mark and really gross violations of human rights occurred in India. Just to meet out all that criticism and higher up the national image, government of India started codifying various human rights laws.[64]

It is a fact that during 1950 to 1970, there were certain pro-labour, pro-farmer, or pro-poor laws which directly assisted human rights. Government took steps for the legalization of human rights by ordinary legislation. The bonded Labour System(Abolition) Act, 1976(19 of 1976)[65] The Child labour(Prohibition and Regulation) Act, 1986(61of 1986)[66] SC and ST (Prevention of Atrocities) Act, 1989 and Rule, 1995, along with The Protection of Civil Rights Act, 19[67] The Juvenile Justice(Care and Protection) Act, 2000[68] The Protection of Women from Domestic Violence Act, 2005[69] prevent crimes against Children, Women, Labourers, SCs and STs. National Commission for Women Act 1990 helped a lot to advance the social position of women. National Commission for Minorities, 1992, is a positive signal for the upliftment of Muslims, Christians, Jews and Parsis, etc. Lastly, The Protection of Human Rights Act, 1993[70] created a total atmosphere of human rights in society within few years. National Human Rights Commission and a few state human rights commissions which have been established so far have created a fear in the minds of human rights violators. It has raised the respect for human rights throughout the nation[71]

It is thus evident that during the period of 1946 to 1949, India had formulated the elaborative concept of human rights. In the substantive provisions of the Constitution, the human rights were divided into two parts, in the same way as the International Covenant on Civil and Political Rights and on Economic, Social and Cultural Rights did later in 1966. In the Indian Constitution, the justiciable human rights are included in part III, while the non-justciable rights in the form of Directive Principle of State Policy were included in the part IV of the Indian Constitution. Part III of the Indian Constitution shows that the State has been put under certain limitations which are essential for the preservation of civil and political human rights. Part IV of the Constitution is a mirror which reflects the image of an egalitarian society aiming at the betterment of the individual as an integrative component of the society. The State is enjoined within the limits of its economic capacity to provide for securing the right to work, to education and public assistance in cases of unemployment, old age, sickness, disablement and to secure just and humane conditions of work and maternity relief.[72]

To conclude, however, the theory of *a priori* or natural rights doctrine of West is not the source of Indian conception of human rights, rather it has its own experience and overview of human rights. That experience and overview develops from its culture and civilization, which is oldest, greatest and unique of the whole world. The freedom of the individuals in the Western societies was secured after a long and bitter struggle against the Church and the State; in India those freedoms were seen as the very substance of human existence. Therefore, it is only a misconception created by the pro-western scholars that the West possesses rich literature, and the same is absent in India. It would be totally wrong to conclude that the idea of rights and freedoms is chiefly a Western one.[73] The Indian conception of human rights does not vision the man as an isolated individual, but the individual is a total person whose interdependent rights and duties are determined by his/her position within a hierarchical network of relationship.[74] In

India, human rights movement does not develop as unrest against the political authority, but there are several social, cultural and religious circumstances which have played prominent role in the formation and practice of human rights in India. Humanistic vision of ancient scriptures, impact of religious philosophies, reform movements, British colonialism and the nationalist movement for independence influenced the perception of human rights in India and characterized the Indian human rights conception with perspective different and unique to the Western and Third World perspective.

## References

1. Arun Ray Mohapatra, *National Human Rights Commission of India*, Radha Publications, New Delhi, 2001., p. 27.
2. Thomas. M. Franck, "Human Rights in Third World Perspective", *Human Rights Quarterly*, Vol. V, No. 3, August 1983, pp. 374-376.
3. Arun Ray Mohapatra, *op. cit.*, p. 27.
4. Thomas M. Franck, *op. cit.*, pp. 374-376.
5. Yogesh Kumar Tyagi, "Third World Response to Human Rights", *Indian Journal of International Law*, Vol. 21, 1981, p. 40.
6. K.M. Mathur, *Management of Internal Security and Related Issues*, Gyan Publishing House, New Delhi, 1995, p. 182.
7. Vaman Shivam Aapte, *Sansktir-Hindi Dictionary*, Kamal Parkashan, New Delhi, 2005, p. 30.
8. Gukulesh Sharma, *Human Rights and Legal Remedies*, Deep & Deep Publications, New Delhi, 2000, pp. 98-99.
9. K.M. Mathur, *Crime, Human Rights and National Security*, Gyan Publishing House, New Delhi, 1996, p. 159.
10. Arun Ray Mohapatra, op. cit., pp. 28-29.
11. Gukulesh Sharma, *op. cit.*, p. 102.
12. *Ibid.*, p. 103.
13. V.T. Thamilmaran, *Human Rights in Third World Perspective*, Har- Anand Publishers, New Delhi, 1992, p. 46.
14. Gukulesh Sharma, *op. cit.*, p. 104.
15. *Ibid.*, p. 104.
16. *Ibid.*, pp. 104-105.
17. V.T. Thamilmaran, *op.* cit., p. 46.
18. *Ibid.*, p. 47.
19. *Ibid.*, p. 48.
20. R.C. Pandaya, *Human Rights: An Indian Perspective in Philosophical Foundations of Human Rights*, UNESCO, Paris, 1986, pp. 267-277.
21. Arun Ray Mohapatra, *op. cit.*, p. 30.

22. *Ibid.*, p. 31.
23. Sutta Nitapa, "136 Mahaparinibbna-Sutta of the Digha-Nikaya", as quoted by G. S. P. Misra, *Development of Buddhist Ethics*, Munshiram Monoharlal Publications, New Delhi, 1995, p. 73.
24. Prabha Chopra, "Contribution of Buddhism to Human Rights and Status of Women", in P. N. Chopra (ed.) *Contribution of Buddhism to World Civilisation and Culture*, S. Chand & Company, New Delhi, 1983, p 127.
25. L.N. Basu, *Human Rights: Practice and Limitations*, Pointer Publishers. Jaipur, 2006, p. 4.
26. Abha Singh, "Human Rights in Buddhist Perspective", *Indian Philosophical Quarterly*, Vol. XXXIII, No. 3, July-October 2006, p. 331.
27. Gukulesh Sharma, *op. cit.*, p 105.
28. Syed Maududi, "Human Rights in Islam", *Islam 101*, http://www.islam101.com/rights/index.htm.
29. M. M. Rehman, *op. cit.*, pp. 4-5.
30. Yogesh Kumar Tyagi, "Third World Response to Human Rights", *Indian Journal of Law*, Vol. 21, 1981, p. 123.
31 Arun Ray Mohapatra, *op. cit.*, pp. 59-60.
32. Gukulesh Sharma, *op. cit.*, p. 60.
33. Arun Ray Mohapatra, *op. cit.*, p. 32.
34. *Guru Granth Sahib*, p. 1349.
35. *Guru Granth Sahib*, p. 1375.
36. *Guru Granth Sahib*, pp. 722-723.
37. *Guru Granth Sahib*, p. 1288.
38. *Guru Granth Sahib*, pp. 1127-1128.
39. *Guru Granth Sahib*, p. 949.
40. Charanjit Ajit Singh, *Human Rights and Minorities*, World Council of Churches, http://www.wcc- coe.org/wcc/what/interreligious/cd33-17.html.
41. Arun Ray Mohapatra, *op. cit.*, p. 32.
42. Gukulesh Sharma, *op. cit.*, p. 60.
43. Indian Heroes: Social Reformers: Jyotiba Phule, http://www.iloveindia.com/indián-heroes/jyotirao-govindrao-phule.html.
44. Philip Constable, "Early Dalit Literature and Culture in Late Nineteenth and Early Twentieth Century Western India", *Modern Asian Studies*, Vol. 31, No. 2, 1997, p. 317.
45. A.K. Gautam, *Human Rights and Justice System*, A.P.H. Publishers, New Delhi, 2000, p. 50.
46. G. Austin, *The Indian Constitution: The Corner Stone of a Nation*, Oxford University Press, Oxford, 1966, pp. 53-54.
47. Gukulesh Sharma, *op. cit.*, p. 63.
48. *Ibid.*, pp. 63-64.
49. S. Subramanian, *Human Rights: International Challenges*, Vol. I, Manas Publications, New Delhi, 1997, p. 56.

50. *Ibid.*, p. 57.
51. *Ibid.*, p. 57.
52. S. Subramanian, *op. cit.*, p. 58.
53. D. D. Basu, *Human Rights in Constitutional Law*, Princtene Publications, New Delhi, 1994, p. 14.
54. *Ibid.*, p. 3.
55. *Ibid.*, p. 14.
56. G.S. Bajwa, *Implementation of Human Rights in India*, an unpublished Ph. D. Thesis, Department of Law, Punjabi University, Patiala, 1993, pp. 71-72.
57. Gukulesh Sharma, *op. cit.*, pp. 67-68.
58. V.N Shukla, *Constitution of India*, 10th Edition (Revised by Mahendra P. Singh), Eastern Book Company, Lucknow, 2006, p. 202.
59. *Ibid.*, p 298.
60. Statement by Dr. Manmohan Singh, then Minister of Finance at the 50th World Conference on Human Rights, *The Observer*, 22nd January, 1993.
61. Statement by Ghulam Nabhi Azad, then Minister of Civil Aviation and Tourism, at the 51st Conference of Human Rights in Geneva, *The National Herald*, New Delhi, March 14, 1995.
62. H.O. Agarwal, *Internatonal Law and Human Rights*, 11th Edition, Central Law Publications, Allahabad, 2004, p. 886 .
63. S.K. Kapoor, *International Law and Human Rights*, 15th Edition, Central Law Agency, Allahabad, 2004, pp 892,893.
64. Gukulesh Sharma, *op. cit*. p. 69.
65. 67. Krishna Arora, *The bonded Labour System(Abolition) Act, 1976(19 of 1976)* BARE ACT, Professional Book Pub., 2007.
66. Krishna Arora (ed.)*The Child labour(Prohibition and Regulation) Act, 1986(61of 1986)* BARE ACT, Professional Book Pub., 2007.
67. Krishna Arora (ed.)*The Protection of Civil Rights Act, 1955*,BARE ACT Professional Book Pub., 2007.
68. Krishna Arora(ed.) *The Juvenile Justice(Care and Protection) Act, 2000*, Professional Book Pub. BARE ACT, 2007.
69. Krishana Arora (ed.) *The Protection of Women from Domestic Violence Act, 2005*, BARE ACT, 2007.
70. *The Protection of Human Rights Act 1993*, BARE ACT, 2007.
71. Gukulesh Sharma, *op. cit*. p. 70.
72. Distance Learning Post-graduate Programme in Human Rights, *Indian Constitution and Human Rights*, Indian Institute of Human Rights, New Delhi, p. 9.
73. Badrinath Chaturvedi, "Dharma and Jainism", *Times of India*, September 25, 1995.
74. Chiryankandth Jamas, "Human Rights in India: Concepts and Contexts", *Contemporary South Asia*, Vol. 2, No. 3, p. 224.

# PART–2

# 5

## Custodial Torture and Deaths in India: A Lethal Violation of Human Rights

Human rights are the prerequisite conditions indispensable for all human being for the existence and fullest exposure of the innate features of their personality. Negation of human rights is not only an individual tragedy but it is also contrary to the objective of social welfare presumed by the democratic nations. Violation of human rights is the most severe and lethal form of crimes against the humanity. Violation of human rights does not only hinder the chances of human beings for development but even curtails their opportunities for existence and survival.

The term 'violation' is generally defined as an act that disregards an agreement or a right.[1] It is an unwanted intrusion by a person, object or ideology into one's life that leaves someone feeling without value and protection.[2] Violation is considered as infringement or breach, as of law, rule, right etc.[3] Amongst scholars and international organizations concerned with human rights, there is little or no agreement about the meaning of the concept of 'violation of human rights'. In broader terms, violation of human rights includes all inhuman, illegal acts which mitigate the rights and liberties of the human beings. Violation of human rights is actually the contravention of those conditions which are acknowledged by the moral and legal values, the paramount requirement for existence, survival and development of human beings. It includes hindering, restraining or abolishing those civil, political, economic and social opportunities which are needed by individuals, recognized by the State and protected by the law. However, the terms 'gross violation of human rights' means the acts of torture, disappearances and extrajudicial executions.[4]

It is said in personal terms, that a man is treated exactly the way he allows himself to be treated. In case of the nation, it will be treated just the way it allows itself to be treated. India has done of course, significant progress in the field of establishing almost all necessary legal provisions to safeguard human rights since independence. But an alarming question still arises that how all this legal mechanism measures in the context of availability of minimum conditions essential for the development of innate characteristics, which nature has bestowed every Indian with as a human being irrespective of one's race, caste, creed, colour, gender or social origin, birth or any other status ? Unfortunately, the answer is not much encouraging. Violations of human rights now have been taking place in almost every part of the country. Violations of human rights in India are now seen as violations of the democratic principles enshrined in the Indian Constitution as well as violation of India's international commitment of humanitarian international law, international Covenants and Conventions.

India has made the sincere efforts for the protection and promotion of human rights and is acknowledged as the champion of human rights in the Third World. The impact of the Universal Declaration of Human Rights can be explicitly seen on the drafting of chapters (Part III and IV) of the Indian Constitution. Besides that, India has signed and ratified all major international covenants, protocols and conventions for the promotion and protection of human rights. The National Human Rights Commission at central level and the State Human Rights Commissions at regional level have been working to protect the human rights of Indian masses. Moreover, there exists an independent judiciary to provide justice to the victims of human rights abuses and check the governmental authorities to infringe the rights of the people. However, the fact remains that there is a wide gap between theory and practice. All that is practiced is not always put into practice and India is no more exception. The denial of fundamental freedoms and human rights by the states creates the conditions of social and political unrest. It definitely sows the seeds of violence and conflicts within and between societies and nations.

Police atrocities are a common feature of Indian scenario. These violations are committed under the shields of uniform and authority between the four walls of the police stations, lock-ups and prisons, where the victims are totally helpless. Abuse of power, arbitrariness, failure in taking lawful action, illegal arrest and detention are the most common feature of violation of human rights by the Indian police. Other severe forms of human rights violations by the police are the torture of arrested persons, the disappearances of suspects who ought to have been in regular police custody, deaths in fake encounters and at police stations, and under-trials detained in jails for years without trials.

## Custodial Torture and Custodial Deaths

Among all these worst forms of human rights violations, custodial torture has become a serious and alarming problem in India. Brutal atrocities perpetuated by the police, jail authorities, and other law enforcing agencies on the suspects/ accused persons are menacingly on the increase day by day. The State and the police remain in worrying denial. Torture in police custody remains a widespread and systematic practice in India.[5] The lack of effective system of independent monitoring of all places of detention facilitates torture.[6] It would be hard to find any police station or jail where the inmates are not subjected to torture and other cruel, inhuman or degrading treatment or punishment.[7]

### *Custodial Torture: Major Cause of Custodial Deaths*

The methods as well as the equipments used by the Police to torture the accused are brutally violent. Police personnel, before torturing and even while torturing the accused, forget or deliberately neglect that the lethal equipments and methods of torture may cause the death of the person tortured by them. The unaccountability, dearth of active criminal justice system and the unrestricted impunity by higher authorities and political elites encourages the police to torture the indicted in a cruel manner. The inhuman and lethal custodial torture, most of the times, result in custodial deaths, where the accused dies in the police lock up, while reaching to the hospital or even after reaching the hospital.

Torture is the most naked assault on human dignity that ruins the victim physically, psychologically and mentally. Hence, torture is recognized worldwide as a crime against humanity. Considering the wide-spread violations, the UN General Assembly adopted the 'UN Declaration on the Protection of all persons from being subjected to Torture and Other Cruel, Inhuman or Degrading Treatment or Punishment' on 9th December, 1975. Article 1 of the Convention against Torture and Other Cruel, Inhuman or Degrading Treatment or Punishment provides that no one should be subjected to torture or other cruel, inhuman or degrading treatment or punishment. This has been reiterated in numerous international human rights laws and international humanitarian laws. When even this Declaration did not satisfy the world community, the UN General Assembly adopted the 'Convention Against Torture (CAT)' on 10th December, 1984 and brought the same into force on 26th June, 1987. It defines the torture as "any act by which severe pain or suffering whether physical, mental, is intentionally inflicted on a person for such purposes as obtaining from him/her or third person, information or a confession, punishing him for an act he or a third person has committed or is suspected of having committed, or intimidating or coercing him or a third person, or for any reason based on discrimination of any kind, when such pain or suffering is inflicted by or at the instigation of or with the consent or acquiescence of a public official or other person acting in an official capacity".[8] However, it does not include pain or sufferings arising only from inherent in or incidental to Lawful Sanctions.

## Legal Provisions in India to check Custodial Torture

Torture is neither defined in the Indian Constitution or in any penal law in India. But Indian law provides certain rights to the prisoners/suspects/ accused persons while in custody. Unlike the International Covenant on Civil and Political Rights, the Indian Constitution does not specifically provide any right against custodial torture. However, certain fundamental rights enumerated in Part III of the Indian Constitution and mainly contained in articles 19, 20, 21, 22, 32 and 226 of the Constitution are available to them. Though, sections 220 and 330 of Indian Penal Code have been held to be inadequate in as much as they only punish the culprit without giving any benefit to the victim. Besides that Government of India has also signed the Convention Against Torture (CAT) in October 1997.

### *Guidelines of the Supreme Court of India*

The Indian Supreme Court, in number of cases has not only acknowledged these rights but also expanded their scope through the process of judicial activism giving new and liberal interpretation. According to the Supreme Court, "Torture of a human being by another human being is essentially as instrument to impose the will of the strong over the weak by suffering."[9] Moreover in a landmark judgment in 1996 in the case of *D.K.Basu Vs State of West Bengal,* the Supreme Court laid down specific guidelines required to be followed while making arrests with the aim to eliminate violations of human rights in police custody. The Indian Supreme Court has said that, "dehumanizing torture, assault and death in custody" are so "widespread" as to "raise serious questions about credibility of rule of law and administration of criminal justice."[10]

### *National Human Rights Commission Guidelines*

In recognition of the scale of the problem of use of torture, on 14 December 1993, the National Human Rights Commission (NHRC) issued guidelines directing all District Magistrates and Superintendents of Police in every district to report to the Secretary General of the NHRC about custodial deaths/rapes within 24 hours. The NHRC warned that: "Failure to report promptly would give rise to presumption that there was an attempt to suppress the incident".

The preventative actions of the Supreme Court and the NHRC have not ended deaths in police custody due to torture. The law prohibits torture, but there is credible evidence that it is common throughout India. The data collected by the National Human Rights Commission (NHRC) and the National Crime Record Bureau (NCRB) of the Ministry of Home Affairs, Government of India to a limited extent indicates the intensity of torture in India.

**Magnitude of Custodial Deaths in India**

While studying the statistics of custodial deaths given in the annual reports of the NHRC, it has been found that cases of custodial deaths are on the rise year after year. The NHRC had registered only 62 cases (37 in Police Custody (PC) and 25 in Judicial Custody (JC)) of custodial deaths during 1993-94. There was an alarming increase in the number of cases in one year and the NHRC registered 162 cases (111 in PC and 51 in JC) of custodial deaths in 1994-95. The number of custodial deaths was 444 (136 in PC and 308 in JC) in 1995-96 which had doubled in one year with total number of 888 complaints (188 in PC and 700 in JC) in 1996-97. During 1997-98, the deaths of 1012 persons in custody (193 in PC and 819 in JC) were reported to the NHRC, which was followed by 1297 complaints (183 in PC and 1114 in JC) during 1998-99 and 1093 complaints (177 in PC and 916 in JC) during 1999-2000. In 2000-01, there was a trivial decrease in the number of complaints and the NHRC had registered 1037 cases (127 in PC and 910 in JC). It was followed by 1277 cases (160 in PC and 1117 in JC) in 2001-02, 1340 cases (183 in PC and 1157 in JC) in 2002-03 and 1462 cases (162 in PC and 1300 in JC) of custodial deaths in 2003-04. The rise in the number of complaints had constantly increased and the NHRC had registered 1493 cases (136 in PC and 1357 in JC) of custodial deaths during 2004-05, as many as 1730 cases (139 in PC and 1591 in JC) in 2005-06, and 1620 cases (100 in PC and 1518 in JC) in 2006-07.

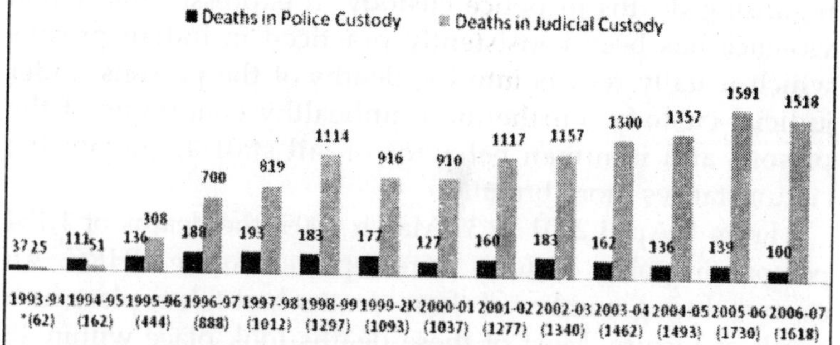


(*Data in Brackets Represents Total Number of Complaints in a Year.)

*Source:* Annual Reports of National Human Rights Commission.

**Figure 1: Cases of Custodial Deaths Registered by NHRC (1993-94 to 2006-07)**

The NHRC from 1993-94, the initial year of its inception, to 2006-07, has registered 14915 cases of custodial deaths from different regions of India. It confirms that the NHRC registers average 1 complaint of custodial deaths in every three days. Among total 14915 complaints of custodial deaths, 2032 are regarding deaths in Police Custody and 12883 are regarding deaths in Judicial Custody. It asserts that approximately 14 per cent of total number of complaints is regarding deaths in Police Custody while worryingly 86 per cent of total number of complaints is regarding deaths in Judicial Custody.

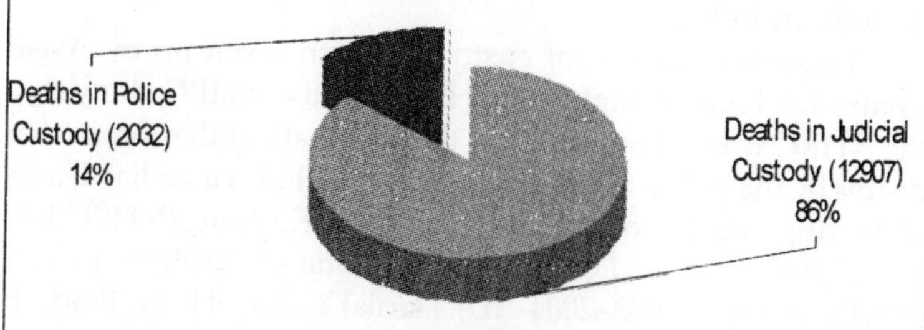


*Source:* Annual Reports of National Human Rights Commission

**Figure 2: Cases Registered by NHRC Regarding Custodial Deaths (1993-2007)**

The data reveals that the number of complaints registered by the NHRC regarding deaths in judicial custody is more than 6 times in comparison with the total number of complaints regarding deaths in police custody. It expresses that lethal violence has been consistently practiced in Indian prisons which usually results into the deaths of the persons under judicial custody. Furthermore unhealthy conditions of the prisons and inhuman behavior of jail staff aggravate the circumstances more brutally.

From 1 April 2001 to 31 March 2009, the deaths of 1,184 persons in police custody were reported to the NHRC. An overwhelming number of these deaths had taken place as a result of torture. Most of these deaths took place within 48 hours of the victims being taken into custody by the police. During this period (1 April 2001 to 31 March 2009), the highest number of custodial deaths was reported in Maharashtra (192 cases) followed by Uttar Pradesh (128), Gujarat (113), Andhra Pradesh (85), West Bengal (83), Tamil Nadu (76), Assam (74), Karnataka (55), Punjab (41), Madhya Pradesh (38), Bihar and Rajasthan (32 each), Haryana (31), Kerala (30), Jharkhand (29), Delhi (25), Orissa (24), Chhattisgarh (23), Uttarakhand and Meghalaya (16 each), Arunachal Pradesh (11), Jammu and Kashmir and Tripura (9 each), Puducherry and Chandigarh (3 each), Himachal Pradesh (2) while Manipur, Goa, Sikkim, and Dadra & Nagar

Haveli recorded one case each.[11] However, the above figures do not represent the actual number of deaths in police custody in India.

A number of cases of custodial death taken up by Asian Centre for Human Rights (ACHR) with the NHRC show that the NHRC was not informed by the police about these custodial deaths by the police. Some of these cases include custodial deaths of Tsering Tondup of Leh in Jammu and Kashmir (NHRC File No. 27/9/9/07-08-AD); Boya Venkatanna of Andhra Pradesh (NHRC No. 6/1/2003- 2004-AD); Harilal Yadav of Uttar Pradesh (NHRC No. 704/24/2003-2004-CD); Jarupula Srinu of Andhra Pradesh (NHRC No. 60/1/2005-2006- AD-SCN); and Dwipen Bayan of Assam (NHRC No.133/3/2004-2005-AD).[12] The NHRC has expressed its anguish against the failure to report these cases of custodial death to the NHRC. But unfortunately, the NHRC's guidelines continue to be flouted.

According to the annual record of the data of crime published by the National Crime Record Bureau, in the 2000 there were total 78 reported cases of custodial deaths through out India. In 2001 the number increased to 90 and decreased to 84 in 2002. There were 94 cases of custodial deaths in 2003, total 86 cases in 2004 and 128 cases in 2005. The number of cases of custodial deaths was 89 in 2006 which had increased to 108 in 2007. In the year 2008 there were total 101 reported cases of custodial deaths in India as NCRB.

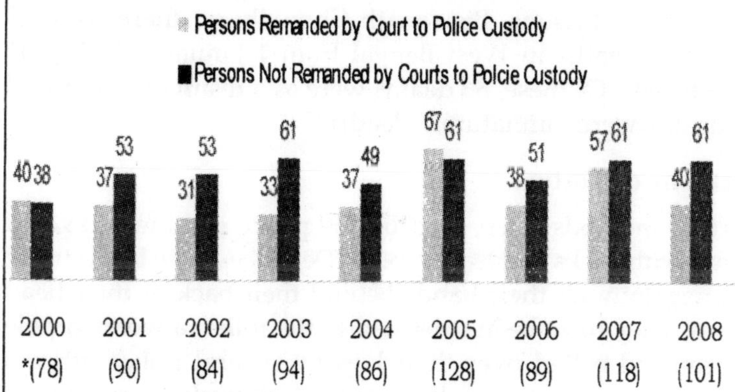


*Data Given in the Brackets Represents the Total Number of Custodial Deaths.
*Source:* National Crime Record Bureau of India.

**Figure 3: Custodial Deaths in India (2000-2008)**

The data asserts that there were as many as 868 reported cases of custodial deaths in India since 2000 to 2008. It means an average approximately 96 persons die in the police custody every year in India. Noticeably there is a steep increase in the number of custodial deaths every year. From 868 persons died in the police custody, 380 among them were those who were formally remanded to the police custody by the courts as per law, and 488 were those who were not remanded to police custody by the courts and had died while in an illegal confinement or detention. The data reveals that 56.22 per cent of the total persons died in the police custody (868) had died while in illegal confinement or detention by the police.

### *Torture in Prison Custody*

Torture remains widespread in Indian prisons. The National Human Rights Commission registered 1,996 cases of torture of prisoners in 2006-2007, 2,481 cases in 2007-2008 and 1,596 cases in 2008-2009 (up to 11 December 2008).[13] According to National Crime Records Bureau (NCRB) under Ministry of Home Affairs, 1,424 prisoners died in 2006, 1,387 prisoners in 2005, 1,169 prisoners in 2004,[14] and 1,060 prisoners in 2003[15]in India. Of the 1,423 prisoners who died in 2006, 80 died as a result of "unnatural" causes.[16] According to West Bengal's Minister for Prisons, Biswanath Chowdhury, there were 97 custodial deaths in West Bengal from 1 January 2007 to 31 March 2008. Of these, 86 deaths were as a result of illness and 14 deaths were "unnatural" deaths.[17]

### Methods of Torture

Torture methods often used by the police include kicks and blows with sticks and leather belts. Detainees have been strung up, usually with their hands behind their back or their head down. They have been subjected to the roller, a wooden pole or iron rod rolled over their legs by several police officers leaning on it with their full weight, which leads to crushing of muscle tissue and subsequently kidney complaints. Detainees have been tortured with electric shocks to the genitals and other areas such as ear lobs and fingers. They have been beaten on the soles of their feet, burned with a hot iron or boiling water.[18] As a result of torture, victims have suffered serious physical disabilities, deep states of depression, disturbed sleep and nightmares.[19]

Several types of instruments and equipments are used by the Police to torture the people in custody. It includes the instruments to give electric shocks, wooden locks to make the suspects immobile and then torture them, instruments to put pressure on the epidermal layers of the skin that gives a lot of pain to the victims and the belts attached with wooden handles to beat up the accused. The deadly torture applied on victims does not cause only physical pain or injury, but also results in emotional humiliation and psychological disorder. The physical agony and the psychological torment leave an endless negative impact on the personality of victims.

### Vulnerability of Certain Groups

Custodial torture is not confined to severely anti-social and violent people like terrorists, dacoits and other hardened criminals as certain police officials would like to make out. Economically poor and socially deprived sections of the society form the majority of torture victims. Torture is widespread and endemic in India but those living in armed conflict situations, Dalits, indigenous/tribal peoples, minorities, economically downtrodden, women and children[20] remain more vulnerable to torture, inhuman and degrading treatment because of their location, caste, ethnic origin, religious belief and gender. Hence, every year thousands of people are taken into custody by the police and subject to torture and custodial violence.[21]

### Causes of Custodial Violence

In India, torture is often used by the Police on the persons in the custody to solve criminal cases quickly, without investigations, to obtain a confession or the information needed to solve a case. Torture rather has increased today because police lack investigative capabilities which are also a direct result of inadequate resources, insufficient budget, poor investment in infrastructure, training, research, modernization of investigative techniques and unaccountability.

#### *Impunity Provided by the Government to the Police*

The governmental regimes which have ruled over India since independence were certainly opposite to each other in their ideology and functioning, but they have complemented each other in shielding the guilty police personnel from the grip of law and adjudicating system. None of the government has expressed any endeavour to expose the cases of human rights violations by the police and book the accused police officials as per law. Nevertheless, the governments have declared an amnesty sometimes hidden and sometimes open, for the police officials guilty of violating the rights of people.[22] The impunity provided by the government to the accused police personnel has spread out a fallacy among the police that they are beyond and above the law and can breach the rights of people anytime, anywhere.

### *Out-Dated Legislations advocating Strained Relationship with the Public*

The history of the Indian police discloses that the police have long had a strained relationship with the public. India's state and central police services were organized based on the Police Act of 1861, a law drafted in the wake of the 1857 uprising against British rule that remains in force in the union territories and is the basis for most state police laws.[23] While reformists frequently prioritize replacing the Police Act of 1861, important police structural characteristics in fact arose from the Police Commission of 1902.[24]

India retained the Police Act of 1861 after it gained independence from British rule in 1947, along with many of the structural characteristics described. In the decades that followed, the Indian police remained a force deployed to maintain law and order and support the state, and failed to develop the public service orientation of modern policing.[25] A dangerous anachronism, the police have largely failed to evolve from the ruler-supportive, repressive forces they were designed to be under Britain's colonial rule.

### *Colonial Mind-Set of the Police*

The colonial mind-set of the police arouses them not to treat the people as the human beings, but to use and abuse them according to their personal will and wish. The same repressive and suppressive attitude of the police still continues in India, because none of the government has made any sincere efforts to amend and improve the Police to work faithfully for the well-being of the people. Generally since the post-independence period, the police force has been used by the government as an effective force to maintain a threat and panic in the minds of the people.

### *Torture-A Substitute for Police Investigations*

Custodial torture is often used to solve criminal cases quickly, without time consuming investigations. It is widely reported that many police officials torture the suspects or the potential informants, or even persons totally unconnected with the case under investigation, in order to obtain a confession or the information needed to solve a case. The torture continues to be used today in India because professional investigative skills have been sapped and no other method of conducting an investigation is familiar to most of the police force in India.[26]

### *Extortion*

News of media and social commentators widely report that recruitments, transfers and promotions within the police take place on payment of large sums of money by the candidates at all levels. In these circumstances, police officers see the payment of a large bribe for their recruitment or promotion as an investment which they try to recover by demanding bribes in their turn in return for police services once they get the desired posting. In criminal cases, officers may be bribed by one or other of the parties, or may extort money from detainees not to torture them or to release them.[27]

### *Crumbling Police Infrastructure*

Although the police are tasked with battling India's most pressing problems—including armed insurgency, terrorism, and organized crime—a lack of political commitment and investment by the state has left the police overstretched and ill-equipped. There is just one civil police officer for every 1,037 Indian residents, far below Asia's regional average of one police officer for 558 people and the global average of 333 people[28] Police infrastructure is totally degenerated. Decaying, colonial-era police stations and posts across India are stocked with antiquated equipment and lacking sufficient police vehicles, phones, computers, and even stationery.

### *Strained Schedule and Dreadful Working Conditions*

The major problem lies in the working conditions of individual police officers. The police stations, where junior and low-ranking police officers often reside and deal with suspects or victims are in abysmal conditions. Police officials are often exhausted and demoralized, always on call, working long hours without shifts and necessary equipments, only to return to government-provided tents or filthy barracks for a few hours' sleep. The Director General of Police in Uttar Pradesh had once unveiled the exhausted schedule of Indian police while replying on the issue of comparison between Indian Police and Western police. He said that, "If you bring a US policeman here he would commit suicide within one day. [Here], you are literally thrown against the wall. We don't have a shift of 8 to 10 hours, it is the system we have; we work 24 hours a day."[29]

### *Political Pressure and Unnecessary Interference*

It has been observed that the political leaders have become bosses of the police and they use the police as means to threaten and torture their opponents. In 2003, then DGP of Punjab had disclosed to the media that a 'policeman, who is trained to obey the orders, is in dilemma, whether to obey the wrong orders of the political boss or to suffer by displeasing the political boss. And the policeman chooses the way which pleases to him and the political boss.'[30] Hence, the policemen, when used by the political elites for their personal and selfish interests, violate the human rights of the people on the behest of the political elites.

## Suggestions and Recommendations

Thus it has been established as a fact that the human rights of the people in India have been continuously and consistently violated by the police during the police or judicial custody of the accused/suspects. The number of custodial deaths has been growing rapidly day by day, instead of declining. The graphs of the complaints received by the governmental and non-governmental human rights organizations have been increasing constantly. But still there is time to control the situation, before it gets exploitive and incurable. There are some suggestions and recommendations, which if acknowledged, can prove a great help to curb the problem of custodial deaths in India.

- There is no disagreement on the urgent need for police reform in India. In October 2005, the central government set up a Police Act Drafting Committee (PADC) - commonly known as the Soli Sorabjee Committee – to draft a new model bill which would guide state government's adoption of new police laws. The PADC submitted its Model Police Act to the Ministry of Home Affairs on 30 October 2006.[31] Moreover, Police reforms however were started by the judgment of the Supreme Court of 22 September 2006 in *Prakash Singh vs. Union of India* case. The apex court directed the central and state governments to comply with its set of Seven Directives for police reform.[32] The seven points of the directive, if acknowledged by the Centre as well as State governments, can help in diminishing police torture and custodial deaths through out India.
- A critical step is holding abusive officers accountable. Those who commit torture or other abuses must be treated as the criminals they are.
- Improve conditions for rank and file officers: low-ranking police are overworked and often exhausted due to the requirement they be available for duty 24 hours a day. Minimum standards for housing and work hours should be developed, for instance, a requirement that station house officers announce and adhere to a monthly work schedule with maximum hours of work and provide for mandatory leave.
- Training and equipment of the police should be improved. Increasing the number of junior-ranking officers trained and authorized to conduct investigations and register complaints, and training constables to assist in crime investigations, is critical. The training and roles of low-ranking police should be enhanced to include investigation assistance.
- A system of effective independent investigations into complaints of police abuse and misconduct should be

created. To reduce impunity, the central and state government should bolster the capacity of the national and state human rights commissions to undertake independent investigations, including the number of investigative staff. The central and state governments should also comply with the Supreme Court's orders and directives regarding the arrest and detention of the suspects/accused.

- Strong domestic laws against torture are sturdily needed to be enacted. The Indian parliament should ratify the Convention Against Torture.
- The government should repeal laws that encourage impunity. Section 197 of the Criminal Procedure Code continues to effectively shield many abusive police officials from prosecution for actions taken on 'official duty', permitting abuse to frequently go unpunished and undeterred. The Indian parliament should repeal Section 197, or retain it but define "official duty" to exclude unconstitutional conduct such as arbitrary detention, custodial torture and ill-treatment, and extrajudicial killings.
- Existing laws regarding arrest and detention are frequently flouted, regarded by some police as impractical. To encourage institutional acceptance of these safeguards and reduce abuse, require police to formally recite the suspect's rights upon arrest or any informal detention.
- The government of India should send the Prevention of Torture Bill, 2008 to Parliamentary Standing Committee for organizing public hearing to ensure its conformity with the UN Convention against Torture and Other Cruel, Inhuman or Degrading Treatment or Punishment. The government of India should ratify the UN Convention against Torture and Other Cruel, Inhuman or Degrading Treatment or Punishment and its Optional Protocol.

- The government of India should extend an invitation to the UN Special Rapporteur on Torture and Other Cruel, Inhuman or Degrading Treatment or Punishment.

Undoubtedly, the lethal custodial torture, a routine practice in Indian police stations and the Prisons, frequently results in the custodial deaths, a worst crime against the humanity. But the considerable point is that the police alone cannot be acknowledged as guilty of the miserable scenario. In fact, the unawareness of the rights among masses, continuity of colonial mind-set among people, lackadaisical approach of criminal justice system and unenthusiastic attitude of government are equally responsible for consistently increasing graph of custodial deaths. Thus, the need of the hour is to awaken the masses, generate enthusiasm among the political leadership and bring about radical reforms in the police and adjudicating process to curb the misery of custodial deaths.

## References


1. The Free Dictionary, http://www.thefreedictionary.com/violation.
2. The Urban Dictionary, www.theurbandictionary.com/define.php?term=violation.
3. The Oxford Dictionary, www.yourdictionary.com/violation.
4. Hilde Hey, *Gross Human Rights Violations: A Search for Causes- A Study of Guatemala and Costa Rica*, Martinus Nijhoff Publishers, Boston, 1995, p. 18.
5. Human Rights Watch, *India: Broken System- Dysfunction, Impunity and Abuse in the Indian Police*, 2009, pp.3- 4.
6. Asian Centre for Human Rights, *Torture in India: 2009*, p. 22.
7. Asian Centre for Human Rights, "Need for a National Law for Prevention of Torture", A Background Paper, *National Convention on Prevention of Torture in India*, June 2007, India International Centre, New Delhi, p. 1.
8. Article 1, *United Nations Convention against Torture*, 1984.
9. *Supreme Court Cases*, 1997, pp. 424.
10. Dalbir Singh v. State of U.P. and Others, Writ Petition (Crl.) NO. 193 OF 2006, decided 2/3/2009, paras. 8-9. The Court noted that procedural safeguards for arrest and detention established in D.K. Basu v. State of West Bengal, JT 1997 (1) SC 1) "seem to have caused not even any softening attitude to the inhuman approach in dealing with persons in custody."

11. The Data is based on the Annual Reports of National Human Rights Commission of India (NHRC) from 2001 to 2007.
12. Asian Centre for Human Rights, *Torture in India: 2009*, p. 3.
13. The statement of Minister of State in the Ministry of Home Affairs, Mr Shakeel Ahmad while answering to question No. 2624 in the Lok Sabha on oppression of prisoners on 16.12.2008
14. The statement of Minister of State in the Ministry of Home Affairs, Mr Shakeel Ahmad while answering to question No. 5075 in the Lok Sabha on death of prisoners on 29.04.2008
15. The statement of Minister of State in the Ministry of Home Affairs, Shri Manikrao H Gavit while answering question No. 461*(deaths of prisoners) on 14.08.2007
16. National Crime Records Bureau, "Prison Statistics India 2006", Chapter 9, available at http:// ncrb.nic.in/PSI2006/prison2006.htm
17. 97 custodial deaths in WB jails, 3 December 2008, available at: http:// news.indiainfo. com/2008/12/03/0812030039_custodial.html
18. 50 cases of Custodial Torture and Custodial Deaths registered and adjudicated by the NHRC and disclosed in its Annual Reports from 1993 to 2007 are studied which have revealed the use of these methods by the police to Torture the Prisoners/Accused/Suspects or their Relatives.
19. Vitul K. Gupta, "Institutionalization of Torture and Post-Conflict Situations: The Experience of Punjab", *PUCL Bulletin*, Vol. XXVII, No. 8, August 2007, pp. 307-308.
20. 50 cases of Custodial Deaths revealed in the leading daily Newspapers (The Hindu, The Tribune) from 2000 to 2009 were studied. It has been found that 35 % of the 50 victims belonged to the above mentioned groups.
21. David Milton, "In Defense of Human Rights", *Indian Express*, Chandigarh, December 9, 1991, p. 6.
22. Several human rights NGOs and the activists had filed cases against the police personnel of Punjab who were reportedly responsible for killing and torturing the accused/suspected or their relatives during the terrorism and counter-terrorism era in Punjab. But police personnel were provided open amnesty by the then state as well as central governments.
23. Police Act of 1861 Sec. 3-4. At the state level, the Chief Minister has "superintendence" authority over police. Each state police service is organized territorially into administrative districts; at the district level, the chief police official's administrative authority is subject to the "general control and direction" of district administrative officials.
24. Arvind Verma, *The Indian Police: A Critical Evaluation*, New Delhi: Regency Publications (2005), pp. 10-40.
25. Farrukh Hakeem, "Emergence of Modern Indian Policing" in Maki Haberfeld and Ibrahim Cerrah, (eds.) *Comparative Policing*, SAGE Publications, Los Angeles, London, 2008, p. 179.

26. Amnesty International, *India: Break the Cycle of Impunity and Torture in Punjab*, 2002, p. 20.
27. *Ibid.* p. 21.
28. Human Rights Watch, 2009, *op.cit*, p. 7.
29. Interview of the DGP, Uttar Pradesh by Activists of Human Rights Watch, *Ibid.* pp., 7-8.
30. Varinder Walia, "Criminals have Become Part of Governance: DGP", *The Tribune*, October 12, 2003.
31. Commonwealth Human Rights Initiative (CHRI), http://www. humanrightsinitiative.org/programs/aj/police/india/initiatives/model_police_act_2006.htm
32. Commonwealth Human Rights Initiative (CHRI), http://www.humanrightsinitiative.org/programs/aj/police/india/initiatives/seven_steps_to_police_reform.pdf

# 6

## Extra Judicial Killings in India: A Brutal Violation of Human Rights

The political and Extra-judicial killings by government forces have certain common features. Political killings are summed up in the definition that Amnesty International uses: "unlawful and deliberate killings of persons by reason of their real or imputed political beliefs or activities, religion, other consciously held beliefs, ethnic origin, sex, colour or language, carried out by order of a government or with its complicity." The alternative term extrajudicial execution is also used to refer to these killings. They are committed outside the judicial procedure and in violation of national laws and international standards forbidding the arbitrary deprivation of life. They are unlawful and deliberate. This distinguishes them from accidental killings and from deaths resulting from the use of reasonable force in law enforcement.

The pattern of killings in the North-east region of India has pointed to an official policy sanctioning extrajudicial killings. On March 1, 1997, the bodies of six residents of a Manipur Fishing Community, including two women, were found dead in a river near *Serou* village in *Thoubal* district. They were last seen alive near the village on February 25, 1997. The evidences suggested that soldiers who were hunting for members of the People's Liberation Army of Manipur, who had been active in the area, killed them.[1]

According to the NHRC's Annual Report of 1997, 259 complaints of alleged human rights violations by the Border Security Force had been registered between January 1, 1990 and March 31 1997. During the same period, only 31 investigations into allegations of human rights abuses by members of the army had been completed, including 29 officers.[2]

Scrutiny by the NHRC and international human rights organizations, when permitted, and the persistence of individual magistrates have resulted in greater accountability of the security forces in Jammu and Kashmir over the years. The NHRC in its 1996-97 report noted that the security forces are making a conscious and serious effort to exercise restraint. Despite this effort, the NHRC continues to receive complaints alleging human rights violations by the security forces, especially from Jammu and Kashmir and the North-Eastern states. The vast majority of violations by security forces has gone and continues to go uninvestigated and unpunished.

There are many allegations that military and paramilitary forces in the North-East engage in arbitrary detention, abduction, torture, and extrajudicial execution of militants. The reports of extrajudicial killings are described as having occurred during 'encounters' between insurgent groups and security forces. But several human rights NGOs and human rights activists allege that in fact the 'encounters' are staged and that those insurgents reported dead are killed after being detained by security forces.[3]

Throughout the period of terrorism, Indian security forces-particularly the Central Reserve Police Force (CRPF) and the Border Security Force (BSF) have committed regular and deliberate violations of human rights in Kashmir. The level of abuses by Indian government forces has been rising significantly, with large numbers of summary executions of suspected militants and increased killings of civilians in reprisal attacks.

### Extrajudicial Killings in Punjab

In Punjab, during the era of terrorism and counter-terrorism (1984-1995) there were innumerable cases of extrajudicial killings including faked encounters. In the typical scenario, the Police took into custody a suspected terrorist or supporter of terrorists, without filing an arrest report. If the detainee died during interrogation or was executed, the officials denied that the person had never ever been in the custody. They also claimed that the person had died during an armed encounter with Police or security forces.[4] Scores of people are reported to have disappeared between 1992 and 1995. There are a lot of cases in which the security forces illegally arrested the suspected terrorists or the relatives and supporters of terrorists[5] The people arrested were neither produced before courts and nor came back to their homes. They had either died in the police custody due to torture or were shown killed in the encounters.

The persons who were shown disappeared or killed in the encounters, in most of the cases were those who were captured by the police due to their involvement in terrorist movement, due to their relationships with terrorists or their support to the cause of militancy. They were illegally detained, tortured and eventually shown killed in the fake encounters. Security forces reported many extra-judicial executions and enforced disappearances as encounters or escapes from the custody, in order to conceal extrajudicial killings.[6] The noticeable feature of the encounters which took place especially after 1992 was that only terrorists had faced the causalities during any armed encounter and there were very rare reports of death or even injuries to the police personnel. For example, 76 alleged terrorists were reportedly killed in armed encounters during 1994, but no police or other security personnel were killed in such encounters.[7] Several examples show that the persons killed in the same encounters did not know each other. Nor were they abducted at the same time. There are numerous examples which show that the police shot and killed young men without warning, despite no signs of danger; they shot people at public places in broad daylight.[8] There are several illustrative cases which depict that fake encounters and extrajudicial killings were the part of a systematic and pre-planned strategy to demolish terrorism in Punjab at any cost. The illustrative cases of extra-judicial killings reported from

Punjab by the governmental human rights organizations, NGOs, newspapers and personally interviewed and studied are mentioned below.

### *Case of Harvinderjit Singh and Mandeep Singh*[9]

On May 22, 1992, around 1:30 p.m., 20 year old Harvinderjit Singh Gill and his friend Mandeep Singh went to the Shiromini Gurudwara Prabandhak Committee (SGPC) office within the Golden Temple complex in Amritsar. Both of them were carrying their student identity cards and Harvinderjit Singh had, in addition, his educational concessions entitlement card No. 7624, issued to children of ex-servicemen. After meeting some SGPC functionaries in their office, Harviderjit and Mandeep left Golden Temple complex. Deputy Superintendent of Police (DSP) Rattan Lal Monga, caught Harvinderjit by his arm and asked him to get himself frisked. Harvinderjit could not recognize that it was an officer in plain clothes who grabbed him, hence he protested loudly. The altercation between two led to a physical scuffle and both of them fell to the ground. DSP Monga ordered his subordinates to shoot Harvinderjit. He was shot and collapsed dead on the road. A shocked, confused and perplexed Mandeep Singh ran into a tea shop to save himself, but DSP Monga came after him, had him dragged out and shot. Mandeep Singh also died on the spot. Amritsar's Sadar police station registered FIR No. 36 to claim the incident as an encounter. Though, the eye-witnesses of the whole scene claimed it a case of cold blood murder by police in daylight.

### *Case of Gurmej Singh*[10]

Gurmej Singh alias Gurbhej, son of Jagir Singh from Buge locality in Tarntaran, and Jasbir Singh s/o Bhajan Singh, resident of Tarntaran were associated with a terrorist movement. They were arrested by the Police at a checkpoint, when they were traveling in a bus. The passengers of the bus were witnesses of their arrest by the police. The next day, the regional newspapers, *Ajit* and *Jagbani* reported the death of Jasbir Singh and two other unidentified terrorists in a police encounter. The police did not inform Gurmej's family about his death. The family was even unable to collect his ashes since they did not know when and where the police carried out the cremations.

### *Case of Harjit Singh*[11]

On April 29, 1992, Harjit Singh, an employee of the Punjab State Electricity Board was arrested by police officials. The police did not have an arrest warrant and subsequently denied the arrest. The police claimed that Harjit Singh and another suspected terrorist were captured on May 11, 1992, after an armed encounter with them. The police said that they took both of them to recover hidden arms and that while doing so; they were attacked by armed militants, during which the two men were killed. However, Harjit Singh was twice seen alive by his father in police custody after the police claimed that his son had been killed.

### *Case of Kulwant Singh*[12]

In another case of extrajudicial killing, Kulwant Singh, a Sikh lawyer, disappeared on January 25, 1993 along with his wife and child, after he was called to the Ropar police station to pick up a client. Following repeated inquiries by local lawyers for over two weeks, the district police superintendent announced that Kulwant Singh and his family were killed on January 25, 1993 by two terrorists who wanted to surrender. The police superintendent further claimed that the terrorists who allegedly confessed to the killings committed suicide by swallowing cyanide shortly before their role in Kulwant Singh's murder was made public. Punjab Chief Minister Beant Singh agreed to order an inquiry into the case but reportedly backed off in the face of police resistance.

## Extrajudicial Killings in Kashmir

India's northernmost state, Jammu and Kashmir, lies in the Himalayas and borders Pakistan, Tibet, and China. The state comprises the administrative regions of Jammu, which lies in the plains below the Pir Panjal range, and has a population of approximately 4.39 million; Ladakh, bordering Tibet, with a population of 0.23 million; and the Kashmir valley between the Pir Panjal and Panjri ranges, with a population of 5.44 million.[13]

Jammu and Kashmir is the only Muslim majority state in India. However, the state is divided roughly along religious lines. 95 percent of the residents of the Kashmir valley are Muslim, the overwhelming majority of whom are Sunni, while 50 percent of the population of Ladakh is Buddhist and 46 percent is Muslim (most of the Muslims of Ladakh are Shia). Jammu has a very different religious make-up, with 66 percent of the population Hindu and most of the rest Muslim.[14] The literacy rate is 54 percent, lower than the national average of 65 percent.[15]

Before the conflict, Jammu and Kashmir had a large and profitable tourist industry, which provided a major portion of the state revenue. But tourist numbers have dropped from more than seven hundred thousand visitors a year before 1989 to fewer than eight thousand per year in the 1990s. With an improvement in the overall security situation, the number of tourists visiting the state is gradually increasing, though those numbers may decrease after the recent deliberate targeting of tourists by militants in 2006.[16]

The conflict has also exacted a heavy toll on the state's infrastructure. Over 1,100 government buildings, 640 educational buildings, eleven hospitals, 337 bridges, and more than ten thousand privates houses and shops have been destroyed in violent incidents since the conflict began.[17] The state's inability to generate sufficient resources has led to an increased dependency on central assistance and borrowings. In an effort to generate employment opportunities and prevent the youth from joining the militancy, the central government has announced several aid packages over the years. The central government spends eight to ten times more on each citizen in Jammu and Kashmir than any other Indian state.[18]

Kashmir has long been a disputed territory between India and Pakistan which have gone to war over Kashmir twice. Armed opposition groups in Jammu and Kashmir, some of which favour accession of the area to Pakistan while others advocate independence, intensified their activities in the Valley of Kashmir in late 1989. India has consistently claimed that Pakistan provides military support and training to secessionist groups operating in Kashmir while Pakistan has equally consistently denied such claims. There is, however, considerable evidence that Pakistan has indeed provided men and military support to groups seeking accession of Kashmir to Pakistan.

Kashmir, which had been acknowledged as a 'paradise on earth' has been suffering due to the 'paralyses' of terrorism and insurgency. Since the late 1980s, Kashmiri militants have engaged in widespread violations of international human rights and humanitarian norms. These militant groups have been continuously working to install fear in the civilian Hindu population and among Muslim civilians who do not support the militants' aims.

Many of the violent attacks committed by the militant groups have deliberately targeted civilians. Among the worst abuses have been the assassinations of hundreds of civilians, including members of the Hindu community, civil servants and political figures, particularly Muslim political leaders associated with the National Conference Party and other political groups opposed by the militants.[19] Militant organizations have ordered summary punishment, including execution of individuals believed to be government operatives and informers. Militants have launched bombs and grenade attacks on governmental buildings and transport vehicles.[20]

Rapes by members of militant organizations was rare in the early years, however, since 1991, rape has been committed with increasing frequency by members of certain militant groups. In some cases, women have been raped and then killed after being kidnapped by rival militant groups and held as hostages. In other cases, members of armed militant groups have abducted women after threatening to shoot the rest of family unless the woman was handed over to the particular militant leader. Some incidents of rape by militant appear to have been intended as punishment because the victims or their family members were believed to be government informers, opposed to the militants or supporters of rival groups.[21]

The terrorists in Kashmir have been consistently attacking and killing the members of police and security forces.[22] Militants in Kashmir are also accused of kidnapping the relatives of political leaders, governmental officials, foreigners and even the civilians. These abductions are attempted by the militants to fulfill their illegal and unjustified demands, such release of their companions.[23] Doctors claim that militants abduct medical workers to force them to provide treatment to injured militants. Militants have also reportedly abducted patients from hospitals.[24] Reports by the Governmental sources, media and NGOs suggest that militants have violated the international proscription against the use of religious sites as military strongholds. The Muslim shrines and mosques are taken over by militants and used as the base camps or commanding stations by them.[25]

During the night of 30 May, 1997, Ghulam Rasool Wani, a leader of the National Conference was kidnapped by unidentified armed persons at gunpoint and shot dead near his home in Kaskot, in the Banihal area of Doda district.[26] Janata Dal leader Abdul Samad Vakil was shot dead in Ramban area by unidentified men from close range in his car on 21 April 1997.[27] Former National Conference member of the legislative assembly, Ghulam Rasool Bhat and his brother-in-law, Ghulam Nabi Wani were shot dead by armed persons on 3 March 1997 near Sopore.[28] Unidentified armed men on 18 May 1997 forced their way into a house in Mahore area of Udhampur district where sheep development officer S.D. Nayyar and his technical assistant Rattan Singh were staying and shot them both dead.[29]

On 27 March 1996, the dead body of human rights lawyer Jalil Andrabi was found in the river Jhelum, 19 days after he had been seen taken away by military personnel.[30] On 30 March 1996, 23 members of the faction of the Jammu and Kashmir Liberation Front led by Amanullah Khan were killed when police fired mortar shells at their office in Srinagar.[31] On 18 September 1997, 11 people, including women and children, were killed by mortar shelling at Arin Bandipora. In January 1998, nine people, including a woman and child, were killed in Kadrana village, Doda district, when army soldiers opened fire on people protesting an earlier arrest. In July 1998, 40 people, including women and children were killed in and near Surankote. On 28 June 1999, fifteen members of two Muslim families, including women and children, were shot dead at Surankote, Poonch district, by unidentified gunmen wearing army uniforms who shot two more women as they fled.[32]

On March 20, 2000, on the eve of a visit by then U.S. President Bill Clinton to India, armed men in Indian army uniforms entered the village of Chattisinghpora in Anantnag district at night. The villagers, most of them Sikhs, were told that it was a routine investigation and identity check. Male residents were asked to come out of their homes with their identification cards.

Once they were lined up outside, however, the gunmen opened fire, killing thirty-six and injuring several others. It was the first time in more than a decade of violence in Jammu and Kashmir that the Sikh community had come under attack.[33]

On 3 April 2000, seven people demonstrating against the earlier two incidents were shot dead by police. On the night of 1 August 2000, at least 105 people were shot dead in several different incidents. On 15 February 2001, six people were shot dead in Haigam during protests at an earlier death in custody when security forces and/or police opened fire on them.

At least 40 people were killed in the state in June-August 2008 when the Central security forces and the state police used force against protestors defying curfew restrictions as both Jammu and Kashmir regions witnessed demonstrations and counterdemonstrations to boycott the elections in Jammu and Kashmir.[34] The protests in both regions have made the tasks of policing and ensuring safety of civilians wishing to exercise their right to vote even more critical. On August 11, the security forces opened indiscriminate firing at an agitating crowd at Baramulla in which Sheikh Abdul Azeez, a leader of the All Party Hurriyat Conference (APHC) and at least four others were shot dead during a procession.[35]

The Government of India responded to frequent attacks by armed opposition groups with a policy which has resulted in hundreds of arbitrary arrests, torture; including rape, leading to hundreds of deaths in custody, extrajudicial executions and "disappearances". These widespread and grave human rights violations have been perpetrated by law enforcement personnel, including police, paramilitary forces, the army and by the so-called renegades, former members of armed opposition groups who now side with the government and reportedly carry out human rights violations with the acquiescence or connivance of, or on orders by state agents. Its victims have been people alleged to be members of armed opposition groups, people assumed to sympathize with them, their friends and relatives as also lawyers and journalists monitoring human rights violations. Despite a stated commitment to human rights protection and promotion, the Government of India and authorities in Jammu and Kashmir have permitted state agents to perpetrate violations with impunity by failing to bring perpetrators to justice and by not amending or withdrawing special laws operative in the state which facilitate such violations.

Throughout the period of terrorism, Indian security forces-particularly the Central Reserve Police Force (CRPF) and the Border Security Force (BSF) have committed regular and deliberate violations of human rights in Kashmir. The level of abuses by Indian government forces has been rising significantly, with large numbers of summary executions of suspected militants and increased killings of civilians in reprisal attacks.[150]

In addition to summary executions and reprisal killing of civilians, abuses by Indian forces include disappearances,[151] unprovoked shootings of unarmed noncombatants, rape and other attacks on civilians and captured combatants. Legislation authorizing the security forces to shoot to kill and protecting them from prosecution has facilitated such abuses. The security forces have also engaged in wanton destruction and looting of civilian property and have burned down residential neighbourhoods in retaliation for militant attacks.[152]

Governmental forces have also systematically violated human rights by using lethal force against peaceful demonstrations and engaging in widespread and arbitrary arrests of persons suspected of sympathizing with militants and detaining them for extended periods without charge or trial. Torture of detainees is widespread and includes methods such as prolonged beating, electric shocks and sexual abuses.[153] The incidence of rape is also high. Women are often raped in the course of house searches by the security forces and retaliation for militant attacks on the governmental patrols.[154]

The years of armed struggle have taken a heavy toll of lives lost, about which reliable figures are impossible to obtain. According to official handouts 19,866 people have died in Jammu and Kashmir from January 1990, to 1998, including 9,123 members of armed opposition groups, 6,673 victims of armed opposition groups, 2,477 civilians killed by Indian security forces and 1,593 security personnel.[36] On 24 April 1997, Minister of State for Home Affairs, Ali Mohammad Sagar, told the Legislative Assembly that in the seven years of unrest, 16,991 persons, including 7,849 civilians, 1,319 security personnel and 7,823 "militants" including 121 foreign mercenaries, had been killed. He admitted that 454 persons were missing since 1990. The Institute of Kashmir Studies believes that the number of dead since 1989-1990 lies between 40,000 and 50,000.[37]

The official figures conceal that hundreds of victims were not killed as legitimate targets in situations of armed conflict but were deliberately and arbitrarily killed or died as the result of torture inflicted in the custody of state agents. The Jammu and Kashmir Bar Association documented 218 deaths in custody in 1996; all victims had reportedly been arrested first and killed in detention centres inside and outside the state. In the following year, the Institute of Kashmir Studies said that some 200 people died in custody in 1997; in the first half of 1998, around 60 deaths in custody were reported. The real number of such deaths is considered by many observers to be twice as high as the number of reported deaths, i.e. some 350 to 400 deaths per year. Officials have declared in many of these cases that the victims were killed in shoot-outs or "encounters" with police but witnesses have indicated that the victims had been in detention days before the alleged shoot-out or that security forces resorted to shooting even though they could have arrested suspects.[38]

*Case of Javed Ahmad Magray*

In May 2003, Javed Ahmad Magray, a seventeen-year-old student, was murdered one night near his home in Srinagar. An investigation by the district administration concluded that Magray had been abducted and killed by the army. Although the investigation identified the officer responsible, he was never arrested or even compelled to testify during the inquiry, because the army claimed that his unit had been moved out of Jammu and Kashmir.

*Case of the Killing of Mohammad Ramzan Dar, Gundipora, Budgam*

According to his family, Mohammad Ramzan Dar suffered from a psychological disorder and was therefore unfit for regular jobs. The village had appointed him caretaker of the local mosque, to help support his family. Mohammad Ramzan woke as usual at 3:30 a.m. on June 6, 2005, so that he could be in the mosque in time to call to morning prayers. Many of the villagers woke up soon after because they heard gunfire. As is usual, everyone stayed inside as long as the firing continued so that they would not be caught in crossfire. In the morning there was no call to prayer, but some of the villagers went to the mosque on time. Outside the mosque, they found the body of Mohammad Ramzan. He had been shot in the head and chest. After villagers protested, police and district authorities promised an inquiry. According to Mohammad Ismail Dar, brother of Mohammad Ramzan, the authorities later said that the killing was a mistake.

**Unlawful Killings in North-Eastern States**

The situation of human rights is really alarming in the North-East parts. This part of India is infected by insurrections, insurgencies and armed Naxalite and Maoist revolts. The human rights reports by the international NGOs including Amnesty International has assumed that India continues to lag behind in the field of human rights, reporting gross violations of human rights in North-Eastern States, and Naxalite affected States of Chhatisgarh, Madhya Pradesh, Bihar and Jharkhand. According to Amnesty International, Jharkhand is a State, full of human rights abuses.[140] There are continuous reports of the acts of violence and terrorism by the militants. The reports of the killing, injuring or abducting the civilians are common in those areas.[141]

The United Liberation Front of Assam (ULFA) is blamed for perpetrating most of the terrorist strikes targeted at State-run Oil and Tea infrastructures, non-indigenous migrant workers and Indian security forces. According to an estimate there are average 550 incidents of terrorist violence in the region, with nearly 130 civilian deaths recorded almost every year. More than 15 tribal militants' outfits with transnational linkage are active in Manipur. In Nagaland, there are two warring Naga militant groups. These groups are accused of abducting the youth to provide them training for preparing to fight against the security forces and other hostile groups. Besides that, these groups are blamed to abduct and even kill the civilians for extortions.[142] In the neighboring State of Tripura, National Liberation Front of Tripura is active to disseminate the terror and violence in the region. NLFT is accused of setting fire to the villages and opening indiscriminate firings on the innocent and panicked people. Is it common for the members of NLFT to behead the rebellions or even common civilians, torture the children and disrespect the women.[143]

During 1991-1992, there were massive encounter deaths in the North-Eastern states.[39] Since 1980, clashes between police and Naxalite Maoist revolutionaries of the People's War Group (PWG) have taken place in northwestern Andhra Pradesh. Over the past few years, hundreds of policemen and suspected Naxalites have been killed, according to press reports and human rights organizations. According to local human rights groups, 174 persons were killed in faked police encounters in the first 8 months of 1981. The conflict has led to serious human rights abuses by both sides. Human rights groups allege that the police to cover up the torture and subsequent murder of Naxalite suspects, sympathizers, or informers usually stages the faked encounters. These groups further allege that police refuses to hand over the copses of suspects killed in encounters which are often cremated before families can view the bodies. Villagers in PWG dominated area complain if regular harassment and arbitrary detention by the police. Police officials rarely are held accountable for human rights abuses in the region.

**Chhatisgarh**

A lopsided socioeconomic development of the district caused by indirect exploitation through environmental destruction and direct exploitation through cheating and duping, has provided an ideal setting for the Naxalites to take root in the area. They supported the illegal encroachments of forest land and organised some campaigns of encroachment themselves; they repeatedly brought to the fore the issue of tanks and the need to maintain them in a systematic manner for irrigation; they openly opposed the Bodhghat project; they punished corrupt officials; they made the tendu leaf contractors increase the wage rates; and they held health and education programmes among tribals." - Observations of the People's Union for Civil Liberties in the report, Baster: An Investigation into an 'Encounter', June 1985.[40]

The Naxal movement, named after the peasant's armed uprising at Naxalbari in West Bengal, has become synonymous of armed insurrection influenced by Chairman Mao Tsetung of China. Naxalbari Day is celebrated on 25 May to commemorate the unprovoked killing of 11 innocent persons including 7 women and 2 children on 25 May 1967 at Naxalbari bazaar in West Bengal by the Assam Frontier Rifles. The victims were participating in a meeting. The alleged killing was in retaliation for the killing of Mr Sonam Wangdi, an enforcement inspector by a youth's arrow on 24 May 1967. Mr Wangdi was to raid the houses of those suspected of looting foodgrains, arms and taking over lands from the Zamindars.[41]

The West Bengal government responded with unprecedented violence and unlawful measures such as torture, disappearances and extrajudicial executions to crush the Naxalite movement. In 1980, another Naxalite movement was started in the impoverished and underdeveloped Telengana region of Andhra Pradesh by the Peoples War Group (PWG). Killings of the class enemies, petty bourgeois, police informers and sentençing through its Peoples Court became key features of the PWG functioning.

The State government of Andhra Pradesh too reacted with equal lawlessness. The "Guidelines / Procedures to be followed in dealing with deaths occurring in Encounters" of the National Human Rights Commission of India were developed based on systematic extrajudicial executions perpetrated by the Andhra Pradesh Police with impunity. There has been little difference between the security forces and the Naxalites in terms of lawlessness and violations of human rights.

The Naxalite movement from Andhra Pradesh soon spread to neighbouring Madhya Pradesh, Orissa, Jharkhand and Maharashtra. "Commander" Kosa, the secretary for the Naxals in Chhattisgarh hails from Andhra Pradesh.[42] Since the launch of Salwa Judum, an anti-Naxalite campaign, in Dantewada district of Chhattisgarh in June 2005, the Adivasis, who constitute 78.51% of the total population of Dantewada, have become victims of the conflict between the Naxalites and the State government of Chhattisgarh. Since the beginning of 2005, there have been increased attacks from the Naxalites. On 5 September 2005, the Chhattisgarh government banned Naxal organizations in the State following the killing of 24 security personnel in Bijapur Police district on 3 September 2005.7 Official sources estimate the number of cadres of the Naxals in Chhattisgarh to be about 3,000.[43] The Naxals have two units - Dalams and Sanghams. The Dalams are responsible for armed attacks while the Sanghams are hardcore overground cadres.[44]

The Naxalites responded with violence against the Salwa Judum cadres irrespective of whether they are joining on their own volition or by force. Between 5 June 2005 and 6 March 2006, at least 138 Salwa Judum activists have been allegedly killed by the Naxalites.[45] In the Darbhaguda massacre of 28 February 2006 in which 27 persons were killed and 32 others were injured. The Naxalites allegedly killed many injured by stabbing and clubbing. Although the Naxalites have been responsible for more killings, the response of the State government to involve the civilains directlty in the conflict and recruiting children as Special Police Officers is morally and legally untenable.

As on 4 March 2006, a total of 45,958 Adivasi villagers from 644 villages in 6 blocks of Dantewada district have come under Salwa Judum programme. The security forces and Salwa Judum activists have been responsible for gross violations of international human rights and humanitarian laws including torture, killings and rape especially during joint operations to bring scattered villages under the Salwa Judum. But the police do not register such complaints of atrocities as they also commit these crimes. Those who are victims of violations by the security forces and the Salwa Judum activists therefore are not given any compensation. Only the alleged victims of Naxalite violence are given compensation.[46] As many as 227 persons have been killed between 5 June 2005 and 6 March 2006 including 47 security personnel and 30 alleged Maoists, 150 civilians out of which 138 at the hands of the Maoists and 12 at the hands of security forces and Salwa Judum activists. Out of these, 63 persons including 33 security forces and 30 civilians were killed in landmines planted by the Naxalites[47]

### *Killings of the Security Forces*

- On 8 January 2005, alleged Maoists reportedly killed three policemen - Sub- Inspector B S Tirkey, Bhuneshwar Bhagat and Lalit Kumar in an ambush near Indrapuri in Balrampur district.[48]
- On September 28, 2010, three Border Security Force (BSF) personnel, a constable of the Chhattisgarh police and a Special Police Officer were killed in an ambush in Chhattisgarh's Kanker district, 250 km from Raipur.[49]
- The brutal face of Naxals exposed on July 1, 2010 when they killed 27 CRPF personnel in Narayanpur district of

Chhattisgarh with the throats of some of the hapless victims found slit and heads of a couple of them smashed. According to preliminary post-mortem reports, the CRPF personnel were killed by the Maoists in a brutal manner and around three to four bullet wounds were found on the bodies of each of the 27 slain CRPF personnel. The Naxalites reportedly shot dead CRPF personnel from a distance and later, they slit open the throats of three and smashed heads of two other jawans.[50]

- On April 6, 2010, In the bloodiest attack on the security forces, the Naxals trapped and gunned down 75 personnel during a joint "Operation Green Hunt" offensive against the ultras in the thick forests of Mukrana in Dantewada district of Chhattisgarh.[51]
- On 23 May 2005, Maoists killed 6 security personnel in two separate incidents. Five security personnel, including four CRPF personnel were killed in a landmine blast triggered by suspected Maoists near Jhangla village under Bhairamgarh police station of Dantewada district. In another incident, Maoists shot dead Station House Officer, Mr Augustus Kujur of the Mainpart police station of Sarguja district. He was reportedly leading a police party to nab the Naxalites.[52]
- The Maoists, on May 17, 2010, blew up a passenger bus killing at least 36 persons, including 12 Special Police Officers (SPOs), in Dantewada district of Chhattisgarh, That attack their second in six weeks.[53]
- An armed gang of Naxalites killed over 50 security personnel on March 13 2007, at a police outpost in Bijapur district of Chhattisgarh.[54]
- On the night of 3 September 2005, 24 CRPF personnel were killed in a powerful landmine explosion by the Maoists in remote Punjer village in Dantewada district.[55]
- On 17 December 2005, the Maoists killed one Indian Reserve Battallion (Nagaland Regiment) personnel in Pakhanjur of Dantewada district.[56]

- On 6 February 2006, 11 security personnel including nine from the Indian Reserve Battallion (Nagaland Regiment) were reportedly killed in two separate attacks by the Maoists. While nine personnel of the Naga Task Force were killed in a landmine blast in village Kutachera under Bhejji police station of Dantewara, two policemen were killed in an attack by the Maoists at a police outpost in Jashpur district, bordering Jharkhand.[57]
- On the night of 9 February 2006, eight Central Industrial Security Force personnel were killed and nine others injured when the armed Maoists attacked the National Mineral Development Corporation depot at Hiroli in Dantewada district. The Maoists also reportedly looted 50 tonnes of explosives and 17 rifles.[58]
- On 4 March 2006, the Maoists reportedly killed a policeman Jai Singh Thakur and looted his rifle in daylight in front of Benur police station in Narayanpur police district.[59]

*Killings of the Naxalites*

- There have been reports of allegations of extra-judicial executions of Naxalites. For example, the police claimed that between 29 August 2005 and 3 September 2005, 10 alleged Maoists were reportedly killed by the security forces in the dense forest of Bijapur and Bhairamgarh areas under Bijapur police district during a special operation called "Green Hunt".[60]
- On 11 August 2005, two alleged Maoists identified as Lekam Borde and Duhram of Kotrapal were reportedly killed in a gun battle with the jawans of the Nagaland Armed Police patrolling party near Podum under Bhairamgarh police station.[61]
- On 16 November 2005, an alleged Maoist leader identified as Shyam Bihari alias David, zonal commander of the CPI-Maoist, was killed in an alleged shootout by the police in Surguja district.[62]
- On 16 December 2005, three alleged Maoists and a civilian were killed in an encounter with security forces at Bhejji locality in Dantewada district.[63]

- On 18 December 2005, one alleged Maoist was reportedly killed and seven others were arrested during an encounter between police and the Maoists at Rampur in Kanker district.[64]
- On 28 December 2005, six alleged Maoists were reportedly killed in a gun battle with the security personnel on Basaguda-Gangalur road near Korma village in Bijapur police district. The dead body of one Maoist recovered by police was reportedly identified as Sannju Halma.[65]

### *The Counter-Naxals: The Salwa Judum Cadres*

As the Naxalites made their presence felt strongly, especially since the beginning of 2005, a counter- Naxal campaign, named Salwa Judum came up.

In local Gondi Adivasi dialect, the term Salwa Judum means a "purification hunt".[66] The supporters of this campaign translate its meaning as "peace campaign". The Naxalites on their part stated that Judum means "hunting" and Salwa means "group" and therefore, they say, it is a group hunting of innocent Adivasis supporting the "people's movement", the movement of the Maoists.[67]

The persons joining the Salwa Judum camps may be broadly categorised as (1) victims and relatives of victims of Naxalite violence; (2) persons who are induced by free rations and money; (3) persons who want security in the form of recruitment as Special Police Officers and police informers; and (4) persons who support the Naxalites. Soon, the Chhattisgarh State government lent its support to the Salwa Judum led by the Leader of the Opposition in the State Legislative Assembly. In his Independence Day address on 15 August 2005, Chief Minister Dr Raman Singh assured the Adivasis that the government would abide by its commitment to provide full backup to people fighting the Maoists.[68] 52 On 25 August 2005, the State government announced that it had set up a Committee headed by Chief Secretary A.K. Vijayvargiya to provide direct support such as logistics, arms and funding to the Salwa Judum.[69]

### *Human Rights Violations by the Security Forces and Salwa Judum Cadres*

Human rights violations by the security forces and Salwa Judum cadres Bastar region is the most heavily militarised area in Chhattisgarh with the deployment of National Security Guard Commandos, Indian Reserve Battallion (Nagaland Regiment), Central Industrial Security Forces and Central Reserve Police Force, in addition to the State police. On 1 March 2006, Union Home Minister Shivraj Patil confirmed that the Centre had already provided 26 battalions (26,000 personnel) of security forces to Chhattisgarh to deal with the Naxals.[70]

Yet, in the Dantewada district, there is neither law nor order. The State government has abdicated its duty of maintenance of law and order to the Salwa Judum activists.

Members of the Salwa Judum are involved in illegal checking of all vehicles passing through their area, levying of illegal tax like the Naxalites from the drivers or occupants of the vehicles. The Salwa Judum activists, armed with lathis, bows and arrows and other traditional weapons stop the vehicles, direct the occupants to get down and thoroughly check the vehicle and luggages, seized the contents they find objectionable and subject the occupants to extensive interrogations. The ACHR team also received reports of torture of occupants of vehicle, who refused to pay illegal tax, looting of the occupants of vehicles and villagers and torture and killings of villagers not willing to join Salwa Judum. The ACHR researchers personally experienced it. Their vehicle was stopped and checked numerous times by the Salwa Judum activists during the team's visit to different temporary relief camps in the district. At Bangapal relief camp, lathi yielding Salwa Judum activists stopped their vehicle and directed the occupants to get down. The Salwa Judum activists started to rebuke the occupants for delay in vacating the vehicle for checking. They relented only when ACHR team told them that they were visiting the area with due permission of the District Collector, Dantewada and have already met the senior police officers.

In frequent raids jointly carried out by the Salwa Judum activists and the security forces, alleged Naxalite supporters are beaten up, their houses torched, livestock killed or looted. It has been alleged that "in some villages, the raids continue till the entire village is cleared and people have moved to camps while in other cases, only old people, women and children are left. Many villages are coming to camps to avoid these attacks in the first place."[71] Police do not register First Information Reports relating to such atrocities by the Salwa Judum activists, as they also take part in these illegal activities and crimes. Rather it has been reported that the security forces threw dead bodies inside or near villages with a clear motive to frighten the villagers, who are not joining the Salwa Judum against the Naxalites.[72]

- On 1 July 2005, hundreds of police, paramilitary forces and Salwa Judum activists under the leadership of Inspector General of Police Ansari, Bijapur Superintendent of Police Manhar and MLA Mahendra Karma reportedly raided the Kotrapal village in retaliation against the killing of three Salwa Judum activists by the villagers when they had attacked the village on 18 June 2005. Most of the villagers had fled to the forest prior to the attack. The mob allegedly burnt down 8 houses and killed and looted all the chicken, pigs, and animals of the villagers. Two elderly villagers who were returning to the village were allegedly brutally killed by the Central Reserve Police Force personnel, who also shot at and seriously injured an old woman.[73]
- The police, paramilitary personnel and Salwa Judum activists reportedly carried out similar attacks at Pondum and Pallayvaya villages on 20 July 2005; at Munder village on 22 July 2005; Phulgatta village on 25 July 2005; Karrebodli village on 29 July 2005.[74]
- On 8 August 2005, the Salwa Judum cadres accompanied by the police and paramilitary forces allegedly attacked Kotrapal village and killed three innocent peasants and raped four women.[75]

- On 26 August 2005, the forces of Indian Reserve Battalion (Naga Battallion) reportedly attacked Pottnar village but they had to repel when ambushed by the PLGA forces. While fleeing from Pottnar village, the Naga forces met four Adivasis, who were grazing cattle. They allegedly shot dead all the four including a 12-year-old boy.[76]
- On 28 August 2005, personnel of the Indian Reserve Battalion (Naga Battallion) and Salwa Judum cadres allegedly attacked Aakva village and killed one 12-year-old boy after he was found hiding in the village.[77]
- On 1 September 2005, the police and paramilitary personnel allegedly arrested 10 unarmed villagers, including a 12-year-old boy, and killed all of them in cold blood at Haryal village situated just two kilometers from the Mirtul Police Station in West Bastar. The security personnel reportedly raided the village upon complaint by the village Mukhiya, Doru Magu (who was a leader of the Salwa Judum) that the villagers were planning to attack the police station. The security forces later announced that they had killed 10 Naxalites. The bodies of the deceased were allegedly not handed over to their family members but were secretly burnt down by the security forces in the forest.[78]
- In September 2005, around 50 houses were allegedly burnt in Mankeli village, 15 kilometers from Bijapur by gangs purporting to be 'Salwa Judum' activists.[79]
- According to the estimates of Asian Centre for Human Rights, the security forces and the Salwa Judum cadres have killed 330 persons during 2006. Of them, 114 persons were killed in Chhattisgarh, 108 in Andhra Pradesh, 36 in Maharashtra, 27 in Jharkhand, 21 in Bihar, 17 in Orissa, 4 in West Bengal, 2 in Uttar Pradesh and 1 in Karnataka.
- According to the estimates of Asian Centre for Human Rights, the security forces and the Salwa Judum cadres

have killed 330 persons during 2006. Of them, 114 persons were killed in Chhattisgarh, 108 in Andhra Pradesh, 36 in Maharashtra, 27 in Jharkhand, 21 in Bihar, 17 in Orissa, 4 in West Bengal, 2 in Uttar Pradesh and 1 in Karnataka.

According to the estimates, a total of 749 persons - 285 civilians, 135 security personnel and 329 alleged Naxalites - were killed in the Naxalite conflict in various Naxalite affected States of India during 2006. The highest number of killing was reported from Chhattisgarh (363), followed by Andhra Pradesh (135), Jharkhand (95), Maharashtra (60), Bihar (45), Orissa (25), West Bengal (22), Uttar Pradesh (2), Karnataka (1) and Madhya Pradesh (1). Chhattisgarh accounted for 48.5% of the total killings as a direct consequence of the anti-Naxalite Salwa Judum campaign.

The killing of 749 persons in 2006 represents a decrease in the number of killings than in 2005 during which 892 persons were killed according to the 2005-2006 Annual Report of the Union Ministry of Home Affairs (MHA). The MHA report further stated that 653 persons were killed in Naxal violence in 2004, 731 persons in 2003 and 623 in 2002. Despite decrease in the number of killings in 2006 in comparison to 2005, the Naxalite conflict came to centre-stage of the internal armed conflicts in India prompting Prime Minister Dr. Manmohan Singh to declare it as the "single biggest internal security challenge ever faced by our country" at the 2nd meeting of the Standing Committee of the Chief Ministers of the Naxalite affected States on 13 April 2006.[80]

## Manipur

The northeastern part of India is linked to the rest of the country by a narrow corridor through the hill districts of West Bengal state. Surrounded by Bhutan, Bangladesh, Burma, and the Tibetan region of China, the northeast is a strategically sensitive area. A large deployment of troops has long been stationed to guard the borders.

The region is populated by diverse ethnic, linguistic, and religious groups, including a number of indigenous tribes.[81] It makes up roughly 7 percent of India's total area and is home to about 3 percent of its total population.[82] The northeast now includes the states of Manipur, Assam, Nagaland, Tripura, Meghalaya, Arunachal Pradesh, Mizoram, and Sikkim.[83] Many of these states were created to win the allegiance of ethnic groups and to accommodate political aspirations.[84] Integrated into India after the end of British colonial rule in 1947, most people from this region have little ethnically in common with the bulk of the Indian population.

The landlocked region has endured decades of neglect, widespread corruption, and a failure by successive governments to deliver economic growth and sustainable development.[85] Separatist armed groups from the Naga tribes first started resisting integration with India in the mid-1950s.[86] Manipur is an area of roughly 22,000 square kilometers, about half the size of Switzerland, made up of a valley surrounded by hills. Two-thirds of the population lives in the valley, which is roughly 10 percent of the total area. The population of 2.2 million, according to the 2001 census, includes the majority Hindu Meiteis, who occupy the valley, and tribal groups, including the Naga and Kuki tribes, who practice Christianity and live primarily in the surrounding hill districts.[87] Muslim immigrants, known as Pangals, are about 8 percent of the population. There is also a small population of migrants from other parts of India who are called Mayang (outsiders).[88]

Manipur was an independent kingdom until defeated by Britain in 1891. It remained a princely state under British suzerainty until the end of colonial rule. The maharajah (king) of Manipur then signed an Instrument of Accession, placing Manipur within the dominion of India and granting it exclusive power over Manipur's defense, foreign relations, and communications. However, a movement demanding an end to the old feudal system had already begun in Manipur which, in 1948, led to the establishment of an elected legislature with the king becoming only a constitutional head of state.[89] But King Bodhchandra signed a Merger Agreement with the Indian state on September 21, 1949,[90] and Manipur formally merged with India on October 15, 1949. It was directly governed by

New Delhi until January 21, 1972, when it became a state with the right to elect its own legislative assembly.

Because of separatist activity by Naga tribes that spilled over into Manipur, the Indian government enacted the Armed Forces (Assam and Manipur) Special Powers Act in 1958, which provided troops with extraordinary powers during counterinsurgency operations.[91] This law became applicable in the areas of present-day Nagaland and in the hill areas of Manipur. Later, when armed groups from other ethnic communities started their own insurgencies, the law was extended to the remaining parts of Manipur and remains in effect today.[92]

The first armed opposition group in Manipur, the United National Liberation Front (UNLF), formed in November 1964 demanding independence. Since then many armed groups led by Meiteis were established with similar objectives. The People's Revolutionary Party of Kangleipak[93] (PREPAK) was formed in 1977. The People's Liberation Army (PLA), which received arms and training from China, was formed in 1978.[94] The Kangleipak Communist Party (KCP) was formed in 1980. These groups began a spree of bank robberies and attacks on police officers and government buildings.[95]

In 1980, all of Manipur was declared "disturbed" and the Armed Forces (Special Powers) Act was imposed in the state because the state government said that "the use of the Armed Forces in aid of the Civil Powers is necessary."[96] The violence in Manipur has not simply been between security forces and armed groups (called "undergrounds," or "UGs" by Manipuris). There is also a history of differences between the Meiteis, Nagas, Kukis and other tribal groups.[97] Once the Naga tribes in Manipur began to support the separatist groups in Nagaland in their demand for a sovereign "Nagalim"—a large swathe of Naga majority areas that include parts of Manipur, Assam, and Burma—the Meiteis began to form organizations to demand independence and protect their territories from Naga claims. In 2001 widespread protests broke out when Meitei Manipuris feared that a peace agreement between Naga insurgents and the Indian government would lead to the truncation of Manipur.[98] In the riots that followed, a number of government offices came under attack and the Manipur State Assembly building was burned down.[99]

The Kukis and Nagas have had numerous clashes, with hundreds killed in the 1990s.[100] The Kukis support the demand of a separate Kukiland that would include the Kuki tribes of Burma. The Nagas killed over 900 people in the 1990s. Over 350 villages were uprooted. The army has continued human rights abuses. There is particular resentment among the Meiteis for the secessionist demands of the Nagas and Kukis because of the special protections reserved for tribal groups under the Indian Constitution including quotas in universities and government jobs. The Meiteis are not eligible for these privileges. Under Manipuri law to protect indigenous tribes, they are also not allowed to settle in the hill districts.

However, there is no such restriction on Nagas and Kukis settling in the valley. Despite the deployment of the Indian army, the insurgencies have continued.[101] Militant groups have split and new ones formed, all of them representing their own community interests.[102] The three largest Meitei groups—the UNLF, PLA and PREPAK— have operated under a unified platform called the Manipur People's Liberation Front (MPLF) since 1999, though they maintain their independent identities and command structure.[103]

After clashes between Meiteis and Muslims in 1993, Islamist groups such as the People's United Liberation Front, North East Minority Peoples Front, Islamic National Front, Islamic Revolutionary Front, and United Islamic Liberation Army were formed.[104] Conflicts between the Nagas and the Kukis of Manipur led to the emergence of a number of Kuki armed opposition groups such as Kuki National Army, Kuki National Front, Kuki Revolutionary Army, and the United Kuki Liberation Front.[105] The Nagas back the National Socialist Council of Nagaland-IM, which is led by a Manipuri Naga called Thuingaleng Muivah.

There are now an estimated 30 armed groups belonging to various ethnic or religious groups operating in Manipur.[106] At present there is a cessation of hostilities by most of the Kuki groups.[107] The main Naga groups have also ceased hostilities against the state because of ongoing talks with the Indian government.[108] However, counterinsurgency operations have continued against the Meitei and Islamist groups.

The continuing violence in Manipur since separatist conflicts began has led to fear, anxiety, and terror for many residents, greatly impacting daily life and the region's development. Since the beginning of the conflict, the armed groups have been responsible for torture, targeted killings, the indiscriminate use of bombs and landmines, abduction for ransom, and forced recruitment into combat.[109] In the villages, militants also demand food or shelter from civilians. While Manipuris complain about the daily abuse and human rights violations by the state security forces, they are also held hostage by the stranglehold of the militants.

The biggest problem Manipuris face from militants is extortion, euphemistically called "taxes" by various armed groups. Many of these groups are so powerful that even government officials, including very senior officials, allegedly pay these "taxes." Manipuris describe how they have been forced to seek the protection of one group from the threats and extortion of another, thereby risking arrest by the security forces for collusion with militants.

A prevailing lawlessness has prevented private business enterprises from emerging, since traders and entrepreneurs are reluctant to share their profits with a number of different extortionists. In February 2008, transporters went on strike, protesting against extortion demands by some militants.[110] In April 2008, government engineers went on strike following numerous attacks by militants, including the murder of one engineer.[111]

The militants have also imposed moral diktats, such as on the sale of cigarettes and heroin or the screening of Hindi movies, and implement their orders violently. In 2001, there was outrage when one group imposed a dress code for women.[112] Many of them also punish perceived corruption and other crimes without due process.[113] Forced recruitment by militants has been an overwhelming problem since the beginning of the conflict. In July 2008, there were protests against the abduction and recruitment of children into combat.[114]

Unfortunately, the Indian government treats the violence in Manipur as a law and order problem. But it is a political problem. There are sovereignty issues that have to be addressed for the violence to end. According to the army, at least 53 civilians have been killed by militants in Manipur in 2008, while 108 were killed in 2007.[115] The army arrested 771 alleged militants and killed 111 alleged militants in 2007. Through August 2008, 54 alleged militants had been killed and 207 arrested.[116]

A large number of police and other security forces are deployed in Manipur. The state has over 14,000 police. Estimates suggest that at least 50,000 soldiers and paramilitaries are deployed in the state.[117] These forces include the army, the Central Reserve Police Force, the Border Security Force, the Assam Rifles, and Indian Reserve Battalions. According to Manipuri activists, the extent of militarization is such that it is estimated that there is one member of the security forces for every 20 Manipuris.[118]

Because of the overwhelming influence of various militant groups, since the beginning of the conflict, most civilians have been forced to interact with at least some militants. The security forces have not acknowledged their own failure to provide adequate security to Manipuris, which drives civilians to seek the protection of militants. Instead, the security forces have treated ordinary citizens with suspicion and subjected them to random checks, arbitrary arrest, coercive interrogation and torture. There are numerous allegations of custodial deaths, enforced disappearances, and extrajudicial killings disguised as armed exchanges ("encounter killings") with combatants.

When there are protests after a human rights violation by the armed forces or other security forces, typically the Manipur government sets up a commission of inquiry.[119] However, these commissions usually lack transparency during the investigation. The reports are rarely made public, nor is it ever clarified whether any action was taken based on the findings.

The state government also established the Manipur Human Rights Commission over ten years ago, in 1997. The dismal state of the commission reflects the government's lack of commitment to ensure the protection of human rights.

The commission operates without a proper office, with skeletal administrative support, and no investigative staff all. Under section 19 of the national Human Rights Protection Act 1993, the NHRC is not empowered to investigate violations by the Armed Forces.[120] However, it has the right to ask for information from civilian authorities. But actually it is nothing more than a 'signboard' commission."[121]

### *Human Rights Violations by Government Forces in Manipur*

Indian national security law goes far beyond permitting soldiers to use lethal force in genuine combat situations. Instead of complying with international norms, India provides extraordinary powers to military personnel involved in law enforcement operations. The Armed Forces (Special Powers) Act empowers officers in the armed forces, including non-commissioned officers, to arrest and conduct searches without a warrant, and even to shoot to kill if the officer is "of the opinion that it is necessary to do so for the maintenance of public order" and only give "such due warning as he may consider necessary."[122] The National Security Act, 1989 allows authorities broad 112 U.N. Basic Principles on the Use of Force and Firearms by Law Enforcement Officials, U.N. Doc. A/CONF.144/28/Rev.1 (1990); U.N. Code of Conduct for Law Enforcement Officials, G.A. res. 34/169, annex, 34 U.N. GAOR Supp. (No. 46) at 186, U.N. Document A/34/46 (1979), adopted by the U.N. General Assembly on December 17, 1979. 113 In accordance with the commentary to article 1 of the Code of Conduct for Law Enforcement Officials, in countries where police powers are exercised by military authorities, whether uniformed or not, or by state security forces, the definition of law enforcement officials shall be regarded as including officers of such services.[123] The Armed Forces (Special Powers) Act, sec. 4. powers to detain individuals to prevent them "from acting in any manner prejudicial to the defence of India, the relations of India with foreign persons, or the security of India."[124]

India provides immunity to its armed forces by forbidding any criminal prosecution without permission from the federal government. This provision is used to prevent court proceedings when an individual soldier is accused of murder and other offenses.[125] While by its terms the AFSPA only covers the Army and Air Force, the Assam Rifles, which was created by a separate act of parliament but placed under the operational control of the Army, also enjoys full protection under the act. Similarly, section 197 of the Code of Criminal Procedure provides immunity from prosecution to all public officials unless the government approves the prosecution.[126]

For instance, if police officers are to be prosecuted for human rights violations, prior approval is required from the relevant state government; for paramilitary forces, the central Home Ministry must approve prosecution. Thus prosecutions are rare. While the government claims that many cases are dealt with through disciplinary proceedings, it is rare for punishments meted out by internal courts of inquiry to be made public, making it impossible to know whether such disciplinary action actually occurs.[127] It is in this legal context that the following human rights violations have occurred.

### *Extrajudicial Killings*

Indian security forces have been responsible for a number of custodial killings that they later claimed occurred during an "armed encounter." Since 2006 there has been an increase in such killings. There are several cases highlighted by the Human Rights NGOs in which person was taken into custody in front of eyewitnesses, but was later declared to have been killed in an armed encounter. Human Rights Alert, an Imphal-based NGO, has documented 45 cases since 2006 where relatives have alleged that civilians were deliberately killed by security forces.[128] Of grave concern is that the number of such cases has shot up from 17 in 2006 to 23 in the first eight months of 2008.[129]

*Case of Mohammad Ayub Khan*[130]

Mohammad Ayub Khan, a mason left home on August 26, 2007 to collect dues for a church that he was constructing and then to pay his workers. Four others, Makanmi Ashim, Horni Ashim, Shimriha, and Raiping, accompanied him. They rented a vehicle that was being driven by a man named Peter. When Ayub Khan failed to return the next morning, his brother Yahiya Khan went to seek information from the van driver. According to Yahiya Khan, Peter said that Ayub Khan had been arrested by members of the 19th Assam Rifles. Peter told that the 19th Assam Rifles were conducting search operations on the highway. All the cars had been stopped. When they searched the van, they found that Ayub Khan was carrying cash, which he was carrying to pay the workers. The soldiers had allowed the other cars to go through, but they demanded that Peter drive the van to the Assam Rifles camp at Litan. Peter and an attendant driver were asked to drive away as soon as they reached the camp. But the others were told to stay back.122 Yahiya Khan and other relatives immediately went to the Assam Rifles camp at Litan. But the sentry at the gate refused to let them enter. They then filed a missing person complaint at the Litan police station, saying that Ayub Khan was last seen in the custody of the 19th Assam Rifles. At the Litan market, Yahiya Khan bumped into Makanmi Ashim, one of those detained with Ayub Khan. Makanmi told him that at the camp, Ayub Khan was separated from the others. They had all been released, but no one had any information about Ayub Khan. All other workers were located. But none had any information about Ayub Khan.

Several days later, on August 30, 2007, the Litan police contacted the family. They said that the Assam Rifles had informed the police station that a person had been killed in an armed encounter. They suggested that the family check to see if the unidentified person was Ayub Khan. The corpse of Ayub Khan was identified by his father. On the same day, the Assam Rifles issued a statement claiming that a suspected militant had been killed in an armed exchange and weapons had been recovered from him. Ayub Khan's brother went to the police to lodge a complaint of extrajudicial execution against the Assam Rifles. But the police predictably refused to register the case against the army. According to the government autopsy report, the police reported that the deceased had been killed in "a firearm encounter between 19AR [19th Assam Rifles] party and terrorist party... on 30-8-07 at about 5.15 a.m."

*Case of Razak Khan*[131]

There are several cases in which government officials or members of the armed forces later admitted to relatives that a person had been killed by "mistake." For instance, 15-year-old Razak Khan was preparing with his family to break the Ramadan fast on September 13, 2007 when security forces arrived. Mohammad Abdul Hakim, father of Razak Kahan, had alleged that a joint team of police and members of the 32nd Assam Rifles came up to the house and asked for a man called Khajing, an alleged militant. Hakim said he did not know a person by that name. The security forces surrounded the house, and Razak Khan was asked to accompany the soldiers to the back, to a neighboring house. There, according to Mohammad Abdul Hakim, his son was killed. The next morning the family read in the newspapers that a militant named Khajing had been gunned down in an encounter.

*Case of Longjam Surjit*[132]

In similar circumstances, 18-year-old Longjam Surjit was shot and killed by members of the 22nd Maratha Light Infantry battalion of the Indian army on August 31, 2006. At approximately 8:30 p.m. he went outside to stable his horse for the night. Surjit's father, Longjam Mera, said that district authorities later admitted that his son had been killed by mistakeThe army patrolling the area had shot Surjir dead.The army tried to hand over the body to the police and to register that they had killed a militant. But the police recognized Surjit and refused to take the body. They said he was not a militant. So the army dumped his body in the morgue. Initially, the army issued a statement claiming that Surjit had been killed in an armed exchange and that a pistol had been recovered from him.130 The villagers formed a Joint Action Committee to protest against Surjit's killing. On September 2, 2006, the state's chief minister, O. Ibobi Singh, ordered a magisterial enquiry. According to Longjam Mera, some army officers later apologized for the killing of his son:

*Case of Leitanthem Premananda*[133]

The security forces working Manipur are not the only agencies killing the people in an extrajudicial manner, but police too, have been responsible for extrajudicial executions. Leitanthem Premananda's relatives believe that he was killed because police commandos wanted to rob him. Premananda had left his home on the afternoon of January 30, 2006, to make some purchases for his sister's wedding. He was carrying a large amount of money because he had to stop at the timber merchant and place an order for furniture. He was accompanied by his friend, Keisham Boy. They were driving a two-wheeled motor scooter. According to his uncle, Leitanthem was picked up by the Manipur police: Keisham Boy told us that the two of them had stopped on the roadside because they wanted to go to the toilet. They walked a little apart for privacy. Boy saw some police commandos drive up. They stopped and searched Boy. the police had taken Premananda away. Keisham rushed back to inform the family of Leitanthem Premananda. The family waited anxiously for Premananda to arrive. That evening, a local news channel reported that an unidentified militant had been killed by the police in an armed encounter. Since Manipuris are well aware that missing persons can turn up as dead militants, family members immediately rushed to the morgue. They identified the body as that of Premananda. The police did not take action against those responsible for his death.

*Case of Angom Brajamani* [134]

Angom Brajamani was also picked up by the police and then killed. On November 18, 2007, he was standing on the road near his house with some friends. His older brother, Angom

Ingobi, saw a car drive past slowly and then make a U-turn and stop near the group. One man came out and beckoned Brajamani. Ingobi was too far away to hear what was said, but he saw his brother pushed into the car. Another morning, The local police disclosed that they had killed a militant named Angom Brajamani who was a member of the militant group PREPAK.

It has been an undoubted and unavoidable fact of the Indian scenario that terrorism, violence and insurgency are taking place in several parts of the country. Both, the insurgents and the Centre as well State governments of the respective States are equally responsible for aggravating the problem which has caused the loss of thousands of lives and millions' rupees properties. Both of the parties, the insurgents, as well as the governments, have to accept and appreciate that violent activities and counter-violence is not the moral, legal and even permanent solution of the problem. All groups involved must come at a common platform to acknowledge the gravity of the problem and must initiate to trace out peaceful and permanent solutions taking all groups involved into consideration. Some recommendations are given beneath, which if acknowledged, prove to be helpful in mitigating violence in conflict-effected or conflict prone regions of India.

**Recommendations and Suggestions**

- The Government of India must intervene with the conflict-effected State governments to stop that civilians are not involved in the conflict with the armed opposition groups and that no counter-insurgency or security measure be taken which directly or indirectly increases the risks of the civilians.
- Indian Government should take initiatives for holding dialogues between the State governments and the armed opposition groups active iin various parts of the country.
- The Central Government should initiate to create a separate Ministry for the development of the Naxalite affected States in line with Ministry of Development of North Eastern

Region (DoNER) in order to oversee speedy development of the Naxalite affected areas;

- The Centre government should immediately intervene with the State governments not to adopt policies and practices which prolong and accentuate the Naxalite conflict;
- The Central Government should take initiative to hold dialogues with the local regional parties of Kashmir to solve the Kashmir issue permanently and peacefully.
- The Center Government should take initiatives for holding dialogues between the State governments and the Communist Party of India (Maoists) to solve the Naxalite issue in a peaceful manner with a possible consensus of all political and social groups involved in the conflict ideologically or actively.
- The Conflict-effected State Governments should provide relief to both the victims of violence by the insurgents and violence by the security forces.
- The State Governments should start efforts to vacate the schools, and other public/community places which have been turned into the control centers of the armed forces or relief camps.
- The insurgent groups should stop targeting of the civilians and unarmed persons and use of land mines.
- The insurgent groups should stop opening indiscriminate firing and planting explosive at public places.
- The insurgent groups should stop taking of hostages and immediately release those being held as hostages.
- The insurgent groups should ensure full respect for the Geneva Conventions Protocol Additional to the Geneva Conventions of 12 August 1949, and Relating to the Protection of Victims of Non-International Armed Conflicts (Protocol II) and make a public statement committing to ensure respect for the same.
- The insurgent groups should stop the use and recruitment of children and teen agers in hostilities.

- The insurgent groups should immediately abandon the violent activities; should prepare an agenda for a peaceful campaign for their fair and constitutional rights.
- The insurgent groups should give positive response to the offers of peaceful talks called off by the Centre government.

The felony of Extra-judicial killings is not only a crime of Indian domestic law and should not be seen as a violation of Indian Constitution and law. It is in fact a most lethal infringement of the International and moral and thus must be considered as a most brutal and vicious crime against whole humanity. The problem should not be viewed only as considering the police and security agencies the prime accused. But it should be observed as a part of the policy framed by the Indian government to counter the terrorism and insurgency in various parts of India. The impunity provided by the Indian government to the armed forces to combat the insurgency according to their own will, wish and style proves the consistent happenings of extra-judicial killings as the deliberate acts of the government to counter the insurgency and terrorism in its typical and traditional style. But in the scenario, when Indian civil society as well as the international community has started highlighting and condemning the extra-judicial killings explicitly, the Indian government should sturdily revise its policies and methods to combat the terrorism and insurgency. The Indian government cannot afford to put its image and prestige on risk to be branded as an abuser of human rights and a breacher of international norms and laws of human rights, especially when it is quite closer to the primary goal of its foreign policy to emerge as an economic power, an influential actor of international politics, equipped with possible veto power and acknowledgement and cooperation of world community.

## References

1. Amnesty International, *Annual Report: India, 1997*, p. 13.
2. NHRC, *Annual Report 1997-1998*, p. 135.
3. Ram Narayan Kumar, *et al.*, *Enforced Disappearances, Arbitrary Executions and Secret Cremations: Victim Testimony and India's Human Rights*

*Obligation*, (An Interim Report), Committee for Coordination on Disappearances in Punjab, 1998, p. 178.

4. U.S. Bureau of Democracy (Human Rights and Labour), *India Human Rights Practices 1993*, U.S. Department of State, January 31, 1994, p.3.
5. Amnesty International, *Determining the Fate of the Disappeared in Punjab*, October 1995. p.2
6. U.S. Bureau of Democracy (Human Rights and Labour), January 31, 1994, *op. cit.*, p. 3.
7. *Ibid.*
8. Ram Narayan Kumar, et al., *op. cit.* p. 178.
9. *Ibid.*, pp. 178-179.
10. Ram Narayan Kumar, et al., *Reduced to Ashes-The Insurgency and Human Rights in Punjab*, Vol-1, South Asia Forum for Human Rights, Kathmandu, Nepal, 2003, pp. 277-278.
11. National Human Rights Commission, *Annual Report-1993-94*, p. 9.
12. *Ibid.*, pp. 3-4.
13. The Planning Commission of India, *Jammu and Kashmir Development Report*, District-Wise Population of Jammu andKashmir, Chapter II, September 2003, retrieved from http://planningcommission.nic.in/plans/stateplan/sdr_jandk/sdr_jandk.htm
14. Human Rights Watch, *Kashmir: Everyone Lives in Fear*, September 2006, p. 1.
15. *Ibid.*
16. "Valley's Tourist Graph on High," *The Indian Express*, January 9, 2006. also see, Shujaat Bukhari, "Protest against Attacks on Tourists," *The Hindu*, July 15, 2006.
17. International Center for Peace Initiatives, *Costs of Conflict Between India and Pakistan, Costs for Jammu and Kashmir*, July 2004, p. 73.
18. *Ibid.*, p. 75.
19. Asia Watch & Physicians for Human Rights, *Human Rights Crisis in Kashmir-A Pattern of Impunity*, June 23, 1993, p. 147.
20. Human Rights Watch, *Arms and Abuses in Indian Punjab and Kashmir*, September 1994, Vol. 6, No. 10, p. 6.
21. Asia Watch & Physicians for Human Rights, *Human Rights Crisis in Kashmir-A Pattern of Impunity*, June 23, 1993, pp. 160-162 .
22. Amnesty International, *India: Punitive Use of Preventive Detention Legislation in Jammu and Kashmir*, June 2000, p. 3.
23. Barbara Crossette, "Kashmiri Militants Say They May Kill 2 Swedes", *NewYork Times*, April 13, 1991. Also see, "Militant Abduct Farooq Aide", *Times of India*, June 9, 1993.
24. Asia Watch & Physicians for Human Rights, *op. cit.*, pp. 172, 173.
25. "India: Stalemate in Kashmir, Militants Threaten Mosque", *Inter Press Services*, October 18, 1993.

26. Amnesty International, India: *Appeal to armed opposition groups in Jammu and Kashmir to abide by Humanitarian Law*, 1997, p. 3.
27. *Ibid.*
28. *Ibid.*
29. *Ibid.*
30. Amnesty International, *India: Jammu and Kashmir- Remembering Jalil Andrabi*, October 1997, p. 7.
31. Amnesty International, *India: Human rights Abuses in the Election Period in Jammu and Kashmir*, 1996, pp. 21-22.
32. Human Rights Watch, *Everyone Lives in Fear: Patterns of Impunity in Jammu and Kashmir*, September 2006 Volume 18, No.11(C), p. 51.
33. Amnesty International, *India: A trail of unlawful killings in Jammu and Kashmir- Chithisinghpora and its Aftermath*, June 2000, pp. 2-5.
34. Amnesty International, *India: Act with Restraint during Elections in Jammu & Kashmir* (Public Statement), 13 November 2008, p. 1.
35. *Ibid.*
36. Amnesty International, *India: Disappearances" in Jammu and Kashmir*, February 1999, p. 8.
37. *Ibid.*
38. *Ibid.*, p. 9.
39. N. Jayapalan, *Human Rights*, Atlantic Publishers and Distributors, Delhi, 2000, p. 48.
40. Subhash Gatade, *"The Naxalite Left at the Beginning of the Millennium"* http://www.massline.info/India/Gatade.htm
41. Suhas Chakma, "Confronting the Naxalites", *The News Time*, Hyderabad, 26 June 1998.
42. Subrangshu Chowdhury, "In Naxal Heartland", *The Hindu*, 10 April 2005.
43. "Carrot-&-stick policy to keep Naxals at bay", *The Pioneer*, 22 February 2005.
44. "Maoist Shadow Over Chhattisgarh", *The Times of India*, 16 May 2005.
45. State Government of Chhattisgarh Figures up to 31 January, 2006.
46. Asian Centre for Human Rights, *The Adivasis of Chhatisgarh: Victims of the Naxalite Movement and Salwa Judum Campaign*, March 206, p. 9.
47. *Ibid.*, p. 10.
48. "Three policemen killed in Naxal Ambush", *Deccan Herald*, 9 January, 2005.
49. "Three BSF Personnel, Two Others Killed in Ambush", *The Hindu*, September 29, 2010.
50. "Narayanpur Attack: Naxals' Savage Face Stands Exposed", *The Tribune*, July 2, 2010.
51. *"Bloodbath by Naxals: 76 Security Men Gunned Down in Bastion"*, *The Tribune*, April 7, 2010.

52. "Maoists Step up Attack on Policemen, 6 killed in Chhattisgarh", *The Pioneer*, May 24, 2005.
53. "Dantewada Again: Toll 36", *The Tribune*, May 18, 2010.
54. "CRPF Jawan killed in Chhattisgarh Naxal attack", *The Hitavada*, June 18, 2005.
55. "24 CRPF Personnel Killed in Chhattisgarh Landmine Blast", *The Hindustan Times*, September 5, 2005.
56. "Ultras Rise again in Bastar Killing Naga Cop", *The Pioneer*, December 19, 2005.
57. "11 Security Men Killed in Chhattisgarh", *The Pioneer*, February 7, 2006.
58. "Maoists Attack PSU Depot: Kill 8 CISF Men", *The Times of India*, February 11, 2006.
59. "Naxals kill 1, Abduct 16", *The Hitavada*, March 6, 2006.
60. "10 Maoists Killed in 'Green Hunt': DGP", *The Hitavada*, September 6, 2005.
61. "Two Maoists Killed in Police Encounter", *The Hitavada*, August 13, 2005.
62. "Top Maoist Leader Killed in Chhattisgarh, *The Pioneer*, November 18, 2005.
63. Incidents Involving Communist Party of India-Maoist (CPI-Maoist): Chhattisgarh 2005, Retrieved from http://www.satp.org/satporgtp/countries/india/terroristoutfits/CPIM_Timeline.htm#chhattisgarh
64. *Ibid.*
65. "6 Maoists Killed in Gun-Battle", *The Hitavada*, December 30, 2005.
66. State Pulse: Chhattisgarh: The purification Hunt, available at http://www.centralchronicle. com/20060125/2501304.htm
67. "War in Tribal Heartland", *The Indian Express*, February 27, 2006.
68. Raman Singh Asks Locals to Step up Anti-Maoist Fight, Indo-Asian News Service, http://www.eians.com/stories/2005/08/15/15ram. shtml
69. South Asia Intelligence Review, *Weekly Assessments & Briefings*, Volume 4, No.7, August 29, 2005, available at http://www.satp.org/satporgtp/sair/Archives/4_7.htm#assessment2
70. "Central Team to Visit Chhattisgarh, *The Kashmir Times*, March 2, 2006.
71. People's Union for Civil Liberties, *Fact-Finding Report on the Salwa Judum, Dantewara District*, PUCL Chhattisgarh Unit, West Bengal and IAPL, Nov-Dec 2005, available at http://www.pucl.org/Topics/Human-rights/2005/salwa-judum-report.htm
72. *Ibid.*
73. " More Horrors of the Salwa Judum", Peoples March Magazine, Vol. 7, No. 1, January 2006, available at http://www.peoplesmarch.com/archives/2006/Jan2k6/salwa%20judum.htm
74. *Ibid.*
75. *Ibid.*
76. *Ibid.*

77. *Ibid.*
78. *Ibid.*
79. International Federation of Journalists (IFJ), *IFJ Concerned Over Harassment of Journalist in Chhattisgarh,* 16 January 2006, available at http://www.ifj-asia.org/page/india060116.html
80. 'Naxalism: Single Biggest Internal Security Threat', *The Economic Times,* April 14, 2006.
81. Ministry of Home Affairs, Government of India, *Annual Report* 2006-2007, p. 16.
82. According to projections based on 2001 census, the population in India's northeast is estimated to be around 43.56 million out of a total population is 1.14 billion. Census of India, "Projected Population for the year 2008,"http://www.censusindia.gov.in/Census_Data_2001/Projected_Population/Projected_population.aspx#2008 (accessed April 21, 2008).
83. Apart from the kingdoms of Tripura, Manipur and Sikkim, the rest of the northeast was initially part of Greater Assam.
84. Sikkim was an independent kingdom until it merged with India in 1975.
85. B.G. Verghese, "Building Northeastern Futures, Looking East," *Eastern Quarterly,* vol. 4, October 2007-March 2008, Manipur Research Forum, New Delhi, p. 158.
86. South Asia Human Rights Documentation Center, "*Armed Forces Special Powers Act; A Study in National Security Tyranny,*"November 22, 1995, http://www.hrdc.net/sahrdc/resources/armed_forces.htm (accessed April 21, 2008).
87. Population of North-Eastern States, Ministry of Home Affairs, Government of India, http://mha.gov.in/nemain.htm (accessed April 5, 2008). The population in 2008 is estimated to be 2.6 million according to the Census of India, "Projected Population for the year 2008."
88. R.Upadhyay, "Manipur-In a Strange Whirlpool of Cross-Country Insurgency," Paper No. 1210, South Asia Analysis Group, January 3, 2005, http://www.southasiaanalysis.org/papers13/paper1210.html (accessed March 14, 2007).
89. South Asia Human Rights Documentation Center, "Armed Forces Special Powers Act; A Study in National Security Tyranny." Retrieved from, http://www.hrdc.net/sahrdc/resources/armed_forces.htm
90. Agreement between Governer General of India and the Maharajah of Manipur, "Merger of Manipur with India," September 21, 1949, Text of the Agreement, retrieved from, http://lib.ohchr.org/HRBodies/UPR/Documents/Session1/IN/COHR_IND_UPR_S1_2008anx_Annex%20V_ManipurMergerAgreement.pdf (accessed March 13, 2008).
91. Ministry of Home Affairs, "Armed Forces (Special Powers) Act, 1958," http://www.mha.nic.in/actsrules/armed_forces_special_powers_act1958.pdf (accessed April 20, 2008).
92. The Armed Foreces (Assam and Manipur) Special Powers Act was amended in 1972 to extend to the new states that had beenformed in the

region and its name was changed to the Armed Forces (Special Powers) Act.

93. Kangleipak is the historical name for Manipur.
94. The People's Liberation Army is the armed wing of the Revolutionary People's Front, Manipur, retrieved from, http://www.geocities.com/CapitolHill/Congress/4568/ (accessed March 13, 2008).
95. South Asia Terrorism Portal, "Terrorist/Insurgent Groups-Manipur,"http://satp.org/satporgtp/countries/india/states/manipur/terrorist_outfits/index.html (accessed April 24, 2008).
96. Government of Manipur, Home Ministry Notification No. 183, September 8, 1980.
97. Sanjay Hazarika, *Strangers of the Mist*, Penguin Books, New Delhi, 1995, p. 242-245.
98. Subir Bhaumik, "Analysis: Manipur's Ethnic Bloodlines," *BBC News*, June 19, 2001, retrieved from, http://news.bbc.co.uk/2/hi/south_asia/1396751.stm (accessed April 24, 2008).
99. "13 Killed, Indefinite Curfew in Imphal," Press Trust of India, June 19, 2001, retrieved from, http://www.rediff.com/news/2001/jun/18mani5.htm (accessed April 5, 2008).
100. Subir Bhaumik, "Analysis: Manipur's Ethnic Bloodlines," *BBC News*, June 19, 2001.
101. Somini Sengupta and Hari Kumar, "A Forgotten Civil War in Northeastn India," *The International Herald Tribune*, September 3, 2005, http://www.iht.com/articles/2005/09/02/news/india.php (accessed August 21, 2008).
102. Lianboi Vaiphei, "Adressing Multiculturalism for Ethnic Equations in Manipur," *Eastern Quarterly*, vol. 4, October 2007-March 2008, Manipur Research Forum, New Delhi, p. 229-237.
103. Bobby Sarangthem, "Revolutionary People's Front," IPCS Database on Armed Groups in South Asia, Institute of Peace and Conflict Studies, New Delhi, http://www.ipcs.org/agdb12-rpf.pdf (accessed August 22, 2008).
104. Sanjay Hazarika, "100 Dead in India Religious Strife," The New York Times, May 5, 1993, retrieved from, http://query.nytimes.com/gst/fullpage.html?res=9F0CE4DD163CF936A35756C0A965958260
105. Hazarika, *Strangers of the Mist*, Penguin Books Publications, 2000, New Delhi, pp. 242-244.
106. These groups include the Peoples Liberation Army (PLA), United National Liberation Front (UNLF), Revolutionary PeoplesFront (RPF), Peoples Revolutionary Party of Kangleipak (PREPAK), Manipur Liberation Front Army (MLFA), Kanglei Yawol KhnnaLup (KYKL), Revolutionary Joint Committee (RJC), Kangleipak Communist Party (KCP), Peoples United Liberation Front (PULF),National Socialist Council of Nagaland (NSCN-K), National Socialist Council of Nagaland (NSCN-I/M), Naga Lim Guard (NLG),Kuki National Front (KNF), Kuki

National Army (KNA), Kuki Defence Force (KDF), Kuki Democratic Movement (KDM), KukiNational Organisation (KNO), Kuki Security Force (KSF), Chin Kuki Revolutionary Front (CKRF), Kom Rem Peoples Convention(KRPC), Zomi Revolutionary Volunteers (ZRV), Zomi Revolutionary Army (ZRA), Zomi Reunification Organisation (ZRO), andHmar Peoples Convention (HPC).

107. "Manipur Govt. to hold Talks with Underground Groups," *North East News Agency*, August 1-15, 2007, Retrieved from, http://www.nenanews.com/ANE%20Aug%201-15,%2007/mj4.htm (accessed April 3, 2008).
108. "Govt. NSCN (I-M) Agree to Extend Ceasefire," *Press Trust of India*, January 15, 2001, retrieved from, http://www.rediff.com/news/2001/jan/15nscn.htm
109. The abuses have continued even after some groups committed to comply with the Geneva Conventions. The Revolutionary People's Front announced its "unequivocal intention to comply" with common article 3 of the Geneva Conventions in its "Declaration Made by RPF during the 49th session of the Human Rights Sub-Commission at Geneva," August 6, 1997, retrieved from, http://www.geocities.com/CapitolHill/Congress/4568/documents/index.html
110. Neelesh Misra, "Manipur: Going, Going, Nearly Gone," *The Hindustan Times*, July 8, 2007, retrieved from, http://www.hindustantimes.com/StoryPage/Print.aspx?Id=9a00654c-3ec6-4dd6-927d-81f9c646f717 (accessed March 30, 2008).
111. "Engineers Stir, CM Assurance Fails to Cut Ice, Agitation On," *The Sangai Express*, April 5, 2008, retrieved from, http://www.thesangaiexpress.com/News_pages/Local_page-02.html (accessed April 5, 2008).
112. "Islamic Outfit Bans Skirts for Girls in Manipur," *The Times of India*, December 9, 2007, retrieved from, http://timesofindia.indiatimes.com/India/Islamic_outfit_bans_skirts_for_girls_in_Manipur/rssarticleshow/2607419.cms also see, Syed Zarir Hussain, "Militants' Dress Code Outrages Manipuri women," echarcha.com, August 28, 2001, retrieved from, http://www.echarcha.com/forum/showthread. php?t=3021
113. "PULF Alleges, Sets 5 day's deadline from Feb 28," *The Sangai Express*, February 29, 2008, Retrieved from, http://epao.net/GP.asp?src=14..290208.feb08
114. "Many anti-child abduction protests held in state," *The Imphal Free Press*, July 22, 2008, retrieved from, http://www.kanglaonline.com/index.php?template=headline&newsid=42783&typeid=1&Idoc_Session=19fd103cb9afcb01ce03596b25c4d8af Also See, Teresa Rahman, "Jackboots Too Large For Them," *Tehelka Magazine*, vol. 5, Issue 30, August 2, 2008, Retrieved from, http://tehelka.com/story_main40.asp?filename=Ne020808jackboots_toolarge.asp
115. Eastern Command, Indian Army, "Acts of Violence by Militants," Retrieved from, http://www.eastarmy.nic.in/combating-militancy/humanrights.html

116. Eastern Command, Indian Army, "Counter insurgency operations by security forces," retrieved from, http://www.eastarmy.nic.in/combating-militancy/militants-killed.html
117. Committee on Human Rights, *Submission concerning the Universal Periodic Review of the Government of India at the UN Human Rights Council*, April 2008.
118. Laishramcha Jinine, "The Militarization of Manipur," Article 2, vol. 5, no. 6, Asian Legal Resource Center, Hong Kong, December 2006, p. 6.
119. Government of India, Commission of Inquiry Act, 1952, retrieved from, http://www.vakilno1.com/bareacts/comminquiryact/comminquiry act.htm (accessed April 21, 2008).
120. PHRA 1993, Chapter 4, Scetion 19 (1).
121. Human Rights Warch, *India-These Fellows Must Be Eliminated: Relentless Violence and Impunity in Manipur*, September 2008, p. 23.
122. *Ibid.*
123. The Armed Forces (Special Powers) Act, Section 4.
124. The National Security Act, enacted December 27, 1980, retrieved from, http://www.satp.org/satporgtp/countries/india/document/actandordinances/NationalSecurityact.htm
125. The Armed Forces (Special Powers) Act, section 6.
126. Code of Criminal Procedure, 1973, http://www.vakilno1.com/bareacts/CrPc/Criminal-Procedure-Code-1973.htm
127. Section 197(2) of the Code of Criminal Procedure provides that: "No Court shall take cognizance of any offence alleged to have been committed by any member of the Armed Forces of the Union whole acting or purporting to act in the discharge of his official duty, except with the previous sanction of the Central Government."
128. Human Rights Warch, September 2008, *op. cit.* p. 40.
129. *Ibid.*
130. *Ibid.*pp. 40-42.
131. *Ibid.*,pp. 42-44.
132. *Ibid.*, pp. 43-44.
133. *Ibid.*, pp. 45-46.
134 *Ibid.*, pp. 46-47.

# 7

## Enforced Disappearances in India: An Atrocious Violation of Human Rights

According to the United Nations International Covenant for the Protection of All Persons from Enforced Disappearances, an 'enforced disappearance' is considered to be, "the arrest, abduction or any other form of deprivation of liberty by agents of the state or by the persons or groups of persons acting with the authorization, support or consent of the state, followed by a refusal to acknowledge the deprivation of liberty or by concealment of the whereabouts of the disappeared person, which place such a person outside the protection of law."[1] Enforced disappearances in India have often begun with illegal detention.[2] In the majority of cases, security forces abduct the victims in front of witnesses, often family members. Security forces do not officially acknowledge detentions. The family members are not provided any information regarding the causes of illegal detention and whereabouts of the victims. The persons arrested and detained are not presented before magistrate within 24 hours, as required by the law. In many cases, security forces extra-judicially execute victims and dispose off their bodies without acknowledging the deaths or informing family members of the whereabouts of the remains and residues of the deceased.[3] In several cases, the mothers have been still waiting for their young sons, the widows still hoping for their husbands, and the children, still expecting their fathers to come back alive from the confinement of police, and do not believe that their dearly-loved have been murdered a long time ago, by the merciless security forces, just in an inhuman and unlawful manner. Thus, the cases of enforced disappearances in India cannot be viewed only as violation of right to life and personal liberty of the victims under the provisions of Article 21 of the Indian Constitution, but must be acknowledged as a harsh crime against the family members and relatives of the deceased also.

### Cases of Enforced Disappearances in Punjab

For more than a decade, Punjab had been the site of the bloodiest conflicts in India's post-independence history. The conflict had its origins in a power struggle between Sikh political leaders and the Indian government, both of which were eager to maintain control over the resources of one of the country's most prosperous States.

Beginning in 1981, however, Sikh militants regularly engaged in a pattern of serious violations of human rights. Most of these violations involved deliberate attacks on unarmed civilians. Besides that, the violations took various other types and forms. Militant groups deliberately directed attacks against civilians in public areas, shooting randomly, for example, through crowded marketplaces, in residential districts and on congested streets. Sikh militants deliberately attacked on Hindu civilians to force them to leave the region. Selective attacks on Hindu populations were simply because of their religious and cultural affiliation. This was in keeping with the stated aim of the Sikh separatist movement to create an independent State. Militants also attacked Hindu civilians in retaliation for crackdowns by the Indian governments which had deliberately discriminated with the Sikhs just to convince and attract the Hindu majority. Sikh militants frequently attacked civilian passengers on public buses and trains in Punjab and neighbouring States. While the majority of these attacks did not seem to target particular individuals, many of them were directed against Hindus Political and religious leaders, including heads of villages and members of rival Sikh organizations were frequently attacked. Government officials such as judges and state ministers were also common targets. The journalists, human rights activists and members of the families of Police became the targets of militants.

The most unfortunate tragedy of the situation of human rights in the State of Punjab is that the Police and other pare-military forces did not follow the national as well as international norms of human rights to counter the problem of militancy in Punjab. Indian authorities were engaged in a pattern and practice of gross violations of human rights. These abuses included arbitrary arrests, torture, prolonged detention without trial, disappearance and summary killings of Sikh civilians and suspected militants. Attacks by government forces against civilians often were carried out in revenge for the activities of armed opposition groups.

The insurgency was crushed by the early 1990s in Punjab. But even after the end of terrorism and under the regimes of popular governments, the area of human rights violations has more widened and the nature of violations has become more severe and explosive, instead of decreasing. Still there are continuous reports of custodial torture which majority of the times, result in to the custodial deaths. Members of the Dalit, poor and other marginal groups have been continuously abused by the rich, upper caste people and even by the government authorities. There has been an overall increase in crimes against women recorded in Punjab in the recent years. To conclude it can be mentioned that situation of the human rights in Punjab is really alarming. The State of Punjab would no more remain an economically, politically, socially and culturally prosperous region, if the violation of human rights is not eradicated with some sincere and faithful efforts.

In Punjab, during the tragic era of terrorism and counter-terrorism operations, the security forces had been severely involved in the enforced disappearances of alleged terrorists, their relatives or the suspects. Many cases from Punjab have been on the record showing trauma of enforced disappearances faced by the victims as well as their relatives.

### *Case of Ram Singh Bling*[4]

Ajaib Singh, the uncle of Ram Singh Bling, disclosed the alleged enforced disappearance of Ram Singh Bling in the police custody, who was a journalist of *Aj di Awaz*, a daily newspaper published in Jallandhar. Ajaib Singh told that Ram Singh Bling was reportedly arrested near a police checkpoint in Bogiwat village on January 3, 1992. The family members, who saw him at the checkpoint on January 4, 1992, were not allowed to speak to him. A farmers' delegation, including Ajaib Singh went to the police checkpoint on January 6, 1992, to know about the reason of the arrest and detention of Ram Singh Bling. The police officials had told that Ram Singh Bling had been detained temporarily. The officials of the checkpoint promised an enquiry into the causes of arrest. But Ram Singh had disappeared since that day. Ajaib Singh further disclosed that the sources within the police had informally described that he had died in the police custody. However the police did not acknowledge any detention of Ram Singh Bling.

### *Case of Jagwinder Singh*[5]

A human rights lawyer Jagwinder Singh was picked up from his house in Kapurthatla by a group of uniformed policemen on September 25, 1992. His family members and neighbourers were the eye-witnesses of his abduction by police However, the police, when contacted by the father of Jagwinder Singh along with other eminent persons of area, denied his arrest and detention. Although then Chief Minister and the Chief Secretary promised to intervene, Jagwinder Singh had disappeared and never returned.

### *Case of Param Satinderjit Singh*[6]

On May 18, 1992, Amritsar police picked up Param Satinderjit Singh, a student of Guru Nanak Dev University, from the university campus. He was forced to identify suspected sympathizers of the terrorist cause within the university, who were also picked up. The police brought Param Satinderjit Singh in the university campus several times for that purpose.

The university students held a demonstration to protest against the abduction, and his father even went on a hunger strike. But Param Satinderjit Singh was not released. He did not return since that time. There was no trace of him thereafter.

### *Case of Gurdev Singh Kaonke*[7]

Gurdev Singh Kaonke, a 44 year old former high priest of the Akal Takht, allegedly involved in the movement of terrorism, had disappeared from the police custody under the mysterious circumstances and believed by his family members and the neighbours as allegedly killed by the police. Hari Singh, son of Gurdev Singh kaonke revealed in the interview that Gurdev Singh was arrested by the police from village Gurudwara on December 20 1992. He was last seen in police custody on December 28, 1992, apparently in poor condition. His wife filed a petition in the Punjab and Haryana High Court which immediately sent a search party to locate him on January 2, 1993. The search was in vain. He was neither found in Jagraon police station nor in the Criminal Investigation Agency centre in town. On January 3, 1993, the police reported that Gurdev Singh Kaonke had escaped from police custody the previous night, when taken by police party to seize weapons near Kanian village in Sidhwan Bet police station of Jagraon police district. The police claimed that their party was ambushed by terrorists and that during an exchange of fire Gurdev Singh Kaonke escaped with handcuffs on, under the darkness. However, he was never known to have returned to his family and even his body was never found. His relatives are of firm belief that he was tortured to death by the police.

### *Case of Bagicha Singh*[8]

Bagicha Singh, resident of village Rajo-ke of Amritsar district was arrested by local police in September 1992. However the police authorities denied his arrest and detention when the family members approached to know the whereabouts of him. In May 1995, the Punjab and Haryana High Court ordered an inquiry by the Central Bureau of Investigation (CBI) into the whereabouts of Bagicha Singh. The High Court found that an inquiry report presented by the state government had been manipulated and there were reasonable grounds which proved the role of the police negative and suspected. However, all efforts went in vain and Bagicha Singh and his whereabouts could never be known by family members.

### *Case of Sukhpal Singh*[9]

Sukhpal Singh alias Pali, a correspondent of the *Aj di Awaz* newspaper, was taken from his uncle's house in Chular Kalan village of Sangrur district, by Punjab Police on July 13, 1994, in the presence of eyewitnesses. Afterwards, the concerned police officials who had arrested Sukhpal Singh had denied his arrest and detention by the police. Chhota Singh, uuncle of Sukhpal Singh sent a letter to the Supreme Court of India regarding the disappearance of Sukhpal Sigh alias Pali from the police custody. On the orders of the Supreme Court, which treated a letter concerning his disappearance as a Public Interest Litigation (PIL), a magisterial inquiry in December 1994 found the Punjab Police responsible for his abduction. In March 1995, the Supreme Court issued notices to the Home Secretary, Punjab, Director General of Punjab Police and the Senior Superintendent of Police, Sangrur. However, the whereabouts of Sukhpal Singh were never known.

### *Case of Barjinder Singh*[10]

Bajinder Singh alias Pappu had disappeared from the police custody. His whereabouts were never known by the family members, after he was abducted by the Jagraon police on February 5, 1995, from his in-laws' house at village Sidhwan Kalan. Bahadur Singh, father of Barjinder Singh petitioned senior police officers, including Deputy Inspector General of Police (DIG) of Ludhiana, Ranjan Gupta. But no further news was available about the whereabouts of Barjinder Singh. Bahadur Singh, the father, and other family members were of a firm believe that Barjinder Singh had been killed by the police. But the mother was still hopeful that his *Pappu* (nick name of Barjinder Singh) would meet him again.

### *Case of Sukhwinder Singh*[11]

Sukhwinder Singh of village Chhan Noorowal, tehsil Ajnala, district Amritsar, was reported to have been picked up by the Lopoke police on January 7, 1995. According to witnesses including his wife who went to bring him food, Sukhvinder Singh was severely tortured and in a miserable condition in the police station. On February 1, 1995, the police claimed that Sukhvinder Singh had escaped by scaling the walls of police station. However he never returned home and neither could be re-produced by police.

### *Case of Jaswant Singh Khalra*[12]

Jaswant Singh Khalra, a human rights activist and the General Secretary of the Human Rights Wing of Shiromani Akali Dal Party, disappeared after several witnesses saw him being picked up by Punjab Police outside his home in Amritsar.[13] However the police officials had totally denied that Khalra was arrested or detained. Jaswant Singh Khalra's wife, Mrs Paramjit Kaur Khalra, told in her personal interview that she had filed a *habeas corpus* petition in the Supreme Court. The Supreme Court ordered an investigation by CBI into the disappearance of Jaswant Singh Khalra. The CBI presented its investigation report to the Supreme Court identifying nine Punjab Police officials as responsible for the abduction and murder of Jaswant Singh Khalra and recommended their prosecution. The Government of Punjab granted sanction for the prosecution of the police officials.[14] The life imprisonment was awarded to DSP Jaspal Singh and Assistant Sub Inspector of Police (ASI) Amarjit Singh in the Jaswant Singh Khalra murder case by CBI court of Patiala Additional Sessions Judge Bhupinder Singh in 2005 for abducting, torturing and killing Jaswant Singh Khalra.[15] Most embarrassing part of the whole incident is that both of the accused were awarded the prestigious Police Medal for Gallantry in 1994 by then President of India, for their brilliant services during the days of terrorism.

## The Case of Mass Cremations in Punjab

Jaswant Singh Khalra had lost his life just because he took a determined initiative to expose the human rights violations committed by the Punjab Police. He had been involved in a campaign to highlight the plight of hundreds of people who disappeared after being arrested by the Punjab Police during 1980s and early 1990s Khalra had uncovered the proof of the disappearances and extrajudicial executions perpetrated by Punjab Police. The official municipal records and the registers maintained by the crematoria exposed by Khalra, demonstrated that police officers had secretly cremated thousands of bodies in three crematoria in the district Amritsar claiming as unclaimed or unidentified.[16] In January 1995, he was instrumental in filing a petition with the Punjab and Haryana High Court that the bodies of several hundred people who disappeared in police custody between 1991 and 1993 had been cremated by Punjab Police in Amritsar district. The Police had claimed that the corpses were unclaimed or unidentified bodies.[17] The High Court had rejected his writ petition. Khalra was just about to file a writ petition in the Supreme Court of India, when he was abducted and made disappeared forever. After his death, the eminent human rights activists in Punjab had formed an apex body, the Committee for Coordination on Disappearances in Punjab (CCDP), to proceed the case of mass cremations, initiated by Jaswant Singh Khalra. In 1995, the Committee for Information and Initiative on Punjab (CIIP) petitioned the Supreme Court to demand a comprehensive investigation into the case of mass cremations. The Supreme Court ordered the CBI to investigate the case of mass cremations. The CBI limited its investigation to three crematoria in Amritsar district, acknowledging 2,097 cases of secret cremations[18] of which 582 persons were all non-terrorists. The CBI further stated in the report to the Supreme Court that it had found *prima facie* evidence that the Punjab Police had secretly disposed of 984 bodies between 1990 and 1995, of most of the bodies were cremated during the period from 1992 to 1993.[19]

CCDP was the premier NGO, which had done in-depth analysis and investigation of 838 incident reports by the end of July 1999 and sent it to the Supreme Court. The yearly division of 838 incidents proves that even after 1992 onwards, hundreds of people were extra-judicially killed and cremated by the police, claiming them unclaimed or unidentified.

Based on CBI inquiry reports, the Supreme Court appointed the NHRC as its *sui generic* body in the Punjab Mass Cremations Case, to examine all issues raised by the petitioners, granting it the extensive powers of the Supreme Court under Article 32 of the Indian Constitution to redress the fundamental human rights violations.[20] Unfortunately, the NHRC had consistently refused to adjudicate the full extent of human rights violations associated with the practice of disappearances in Punjab. Supreme Court had restricted its mandate to three crematoria in Amritsar district, thus ignoring disappearances and killings throughout Punjab. However, NHRC awarded compensation to the relatives of 1,298 victims of such killings in one district, Amritsar.[21]

However, the CCDP, which had been initiating the mass cremations case, did not get satisfied by the role of NHRC in the matter. Though, NHRC had limited its role only up to three crematoria of only Amritsar district deliberately ignored the cases of mass cremations which took place in other districts. A proposal was given by the Punjab and Haryana High Court in August 1999 that a commission of inquiry could be established by the government itself under the Commission of Enquiry Act, 1952, to investigate reports of hundreds of alleged disappearance in police custody and suspected extrajudicial executors. The State's ruling alliance of Shiromany Akali Dal and Bahujan Samaj Party (BJP), when approached by CCDP in 1998 and asked to set up a Commission of Inquiry in the matter of extrajudicial killings and mass cremations, responded by declaring that the past ought to be buried and forgotten, and that it had no intention to set up a Commission of inquiry to conduct such inquiries.[22]

## Enforced Disappearances in Kashmir

There have been so many enforced disappearances in Kashmir that there is now a term for women with missing husbands: they are called "half widows."[23] The Indian security forces have 'disappeared' countless people in Jammu and Kashmir since

1989 and staged fake encounter killings while fabricating claims that those killed were militants. In Jammu and Kashmir it is an ongoing process; in some years, especially 1990, 1991 and 1992, more people "disappeared" than in other years. Fewer "disappearances" were reported in 1996 and 1997, perhaps because of fear and intimidation following the killing of a well-known human rights activist in early 1996 which led to a virtual suspension of documentation and reporting of human rights violations. The year 1998 has witnessed a lower level of cases of "disappearances" while other human rights violations continue to be reported in large numbers. But the process has not stopped and available mechanisms have failed to provide redress for the hundreds of "disappearances" of earlier years.[24]

While the level of violence has decreased in Kashmir, failure to investigate human rights violations transparently and prosecute those responsible remains a strong reason for public anger. The people of Kashmir believe that many of the thousands "disappeared" over the last two decades were dumped into unmarked graves. The government has ignored calls for an independent investigation by human rights groups to determine the fate of the victims.[25]

In 2008, Amnesty International urged the Government of India to launch urgent investigations into hundreds of unidentified graves discovered since 2006 in Jammu and Kashmir. The grave sites are believed to contain the remains of victims of unlawful killings, enforced disappearances, torture and other abuses which occurred in the context of armed conflict persisting in the state since 1989. The graves of at least 940 persons have reportedly been found in 18 villages in Uri district alone.[26]

A report issued on 29 March 2008 by the Srinagar-based Association of the Parents of Disappeared Persons (APDP), *Facts under Ground,* indicated the existence of multiple graves in localities which, because of their proximity of the Line of Control with Pakistan, are not accessible without the specific permission on the security forces. In response to the report army spokespersons again claimed that those found buried were armed rebels and "foreign militants" killed lawfully in armed encounters with military forces. However the report detailed testimonies from local villagers saying that most of those buried were local residents hailing from the state. These are serious allegations that must be fully investigated. While the report alleges that more than 8,000 persons have gone missing in Jammu and Kashmir since 1989, the central and state authorities state that the total amounts to less than 4.000, and that most of these went to Pakistan to join armed opposition groups. In 2006 a state police report confirmed the deaths in custody of 331 persons and also 111 enforced disappearances following detention since 1989.[27]

According to official estimates, the number of people disappeared in Jammu and Kashmir since 1990 was only 1,017. However, the opposition in the State Assembly claimed that the figure was around 5,000.[28] While the Association of Parents of Disappeared Persons (APDP) put the number of missing persons at over 10,000.[29]

In August 2007, the Jammu and Kashmir State Human Rights Commission (SHRC) stated that it recorded disappearances of 42 persons after arrest by different security agencies during April to July 2007 in the Kashmir division alone. While 10 persons disappeared in April 2007, 15 persons disappeared in May 2007; 11 in June 2007 and 6 in July 2007. These were the records of only those people who registered their cases with the SHRC. The SHRC did not have data from the Jammu division.[30]

### *Case of Riyaz Ahmad Lone*[31]

He was picked up on 20 March 1997 from his home in village Anderbugh Lolab, district Kupwara in the presence of relatives and neighbours by 36 Battalion of Rashtriya Rifles and taken to their camp at Divar Anderbugh. Village elders looking for him there on the next day were told by camp authorities that Riyaz Ahmad Lone was not in the camp. His parents then attempted to file a complaint with police but the police refused to register it. They then reportedly approached the Superintendent of Police at Kupwara who told them that the army had informed him that Riyaz Ahmad Lone had been released. His whereabouts remain unknown.

### *Case of Gulam Mohammad Sheikh*[32]

Gulam Mohammad Sheikh, a 35-year old farmer with seven children, was picked up in April 1997 during a raid of his village Potwari Magam, Tehsil Handwara, district Kupwara in the presence of several family members and taken away, probably to the Rashtriya Rifles' camp at Seelu. His whereabouts are not known to the family memebers.

### *Case of Mohammad Rafiq Palhoo*[33]

He was arrested in the night of 8-9 August 1997, from his home in Mander Bagh, Srinagar, by an unidentified security agency. A First Information Report (FIR) alleging his abduction was filed within an hour. Following protests by local people, the concerned Senior Superintendent of Police assured the protesters that immediate action would be taken. It is not known if any action was initiated.

### *Case of Meraj-ud-Din Peerzada*[34]

Another case of enforced disappearances in Kashmir which gained significant attention of the media was the "disappearance" of Meraj-ud-Din Peerzada, former Secretary General of the Jammu and Kashmir People's League following his arrest on 16 October 1998 by a unit of the SOG on Lal Chowk in Srinagar. Several police stations approached by the family, denied holding Meraj-ud-Din Peerzada and refused to register a complaint of his abduction and disappearance.

### *Case of Abdul Rahman Paddar*[35]

Abdul Rahman Paddar, a carpenter, was reported missing in Srinagar city in December 2006. Police, during routine investigations into his disappearance, traced his mobile phone to an assistant police sub-inspector named Farooq Ahmad. When questioned, Farooq Ahmad admitted that Abdul Rahman had been picked up from Srinagar city by a Gandherbal district police special operations squad and killed.

Although Abdul Rahman had been reported missing by his family, the police later identified him as a Pakistani militant and claimed that he had been killed in an armed encounter during joint operations by the special operations squad and the paramilitary Central Reserve Police Force. Two other deaths mentioned during the interrogation are also being investigated by Jammu and Kashmir police. Nazir Ahmad Deka was allegedly picked up from Srinagar and killed in adjoining Gandherbal district in February 2006. He was identified as a "foreign militant" killed during a so-called encounter between alleged militants and a joint operation of the police and the army. The third man, Ghulam Nabi Wani, was killed in March 2006, and again identified as a "foreign militant" killed during a joint police-army operation.[36]

### *Case of the Disappearance of Manzoor Ahmed Mir, Awuntipura*

On September 12, 2004, Manzoor Ahmed Mir, a thirty-seven-year-old state government employee was arrested by security forces. The next day the family went to the police station to lodge a complaint. Mohammad Akbar, the brother of Manzoor Ahmed Mir was later informed by Sheikh Mohammad, the local police chief, that Manzoor Ahmed was alive and would be released soon. But he never returned. Mohammad Akbar says that a month later Sheikh Mohammad was transferred from the area and the police stopped taking an interest in the case.[37]

### *Case of the Disappearance of Bashir Ahmad Sofi*

On June 17, 2003, paramilitary forces, some in plainclothes and others in uniform, arrived at the home of Bashir Ahmad Sofi in Srinagar at around 1:30 a.m.The security force personnel arrested him by disclosing the family members that he was wanted for questioning. The soldiers told his family that he would be released in the morning. When he failed to return, Bashir Ahmad's relatives filed a police complaint. A week later a police officer named Jala told the family that Bashir Ahmad had been detained by the 61st Battalion of the BSF. However, when Bashir Ahmad's sisters went to the BSF camp, they were told that Bashir Ahmad was not in their custody. The same police officer later told the family that the BSF had denied detaining Bashir Ahmad, or even holding any operation in the area on that date. The police had initially promised that Bashir Ahmed Sofi would be at home soon. But the family could not trace out his whereabouts.[38]

People who have disappeared in the custody of the state are not only deprived of these basic human rights, they are also at risk of further human rights violations which are unconditionally prohibited under international human rights law, the Constitution of India and Indian law. Away from the scrutiny of lawyers, family members and human rights monitors, the "disappeared" are likely to be tortured or killed with impunity.

## Reasons for Disappearing People

Many people appear to be arbitrarily detained during "crackdowns" without any discernible reason. Some are arrested as the only male members found in their homes during raids. Others appear to be arrested in an attempt to force male relatives, assumed to be involved in an armed opposition group, to surrender.

Extortion reportedly also plays an increasing role in many human rights violations, including disappearances in Jammu and Kashmir. The most common motive for disappearing people in custody appears to be to intimidate young people not to join the militancy or to frighten the general population not to shelter or associate themselves with members of armed opposition groups.[39]

Custodial killings in Jammu and Kashmir have been characterized as not so much the unintended outcome of torture inflicted to obtain information but as a "purposeful culmination of torture" constituting a "brutal signal to other Kashmiris that they had better not get into militancy".[40] Disappearances may be an even more potent tool of intimidation, as months and years of enduring hope and despair may render families ready "to do anything if only he comes back alive", as some mothers have said.

No circumstances whatsoever, whether a threat of war, a state of war, internal political instability or any other public emergency, may be invoked to justify enforced disappearances. (Article 7, UNDPPD) Enforced disappearances appear to have been used sometimes as a punitive measure. Following the alleged rape on 22 December 1996 of 16-year old *Atri* in village Hakoora Badasgam in district Anantnag, her family filed a complaint with police and *Atri* made a statement before the Chief Judicial Magistrate in Anantnag. When the Rashtriya Rifles (RR) unit reportedly responsible for the rape learned of this attempt to seek justice, they picked up *Gul Mohammad Shan*, *Atri*'s father, and took him away. His whereabouts could not be established afterwards. According to reports the RR unit threatened remaining family members to the extent that they locked their house and moved away. No one apparently now dares to pursue the complaint about Atri's rape or her father's "disappearance".[41]

Since the beginning of the insurgency, thousands of Kashmiris have gone missing. Of course, not all persons who go missing in Kashmir are victims of "enforced disappearance" by the security forces: some have left without telling their family or friends, often to join the militants, or simply to find jobs. Tellingly, however, the problem of enforced disappearance in Jammu and Kashmir is so widespread that there is possibility of certain persons listed as disappeared who had actually gone away voluntarily to find jobs in other cities, but whose relatives had immediately assumed they were victims of enforced disappearance. Consequently, with such instances of erroneous reporting, substantial controversy remains about the problem's exact prevalence.

The problem of enforced disappearances in conflict-effected regions of India is not a new and unique in India. Earlier, it was practiced in Punjab as an effective instrument of counter-terrorism by the State Police agencies and the armed forces deployed there. It continued till 1995, and ended in Punjab with the end of terrorism and counter-terrorism operations. Now days, same brutal instrument of counter-terrorism has been adopted by the security forces deployed in

Kashmir to counter the insurgency and terrorism. The centre as well as State governments should genuinely acknowledge the seriousness of the dilemma and must take initiatives to stop the occurrences of enforced disappearances, in spite of shielding the police or army personnel guilty of performing these brutal acts. Some recommendations are given underneath, which, if considered, can help in diminishing the crisis of enforced disappearances in all insurgency-effected regions of India.

**Suggestions and Recommendations**

- The Centre government should genuinely acknowledge the United Nations International Covenant for the Protection of All Persons from Enforced Disappearances, and adopt the definition of the 'enforced disappearances as given in that Covenant.
- The Centre government should make legal provisions for imparting more severe and rigorous punishments to all those police/armed/security personnel proved accused of the enforced disappearances.
- The police as well as the other security forces should be mandated to follow the verdict of the Supreme Court of India regarding arrests given in *D.K. Basu V/S State of Bengal* case.
- In all insurgency-effected areas, where there are alleged allegations against security agencies regarding enforced disappearances, the police and security agencies should be provided the particular memo-forms, which should be mandatory for the arresting authorities to fill up while taking any person to the custody. These memo-forms should preferably include the name of person arrested, his alleged crime, address, actual place of his arrest. Besides that the name of the official arresting the accused, his rank, designation, authority, jurisdiction, commanding station; along with the place were the accused is to be detained, should be filled up by the official arresting any person. That memo-form should be duly signed and sealed by the

arresting authority, signed by the person arrested and at least two witnesses, preferably known to the person arrested.

- Separate law to combat with the problem of the enforced disappearances should be executed and implemented enthusiastically.

The consistent occurrence of the alleged cases of enforced disappearance in various parts of the country are very much part of the premeditated governmental policy to counter and collapse the insurgency and terrorism at any cost and with whatsoever means and methods. That is why the personnel accused of these inhuman acts are not prosecuted as per law, but provided a shield and an open impunity, along with rewards and ranks. The Indian government has to immediately condemn these acts, prosecute the guilty persons and restrict its armed forces to follow that ruthless practice of making the people disappeared from the custody in the mysteries conditions. Otherwise it would be too late to recover the indecent image of Indian government, security agencies and criminal-justice system at domestic as well as international level.

## References

1. International Convention for the Protection of All Persons from Enforced Disappearance, adopted by the UN General Assembly resolution 61/177 on 20 December 2006, Article 2.
2. *Ibid.*, pp. 15-16.
3. *Ibid.*, p.16.
4. Romesh Silva, et.al, *op.cit.* p. 16
5. Indira Jai Singh, "A Tale of State Repression", *SikhSpectrum.com Quarterly (Online Magazine)*, No. 14, November 20, 2002, p. 5.
6. *Ibid.*, pp. 5-6.
7. Amnesty International, India: *Three Reports of Deaths in Custody and Disappearances in Punjab*, April 1993, p.3-4. & Personal Interview of Hari Singh, Son of Gurdev Singh Kaonke.
8. Amnesty International, *India: Determining the Fate of the Disappeared in Punjab*, October, 1995, pp.10-11.
9. *Ibid.*, p. 16.
10. Asian Human Rights Commission, *Disappearances in Punjab*, 1999,p.p. 3-4.

11. *Ibid.*, p. 4.
12. Personel Interview of Paramjit Kaur Khalra, wife of Jaswant Singh Khalra.
13. Ram Narayan Kumar, et al., op. cit., p. 61.
14. Amnesty International, *India- A Mockery of Justice: The Case Concerning the Disappearance of Human Rights Defender Jaswant Singh Khlra Severly Undermined*, April 1998, p.2.
15. "Strip Convicted Cops of Medal: IHRO", *The Tribune*, November 20, 2005.
16. Human Rights Watch, *World Report 1997:India*, www.unhcr.org/refworld/docid/ 3ae6a8ad 28html, p.3.
17. Amnesty International, *Annual Report 1996: India*, p. 3-4.
18. Human Rights Watch and Ensaaf, *India: Protecting the Killers- A Policy of Impunity in Punjab, India*, October 2007, pp. 29-30.
19. Human Rights Watch, *World Report 1997: India*, p. 3.
20. Romesh Silva et al., *op.cit.*, p.17.
21. Amnasty International, *Annual Report: India 2008*, p.6.
22. People's Commission Not Needed: Badal, *The Tribune*, September 8, 1998.
23. Human Rights Watch, *Everyone Lives in Fear: Patterns of Impunity in Jammu and Kashmir*, September 2006 Volume 18, No.11(C), p. 86.
24. Amnesty International, 1999, op. cit., pp. 9-10.
25. Human Rights Watch, *India-World Report on Human Rights*: 2009, p. 2.
26. Amnesty International, *india should Investigate all Allegations of Enforced Disappearances in Jammu and Kashmir following Reports of Mass Graves* (Public Statement), April 2008, p. 1.
27. Brad Adams, *India: Investigate all Disappearances in Kashmir*, Human Rights Watch, p. 1.
28. "1,017 people missing since 1990 in Kashmir", *The Pioneer*, 5 February 2007.
29. "Police starts compiling data of missing persons", *The Tribune*, 15 February 2007.
30. "42 disappearances, 19 custodial - deaths prove govt. claims fake", *The Kashmir Times*, 19 August 2007.
31. Amnesty International, India: 1999, *op. cit.* p. 14.
32. *Ibid.*
33. *Ibid.*
34. *Ibid.*, p. 15.
35. Human Rights Watch, *Prosecute Police for Killings in Jammu and Kashmir*, January 2007, p. 1.
36. *Ibid.*, pp. 1-2.
37. Human Rights Watch, *Everyone Lives in Terror: Patterns of Impunity and Torture in Jammu and Kashmir*, September 2006, Volume 18, No.11(C), p. 86.
38. *Ibid.*, pp. 91-92.

39. Amnesty International, *Disappearances in Jammu and Kashmir*, February 1999, p. 13.
40. Civil War and Uncivil Government - Report on Human Rights Violations in Kashmir under the National Conference Government, issued by the Andhra Pradesh Civil Liberties Committee, Hyderabad, the Committee for Protection of Democratic Rights, Mumbai and the People's Union for Democratic Rights, Delhi, in November 1997 following a fact finding visit to the state in May-June 1997, p.22.
41. Amnesty International, 1999, *op. cit.*, p. 13.

# 8

## Violence against Women in India: A Denial of Women/Human Rights

The doctrine of 'women rights' is a worldwide phenomenon however it has been acknowledged and propagated in different words and terms in different societies. Women Rights as a term are also recognized as 'Gender Rights' and 'Feminist Rights'. The term 'gender' is used to describe a set of qualities and behaviours expected from men and women by their societies. A person's social identity is formed by these expectations. These expectations stem from the idea that certain qualities, behaviour, characteristics, needs and roles are 'natural' for men, while certain other qualities and roles are 'natural' for women. Gender is not biological. In other words, girls and boys are not born knowing how they should look, dress, speak, behave, think or react. Their 'gendered' masculine and feminine identities are constructed through the process of socialization, which prepares them for the social roles they are expected to play. These social roles and expectations differ from culture to culture and at different periods in history.[1]

The word Feminism takes its origin from the French word '*Feminisme*' believed to be coined by a French socialist thinker Charles Fourier (1772-1837) in France. He essentially believed that the true liberation of women could only come by eradicating the legal and economic subjugation of women to men. Throughout the Western world, the word 'Feminism' connotes the ideas that advocate emancipation of women and the word 'Feminists' to those who support the cause and attempt to realize it.[2] According to Oxford English Dictionary the word Feminism was not used in English before 1895. But definitely, at least a century prior to the entry of this word into popular political discourse, existed the ideology- a distinct body of ideas and aspirations- in order to protest for the rights of women and against the inequalities of women's condition in the society.[3] Different terms are used to signify the women's struggle especially in the English language. 'Women's Movement', 'Feminism', 'Women's Liberation' and 'Emancipation of Women' are some names for Feminism. During the late 19th century and the early 20th Century, the word Feminism was used mostly to signify the struggles for women's rights.

Feminism is the doctrine of equal rights for women, based on the theory of equality of sexes.[4] Feminism is any struggle designed to elevate women's status, socially, politically, economically and in respect to their self-concepts.[5] Feminism includes any form of opposition to any form of social personal or economic discrimination which women suffer because of their sex.[6] Feminism is not a subject limited to autonomous women's movement but a very general belief that society is unjust to women.[7]

Gender discrimination is a universal phenomenon. Discrimination against women is more predominant in Asian countries. Gender-biased customs, beliefs, superstitions, behavioural training, and mythology are used as tools to subjugate women and maintain them in oppression. Though all human beings are born with equal physical and mental capability and potential, men, who are in power and authority, which is the hallmark of patriarchy, suppress women.[8] Ironically, women are yet to understand the core issues related to gender discrimination and consolidate their resistance in this matter, mainly due to the internalization and reinforcement of certain values of an ideal wife, ideal mother, and ideal daughter imposed by social customs and supported by religious teachings. The discrimination starts even before or right after the birth; female foeticide and infanticide, neglect of health of the female child, and gender-biased feeding practices are rampant in the life of women. Discrimination is extended to all spheres of life - social, political, economic, and cultural.[9] The discrimination against women results in physical, psychological and cultural violence against women which harms the women physically, terrifies them mentally, and puts them inferior culturally.

## Violence against Women

The women of all regions, age groups, and social standings are equally prone to one or the other form of violence against them. As a result, even being equal to men in physical capacity, mental efficiency and specialized virtues, the women as a whole remain underdeveloped due to the ever present threat of violence against them. Violence against women ultimately impoverishes women, their families, communities and eventually the nations.[10] In the words of Kofi Annan, former Secretary-General of the United Nations, "Violence against women is perhaps the most shameful human rights violation. And it is perhaps the most pervasive. It knows no boundaries of geography, culture or wealth. As long as it continues, we cannot claim to be making real progress towards equality, development and peace."[11]

## Meaning and Definition of Violence against Women

Violence against women includes physical, sexual, psychological, and economic abuse. It is often known as 'gender-based' violence also because it evolves in part from women's subordinate status in society.[12] The term 'violence against women' refers to many types of harmful behavior directed at women and girls because of their sex. It is one of the most pervasive forms of human rights violations, denying women the equality, security, dignity, self-worth, and their right to enjoy fundamental freedoms.[13] However there is no universally accepted definition of violence against women. Some human rights activists prefer a broad-based definition that includes 'structural violence' such as poverty, and unequal access to health and education. Others have argued for a more limited definition in order not to lose or distract the actual descriptive influence of the term.[14] In any case, the need to develop a specific operational definition has been realized so that research and monitoring regarding violence against women can become more specific and have greater cross-cultural applicability.

In 1993 the United Nations offered the first official definition of such violence when the General Assembly adopted the 'Declaration on the Elimination of Violence Against Women'. The UN Declaration on the Elimination of Violence Against Women 1993 asserts that "Violence against women is a manifestation of historically unequal power relations between men and women, which have led to domination over and discrimination against women by men and to the prevention of the full advancement of women." According to Article 1 of the declaration, violence against women includes, "Any act of gender-based violence that results in, or is likely to result in, physical, sexual or psychological harm or suffering to women, including threats of such acts, coercion or arbitrary deprivations of liberty, whether occurring in public or private life."[15] Article 2 of the UN Declaration clarifies that the definition of violence against women should encompass, but not be limited to, acts of physical, sexual, and psychological violence in the family and the community. These acts include spousal battering, sexual abuse of female children, dowry-related violence, rape including marital rape, and traditional practices harmful to women, such as female genital mutilation. They also include non-spousal violence, sexual harassment and intimidation at work and in school, trafficking in women, forced prostitution, and violence perpetrated or condoned by the state, such as rape in war.[16]

### *Nature of Violence against Women*

Violence against women is different from interpersonal violence in general. The nature, features causes and patterns of violence against men generally differ from those against women. Contrary to violence against women, the men are more likely to be victimized by a stranger or casual acquaintance. Women are more likely than men to be victimized by a family member or intimate partner.[17] The major cause of violence against women is their 'subordinate gender'. The other fact is that women are often emotionally involved with, socially attached through, and financially dependent upon those males who abuse them. The roots of violence against women lie in historically unequal power relations between men and women and pervasive discrimination against women in both the public and private spheres. Patriarchal disparities of power, discriminatory cultural norms and economic inequalities serve to deny women's human rights and perpetuate violence. Violence against women is one of the key means through which male control over women's agency and sexuality is maintained.[18]

This violence is both of a physical and psychological nature and cuts through all cultures and societies. It is committed within the family setting (battering, sexual abuse of female children, dowry-related violence, marital rape, female genital circumcision, and other traditional practices that have proven to be harmful to women; non-spousal violence, and violence that accompanies various forms of female exploitations)[19]; in communities (sexual abuse, harassment, and intimidation in the workplace and educational institutions, trafficking in women, and forced prostitution);[20] as well as in society at large, in cases when the perpetrators are members of state institutions, or because these institutions are unable to protect women, as may be the case during detention and custody and in armed conflicts.[21] Whilst traditional forms of gender-based violence centered on religion and customary laws that dominate in developing countries, in developed countries, domestic violence with women's partners as perpetrators, is the most frequent type of violent behaviour.[22] Although all women are potential victims, certain groups are more exposed to the violence, such as indigenous women, women from ethnic minority groups, female refugees and internally displaced women, migrant women, women living in rural and remote communities, destitute women, female children and elderly women, and last but not least, women and girls in situations of armed conflicts.[23]

### *Types of Violence against Women*

The above mentioned discussion explores out three main types of violence against women:

(a) Physical, sexual or psychological violence occurring in the family, including battering, physical abuse of the girl children at household, dowry related violence, marital rape, female genital mutilation or other traditional practices harmful to women, non spousal violence, and violence related to exploitation.

(b) Physical, sexual or psychological violence occurring within the general community, including rape, sexual abuse, sexual harassment, and intimidation at work, in educational institutes, and elsewhere, trafficking of women and forced prostitution.

(c) Physical, sexual or psychological violence perpetrated or condoned by the State, wherever it occurs.

## Worldwide Phenomenon

Violence against women is the most pervasive yet least recognized human rights abuse in the world. Violence against women continues to be a global catastrophe that kills, tortures, and hurts the women, physically, psychologically, sexually and economically.[24] Violence against women is present in every country, cutting across boundaries of culture, class, education, income, ethnicity and age. However the nature, forms and causes of violence against women may vary as per different regions and societies.[25] Even though most societies proscribe violence against women, the reality is that violence against women is often sanctioned under the garb of cultural practices and norms, or through misinterpretation of religious tenets.[26] Moreover, when the violence takes place within the home, as is very often the case, it is effectively condoned by the tacit silence and the passivity displayed by the state and the law-enforcing machinery.[27] The global dimensions of violence against women are alarming and no society can claim to be free of such violence.

Violence against women exists in every country of the world in some form. The statistics depicted by UNIFEM (United Nations Development Fund for Women) in its report entitled, "Not a Minute More: Ending Violence against Women", paint a horrifying picture:

- 40 per cent of all female homicide victims in the United Kingdom are killed by their intimate partners
- Every year thousands of women suffer dowry-related deaths or are disfigured by acid thrown in their faces by rejected suitors in Bangladesh, Colombia, India, Nigeria and Pakistan.
- In 2002, the Council of Europe declared violence against women a major cause of death and disability for women 16 to 44 years of age and called it a public health emergency.
- In the United States, the health-related costs of rape, physical assault, stalking and homicide by intimate partners are more than $5.8 billion every single year.
- Globally, the World Bank estimates that violence against women is as serious a cause of death and incapacity among women of reproductive age as cancer and a greater cause of ill-health as traffic accidents and malaria combined.
- One in three women throughout the world will suffer this violence in her lifetime; she will be beaten, raped, assaulted, trafficked, harassed or forced to submit to harmful practices such as female genital mutilation (FGM). In the majority of cases, the abuser will be a member of the woman's own family or someone known to her.

For over three decades, women's advocacy groups around the world have been working to draw more attention to the physical, psychological, and sexual abuse of women and to stress the need for action. They have provided abused women with shelter, lobbied for legal reforms, and challenged the widespread attitudes and beliefs that support violent behavior against women.[28]

## Violence against Women in India

While observing the status of women in India from historical perspective, it is found that women in India definitely had a status, dignity and respect in the society during ancient period.[29] It was said, "*Yatra Narayeshu Pujayante, Ramente Tatra Devata*"- In the age of *Ramayana*, *Sita* was kidnapped by the demon King *Ravan*. He kept her in *Ashoka-Vatica* for one year, provided her all amenities of life, played all tricks to win her confidence, but Sita did not budge an inch. The character of that demon King Ravan, who is allegedly acknowledged as *Rakshas-Ravan*, is an example for the humanity even today. He did not touch person of Sita. That Demon Ravan was far superior in moral values and thoughts. In the Gupta Age, *Kalidas* wrote that the wind did not have the courage to touch the apparel of young beauties sleping on his way and down with intoxication of youthfulness. In the Vedic age many ladies showed their brilliance with incompatible wisdom. Come the 16th century, there was no man available better qualified and more erudite than lady Satyawati to judge and preside over an intellectual battle (Tarka-Shastra) between her husband *Madan Mishra* and great reformer and prodigy Sir *Adi Shankaracharya*.

Medieval India saw a fall in the status of women owing to some extraneous reasons.[30] In that age, a woman might have been subjected to social or educational biases, but she was the Goddess blessing of the home of that era. There are seldom found any references regarding violence or crime against women. Barring rarest of rare cases, neither were they immolated nor were they drowned neither the society sneered at them nor subjected them to eve-teasing or molestation and the brutality of rape. Medieval Indian society was not as sinful towards women and women were at least not sexually abused by their own relatives and family members. Today, it all appears beyond one's imagination.

The struggle against women's oppression in India started during the 19th century through the efforts of early reformers. Raja Ram Mohan Roy of West Bengal tried to abolish *Sati system* legally, in 1829.[31] Another champion of women's cause, Ishwara Chandra Vidhyasagar campaigned against polygamy and propagated widow's re-marriage.[32] The Brahmo Samaj and Arya Samaj opened their doors to women by challenging Hindu orthodoxy. These were followed by other reformists like Mahatma Jyoti Roy Phule and Panditha Rmabai in Maharashtra, Kaisandas Nulji in Gujarat, Swarnakumari from Tagore's family in West Bengal and many others.[33]

During the 20th century the theme changed from reform to uplift the women, with the demand of equal rights with men. Most of the thinking of women's issues was initially influenced by the ideals set by Gandhi. He saw women as agents of social change. He emphasized the wõmen's role in the family as the source of moral support and strength to men.[34] Another hallmark of the time was the birth of the All India Women's Conference in 1927 through the efforts of women such as Annie Besant, Margaret Cousins, Sarojini Naidu, Kamaladevi Chattopadhyaya and Hansa Mehta. It drew many women from different classes and organizations of the Congress, Communist and Socialist parties. They all shared the view that women and men by nature were meant to perform different functions and complementary roles. Each had the right to be supreme in her/his domain. Much of their contribution was towards education, protection of destitute women and their voting rights. Their work resulted in the enactments of various legislations pertaining to re-marriage, Sati, prostitution, child marriage and dowry as well as welfare programmes like residence for destitute women and vocational training for income generation[35]

Along with the struggles of middle class women before independence, there were also other attempts to organize peasant women in West Bengal, Andhra Pradesh and Maharashtra, influenced by leftist ideology. This gave birth to 'Tebhaga', 'Telangana' and 'Warli' upheavals. The major issue was land and its produce. Women left their traditional homes and voluntarily entered into an armed struggle along with their men. Numerous 'Atma Raksha Samities' and 'Mahila Sangams' spontaneously sprang up into action. The contribution of the peasant women was analyzed and understood, not according to the value of importance for women, in their question of equality, but according to the 'use value' for the peasant movement in general.[36]

Right from the time of independence which ensured constitutional protection of women, plane development came into focus. It mostly aimed at maximum production, more employment and economic advance. The Central Social Welfare Board and the Community Development Programmes of 1952 envisaged women's participation and education with the assumption that knowledgeable women could participate better in the process of development.[37] Greater emphasis was given to women's education during the third and the fourth Plan periods, especially in the areas of health, hygiene, nutrition and family planning. High priority was given for immunization and nutrition of children and intending mothers. However, this attention on women seemed to have come only as an after-thought as in the case of ICDS programmes, in which women were 'incidental beneficiaries' as mothers.[38]

The latent base on consciousness of women began to get a public recognition with the emergence of the Report of the Committee on Status of Women in India (1974) and the Declaration of Women's Decade by United Nations.[39] The above report indicated that the majority of women still remained under bondage and were far from enjoying the equal rights and opportunities guaranteed to them by the Constitution and Government Welfare programmes. It said that the administrative programmes, introduced with the objective of promoting women's welfare and development had suffered various drawbacks as there was no single agency to co-ordinate the government measure, both legislative and administrative, and provide expert advice on the methods of implementation. It observed under the rules of business in the government of that time, the women's affairs were really nobody's concern. It brought into focus the developmental policies and programmes constantly neglecting the issues of declining sex-ratio, women's lower life expectancy, increasing maternal mortality, decreasing women's work participation, female illiteracy, women headed households, dowry, migration, domestic violence and trafficking.

The World Conference of UN Decade of Women held at Copenhagen in July 1980, perceived women as an essential component in 'every dimension' of development as a whole[40] The same Conference held in 1985, in Nairobi, emphasized the participation of women in the political processes of development, having and 'equal share of power' as well as strategies 'to enhance women's autonomy' in order that they integrate themselves in the 'total development efforts'.[41]

The year 1988 brought the National Perspective Plan for Women 1988-2000 (NPPW).[42] Its salient features were, the establishment of an inter-ministerial body for monitoring women's programmes, higher rate of public investments in women preferred industries, state and district level coordinating bodies, women's access to land, co-operative economic programmes, ban on sex determining tests and 30 per cent reservation in panchayats and municipal bodies. This plan came under strong criticism by several women's organizations.

Today, the reported crime against women indicates that cruelty to women, molestation, rape, abetment to suicide, all are increasing year after year. Despite that we have more and more legislations to inflict harsher punishment on the guilty, more and more feminist liberation movements, news papers and magazines celebration of International Women Year and Day and howsoever high we try to bring women on par with men, the intensity of crime against women is increasing.[43]

States have concrete and clear obligations to address violence against women, whether committed by state agents or by non-state actors, and are accountable to women themselves, to all their citizens and to the international community regarding this prerequisite responsibility. India, while acknowledging that obligation, has made several efforts in its Constitution and the law to improve the status of women.

However the constitutional dream of gender equality is miles away from becoming a reality.[44] Even today, 'the mainstream remains very much a male-stream'. The dominant tendency has always been to confine women and women's issues in the private domain. The traditional systems of control with its notion of 'what is right and proper for women' still reigns supreme and reinforces the use of violence as a means to punish its defiant female 'offenders' and their supporters.[45]

## Constitutional and Legal Provisions to Prevent Violence against Women

There are several provisions in the Indian law to prevent and prohibit violence against women. Various new legislations have been brought and amendments have been made in existing laws with a view to handle the violence effectively. These are broadly classified under two categories.

### *The Crimes under the Indian Penal Code (IPC)*

- Rape (Sec. 376 IPC)
- Kidnapping & Abduction for specified purposes (Sec. 363-373 IPC)
- Homicide for Dowry, Dowry Deaths or their attempts (Sec. 302/304-B IPC)
- Torture - both mental and physical (Sec. 498-A IPC)
- Molestation (Sec. 354 IPC)
- Sexual Harassment (Sec. 509 IPC)
- Importation of girls (up to 21 years of age) (Sec. 366-B IPC)

### *The Crimes under the Special & Local Laws (SLL)*

The gender specific laws which prevent and prohibit violence against women in the country are:

- Immoral Traffic (Prevention) Act, 1956
- Dowry Prohibition Act, 1961
- The Child Marriage Restraint Act, 1929
- Indecent Representation of Women (Prohibition) Act, 1986

- Commission of Sati (Prevention) Act, 1987
- Protection of Women from Domestic Violence Act, 2005.

Despite all aforesaid safeguards, the violence against women is on constant rise in the country. India has an elaborate system of Constitutional provisions and legislative safeguards to protect the rights of women, including the Equal Remuneration Act, the Prevention of Immoral Traffic Act, the Sati prevention Act, Dowry Prohibition Act. However, the Government often is unable to enforce these laws, especially in rural areas where traditions and rituals are deeply rooted. Female bondage and forced prostitution are widespread in parts Indian society. Crimes against women- including molestation, rape, kidnapping, sexual harassment and killing of brides for dowry- has been increasing, in spite of declining. There is huge dearth of respect and status for women in Indian society. These factors have further increased the evils of female infanticide and female foeticide.

It is an evident fact that the women in India have been consistently becoming the victims of torture, discrimination, molestation, sexual abuse, dowry deaths, honour killings, selling, buying, kidnapping and abduction and other forms of violations of the rights provided to them by the Indian Constitution, Indian domestic/municipal law, as well as International Law. To obtain a thorough understanding of all aspects of the violation of women's rights, an in-depth analysis of all forms of violence against women becomes essential. Violence against women is a serious problem in India. Overall, one-third of women age 15-49 experience physical violence and about 1 in 10 experience sexual violence. In total, 35 percent do experience physical or sexual violence. This figure translates into millions of women who have suffered, and continue to suffer, at the hands of husbands and other family members.[46] Not only the civil society and the NGOs, but even the formally concerned government agencies have been depicting the worrisome consistent growth in the number of cases of violence against women. To elucidate the subject, it is noteworthy to look at some government data presenting the reported cases and complaints of violence against women throughout India.

## Magnitude of Violence against Women in India

However, it is an impossible task to trace out the exact number of cases of violence in any society, especially when the violence has been practiced against a vulnerable section of the traditional and bigoted society. Even though, an attempt has been made to collect and compile the statistical data maintained by various governmental organizations concerned to data collection regarding violence against women.

### *Statistical Data of NCW*

In India, the NCW (National Commission for Women) is the nodal and formally ratified agency to redress all types of grievances regarding the violence and crime against women. The NCW, functioning since 1992 for the cause of women rights, has received a massive number of cases in 17 years since 1992 to 2008[47].

The NCW, in 1992, (year of its inception) had received total 122 cases regarding all types of atrocities against women. The number was 175 cases in 1993, which reached to 215 cases in 1994 and 177 cases in the year 1995. In 1996, the NCW had received 233 cases; while a swift increase in the number of cases was witnessed in the following years and the NCW received

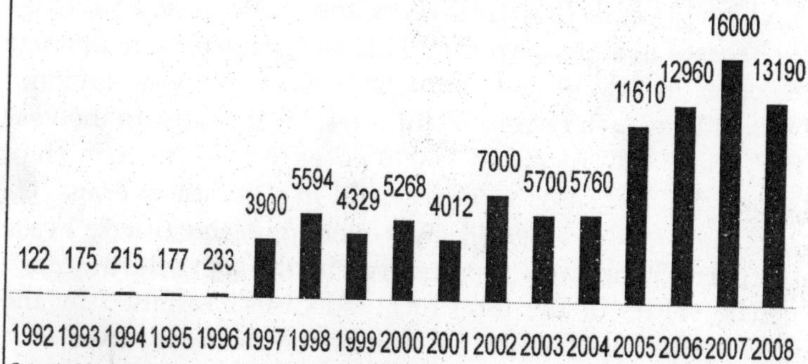


*Source:* National Commission for Women of India.

**Figure 1: Number of Cases Received by NCW (1992-2008)**

respectively 3900 and 5594 cases in the years 1997 and 1998. Total 4329 cases in 1999, 5268 cases in 2000, and 4012 cases in 2001 were received by the NCW. The NCW, in 2002 had received 7000 cases. The number of cases was followed by 5700 cases in 2003, total 5760 cases in 2004, and 11610 cases in 2005. In the year 2006, the NCW received 12690 cases, in 2007, it received record 16000 cases; and in 2008, total 13190 cases were received by the NCW regarding various forms of crime and violence against women.

The data asserts that the NCW had received 96245 complaints regarding atrocities against women in 17 years (1992-2008). It means that in these 17 years, average 5662 cases are received by the NCW every year. The data further confirms that average 472 cases are received by the NCW in a month, average 118 cases in a week; while average 17 cases are received by the NCW every day. In first five years of its functioning (1992-1996), when the NCW was not much known and acclaimed resort to the grievances of women, had received only 922 complaints which constitutes only 0.95 per cent of the total number of 96245 complaints. In next four years (1997-2000), the NCW had received 19.83 per cent of the total number of complaints. In further four years (2001-2004), the NCW received 23.34 per cent of the total number of complaints. Alarmingly, in succeeding most recent 4 years (2005-2008), the number of cases received by the NCW was much more than the double (55.85 per cent) of the total cases received in previous 13 years. In these 4 years, the NCW received average 13440 cases in a year; average 1120 cases in a month; average 280 cases in a week; while average 40 cases every day; and average 1 case after every 36 minutes. Worryingly, in the year 2007, the NCW received 16000 cases which confirm that, average 1333.33 cases were received in a month; average 333 cases in a week; average 48 cases every day; and exactly 1 case after every 30 minutes was received by the NCW during 2007.

The statics of the total received cases presented by the NCW are far less than actual number of incidents of violence against women taking place in India. That data do not even depict the exact or approximate number of total reported cases of violence against women. The prior reason is that the NCW has not yet been able to establish itself as a prime and most preferred resort of the grievances of the women. Hence only a limited number of complaints of violence against women are received by the NCW. On the other side the NCRB (National Crime Record Bureau of India) under the ministry of Home Affairs, is a most reliable agency which maintains the record of all categories of crimes reported in all police stations throughout India.

It has been since 2002-03 that the NHRC seems to get sincerely concerned with the gender issue of violence against women in more versatile manner by considering various categories of violence against women. Since 2002-03, the statics of various forms of violence against women such as rape, sexual harassment, indignity of women, dowry demands, dowry deaths/attempts, exploitation of women, murder after abduction and rape have been presented by the NHRC in its annual reports. The statistical data maintained by the NHRC regarding all aforesaid categories of violence against women has been systematically arranged in the underneath table.

**Table 1**
**Various Categories of Cases Disposed of by the NHRC Regarding Violence Against Women (2002-03 to 2006-07)**

| *Categories of Cases* | *2002-03* | *2003-04* | *2004-05* | *2005-06* | *2006-07* | *Total* |
|---|---|---|---|---|---|---|
| Rape of Women | 400 | 176 | 392 | 453 | 332 | 1753 |
| Sexual Harassment | 159 | 92 | 320 | 281 | 150 | 1002 |
| Indignity of Women | 118 | 61 | 196 | 196 | 155 | 726 |
| Dowry Deaths & its Attempts | 845 | 616 | 1115 | 1196 | 956 | 4728 |
| Dowry Demands | 448 | 266 | 708 | 664 | 330 | 2416 |
| Murder after Abduction & Rape | 289 | 209 | 634 | 783 | 667 | 2582 |
| Exploitation of Women | 200 | 139 | 279 | 250 | 174 | 1042 |
| Total | 2459 | 1559 | 3644 | 3823 | 2764 | 14249 |

*Source:* National Human Rights Commission of India.

### *Year-Wise Analysis*

The year-wise analysis of the data asserts that total 14249 complaints were disposed of by the NHRC in five years (2002-03 to 2006-07) regarding various categories of violence against women. The NHRC had disposed of 17.25 per cent of the total number of complaints during 2002-03; while 10.94 per cent of the total complaints were disposed of in 2003-04. In 2004-05, the NHRC had disposed of 25.57 per cent of the total cases; while 26.82 per cent of the total number of cases was disposed of in 2005-06; and 19.39 per cent of the total number of cases was disposed of in the year 2006-07. Decrease of 36.6 per cent was noticed in the number of cases during 2003-04 as compared to 2002-03. However during 2004-05, increase of 133.73 per cent was observed in comparison with the year 2003-04. The year 2005-06 witnessed the increase of 4.91 per cent in comparison with the year 2004-05; contrarily the decrease of 27.7 per cent was noticed in 2006-07 in contrast to the year 2005-06. It confirms that average increase of 79.25 has been noticed in the five years (2002-03 to 2006-07). The data further corroborates that average 2849 cases are disposed of by the NHRC in a year; while average 237 cases every month; average 59 cases every week; average 8 cases every day; and average 1 case after every 3 hours has been disposed of by the NHRC regarding violence against women.

### *Category-Wise Analysis*

The category-wise analysis of the data divulges that 33.18 per cent of total 14249 cases disposed of by the NHRC in five years (2002-03 to 2006-07) have been regarding 'Dowry Deaths and its Attempts'. 18.12 per cent of total number of cases has been regarding the category of 'Murder after Abduction and Rape'. 16.95 per cent of total number of cases is regarding dowry demands; while 12.30 per cent is regarding 'Rape of Women'; while 7.31 per cent of the total number of cases has been occupied by the category of 'Exploitation of Women'. 7.03 per cent cases are regarding 'Sexual Harassment of the Women', and 5.09 per cent of the total number of cases is regarding 'Indignity of Women'. The data further establishes that in these five years there is average increase of 55.57 per cent in the number of cases regarding rape of women; Increase of 146.9 per cent has been noticed in the number of cases regarding sexual harassment of women; while 143.4 per cent decrease has been witnessed in the number of cases regarding indignity of women. Similarly, the cases regarding dowry deaths or its attempts have observed the increase of 41.1; and increase of 69.03 per cent in the total number of cases in five years have been witnessed regarding the cases of dowry demands. Noticeably, the crime of murder of women after abduction and rape has increased to 184.35 per cent in these five years. Furthermore, increase of 29.41 per cent has been observed in the number of cases regarding exploitation of women.

**Table 2**
**Proportion of Complaints Regarding VAW Towards Total Complaints Disposed of by NHRC**

| *Year* | *Total Complaints* | *Complaints Regarding VAW* | *% to Total Complaints* |
|---|---|---|---|
| 2002-03 | 38438 | 2459 | 6.42 % |
| 2003-04 | 8620 | 1559 | 18.08 % |
| 2004-05 | 24936 | 3644 | 14.61 % |
| 2005-06 | 17534 | 3823 | 21.80 % |
| 2006-07 | 17341 | 2764 | 15.93 % |

*Source:* National Human Rights Commission of India

The data divulges that the cases disposed of regarding VAW constitute 13.33 per cent of total 106869 cases 'disposed of by the NHRC since 2002-03 to 2006-07. Furthermore the cases disposed of regarding VAW comprise an overall increase of 9.51 per cent in five years in proportion to total cases disposed of by the NHRC. Interestingly, after 5 years there is increase of same 9.51 per cent in the cases of VAW in proportion to total number of cases from 6.42 per cent cases during 2002-03 to 15.93 per cent cases during 2006-07.

### *Statistical Data of NCRB*

The NCRB is the formal government agency which has been consistently (since 1953) maintaining and publishing in its year-wise reports, the exact statistical data of the total number of the incidents of crime reported in all police stations of India. To be acquainted with the gravity and growth of the total reported incidents of 'crime/violence against women'[48]

The statistical data of National Crime Record Bureau of India (NCRB) regarding crime against women has been analyzed from 1996 to 2008, which has depicted that huge number of crimes are committed in India every year. According to the NCRB data there were total 115723 reported cases of crime against women, in 1997, the number increased to 121265 and in 1998, it further increased to 131475. The NCRB, in 1999 had reported 135771 cases, in 2000, 141375 cases and in 2002, total 143034 cases of crime against women throughout India. The number of crimes against women kept on increasing in the successive years and the NCRB reported 140601 cases in 2003, total 154333 cases in 2004 and 155553 cases in 2005. In the year 2006 the number of cases was 164765, in 2007 the number was 185856 and n 2008, total 195856 cases of crimes against women were reported by the NCRB of India.

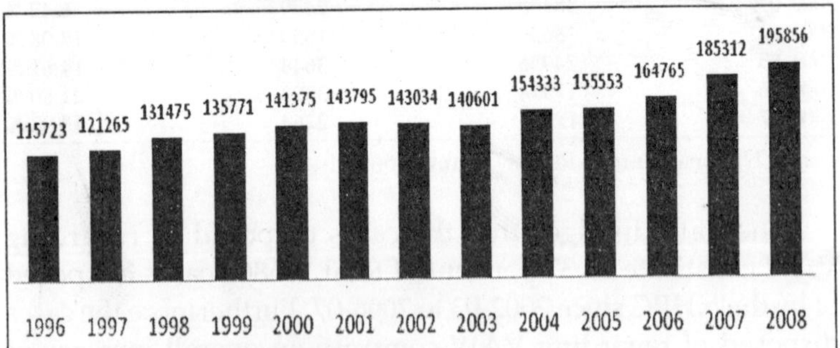


*Source:* National Crime Record Bureau of India.

**Figure 2: Total Reported Cases of Crime Against Women (1996 to 2008)**

The data asserts that there were total 1928858 reported cases of crime against women since 1996 to 2008. It means that average 148374 crimes against women in a year are reported throughout India. The analysis of the data of these 13 years divulges that in these 13 years average 406.50 crimes against women are reported everyday in India. While analyzing more in depth, the date establishes that average 17crimes against women are registered in India every hour. It means that at least one crime against women is registered in India after every three minutes. The graph of the crime against women has been increasing every year. The number of reported cases of crime against women had increased from 115723 cases in 1996 to 19556 cases in 2008. It means there was an increase of 80133 cases in 13 years which confirms average 24 per cent increase in the reported crimes against women after 13 years. Moreover the analysis of ten years of the data of NCRB confirms that there was a huge increase of 60085 cases in ten years with 135771 cases in 1999 to 195856 cases in 2008. It confirms that in ten years, there is average increase of 38.21 per cent reported crimes against women in India. The profound analysis of the data asserts that there is an increase of average 6080 reported cases in India every year in comparison with the previous year.

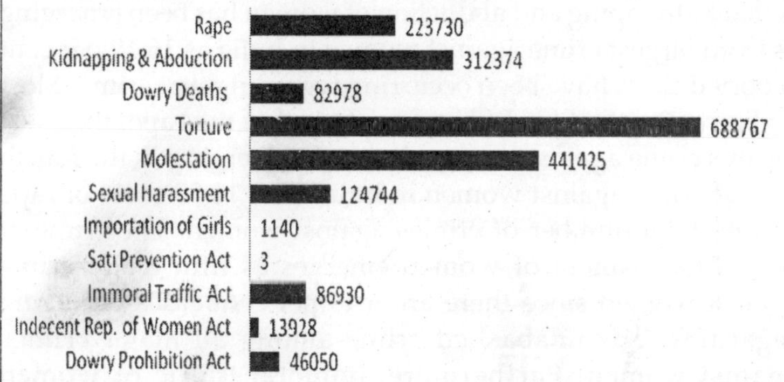


*Source:* National Crime Record Bureau of India.

**Figure 3: Major Categories of Reported Crime Against Women (1996-2008)**

Further observation of the data of NCRB of India (1996 to 2008) divulges that crimes against women in India have been committed in several separate categories such as rape, kidnapping and abduction, dowry demands and deaths, torture, molestation, sexual harassment etc. The statistical data of NCRB (1996 to 2008) reveals that 223730 cases of rape, 312374 cases of kidnapping and abduction and 82978 cases of dowry deaths were reported throughout India since 1996 to 2008. Furthermore 441425 cases of molestation, 124744 cases of sexual harassment, and 1140 cases of importation of girls were reported since 1996 to 2008. Worryingly 3 cases of Sati system violating Sati Prevention Act, which has been considered as most brutal and inhuman crime against women, were registered in these 13 years. Besides that 86930 cases violating Immoral Traffic Act, 13928 cases violating Indecent Representation of Women Act, and 46050 cases violating Dowry Prohibition Act were reported throughout India.

The data reveals that there are a largest number of cases of torture of women (37.70 per cent) among all major categories of crimes against women (1928858 cases). After the torture, the molestation of women occurs as second largest crime against women with 22.88 per cent cases of such crime occurring among total crime against women in India. Another noticeable aspect of the statistics about crime against women is that kidnapping and abduction of women has been emerging as third largest crime against women in India as 16.19 per cent reported cases have been occurring regarding that crime. Most embarrassing fact for Indian society is that the rape, the most vicious crime against women, has been emerging as the fourth largest crime against women in India with 11.59 cases of rape among total number of crimes against women. The crime of sexual harassment of women emerges as fifth major crime against women since there are 6.46 per cent cases occurring regarding that unabashed crime among all major crimes against women. Furthermore, immoral traffic of women emerges as sixth largest crime against women (04.50 per cent cases), while dowry deaths (4.30 per cent) and dowry related crimes (2.38 per cent) unfortunately emerge as seventh and eighth largest crimes against women. Indecent representation of women (0.72 per cent) emerge as ninth largest crime and importation of girls emerges as the tenth largest crime against women among all major crimes against women in India. Although, the crime of Sati emerges as the least occurring crime, but the occurrence of even three incidents of Sati in thirteen years exists as a black blot on the boasting profile of social development of India.

### *Torture of Women in India*

Torture of women as domestic violence and torture in custody is reported regularly in India. Custodial torture remains one of the worst forms of torture perpetrated on women by law enforcement personnel. Official reporting is nothing short of appalling. As per NCRB of India, there were total 35246 reported cases of torture against women in India in the year 1996. The number increased worryingly and there were total 36592 of such type in 1997, as many as 41376 reported cases in 1998, and 43823 reported cases in 1999. In the successive years the number of cases regarding torture on women was 45778 in 2000, total 49170 in 2001, and 49237 in 2002. The NCRB had further reported 50703 cases of torture of women in 2003, as many as 58121 cases in 2004, and 58319 cases in 2005. In the year 2006, there were total 63128 cases, in 2007, total 75930 cases, and in 2008, there were total 81344 reported cases of torture of women in India.

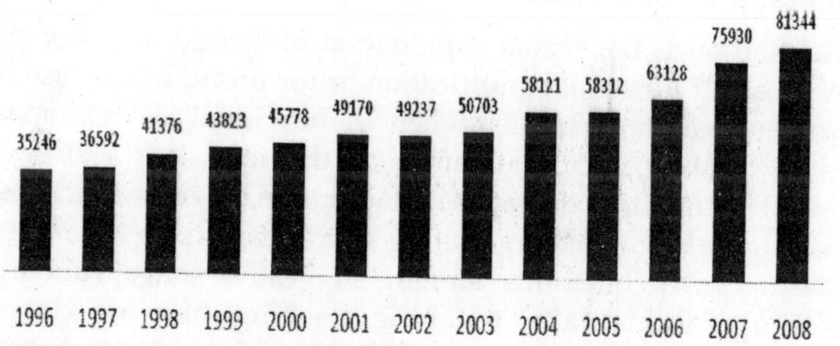


*Source:* National Crime Record Bureau of India.

**Figure 4: Total Reported Cases of Torture of Women in India (1996 to 2008)**

The data asserts that total 688767 cases of torture of women were registered in India in India in 13 years since 1996 to 2008. It constitutes 37.70 per cent of the total reported cases of crime against women in India which formulates 'torture against women' as the largest crime against women in India. It means that average 52983 cases of the torture of women are reported in India every year. It further establishes that average146 cases of the torture of women are registered in India every day. Further analysis of the data confirms that average 6.083 cases of the torture of women are registered in India every hour, and average 1 case of the torture of woman is reported in India after every 10 minutes. The analysis of the data has divulged that there is a consistent increase in the cases of torture of women in India. There is a worrying increase of 46098 cases (130.78 per cent) in the total number of reported cases of torture of women after 13 years from 35246 cases in 1996 to 81344 cases in 2008. After ten years, there is a perturbing increase of 37521 cases (85.61 per cent) in the total number of reported cases of torture of women from 43823 cases in 1999 to 81344 cases in 2008. The analysis of the data of the year 2008 (81344 cases) asserts that in recent times average 6779 cases in a month; average 1695 cases in a week; while average 242 cases in every day; average 10 crime every hour and average 1 case after every 6 minutes has been reported in India regarding torture against women.

### *Molestation of Women*

Molestation is the sexual exploitation of a child or a woman by an adult for sexual gratification or for profit. In the case of women molestation occurs when an individual sees a woman as a sexual object and advances on this idea. It is a form of sexual assault or sexual abuse. Molestation of women includes making staring whistling, staring at breasts, talking to breasts, passing lewd comments, singing suggestive songs, rubbing, groping, 'accidentally' touching, flashing, blowing kisses, rating/making kissing sounds, stalking, rubbing, masturbating in open view, adjusting rearview mirror, unsolicited conversation, unsolicited photography, blowing kisses, winking, following a woman driver, making vulgar gestures to the women, making vulgar comment on the body or physique of a woman, touching any women with sexual intention, showing pornography to the women, any form of sexual harassment etc. The severe forms of molestation of women include fondling of the victim or the abuser, sexual kissing, or forced sexual exposure to media. Molestation other than covering everything mentioned earlier may also cover Eve teasing. Eve teasing refers to all forms of harassment women face in public spaces that are considered trivial, funny and a part of day to day life, and reduce the modesty of the victims. The tragedy of women is that strangers, alleged immoral elements are not the only accused of these crimes but most of the times, the parents, relatives, sibling, teachers, physicians, wardens, police officials are the reported as accused of their molestation by the women themselves.[49]

The statistical data of the NCRB of India asserts that there were total 28939 reported cases of molestation of women through out India. In the year 1997, there were 30764 cases, in 1998, the number of cases was 30959, and total 32311 cases of molestation of women were reported in 1999. The number of reported cases was 32940, 34124, and 33943 in 2000, 2001 and 2002 respectively. In the year 2003, there were as many as 32939 cases of molestation. The number increased to 34567 cases in 2004 and total 34175 cases in 2005. As many as 36617 cases of molestation of women were reported in 2006, total 38734 and 40413 cases were reported of such type in the years 2007 and 2008 respectively.

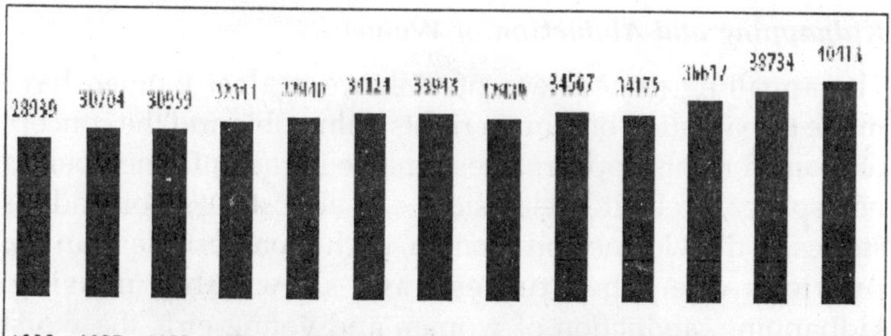


*Source:* National Crime Record Bureau of India.

**Figure 5: Total Reported Cases of Molestation of Women in India (1996 to 2008)**

The data reveals that total 441425 cases of molestation of women are reported in India in 13 years since 1996 to 2008. It confirms that 22.88 per cent of the total number of reported cases regarding crime against women is related to molestation of women. It establishes 'molestation of women as the second largest crime against women in India after the crime of 'torture against women'. The analysis of the 13 years' data reveals that average 33956 cases of molestation of women are reported in

India every year. It means that average 93 cases of the molestation of women are reported in India every day. The in depth analysis of the data asserts that average approximately 4 cases of the molestation of women are reported in India every hour which confirms that average 1 case of the molestation of women is reported in India after every 15 minutes. The data divulges that there is continuous increase in the number of cases regarding molestation of women year by year. There is an increase of 11474 cases (39.64 per cent) in the cases after 13 years from 28939 cases in 1996 to 40413 cases in 2008. After ten years, the crime of molestation of women increases to 8102 (25.07 per cent) cases from 32311 cases in 1999 to 40413 cases in 2008. Total 40413 cases of molestation of women reveal that in recent time, average 3368 cases in a month; average 842 cases in a week; average 120 cases in a day; while average 2 cases every hour and average 1 case after every 30 minutes has been reported in India.

### *Kidnapping and Abduction of Women*

The appalling dimensions of violence against women have made the situation of human rights vulnerable and the concept of women rights appears questionable in India. If one opens a newspaper, web site, television, one almost sees horrendous stories of the violence on women, each more terrible than the previous one. The studies have shown that missing, kidnapping, abduction of women and young girls the worst forms of violence are on the increase in recent times in India due to negligence and corruption of the law enforcing agencies coupled with political malice. Kidnapping and abduction of women, particularly the girls is a new form of contemporary slavery. Reportedly, the young girls and women are being trafficked across well beaten paths within South Asia and further a field.[50]

Kidnapping and abduction of women is another embarrassing and indecent crime against women which not only deprives them of right to freedom, but violates their inherent and inalienable rights to equality, dignity, exposure, and distinguished existence. In India, the women and even the minor girls are kidnapped or abducted to traffic them to other parts for enforced prostitution. Several times, the women or the minor girls are forcefully abducted for raping and sexually abusing them. The minor, young girls and women are also kidnapped and abducted in India to engage them in forceful bonded labour or slavery.

The NCRB of India had reported 114877 cases of kidnapping and abduction of women in 1996, total 15617 cases in 1997 and 16351 cases in 1998. The number of cases of kidnapping and abduction throughput India was further reported as 15962 cases in 1999, 15023 cases in 2000, and 14645 cases in 2001. The NCRB further reported 14506 cases in 2002, total13296 cases in 2003 and as many as 15578 cases in 2004. The number of cases related to kidnapping and abduction of women was reported as 15750 in 2005, which has increased to 17414 cases in 2006, total 20416 cases in 2007, and 22939 cases in 2008.

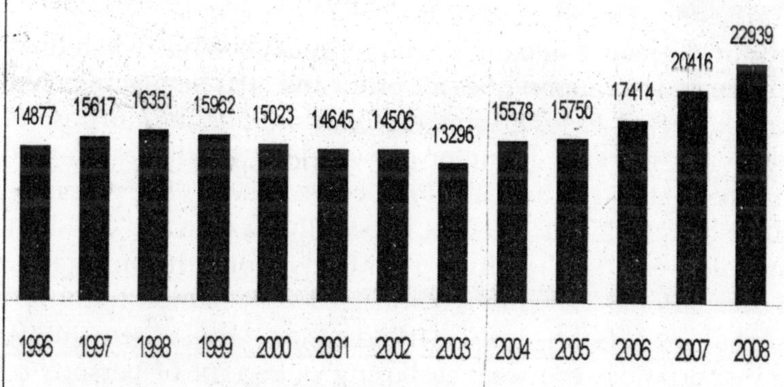


*Source:* National Crime Record Bureau of India.

**Figure 6: Total Reported Cases of Kidnapping & Abduction of Women (1996 to 2008)**

The data reveals that there happened total 312374 reported cases of kidnapping and abduction of women in India in 13 years from 1996 to 2008. It comprises 16.19 per cent of total number of reported cases of total crimes against women in India. The healthy percentage makes the crime of 'kidnapping and abduction of women' as the third largest crime against women in India. The data further asserts that during these 13 years average 24029 cases regarding the kidnapping and abduction of women are reported in India every year. Further, average 66 cases regarding same crime against women are reported every day, average 3 cases are reported every hour; and average 1 case of such type is reported after every 20 minutes in India. The number of reported cases regarding kidnapping and abduction of women has been increasing in India. In 13 years, the number of cases has increased to 8062 cases (54 per cent) from 14877 cases in 1996 to 22939 cases in 2008. In ten years, the number of reported cases has increased to 6977 cases (43.71 per cent) from 15962 cases in 1999 to 22939 cases in 2008.

### *Trafficking of Women*

In its dictionary meaning, the concept of trafficking denotes a trade in something that should not be traded in. Thus, we have terms like drug trafficking, arms trafficking and human trafficking. The concept of trafficking in people refers to the criminal practice of exploitation of human beings where they are treated as commodities for profit and after being trafficked, are subjected to long term exploitation. For the purpose of study, the working definition of trafficking which was adopted has been stated in the U.N. Protocol to Prevent, Suppress and Punish Trafficking in Persons, Especially Women and Children, supplementing the United Nations Convention against Transnational Organised Crime, 2000, to which India is a signatory. It defines trafficking as "the recruitment, transportation, transfer, harboring or receipt of persons by means of the threat or use of force or other forms of coercion, of abduction, of fraud, of deception, of the abuse of power or of a position of vulnerability or of the giving or receiving of payments or benefits to achieve the consent of a person having control over another person, for the purpose of exploitation. Exploitation shall include, at a minimum, the exploitation of the prostitution of others or other forms of sexual exploitation, forced labour or service, slavery or practices similar to slavery, servitude or the removal of organs".[51]

Trafficking in women is the most abominable violation of human rights. Perhaps not many crimes are as ghastly as trading in human misery. Human rights guaranteed by the Indian Constitution are inalienable, non-negotiable and universal. Trafficking in women is a violation of several human rights including the very right to life, the right to liberty and human dignity, and security of person, the right to freedom from torture or cruelty, inhuman or degrading treatment, the right to a home and family, the right to education and proper employment, the right to health care and everything that makes for a life with dignity. Trafficking in women and children is on the rise. And yet, the redressal mechanisms are woefully inadequate and the way the various governmental agencies have dealt with this gross violation of human rights has left much to be desired. This dichotomy calls for an in-depth understanding of the dimensions of trafficking in India as also the need for creating an authentic database, which would help devise appropriate measures to protect human rights with greater vigour.[52]

Press, police and NGO reports on trafficking has given a clear and unequivocal indication that buying and selling of women for sexual and non-sexual purposes is an expanding activity and involved gross violation of human rights. What is even more worrisome was the indication that India is fast becoming a source, transit point as well as a destination area for traffickers. A substantial body of newspaper reporting as well as reports of voluntary agencies suggests that apart from Nepal, Bangladesh and the poverty-stricken districts within India, trafficking from the Commonwealth of Independent States (CIS) countries is also on the increase. This is a significant pointer towards the complex, organised nature of the crime.[53]

According to NCRB's statistical data since 1996 to 2008, there is huge violation of Immoral Traffic (Prevention) Act in India resulting innumerous number of cases of trafficking of women in India. In 1996 there were 7706 reported cases of women Trafficking which was followed by 8323 cases in 1997, total 8695 cases in 1998 and 9363 cases in 1999. The number of cases was 9515 in 2000, 8796 in 2001, and 6598 in 2002. The number of cases was on steep decline and total 5510, 5748 and 5908 cases were reported in 2003, 2004 and 2005 respectively. The NCRB had further reported 4541 cases of women trafficking in 2006, total 3568 cases in 2007, and 2659 cases in 2008.

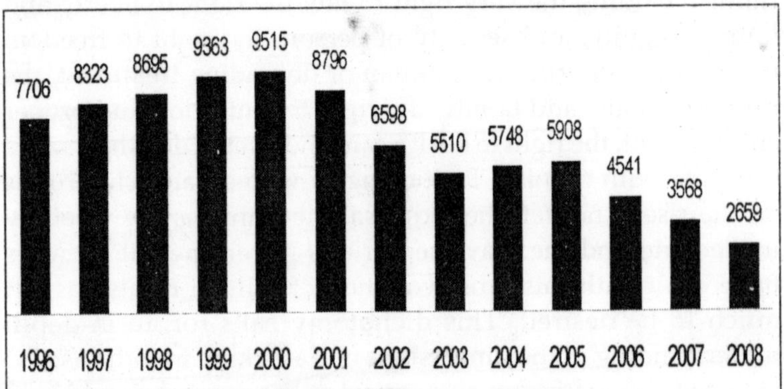


*Source:* National Crime Record Bureau of India.

**Figure 7: Total Reported Cases of Violation of Immoral Traffic Against Women (CP) Act (1996 to 2008)**

The data asserts that there are total 86930 reported cases of trafficking of the women violating Immoral Traffic (Prevention) Act in 13 years since 1996 to 2008. Noticeably 04.50 per cent cases of total reported cases of crime against women (1928858) have been constituted by the crime of the violation of Immoral Traffic (P) Act, which confirms this vicious crime as the sixth largest crime against women in India. The data establishes that in these 13 years average 6687 crimes against women violating the above said Act are reported in a year; average 18 cases every day, and average 1 case is reported after every 90 minutes. The data expresses several ups and downs in the number of cases since 1996 to 2008. The number of cases had increased to 1809 (23.47 per cent) cases from 1996 to 2000. But fortunately since 2001 to 2008, the number of cases decreased noticeably.

*Importation of Women/Girls*

Importation of women, particularly the girls is also a nasty crime against women and a gross violation of human rights.

The importation of women/girls in India is not a new phenomenon, but this cruel crime against women has been increasing very rapidly in the country, due to the absence of legislation of appropriate laws, and poor implementation of the law that exist in the country to curb the ferocious crime. If the investigations, studies and estimations of the NGOs and other non-governmental sources are to be believed, thousands of girls are imported to India every year from different parts of the world, particularly from Bangladesh, Sri Lanka, and Nepal etc. It is almost an impossible task to assess the exact or nearly precise number of the cases of importation in India. However, the data displayed by NCRB in its annual proceedings/reports, is the most reliable and most correctly the only official source to make one acquainted with the number of cases reported regarding the importation of women/girls in India.

As per NCRB, there were total 182 reported cases in India I 1996. In 1997, the number of cases was 78 which was followed by 146 cases in 1998, only 1 case in 1999, and 64 in 2000. In 2001 and 2002, the number of cases regarding importation of girls was 114 and 76 respectively. The NCRB had reported 46 cases in 2003, total 89 cases in 2004, and 149 cases in 2005. In 2006 the number of reported cases regarding importation of women was 67, which was followed by 61 cases in 2007 and 676 cases in 2008.

The data shows that total 1140 cases of importation of girls are reported throughout India in 13 years from 1996 to 2008.

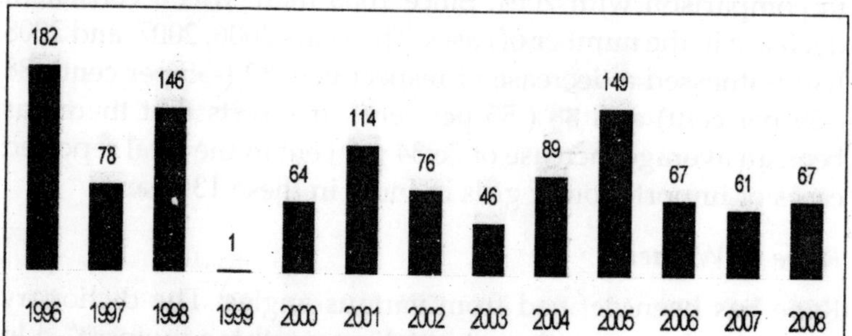


*Source:* National Crime Record Bureau of India.

**Figure 8: Total Reported Cases of Importation of Girls in India (1996 to 2008)**

The number constitutes 0.059 per cent of the total reported cases of crime against women in India since 1996 to 2008, which confirms the crime of 'importation of women' as the tenth largest crime against women in India. The data further asserts that average 88 cases of importation of women are reported in India every year; average 7.5 cases are reported every month in India regarding aforesaid crime against women. It further establishes that average 2 cases of importation of girls in India are reported in a week. Perceptibly, the number of cases regarding the importation of girls has several ascends and descends as far as the analysis of the data since 1996 to 2008 is concerned. In 1997 (182 cases) there was a decrease of 104 (-57.14 per cent) cases in comparison with 1997 (78 cases). While in 1998 (146 cases) there was an increase of 68 (+87.17 per cent) cases in comparison with 1997 (78 cases). In 1999 (1case) a huge decrease of 145 (-99.31 per cent) was noticed in comparison with 1998 (146 cases). In the year 2000 (64 cases) there was again a massive increase of 63 cases (+98.43 per cent) in contrast with 1999 (1 case). The year 2001(114 cases) had witnesses the increase of 50 (+78.12 per cent) cases in comparison with 2000 (64 cases). Contrarily, the year 2002 (76 cases) noticed a decrease of 38 (-33.33 per cent) cases in comparison with 2001 (114 cases). The decrease in the number continued and a further decline of 30 (-39.47) cases was noticed in 2003 in comparison with 2002. The year 2004 witnessed an increase of 43 (+93.46 per cent) cases in comparison with 2003. In 2005 the increase in the number of cases was noticed as 60 (+67.41 per cent) cases in comparison with 2004. Since 2006 there was a consistent decrease in the number of cases. The years 2006, 2007, and 2008 had witnessed a decrease of respectively 82 (-55 per cent), 88 (-59 per cent) and 88 (-55 per cent). It asserts that there has been an average increase of 26.34 per cent in the total reported cases of importation of girls in India in these 13 years.

### *Rape of Women*

Rape has been defined from various angles. The dictionary meaning of rape is "the act of taking anything by force".[54] In legal terms rape is a serious offence of indecent assault on a female committed with the intent of knowledge to outrage her modesty. Generally rape means an act of sexual intercourse by a man or men with the women/women without her consent.[55] In the Indian Penal Code, rape is categorized under 'offences against human body'. But no separate law exists for rape. Rape is the vilest form of violence against a woman where the victim, the woman, has to carry the stigma of the society for the rest of her life in spite of the fact that she is not a consenting party to it. Rape is an assertion of power and not an act of lust. Violence on women is an extension of 'patriarchy', which means 'male rule'. The two main features of patriarchy are sexual power and supremacy. By rape it is asserted that "dominance is the male temperament and subordination the women's. Rape is a conscious process of intimidation by which man keeps woman in a state of fear in the confidence that the victim will not reveal the event to others. It is not like murder to him, though in actuality he murders the life of a woman.[56]

Rape is universally considered an enormous crime against women. In reality, rape has been described as a primary mistrust of control in a patriarchal society and often used as a mechanism of revenge or punishment.[57] At the same time, rape is also used as a challenge of the honour of the male members of the family in various circumstances. The act of rape occurs usually due to various reasons such as an explosion of pent-up sexual impulse, which is motivated by sex desire, an impulse to punish or hurt the victim, or as part of robbery or terrorist activity by an aggressive criminal. In the Indian Penal Code, rape is defined in Sections 375 and 376 as an offence cognizable, non-bailable and non-compoundable.[58] The offence of rape is legally established by the fact of penetration, however slight. In this context, the term 'consent' becomes important and has been misinterpreted often. Thus the trial of rape cases is an interpretation of legal terminologies with a human touch.

The cases of rape have risen alarmingly in recent years despite the government's monitoring and the constitutional and legal safeguards provided for women. According to the all-India figures from the National Crime Records Bureau

(NCRB), the number of rape cases is spiraling to dizzying heights each year.

According to the statistical data of NCRB of India (1996 to 2008) total 14846 cases of the rape of the women were reported throughput India in 1996. The number of the cases of rape in 1997was 15330; in 1998 the number was 15151, which further reached to 15468 in 1999. The number of cases of rapes throughout India was 16496 in 2000, 16075 in 2001 and 16373 in 2002. The NCRB had reported 15847 cases of rape in 2003, total 18233 cases in 2004 and 18359 cases in 2005. The number of cases of rape in India kept on increasing every year and it reached to 19348 cases in 2006, total 20737 cases in 2007, and 21467 cases in 2008.

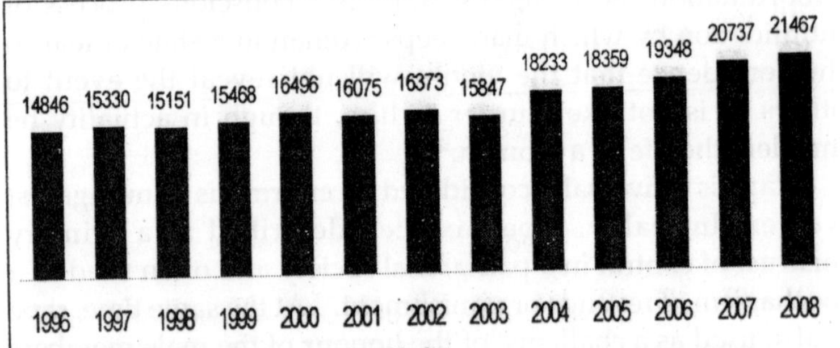


*Source:* National Crime Record Bureau of India.

**Figure 9: Total Reported Cases of Rape of Women (1996 to 2008)**

The data discloses that there are total 223730 registered cases of rape in India in 13 years since 1996 to 2008. It constitutes 11.59 per cent of total number of cases regarding crime against women in India, which confirms the crime of 'rape of women' the fourth major crime against women in India. The data further corroborates that average 17210 cases of rape are reported in India every year; average 47 cases of rape are reported every day; average 2 cases of rape are reported every hour and average 1 case of rape is reported in India after every 30 minutes. Furthermore, there is a constant increase in the number of reported cases of the rape of women in India. The number of cases has increased to 6621 (44.59 per cent) cases after 13 years from 14846 reported cases to 21467 cases in 2008. After ten years, the number of total reported cases of rape has increased to 5999 (38.78 per cent) cases from 15468 cases in 1999 to 21467 cases in 2008.

### *Sexual Harassment of Women*

Sexual harassment is a violation of a woman's freedom of her person, her dignity, bodily integrity and sexual autonomy. A woman may be sexually harassed virtually anywhere: in the workplace, educational institutions, hospitals, marketplace, shops, bars, discos, elevators, Internet bars, public buses, trains and even in planes. Sexual harassment occurs if the impugned act is unwelcome or unsolicited.

In China, 80% of working women experienced sexual harassment at some stage of their career. In Germany, a survey indicated that 93% of working women were victims of sexual harassment as of 1998. Approximately 6 of 10 nurses in Australia have experienced sexual harassment. In Hong Kong most complaints received by the Equal Opportunities Commission (EOC) in some recent years were of sexual harassment. In the United States over 50% of employed women had been sexually harassed. In Canada 51% of women reported having experienced sexual violence at least once and in Singapore almost 50% women have been victims of sexual harassment. The above statistics affirms that sexual harassment is a global problem.[59]

India, in particular, presents irreconcilable contradictions. India produced the world famous book, Kama Sutra on the art of love making. Deriving inspiration from this classic on sex, in the 10th or 11th century, were built Khajuraho stone temples. On these temples are carvings explicitly depicting sexual acts by two or more persons in provocative postures. Women are also worshipped as goddesses in India. But on the other hand, they are objects of torture and harassment.[60]

India does not have any specific legislation on sexual harassment yet. However, the Supreme Court of India in Vishakha15 has declared sexual harassment to be unlawful under constitutional guarantee of the right to life and gender equality, other constitutional provisions, and international conventions. The Supreme Court defines sexual harassment to include any unwelcome physical contact or advances, demands or requests for sexual favours, sexually coloured remarks, displaying of pornography and other unwelcome physical, verbal or nonverbal conduct of a sexual nature.[61] (The Supreme Court requires all workplaces, educational institutions and organised service sectors, private or public with more than 50 employees to introduce sexual harassment prevention policy and set up a complaints committee to investigate into sexual harassment complaints. The complaints committee is required to submit an inquiry report which is treated as the last word on the incident. Prior to Vishakha, the only remedy for sexual harassment was to initiate a criminal proceeding. The then law did not specifically provide for awarding monetary compensation. In Vishakha, the Supreme Court did not deal with the question of compensation to the victim. However in subsequent cases the courts have granted tort damages to sexual harassment victims.[62]

The National Commission for Women (NCW) can intervene where the Vishakha guidelines are not followed by an employer.[63] The NCW drafted the Sexual Harassment of Women at their Workplace (Prevention) Bill which is still pending before Parliament. The Bill does not apply to agriculture, construction and home based unorganised work sectors, among others and excludes men and same sex harassment from its purview.[64] However it relaxes the burden of proof on a woman complaining of sexual harassment, and there is a proposal to amend the Bill to specifically cover students, research scholars and those working in unorganized sector.[65]

According to the NCRB, there 5671 reported cases of sexual harassment through out India. The number was followed by 5796 cases in 1997, total 8054 cases in 1998, and 8854 cases in the year 1999. In 2000, there were total 11024 reported cases of sexual harassment of women. The NCRB had reported 9746 cases in 2001, as many as 10155 cases in 2002 and 12325 cases in 2003. Sexual harassment of women had narrowly declined afterwards with 10001 cases of such type in 2004, total 9984 in

2005, and 9966 cases in 2006. In the year 2007 and 2008, there were respectively 10950 and 12214 cases of sexual harassment of women.

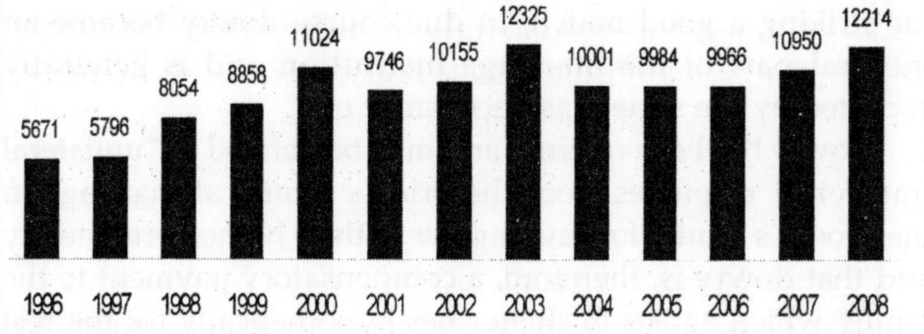


*Source:* National Crime Record Bureau of India.

**Figure 10: Total Reported Cases of Sexual Harassment of Women (1996 to 2008)**

The data states that total 124744 cases of sexual harassment of women are reported in India in 13 years from 1996 to 2008. The number of cases constitutes 6.46 per cent of the total number of crime against women, which establishes 'sexual harassment of women' as the fifth largest crime against women in India. The data adds that average 9596 cases are reported in India in a year and average 26 cases every day in India, regarding the sexual harassment of women. It confirms that average at least 1 case of sexual harassment of women is reported in India every hour. The data of the year 2008 depicts that in recent times, average 1018 cases of sexual harassment of women in a month; average 254 cases in a week; while average 36 cases every day; and average 1 case after every 45 minutes has been reported throughout India. The number of cases regarding sexual harassment of women in India is increasing year after year. After 13 years, there is increase of 6543 cases (115.37 per cent) from 5671 cases in 1996 to 12214 cases in 2008. After ten years, the number of cases has increased to 3356 cases (37.88 per cent) from 8856 cases in 1999 to 12214 cases in 2008.

## *Dowry Related Crimes against Women*

Dowry system is as old as man is. The dowry system is a social evil. It is prevalent in all parts of India and almost in all the countries of the world. In India many of the traditional customs have been given up, but the custom of dowry has not only continued, but flourished over the years. Even in the old age the dowry system was in vogue and dowry was used as means for striking a good match. In due course dowry became an integral part of the marriage institution and is generally accepted by the society as necessarily evil.

Dowry has been referred and may be defined as "unilateral transfer of resources from the bride's family at marriage to the groom's family for inviting her to their home permanently and that dowry is, therefore, a compensatory payment to the family which agrees to shelter her hypothetically for the rest of her life.[66]

Even though India has legally abolished the institution of dowry, dowry-related violence is actually on the rise. Dowry system as a social problem has acquired grave dimensions in recent years and all attempts for a legal solution have not produced the desired result. The gravity of the situation may also be judged from the fact hat the National Commission of the Women has recommended for the scraping of the dowry Prohibition Act. It only shows that the reality of the situation is beyond the legislative and enforcement activities.

The dowry custom has been practiced in Indian society since centuries. Although, the law has made the provision of equal inheritance rights for the girls from the property of their parents, but in majority of Indian families the boy has inheritance rights while the girl is given a hefty sum at the time of her marriage.[67] The problem of dowry is complex enough that it is quite difficult to trace out all causes of dowry. Though, there are several reasons for the prevalence of the dowry system, but the chief among all is that it is a necessary precondition for marriage. There is a widespread fear among the parents of the girls that their daughters will never get married without dowry.[68] Moreover, the prevalence of globalized economy has made the Indian society more materialistic and more possessive about financial and materialist benefits. The price tag for the groom is now bigger and bolder. The emergence of an affluent middle class, the torchbearer of social change in modern India, is the main factor for the perpetuation of the dowry system.[69] The daughter's parents are ready to pay a handsome amount as dowry and they run behind the eligible educated grooms. Most marriages are arranged by families, and a man who does not marry for love, he can marry for other considerations such as possessions. For this man and his family, a woman becomes the ticket to his shortcut richness through the system of dowry. There are a number of things people desire to have in their own houses but cannot afford; they use the opportunity of a son's marriage to get them.[70]

Seldom has there been so firm a consensus on a social issue in India as the one among scholars, journalists, feminists, politicians, legislators, and the police today that the custom of dowry has a causal relationship to prejudice and violence against women. The view that the murders of young wives are a special category of "cultural crime" linked to a high-caste Hindu cultural practice of dowry is unshakably entrenched. Women's organizations have designated the burning of wives baldly as "dowry murder." Although it is true that dowry—clothes, jewelry, household goods, cash, and property that a bride brings to a marriage—is neither new nor unique to India, just as violence against women is not an Indian cultural peculiarity, the view that dowry is a harmful, even dangerous institution has more credence in India than elsewhere.[71]

*Dowry Deaths*

According to the statistical data of NCRB of India, there occurred total reported 5513 cases of dowry deaths in India in the year 1996. As many as 6006 cases in 1997, total 6975 cases in 1998, and 6699 cases in 1999 regarding dowry deaths were reported in India. In the year 2000, 2001 and 2002, there were respectively 6995, 6851, and 6822 reported dowry deaths. The number of total reported dowry deaths was further reported by NCRB as 6208 in 2003, total 7026 in 2004 and 6787 in 2005. The number further increased in the succeeding years and there were total 7618 and 8093 reported dowry deaths in the years 2006 and 2007 respectively. In the year 2008, there were as many as 8172 cases of dowry deaths reported throughout India.

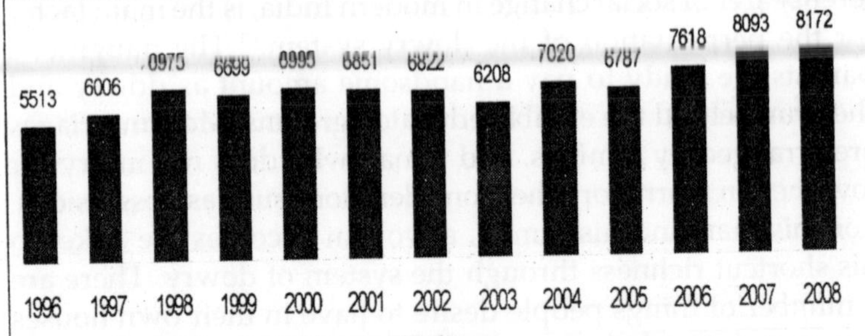


*Source:* National Crime Record Bureau of India.

**Figure 11: Total Reported Cases of Dowry Deaths in India (1996 to 2008)**

The data asserts that total 82978 cases of dowry deaths are reported in India since 1996 to 2008. It constitutes 4.30 per cent of the total reported cases of 'crime against women', which establishes the crime of 'dowry deaths' as the seventh largest crime against women in India. The data further reveals that average 6383 cases of dowry deaths are reported in India every year; average 18 cases of dowry deaths are reported in India every day; and average 1 case of dowry deaths is reported in India after every 80 minutes. There are several ascends and descends in the number of cases year after year. There was an increase of (+8.94 per cent) cases in 1997 in contrast to 1996. The year 1998 noticed increase of (+16.13 per cent) in comparison with 1997. In 1999, there was a decrease of 276 (-3.95 per cent) cases in comparison with 1998. In 2000 the number of cases had increased to 296 (+4.71 per cent) in comparison with 1999. Since 2001 there had been a constant decrease in the number of cases for three years. The number of cases had decreased to 787 (-11.25 per cent) in 2003 (6208 cases) in comparison with 2000 (6995 cases). There was an increase of 818 (-13.17 per cent) cases in 2004 in comparison with 2003. In 2005 there was a decline of 239 (-3.40 per cent) cases in comparison with 2004. In 2006 there was an increase of 831 (+12.24 per cent) cases in comparison with 2005; a further increase of 475 (+6.23 per cent) was witnessed in 2007 in comparison with 2006; and an increase of 79 (+0.97 per cent) cases was noticed in 2008 in comparison with 2007. There was an over all increase of 17.45 per cent cases regarding dowry deaths throughout India since 1996 to 2008.

*Violation of Dowry Prohibition Act*

According to the NCRB of India, total 2647 cases were reported regarding violation of Dowry Prohibition Act throughout India. In 1997, the number of reported cases was 2685, which was followed by 3578 cases in 1998, total 3064 cases in 1999, and 2876 cases in 2000. There were 3222 cases in 2001, overall 2816 cases in 2002, and 2684 cases in 2003 regarding the violation of Dowry Prevention Act. As per NCRB, 3592 cases in 2004, total 3204 cases in 2005, and 4504 cases in 2006 were reported. A huge increase was observed afterwards and the NCRB had reported 5623 cases in 2007 and 5555 cases in 2008 regarding the violation of the above mentioned Act.

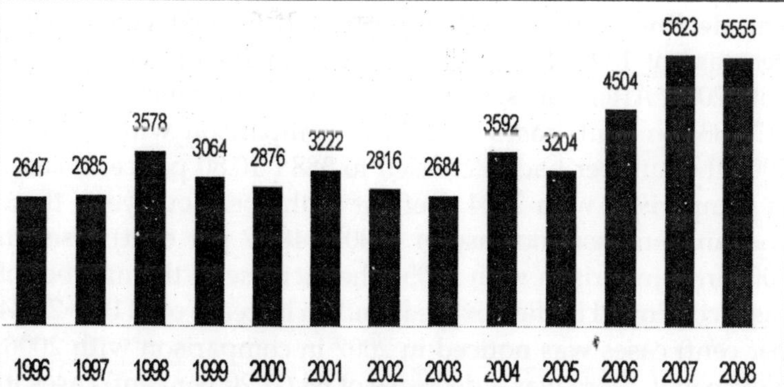


*Source:* National Crime Record Bureau of India.

**Figure 12: Total Reported Cases of Violation of Dowry Prohibition Act (1996 to 2008)**

The data divulges that total 46050 cases are reported throughout India regarding violation of Dowry Prohibition Act in 13 years from 1996 to 2008. It constitutes 2.38 per cent of the total reported crime against women in India, which confirms reported crime of dowry demands, and dowry related violence as the eighth largest crime against women in India. The data further confirms that in these 13 years, average 3542 cases are reported regarding dowry demands, and dowry related violence in India every year; average 10 crimes of such type are reported every day; and average 1 case regarding such type of crime against women is reported in India after every 144 minutes. The number of cases related to violation of Dowry Prohibition Act depicts several ups and downs year after year. There was a thin increase of 38 (+1.43 per cent) cases in the number 1997 in comparison with 1996. But the number had increased to 893 (+33.25 per cent) cases after one year in 1998 in comparison with 1997. In 1999, the number of cases had decreased to 514 (-14.36 per cent) cases in comparison with 1998. The year 2000 had further witnesses a decrease of 188 (-6.13 per cent) cases in comparison with 1999. Contrary to the decrease witnessed consistently in two years, there was increase of 346 (+12.03 per cent) cases in 2001 in comparison with the year 2000. Noticeably, there was again a decrease of 406 (-12.06 per cent) cases in 2002 in comparison with 2001. The decline in the number continued in next year with a decrease of 132 (-4.68 per cent) cases in 2003 in comparison with 2002. Afterwards, there was a noteworthy increase of 908 (+33.83 per cent) cases in 2004 in comparison with 2003. In 2005 the number had decreased to 388 (-10.80 per cent) cases in comparison with 2004. Defiant to the pervious year, there was an immense increase of 1300 (+40.57 per cent) cases in 2006 in comparison with 2005. The increase in the number of cases continued in the next year and an increase of 1119 (+24.84 per cent) cases was noticed in 2007 in comparison with 2006. Noticeably, there was a decrease of 68 (-1.20 per cent) cases in 2008 in comparison with 2007. There is an overall increase of 96.72 noticed in the total reported cases of violation of Dowry Prohibition Act throughout India since 1996 to 2008.

### *Indignity of Women*

According to Oxford Compact Dictionary and Thesaurus, "indignity is a thing that causes you to feel ashamed or embarrassed."[72] The word indignity is generally interpreted to include any kind of inappropriate behavior such as thievery, verbal abuse cursing, ridicule, mistreating and misbehaving.[73] Indignity of women includes lack of voice and dignity in the family and/or society, to be treated as a domestic servant at home to be treated as a sex symbol in the society, not being respected by parents, husband, in-laws or children.[74] In other words indignity towards women includes all activities, feelings, gestures etc. that may feel a woman ashamed, embarrassed, and undignified.

In India, where woman is acknowledged as *Mata, Devi, Shakti, Annapurna* in theological and mythological literature, almost all women daily feel undignified and embarrassed just due to their sex. The graph of the complaints against the violation of the rights of women has been increasing consistently. The perturbing increase can be noticed from the fact that the NHRC, during 1998-1999, had registered only 27 complaints regarding indignity of women ; during 1997-1998, 17 complaints; during 1996-1997, total 317 complaints; during 1995-1996, total 93 complaints; during 1994-1995, total 69 complaints; and during 1993-1994, only 3 complaints related to Indignity of Women. The data shows that the NHRC had registered 526 complaints of Dignity of Women in first six years (1993-94 to 1998-99) of its establishment. In the successive years, that huge number was crossed by a noticeable margin of 31 complaints with 547 complaints in just three years (2004-05 to 2006-07).[75]

### *Violation of Indecent Representation of Women (Prevention) Act*

The Act prohibits indecent representation of women through advertisements or in publications, writings, paintings, and figures or in any other manner and for matters connected therewith or incidental thereto.

According to the NCRB of India, there were total 96 reported cases of the violation of Indecent Representation of Women (Prevention) Act in the year 1996. In 1997, the number of reported cases was 73; in 1998 the number had reached to 190, which was followed by 222 cases in 1999. Afterwards, there had been a consistent and noteworthy increase in the reported cases of the violation of above said Act and the NCRB had reported 662 cases in 2000, total 1052 cases in 2001, and 2508 cases in 2002. There was a slight decrease in the number in the successive years with 1043 reported cases in 2003, and as many as 1378 cases in 2004. The number of reported cases was 2917 in 2005, which had declined to 1562 cases in 2006 and 1200 cases in 2007. The decline continued and the number of reported cases regarding violation of Indecent Representation of Women (Prevention) Act was 1025 in 2008.

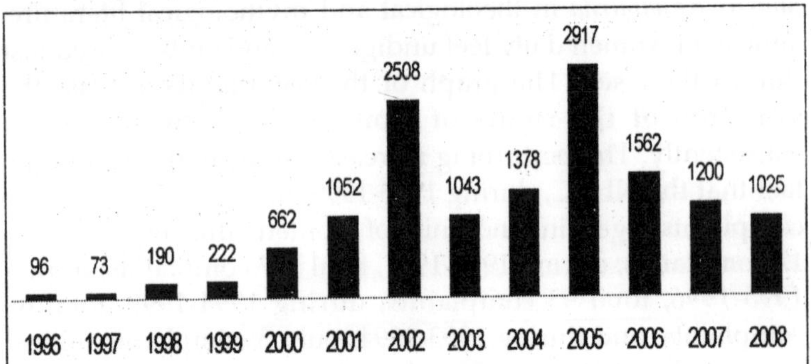


*Source:* National Crime Record Bureau of India.

**Figure 13: Total Reported Cases of Violation of Indecent Representation of Women Act (1996 to 2008)**

The data expresses that there are total 13928 cases reported in India regarding violation of Indecent Representation of Women Act in 13 years since 1996 to 2008. It formulates 0.72 per cent of the total reported cases of crime against women in India since 1996 to 2008. This percentage confirms the crime of violation of Indecent Representation of Women Act as the ninth largest crime against women. The data depicts that average 1071 cases are reported throughout India regarding the aforesaid crime against women in a year. It further establishes that average 3 cases of such crime against women are reported in India every day; while average 1 case of indecent representation of women is reported in India after every 8 hours. There are several ups and downs in the number of reported cases regarding violation of Indecent Representation of Women Act since 1996 to 2008. The year 1997 witnessed a decrease of 23 (-23.95 per cent) in comparison with 1996. The year 1998 noticed an increase of 117 (+160.27 per cent) In contrast with 1997. Afterwards, there was a consistent, rapid and massive ascendance of the number of cases since 1999 to 2002. There was an enormous increase of 2286 (+1029.72 per cent) cases in 2002 in comparison with 1999. The year 2003 witnessed a decrease of 1465 (-58.41 per cent) cases in contrast with 2002. However, the year 2004 noticed an increase of 335 (+32.11 per cent) over 2003. Similarly, in 2005 there was an increase of 1540 (+111.75 per cent) in comparison with 2004. However, the years 2006, 2007 and 2008 noticed a constant decrease. The year 2006 witnessed a decrease of 1355 (-46.45 per cent) cases in contrast with 2005. The year 2007 noticed a decrease of 362 (-23.17 per cent) cases in comparison with 2006; while in 2008, a decrease of 175 (-14.58 per cent) cases was witnessed in contrast with 2007.

### *Female Foeticide and Infanticide*

Female Foeticide has been a common practice in India since centuries. Indian census has always shown a gendered imbalance. This marked gap between boys and girls which has nationwide implications is the result of decisions made at the most local level- the family. Sex selective abortion is a fairy recent phenomenon but its root can be traced back to the age old practice of female infanticide.

Sex selective abortions cases have become a significant social phenomenon in several parts of India. It transcends all castes, class and communities and even the North-South dichotomy. The girl children become the target of attack even before they are born. The advent of technology and misuse of pre-natal sex detection and also attitude of the unscrupulous medical practitioners, who are facilitating the female foeticide through induced abortions. There are strict laws and penal actions against violators, but the laws have not worked. Over 10 million female fetuses have been aborted in India in the past two decades. It is reported that about 4,000 female babies are aborted in Tamil Nadu every year. Since most deliveries in rural areas take place at home or unrecognized delivery homes, there is no record of the exact number of births and deaths that take place.[76] Government officials even suspect that the disproportionate abortion of female foetuses may be major underlying cause of the recent decline in the nation's sex ratio. In 1971 there were 930 females for every 1,000 males. A decade later this figure had increased to 934, but by 1991, instead of continuing to rise, the ratio dropped to 927, lower than the 1971 figure. Up to 2004, India has 882 girls per 1,000 boys. This sex ratio is one of the lowest in the world.[77] The following is the sex ratio chart from 1901 to 2001.

| *Year* | *Sex Ratio (Female per 1,000 males)* |
|---|---|
| 1901 | 972 |
| 1911 | 964 |
| 1921 | 955 |
| 1931 | 950 |
| 1941 | 945 |
| 1951 | 946 |
| 1961 | 941 |
| 1971 | 930 |
| 1981 | 934 |
| 1991 | 927 |
| 2001 | 933 |

*Source:* Census of India, 2001.

The sex ratio as per 2001 census the females are 933 per 1000 males. Although, a marginal improvement of six points in the overall female to male sex ratio in India from 927 in 1991 to 933 in 2001 is an encouraging development, the massive decline of 18 points in the juvenile sex ratio (age group of 0 to 6) from 945 to 927 in the country after 1981 is what shows the extensive female foeticide in India.It is pertinent to note that the figures show the fall in the juvenile sex ratio is much higher in the economically developed States in India. There is step fall in sex ratio in the States like Punjab, Haryana, Gujarat and Maharashtra, along with the Union Territories of Delhi and Chandigarh. The situation is worse in the northern States including Punjab and Haryana. In Punjab there are only 874 females per 1000 males.[78] The situation in Haryana, Gujarat and Maharashtra is also similar- the females are 861, 921 and 922 respectively per 1000 males.[79] Kerala is the only state where females are 1058 per 1000 males.[80]

It is a matter to be anxious that Sex selective abortion cases have become a significant social phenomenon in several parts of India. It transcends all castes, class and communities and even in the North South dichotomy. The girl children become target of attack even before they are born. Reportedly in a well known Abortion Centre in Mumbai, after undertaking the sex determination tests, out of the 15914 abortions performed during 1984-85, almost 100 per cent were those of girl fetuses. Similarly, a survey report of women's centre in Mumbai found that out of 8000 foetuses aborted inn six city hospitals 7999 foetuses were of girls. It is reported that about 4000 female babies are aborted in Tamil Nadu every year.[81] Sex determination tests are widely resorted to even in the remotest rural areas. Since most deliveries in rural areas take place at home there is no record of the exact number of birth/deaths that take place. Therefore, it is difficult to success the magnitude of the problem. However, the fact remains that the natural right to be born are being denied to the female child. Since all religions treated abortion as immoral, and contrary to divine law, this blanket ban on abortion, resulted in illegal abortions and risking the life of the woman.

### *Female Infanticide*

Another form of eliminating the girl child has been the practice of female infanticide. It is a deliberate and intentional act of killing a female child within one year of its birth either directly by using poisonous organic and inorganic chemicals or indirectly by deliberate neglect to feed the infant by either one of the parents or other family members.[82] It is reported that female infanticide existed in India since 1789 in several districts of Rajasthan, along the western shores of Gujarat- Surat and Kutch- among a clan of Rajputs in eastern part of Uttar Pradesh. Prevalence of female infanticide, in the post independence period, has been reported from Tamil Nadu, Bihar, Orissa, Rajasthan and Maharashtra.[83] Legally infanticide amounts to homicide and all legal provisions applicable to the offence of homicide are applicable to infanticide. Female infanticide has been still in practice killing thousands of female babies every year, but it happens very rare that the accused of female infanticide are traced and punished by the law. India is one of the few countries where males significantly outnumber females, and this imbalance has increased over the time. India's maternal mortality rates in rural areas are among the world's highest. From a global perspective, Indian accounts for 9 percent of all lives births and 27 percent of all maternal deaths.[84] There seems to be a consensus that higher female mortality between ages one and five and high maternal mortality rates result in a deficit of females in the population. Deaths of young girls in India exceed those of young boys by over 300,000 each year, and every sixth infant death is especially due to gender discrimination.[85] Of the 15 million baby girls born in India each year, nearly 25 percent will not live to see their 15th birthday.[86]

According to a report by the United Nations Children's Fund, up to 50 million girls and women are missing from India's population as a result of systematic gender discrimination in India. The disastrous impact of the consumerist culture spawned by globalization has been widely held to account by social scientists for the spread of infanticide in India.[87]There are instances like leaving a few days' old girl-child near the gates of governmental Health Centers, Juvenile Centers, Temples and Churches leaving baby's fate to God. Selling girl child for a few hundred rupees to childless couples is another atrocity.

Several incentives and schemes are introduced by the Government of India to reduce Infant Mortality Rate in India and to discourage the practice of female infanticide. To combat the situation, Government has enacted Pre-natal Diagnostic Techniques (Regulation and Prevention of Misuse) Act, 1994 to provide for the regulation of the use of pre-natal diagnostic techniques for the purpose of detecting genetic or metabolic disorders or chromosomal abnormalities or certain congenital malformation or sex linked disorders and for the prevention of the misuse of such techniques for the purpose of pre-natal sex determination leading to female foeticde. Later, the Act was amended with effect from February 14, 2003, and was renamed the Pre-Conception and Pre-Natal Diagnostic Techniques

(Prohibition of Sex Selection) Act (PCPNDT Act). Section 6 of the said Act, says about determination of sex prohibited. Further, Section 22 prohibits advertisements relating to pre-natal determination of sex and punishment for contravention. Section 23 (3) of the said Act lays don that any person who seeks the aid of a genetic counseling centre, a genetic laboratory or a genetic clinic, or of a medical geneticist, gynecologist or registered medical practitioner, for applying pre-natal diagnostic techniques on any pregnant women (unless there is evidence that she was compelled to under go such diagnostic techniques) for purposes other than those specified, shall be punishable with imprisonment or term that may extend to 3 years and with a fine which may extend to Rs. 10,000 and any subsequent conviction may involve imprisonment which may extend to 5 years and a fine of up to Rs. 50,000. The Supreme Court of India in its judgment has observed and issued directions to central and State governments, Union Territories, Central Supervisory Board and Appropriate authorities for proper implementation of the Act.

It is unfortunate that for one reason or the other, the practice of female infanticide still prevails despite the fact that gentle touch of a daughter and her voice has soothing effect on the parents. One of the reasons may be the marriage problems faced by the parents compelled with the dowry demand by the so-called educated and/or rich persons who are well placed in the society. The traditional system of female infanticide where by female baby was done away with after birth by poisoning or letting her choke on husk continues in a different form by taking advantage of advance medical techniques. Unfortunately, developed medical science is misused to get rid of girl child before birth. Knowing fully well that it is immoral and unethical as well as it may amount to an offence; foetus of a girl child is aborted by qualified or unqualified doctors or compounders. This has affected overall sex ratio in various States where female infanticide is prevailing without any hindrance.

Indian society, like most of the societies worldwide, is *patri-linear*, patriarchal and *patri-local*. According to Manu, a man has to be reborn as a man to attain *moksha* (redemption). A man cannot attain moksha unless he has a son to light his funeral pyre. Also, it says a woman who gives birth to only daughters may be left in the eleventh year of marriage. Obviously, it shows the gender bias in our male dominated society. The age old preference for sons is motivated by economic, religious, social and emotional desires and norms that favour males and make females less desirable. Parents expect sons- but not daughters- to provide financial and emotional care, especially in their old age. Sons add to family wealth and property, while daughters are married away to another husband. Sons perform important religious role and sons defend or exercise the family's power while daughters have to be defended and protected, creating a perceived burden on the household. This stereotype notion of women as 'burden' is one of the main reason behind female foeticide and infanticide. Other main reasons behind in rise of female foeticide and infanticide, emerging trend of the small family norm, practices like tradition of giving dowry, laws that govern property inheritance and the cultural perception about the familial name through the male line. The mortality of girl child is also high because of paternal discrimination against their daughters in terms of health care and nutrition. Another major reason behind female foeticide and infanticide is the centuries old tradition of considering the females as honour and pride of the families and clans. If any female is found to be involved in socially objectionable and unaccepted relations with any male, it is considered as the social dishonor, humiliation and a severe disrespect of the family and the whole clan which the female belongs to. There occur several cases of honour killings generally in India and particularly in Punjab and Haryana. The fear of the possibility of social humiliation in case of their daughters' pre-marital relations with any male, forbade the families to give birth to the girls.

### Personal Status Laws: Discriminatory to Women

The personal status laws of the religious communities discriminate against women in India. Under the Indian Divorce

Act of 1869, a Christian woman may demand divorce only in the case of spousal abuse and certain categories of adultery while for the man, adultery alone is sufficient. Under Islamic law, a Muslim husband may divorce his wife spontaneously and unilaterally, but there is no such provision for women. Islamic law also allows a man to have up to four wives but prohibits polyandry. The Hindu Succession Act provides equal inheritance rights to Hindu women, but married daughters are actually seldom given a share in parental property. Islamic law recognises a woman's right of inheritance but specifies that a daughter's share should be only one-half that of a son. In tribal land systems, notably in Bihar, tribal women do not have the right to own land. Other laws relating to ownership of assets and land accord women have little control over land use, retention or sale.[88]

Numerous laws exist to protect women's rights, including the Equal Remuneration Act, the Prevention of Immoral Traffic Act, the Sati (Widow Burning) Prevention Act, and the Dowry Prohibition Act. However, the Government often was unable to enforce these laws, especially in rural areas in which traditions were deeply rooted. According to press reports, the rate of acquittal in dowry death cases was high, and because of court backlogs it took 6 to 7 years on average to rule on such cases.

Prostitution has been common, with an estimated 2.3 million prostitutes in the country, some 575,000 of who are children. Many indigenous tribal women are forced into sexual exploitation. In recent years, prostitutes began to demand legal rights, licenses, and reemployment training, especially in Mumbai, New Delhi, and Calcutta. In January the Government signed the South Asian Association for Regional Cooperation (SAARC) Convention on Prevention and Combating Trafficking in Women and Children for Prostitution. The country is a significant source, transit point, and destination for many thousands of trafficked women.

The law prohibits discrimination in the workplace, but enforcement is inadequate. In both rural and urban areas, women are paid less than men for doing the same job. Women are experiencing economic discrimination in access to employment and credit, which acted as an impediment to women owning a business. The promotion of women to managerial positions within businesses often is slower than that of males. State governments have supported micro credit programs for women that have begun to have an impact in many rural districts.

The Government has continued to review legislation on marriage; it passed the Indian Divorce (Amendment) Act during 2001; the act widely had been criticized as biased against women. The Act has placed limitations on interfaith marriages and specified penalties, such as 10 years' imprisonment, for clergymen who contravened its provisions. Under the Act, no marriage in which one party is a non-Christian may be celebrated in a church. Under many tribal land systems, notably in Bihar, tribal women do not have the right to own land. Other laws relating to the ownership of assets and land accorded women little control over land use, retention, or sale. However, several exceptions do exist, such as in Ladakh and Meghalaya, where women have several husbands and can control the family inheritance.

In the circumstances, when the terms like 'women rights', 'women emancipation', 'feminism', 'gender rights' have been gaining much more recognition and reputation at global level. In the scenario where all developed democracies, especially the Western World has been becoming more and more liberal in favour of women rights, India has so far failed to complement with the countries boasting to establish a conducive legal, social, political, economic and cultural environment to make the women rights a reality. There are some suggestions and recommendations to improve the state of women rights in India.

**Suggestions and Recommendations**

- Empowering women and girls is not only a worthy goal in its own right but also a key strategy for eliminating violence. Women will never escape violence as long as they are financially dependent on men and derive their social value exclusively from their role as wife and mother.

- Eliminate laws that discriminate against women and children.
- Strengthen women in leadership and decision-making.
- Increase access to education for women and girls.
- Increase women's access to and control over economic resources.
- Increase women's access to health information and women's control over their own bodies.
- Improve women's self-esteem and sense of personal power.
- The needs of the victims should be taken proper care. The needs of victims are complex. A woman in crisis needs physical safety, emotional support, and assistance in resolving such issues as child support, custody, and employment.
- To change the pshyche of the men, there is a huge need to approach ot the men. Working with men to change their behavior is an important part of any solution to the problem of violence against women. To date,
- The useless and feminine-contrary cultural ritual and paradigms should be changed in the women's favour. Ending violence against women means changing the community norms and cultural attitudes and beliefs that give rise to men's abusive behavior toward women and that permit it to persist.
- Systematic efforts should be made to organise large-scale awareness programmes and campaigns in order to disseminate gender-just values that should counter the ideology of patriarchy and conservative thinking about sex and sexuality. In order to achieve these, the following measures may be considered.
- National Commission for Women should be given more and real powers. It should more enthusiastically collaborate with human rights organizations and NGOs.
- The capacity and dignity of the law forcing agencies should be strengthened. The NGOs, especially those working for

the welfare of women should be given more administrative assistance in terms of financial and logistic support so that they can combat the crime and violence agaisnt women at the grass-root level.

- A massive community awakening programme against the trafficking of women should be launched at the grass-root level by forming Community Based Anti-Trafficking Watch Group (CBAWG).

Despite the magnitude of the problem, India has not adopted a holistic approach to deal with the problem of violation of women rights. Legislations declaring various acts violating women rights, unlawful, judicial decisions awarding damages, or complaints committees giving out punishment cannot control the widespread prevalence of violence and crime against women. The whole society, including political leaders, social scientists and religious reformers should be involved in spreading the message that women are the equal dignified, important and necessary part of the society as comparison to men, and violation of their rights and liberties is a heinous and demeaning practice. The media, the television, radio and newspapers must engage in concerted attempts to change the mindset of harassers.

## References

1. SWAYAM (NGO), *The Status of Women: A Reality Check*, SWAYAM Publications, Kolkata, 2003, p. 1.
2. Karen M. Offen, "Defining Feminism: A Comparative Historical Approach", *Journal of Women in Culture and Society*, 14:1 Autumn, 1988, p. 45.
3. Rhonda Y. Williams, *The politics of Public Housing: Black Women's Struggles Against Urban Inequality*, Oxford University Press, London, 2004, p. 11.
4. Richard J. Evans, *The Feminists: Women's Emancipation Movements in Europe, America, and Australia*, Taylor & Francis, UK, 1977, p. 39.
5. Naomi B. Lynn, *United Nations Decade for Women World Conference* (Volume 4), Routledge Publications, New York, 1984, p. 70.
6. Stephanie Garrett, *Gender*, Routledge Publications, New York, 1987, p. 129.
7. Judith Worell, *Encyclopedia of Women and Gender: Sex Similarities and Differences* (Volume 2), Academic Press, London, 2001, p. 1052.

8. Usha Venkitakrishnan & Sunil George Kurien, *Rape Victims in Kerala* (Discussion Paper No. 52), Kerala Research Programme on Local Level Development, Centre for Development Studies, Thiruvanathapuram, 2003, p. 7.
9. *Ibid.*
10. United Nations, *Ending Violence against Women: From Words to Action*, United Nations Publications, 2006, p. iii.
11. Kofi Annan as quoted in UNIFEM, *Not a Minute More: Ending Violence Against Women*, UNIFEM New York, 2003, p. 8.
12. Lori Heise, et al., "Ending Violence against Women" (A Report), published in *Population Reports* (Research Journal by the Population Information Program, Johns Hopkins University School of Public Health), Serial L, No. 11, December, 1999, p. 1.
13. Cheywa Spindel, Elisa Levy & Melissa Connor, *With an End in Sight: Strategies from the UNIFEM (United Nations Development Fund for Women) Fund to Eliminate Violence against Women*, UNIFEM, New York, 2000, pp. 10-12.
14. UNICEF, "Domestic Violence against Women and Girls", *Innocenti Digest*, No. 6, June 2000, p. 2.
15. United Nations General Assembly, *Declaration on the Elimination of Violence against Women*, Proceedings of the 85th Plenary Meeting, Geneva, December 20, 1993.
16. *Ibid.*
17. A. Butchart & D. Brown, "Non-Fatal Injuries due to Interpersonal Violence in Johannesburg-Soweto: Incidence, Determinants and Consequences", *Forensic Science* International, Vol. 52. 1991, pp. 35-51. Also see, N. Crowell, and A.W. Burgess (eds.), *Understanding Violence Against Women*, National Academy Press, Washington D.C., 1996, p. 225. Also see, P. Tjaden, and N. Thoennes, *Prevalence, Incidence and Consequences of Violence against Women: Findings from the National Violence against Women Survey*, Washington, D.C., National Institute of Justice, Center for Disease Control and Prevention, November 1998, p. 16.
18. United Nations, 2006, *op. cit.*, p. ii.
19. Charlotte Watts & Cathy Zimmerman, "Violence Against Women: Global Scope and Magnitude", *Lancet*, April 6, *2002*, Vol. 359, p. 1232.
20. Tianfu Wang, et al., "Partner Violence and Sexual Jealousy in China: A Population-Based Survey", in *Violence Against Women*, Vol. 15, No. 7, July 2009, p. 776-777.
21. Marie Vlachová & Lea Biason, *Making the World a More Secure Place: Combating Violence Against Women* (Policy Paper), Geneva Centre for the Democratic Control of Armed Forces (DCAF), Geneva, March 2004, pp. 4-5.
22. Catherine Su-Kum Tang & Fany Miu-Ching Cheung, "Definition of Violence Against Women: A Comparative Study in Chinese Societies

of Hong Kong, Taiwan, and the People's Republic of China" in *Journal of Interpersonal Violence*, Vol. 17, No. 6, June 2002, pp. 673.
23. Charlotte Watts & Cathy Zimmerman, 2002, op. cit, p. 1232.
24. United Nations Special Rapporteur on Violence against Women, Its Causes and Consequences, *15 years of The United Nations Special Rapporteur on Violence against Women (1994-2009): A Critical Review*, 2010, pp. 4-6.
25. United Nations, *Indicators to Measure Violence Against Women* (Report of Expert Group Meeting), October 2007, p. 5.
26. Jeffrey L. Edleson, et al., *Source Book on Violence against Women*, SAGE Publications, California, 2010, p. 152.
27. UNICEF, 2000, *op. cit.*, p. 2.
28. Lori Heise, "Violence against Women: Global Organizing for Change", in J.L. Edleson, and Z.C. Eisikovits (eds.), *Future Interventions with Battered Women and Their Families*, Sage Publications California, 1996, pp. 7-33.
29. Amitabha, Mukhopadhyaya, *Women in Indian Life and Society*, Punthi Pustak and Institute of Historical Studies, 1996, p. 77.
30. S.R. Bakshi, *Advanced History of Medieval India*, Anmol Publishers, New Delhi, 2003, p. 137.
31. Behula Khan, et al., (eds.) *History & Civics* (Volume 8), Ratna Sagar Publications, New Delhi, p. 80.
32. Reddy, *General Studies: History*, Tata McGraw Hill, New Delhi, 2004, p. 116.
33. Cherish Kramarae & Dale Spender, *International Encyclopedia of Women: Global Women's Issues and Knowledge*, (Volume 1), Routledge Publications, 2005, p. 144.
34. Malvika Singh, *Seminar: The Monthly Symposium*, Issue 377, RomeshRaj Trust, Delhi, 1991, p. 398.
35. Bhupendra Kumar Nagla, *Women, Crime and Law*, Rawat Publications, New Delhi, 1991, p. 87.
36. Vina Mazumdar & Kumud Sharma, "Sexual Division of Labour: Subordination of Women", in Mala Khullar, *Writing the Women's Movement: A Reader*, Zubaan Publications, New Delhi, 2005, p. 529.
37. M.K. Rao, *Strategies for Empowerment of Women in India*, Discovery Publishing House, New Delhi, 2005, p. 409.
38. Raj Bhanti, *Awareness Among Rural Women*, Himanshu Publications, Udaipur, 1994, p. 77.
39. Devaki Jain & C.P. Sujaya, "Development Planning for and by Women: Over Five Decades of Indian Experience", in Ganapathy Palanithurai (ed.), *Dynamics of New Panchayati Raj System in India: Empowering women* (Volume 4), Concept Publishing Company, 2004 p. 8.
40. United Nations, *Year-Book of the United Nations*, Department of Public Information, United Nations Staff, 1985, p. 937.

41. Ramesh Chandra Mishra (ed.), *Role of women in legislatures in India: A Study*, Anmol Publications, New Delhi, p. 207.
42. Hajira Kumar & Jaimon Varghese, *Women's Empowerment: Issues, Challenges, and Strategies: A Source Book*, Daya Books Publications, New Delhi, p. 274.
43. Satya Pal Singh, "Crimes against Women", *C.B.I. Bulletin*, Vol. V, No. 1, January 1997, p. 24.
44. Pamela Jumper Thurman, *Violence Against Indian Women*, (Final Revised Report), submitted to United States National Department of Justice, January 2003, pp. 37-38.
45. SWAYAM (NGO), *The Status of Women: A Reality Check*, 2004, p. 3.
46. National Family Health Survey (NFHS), *Domestic Violence*, NFHS-3, Government of India, 2005-2006, p.1.
47. The NCW has made available the statistical data of the total number of received complaints only up to the year 2008.
48. The term 'Crime against Women' used by the NCRB includes all acts of physical, sexual, and psychological violence against women such as torture, molestation, spousal battering, rape, sexual harassment, trafficking, kidnapping & abduction of women, incorporated in the definition of 'Violence against Women' as depicted by Article 1 and 2 of the UN Declaration on the Elimination of Violence Against Women 1993 and the standard definition undertaken in the paper while defining the term.
49. Lori Heise, et al., *op.cit.*, pp. 5-12.
50. Ishrat Shamim, *Mapping of Missing, Kidnapped and Trafficked Children and Women: Bangladesh Perspective*, Centre for Women and Children Studies, Published by International Organisation for Migration, Dhaka, 2001, p. X.
51. U.N. Protocol to Prevent, Suppress and Punish Trafficking in Persons, Especially Women and Children, supplementing the United Nations Convention against Transnational Organised Crime, 2000, Article 3 (Use of Terms).
52. Sankar Sen & P.M. Nair, *A Report on Trafficking in Women and Children in India 2002-2003*, (Volume 1), Institute of Social Sciences, National Human Rights Commission, UNIFEM, p. vi.
53. *Ibid.*, p. 1.
54. Hans Kurath, et al., *Middle English Dictionary*, (Volume 19), University of Michigan Press, 2001, p. 972.
55. Robert James McWhirter, *The Criminal Lawyer's Guide to Immigration Law: Questions and Answers*, American Bar Association, 2006, p. 163.
56. Usha Venkitakrishnan & Sunil George Kurien, op.cit., p. 6
57. *Ibid.*
58. THE INDIAN PENAL CODE, 1860, Act No. 45 OF 1860, [6th October, 1860.], p. 16-17.

59. D.K Srivastva, "Progress of Sexual Harassment Law in India, China and Hong-Kong: Prognosis for Further Reform", *Harvard International Law Journal*, Vol. 51, August 11, 2010, p. 172.
60. *Ibid.*, p. 172-173
61. "Vishakha & Others v. State of Rajasthan", *All India Reporter*, 1997 S.C. p. 3011.
62. D.K. Srivastva, *op.cit.*, pp. 173-174.
63. The National Commission for Women Act, No. 20 of 1990; INDIA CODE (1990).
64. D.K. Srivastva, *op.cit.*, p. 175.
65. Himanshi Dhawan, "Sexual Harassment Bill to Cover Students", *Times of India*, June 18, 2010.
66. Rani Jethmalani (ed.), *Kali's Yug: Empowerment, Law and Dowry Deaths*, Har-Anand Publications, New Delhi, 1995, pp. 23-24.
67. Sita Kapadia, *A Tribute to Mahatma Gandhi: His Views on Women and Social Change*, Souvenir of the First International Conference on Dowry and Bride-Burning in India, Harvard Law School, September 30, October 1 & 2,1995.
68. Julia Leslie, "Dowry, Dowry Deaths' and Violence Against Women", in Werner Menski (ed.), *South Asians And the Dowry Problem*, Trentham Books Publications, London, 1999, pp. 22-24.
69. Rinki Bhattacharya, *Behind Closed Doors: Domestic Violence in India*, SAGE Publications, New Delhi, 2004, p 37.
70. Nehaluddin Ahmad, "Dowry Deaths (Bride Burning) in India and Abetment of Suicide: A Socio-Legal Appraisal", *JEAIL* 2008, pp. 275-276.
71. Veena Talwar Oldenburg, *Dowry Murder: The Imperial Origins of a Cultural Crime*, Oxford University Press, 2002, p. 3.
72. Maurice Waite, *Compact Oxford Dictionary and Thesaurus*, Oxford University Press, London, 2009, p. 474.
73. Roseann Reinemuth, *Kentucky Ancestry: A Guide to Genealogical and Historical Research*, Ancestry Publishing, 1992, p. 137.
74. Chris Corrin, *Gender and identity in Central and Eastern Europe*, Routledge Publications, 1999, p. 94.
75. NHRC, *Annual Reports*, 1993-94 to 2006-2007.
76. Sneh Lata Tondon and Renu Sharma, "Female Foeticide and Infanticide in India: An Analysis of Crimes against Girl Children", *International Journal of Criminal Justice Science*, Vol. 1, Issue 1, January 2006, p. 7.
77. Carol S. Coonrod, *Chronic Hunger and the Status of Women in India*, Condition of Women in India, www.thp.org/reports/indiawom. htm
78. Michael J. Papa, Arvind Singhal & Wendy H. Papa, *Organizing for Social Change: A Dialectic Journey of Theory and Praxis*, SAGE Publications, California, 2005, p. 125.
79. Maitrya Ghatak, "Health and Nutrition", in Jasodhara Bagchi, & Sarmistha Dutta Gupta (eds.), *The Changing Status of Women in West*

*Bengal, 1970-2000:The Challenge Ahead*, SAGE Publications, New Delhi, 2004, p. 36.

80. Sneh Sangwan & Randhir Singh Sangwan, *Rural-Urban Divide: Changing Spatial Pattern of Social Variables*, Concept Publishing Company, New Delhi, 2003, p. 95.
81. Bharat Singh, *Crime Against Children*, Anmol Publications, New Delhi, 2004, p. 142.
82. R. Muthulakshmi, *Female infanticide, its causes and solutions*, Discovery Publishing House, New Delhi, 1997, p. 20.
83. A.M. Shah, *Women in Indian Society*, SAGE publications, 1996, p. 21-22.
84. Usha Sharma, *Women in South Asia: Employment, Empowerment, and Human Development*, Authors Press, New Delhi, 2003, p. 34.
85. Mudhumuri Laskshmipathi Raju, *Women Empowerment: Strategies and Challenges*, Regal Publications, Launceston, 2007, p. 217.
86. T. Sreenivaas, *Globalisation and Emerging India*, Discovery Publishing House, New Delhi, 2006, p. 146.
87. K.V. Ramana Murthy, "Female Foeticide in India", *Article Alley*, www.articlealley.com/article_74633_28.html
88. *Ibid.*, p. 25 .

# 9

## Violation of Child Rights in India

Children and childhood across the world, have broadly been construed in terms of a 'golden age' that is synonymous with innocence, freedom, joy, play and the like. But, then, it is also true that children are vulnerable, especially when very young. The fact that children are vulnerable, they need to be cared for and protected from 'the harshness of the world outside' and around.[1] Children signify eternal optimism in the human being and provide potential for the development. Every nation whether developed or developing links its future with the status of the child. A child of today cannot develop to be a responsible and productive member of tomorrow's society unless an environment, which is conducive to his social and physical health, is assured to him. Neglecting children means loss to the society as a whole.[2] If the children are deprived of their childhood-socially, economically, physically and mentally the nation gets deprived of the potential human resources for social progress, economic empowerment, peace and order, social stability and good citizenry.

India is home to almost 19 percent of the world's children.[3] More than one third of the country's population, around 440 million, is below 18 years. According to one assumption 40 percent of these children are in need of care and protection, which indicates the extent of the problem. In a country like India with its multicultural, multi-ethnic and multi-religious population, the problems of socially marginalized and economically backward groups are immense. Within such groups the most vulnerable section is always the children.[4]

India's commitment to its children could be gauged by the constitutional provisions, policy measures and a plethora of welfare and development programmes. The Government has enacted legislations to the cause of children's survival, development and protection. The Government of India ratified the UN Convention on Rights of the Child (UNCRC) on November 12, 1992. The major significance of the ratification is that it represents a commitment on the part of the Indian Government to improving the situation of children in India. The first report of the Government of India on the UNCRC was submitted to the Committee on Rights of the Child in February 1997. The report reviewed the situation of children in the country with reference to the articles of the Convention. The report states that with India's ratification of the UN Convention on the Rights of the Child, the 'rights approach' to child development is gradually gaining importance and will henceforth form the basis of government's strategy towards child development. The Indian government has taken several measures, policy initiatives, plans and programmes to improve the situation of children in the country. Some of the major policies and plans are:

- National Policy for Children 1974
- National Policy on Education 1986
- National Policy on Child Labour 1987
- National Plan of Action for Children 1992
- National Nutrition Policy 1993
- National Health Policy 2001
- Draft National Policy and Charter for Children 2001

However, all the above provisions, policy measures and programmes mean nothing much to a vast majority of Indian children, as they are unable to enjoy their rights for a plethora of reasons. There are 375 million children in India, more than in any country in the world. Majority of these children are deprived of their rights to survival, health, nutrition, education and safe drinking water. The Under 5 Mortality Rate (U5MR) is still very high standing at 85 and the Infant Mortality Rate (IMR) at 62. 18 per cent of below five years of age are severely underweight while 47 per cent of children are moderately underweight.[5]

Primary education is still far from being universalized. Inaccessibility, poor quality of primary education and its non-relevance to the learning needs of children are the major keep-out and push-out factors that deprive children of basic education. Only 61per cent of children enrolled in primary school reach grade five. The incidence of child labour is very high. Estimates vary between 14 million (UNICEF) to 40 million (NGOs) as working children. Children continue to work in the large unorganized sector-agricultural operations, animal husbandry, numerous small and cottage industries and establishments within the family or in household based units and as domestic labour.[6]

**Child Labour**

The issue of child labour is a complex issue and cannot be viewed in isolation. It needs to be viewed from a socio-economic perspective. Every child has the inherent right to life of dignity and to education. Exclusion at social, economic or political level needs to be addressed and any solution must be based on promoting the rights of the child. Children bear the testimony to the future of the world. It is clearly in the hands of various stakeholders today who are conscious or hidden decision makers for the children of any society. It is of paramount importance to ensure and safeguard the rights of every child. This can only be achieved by collective, collaborative and responsible action.

With one of the Millennium Development Goals as 'Achieving Universal Primary Education', schooling and quality education assumes an even greater role. However, it still remains a challenge. Child labour, an important facet of the child rights is a pervasive problem throughout the world, especially in developing countries. Africa and Asia together account for over 90 percent of total child employment. This

ILO estimates further indicate that 246 million children are engaged in child labour throughout the world. India, the biggest democracy of the world is home to the highest number of child labourers. The estimates of child labour in India range between 11 million (Government) to 100 million (NGOs/TUs).[7] Child labour deprives children of their very basic rights and results in extreme exploitation in terms of long working hours in hazardous settings and for minimal economic gain. In today's times, children in many countries are working alongside adult workers and in the process are losing on precious years meant for them to be in school. The informal sector embraces most of these children and offers cheap employment in small hotels, restaurants, construction sites, stone quarries, carpet-weaving, domestic labour and so on - the job list is quite exhaustive.

Child labour is socially condemned and legally prohibited in most parts of the world. But today about 250 million children aged between 5 to 14 years are estimated to be working in the developing countries of whom at least 120 million are working full time according to the International Labour Organisation. Of these 250 million, 61 per cent are I Asia, 32 per cent in Africa and 7 per cent in Latin America.[8] Relatively few children work in developed countries. The incidence of child labour varies across regions and sectors. The statistics on working children between the age group of 10 to 14 years is as follows: 4,92,87,000 children, that is 69.5 pre cent of the total working children of the world are in Asia; 1,66,80,000 that is 23.5 per cent are in Africa; 47,23,000, that is, 6.7 per cent are in America; 1,48,000 that is, 0.2 per cent are in Oceania and 89,000 child workers, that is 0.1 per cent are in Europe.[9]

India has the largest child labour force in the world. Child labour is comparatively cheaper that adult labour. According to the opinion of V.P. Sawhey, former Labour Secretary, Ministry of Labour, child labour is not only a problem but a misfortune too. India continues to host the largest number of child labourers in the world today. According to the Census 2001, there were 12.7 million economically active children in the age-group of 5-14 years. The number was 11.3 million during 1991 according to the Population Census of 1991, showing an increase in the number of child labourers. Workers in general are classified into main and marginal workers[10] by the population census. Census data shows that there is a decline in the absolute number as well the percentage of children (5-14) to total population in that age group classified as main workers from 4.3 percent in 1991 to 2.3 percent in 2001. But there was a substantial increase in marginal workers in every category of worker irrespective of sex and residence. As a result, despite the number of main workers declining from 9.08 million in 1991 to 5.78 million in 2001, the total number of children in the work force increased. A large part of the increase was accounted for by the increase in marginal workers, which increased from 2.2 million in 1991 to 6.89 million in 2001.[11] The trends between 1991 and 2001 of declining main child workers along with increasing marginal workers may indicate the changing nature of work done by children. This is also to be seen in the context of decelerating employment growth in general in the economy during the last decade.

Approximately, only 59 percent children between the ages of 5 and 14 attend school. According to a UNESCO report, all those children in the age group of 10-14 years, who are not attending schools, are working. There are an estimated 500,000 street children nationwide.[12] Child prostitution occurs in the cities and there are an estimated 57500 child prostitutes nationwide. There is also a growing pattern of traffic in child prostitutes from Nepal. According one estimate 5,000 to 7,000, mostly between the ages 10 and 18, are drawn into this traffic annually.[13] According to an International Labour Organisation estimate, 15 percent of India's estimated 2 million prostitutes are children. Runway children especially in larger cities are at high risk for sexually transmitted diseases and HIV. They work 18 to 20 hour days and suffer sexual and mental abuse. Many children also suffer abuse at school, especially beating by teachers and sexual harassment by teachers.[14] According to official estimates, India has over 12 million child labourers, of these nearly 185,000 work in households and 70,000 in *dhabas* and other eateries. NGOs claim this total number to be as high as 20 million, with National Capital Delhi accounting for one million child labourers.[15] The Child Marriage Restraint (Amendment) Act of 1976 prohibits child marriage, a traditional practice in northern India. The act had raised the age of marriage for girls to 18 from 15, but the Government does not enforce it effectively. According to one report, 50 percent of the girls in Bihar, Rajasthan, Uttar Pradesh and Madhya Pradesh are married at or before age 16.[16] Many scholars opine that in the Indian situation where about 80% of the population lives in rural areas probably each and every child is a working child. If not engaged in directly income-generating activities his or her involvement in the family occupation cannot be questioned.

In 1901 there were as many as 5,147 children below 12 years of age constituting 4.9% of the total Labour force in mines as per the reports of Sharma (1979). By any measure this is a massive abuse of childhood.[17] According to the Census of India of 1961, there were 14.53 million child workers, 13.72 million in rural areas and 0.81 million in urban areas. According to a report of the Registrar General of India, in 1965 the number of child labourers was about 15 million. This in 1971 declined to 10.74 million children below the age of 15 years representing 4.66 per cent of the total child population and 5.95 per cent of the total labour force. Of the total number of working children, 92.8 per cent are employed in rural areas, of which nearly ¾ are males. In urban areas the share of males in the working children is nearly 415. It rose again in 1981 to 11.2 million. The National Sample Survey gives an estimate of 16.25 million children of age group 5-14 years, which consisted of 14.68 million rural, and 1.57 million urban working children. According to an estimate by the Planning Commission in March 1983 the working children of age group 10-14 years were 15.70 million which included 14.03 million rural and 1.67 million urban children and the working children of age group 5-14 years constituted 17.36 million. A 1995 report by .the Indian Commission of Labour Standards acknowledges at least 18.6 million working children in 1990. On the data provided by the Census of 1981, if aggregated to figures of 1991, it is presumed that 14,217,588 children are working on full time basis. This figure may be no real reflection as in 1996, half the population in India was below 22 years of age leading to more child labour.[18]

According to the estimates of the 43rd round of the National Sample Survey, there were 17 million working children in India with a projected 20 million working children by the year 2000 A.D. estimated magnitude for 1991 are full time workers (0-14 years) 2.7 million, full time plus marginal child workers 23.23 million, and non-students and non-workers 74.4 million.[19]

The growth rate of child labour in different states of India varies from 7 per cent in Uttar Pradesh to 0.7 per cent in TamilNadu.[20] At the national level the growth between 1981 and 1991 was 2 per cent.[21] According to the National Sample Survey Organisation (NSSO) 79 per cent of the child labourers were found in rural areas and 21 per cent in urban areas.[22] Two-thirds of the child workers in India are in the age group of 12 to 15 years. Out of the remaining, one-third is below 10 years of age.[23] For every 1000 boys at work, there are nearly 1200 girls.[24] As many as 64 per cent of working children belong to the Scheduled Caste and Scheduled Tribe group, which in turn, constitutes 90 per cent of bonded labour in the country.[25]

The National Commission on Labour comments in its report: "Our evidence reveals that employment of children is almost non-existent in organized industries. It persists in varying degrees in the unorganized sector such as small plantations, restaurants and hotels, cotton ginning and weaving, carpet weaving, stone breaking, brick making, handicrafts and road construction. The Labour Bureau's study also showed the same situation, that is, though child labour has comparatively declined in factory industries it has persisted in small industries such as match manufacture, cashew nut processing, beedi making, carpet weaving either uncertified or having a bogus age certificate.

Poverty, illiteracy, ignorance, speedy growth of population etc. are the main causes of child labour.[26] In India nearly 40 per cent are below poverty line and more than half of the population is illiterate.[27] The unprecedented population growth of India has created a larger share of child labour. Therefore it is obvious that the incidence and extent of child labour is very high. When the child labour is restricted in the organized sector it has been shifted to unorganized sector. The shift of child workers from the organized sector to the unorganized where working conditions are atrocious and welfare- facilities absent has turned child labour into a social problem. Today a countless number of children are working in various unregulated factories like beedi making, tanning, carpet weaving, wool cleaning, bangles manufacturing, slate making, balloon manufacturing, gem polishing, Zari works and a host of unspecified industries. Other industries where children are working are wood and cork, furniture and fixtures, printing publishing and allied trades, leather products, rubber and rubber products, transport equipment and personal services like laundries dying and cleaning.[28] A large number of children are employed as domestic servants, workers in hotels, restaurants, canteens, wayside shops and establishments, lockers, news-paper seller, ice-cream or sweet vendors, coolies, shoe-shines, helpers in service stations etc.[29]

The largest number of child labourers in the country was found to be in Andhra Pradesh, Madhya Pradesh, Uttar Pradesh, Maharashtra, Karnataka, Bihar and Tamil Nadu followed by other states. *Andhra Pradesh has the highest figures of child labour (1.95 million), followed by Madhya Pradesh (1.70 million), Maharasthra (1.56 million), Karnataka (1.3 million), Bihar (1.07 million)* [30] According to one estimate there are nearly 4 lakh child workers in Delhi who comprise about 18 per cent of the child population of the Union Territory. Out of them about 30,000 work in 5,000 registered and 25,000 in unregistered tea shops and dhabas, about 20,000 work in scooter/car repair shops, approximately 30,000 children are working as shop assistants and about 40,000 work as labourers (agricultural, construction and coolies etc) and nearly 1 lakh work as full time or part time domestic servants.[31]

Despite the schemes launched to provide universal education, millions of children in India still have no access to education and work long hours in the worst forms of child labour. India accounts for a significant proportion of the world out-of-school children. This is because many Indian children who work, cannot afford school fees, do not have access to education, or belong to deprived communities such as Dalit or other marginalized castes, tribal groups or minority religions, particularly Islam. In October 2006, the government proscribed the employment of children as domestic servants or in tea stalls and restaurants; while this is a good step, previous experience has shown that without proper implementation and adequate rehabilitation of child workers, such laws are of very limited utility. The government has also announced plans to establish a national commission for children that can prove effective in protecting their rights.[32]

### Child Abuse

Child abuse is a state of emotional, physical, economic and sexual maltreatment meted out to a person below the age of eighteen and is a globally prevalent phenomenon. However, in India, as in many other countries, there has been no understanding of the extent, magnitude and trends of the problem. The growing complexities of life and the dramatic changes brought about by socio-economic transitions in India have played a major role in increasing the vulnerability of children to various and newer forms of abuse. Child abuse has serious physical and psycho-social consequences which adversely affect the health and overall well-being of a child. According to WHO: "Child abuse or maltreatment constitutes all forms of physical and/or emotional ill-treatment, sexual abuse, neglect or negligent treatment or commercial or other exploitation, resulting in actual or potential harm to the child's health, survival, development or dignity in the context of a relationship of responsibility, trust or power." [33] Child abuse is a violation of the basic human rights of a child and is an outcome of a set of inter-related familial, social, psychological and economic factors. The problem of child abuse and human rights violation is one of the most critical matters on the international human rights agenda. In the Indian context, acceptance of child rights as primary inviolable rights is fairly recent, as is the universal understanding of it.[34]

### *Physical Abuse*

Physical abuse is the inflicting of physical injury upon a child. This may include burning, hitting, punching, shaking, kicking, beating or otherwise harming a child. The parent or caretaker may not have intended to hurt the child. It may, however, be the result of over-discipline or physical punishment that is inappropriate to the child's age.

### *Sexual Abuse*

Sexual abuse is inappropriate sexual behaviour with a child. It includes fondling a child's genitals, making the child fondle the adult's genitals, intercourse, incest, rape, sodomy, exhibitionism and sexual exploitation. To be considered 'child abuse', these acts have to be committed by a person responsible for the care of a child (for example a baby-sitter, a parent, or a daycare provider), or related to the child. If a stranger commits these acts, it would be considered sexual assault and handled solely by the police and criminal courts.

### *Emotional Abuse*

Emotional abuse is also known as verbal abuse, mental abuse, and psychological maltreatment. It includes acts or the failures to act by parents or caretakers that have caused or could cause, serious behavioural, cognitive, emotional, or mental trauma. This can include parents/caretakers using extreme and/or bizarre forms of punishment, such as confinement in a closet or dark room or being tied to a chair for long periods of time or threatening or terrorizing a child. Less severe acts, but no less damaging, are belittling or rejecting treatment, using derogatory terms to describe the child, habitual tendency to blame the child or make him/her a scapegoat.

### *Neglect*

It is the failure to provide for the child's basic needs. Neglect can be physical, educational, or emotional. Physical neglect can include not providing adequate food or clothing, appropriate medical care, supervision, or proper weather protection (heat or cold). It may include abandonment. Educational neglect includes failure to provide appropriate schooling or special educational needs, allowing excessive truancies. Psychological neglect includes the lack of any emotional support and love, never attending to the child, substance abuse including allowing the child to participate in drug and alcohol use.

There are some noteworthy findings which display the severe tragedy of child abuse in India.

- Every fifth child in the world lives in India.
- Every third malnourished child in the world lives in India.
- Every second Indian child is underweight.
- Three out of four children in India are anemic.
- Every second new born has reduced learning capacity due to iodine deficiency.
- Decline in female/male ratio is maximum in 0-6 years: 927 females per 1000 males.
- Birth registration is just 62% (RGI-2004).
- Retention rate at Primary level is 71.01% (Elementary Education in India Progress towards UEENUEPA Flash Statistics DISE 2005-2006).
- Girls' enrolment in schools at primary level is 47.79% (Elementary Education in India Progress towards UEENUEPA Flash Statistics DISE 2005-2006).
- 1104 lakh child labour in the country (SRO 2000).
- IMR is as high as 58 per 1000 live births (SRS- 2005).
- MMR is equally high at 301 per 100,000 live births (SRS, 2001-03).

- Children born with low birth weight are 46% (NFHS-III).
- Children under 3 with anemia are 79% (NFHS-III).
- Immunization coverage is very low (polio -78.2%, measles-58.8%, DPT-55.3%, BCG-78% (NFHS-III).

Major Findings by 'A Study on Child Abuse, India 2007', conducted by the Ministry of Women and Child Development of the Government of India has asserted that across different kinds of abuse, it is young children, in the 5-12 year group, who are most at risk of abuse and exploitation. Furthermore the Study has present several shocking findings regarding physical abuse, sexual abuse, emotional abuse and neglect of girl child.[35]

*Physical Abuse*

- Two out of every three children were physically abused.
- Out of 69% children physically abused in 13 sample states, 54.68% were boys.
- Over 50% children in all the 13 sample states were being subjected to one or the other form of physical abuse.
- Out of those children physically abused in family situations, 88.6% were physically abused by parents.
- 65% of school going children reported facing corporal punishment i.e. two out of three children were victims of corporal punishment.
- 62% of the corporal punishment was in government and municipal school.
- The State of Andhra Pradesh, Assam, Bihar and Delhi have almost consistently reported higher rates of abuse in all forms as compared to other states.
- Most children did not report the matter to anyone.
- 50.2% children worked seven days a week.

*Sexual Abuse*

- 53.22% children reported having faced one or more forms of sexual abuse.

- Andhra Pradesh, Assam, Bihar and Delhi reported the highest percentage of sexual abuse among both boys and girls.
- 21.90% child respondents reported facing severe forms of sexual abuse and 50.76% other forms of sexual abuse.
- Out of the child respondents, 5.69% reported being sexually assaulted.
- Children in Assam, Andhra Pradesh, Bihar and Delhi reported the highest incidence of sexual assault.
- Children on street, children at work and children in institutional care reported the highest incidence of sexual assault.
- 50% abuses are persons known to the child or in a position of trust and responsibility.
- Most children did not report the matter to anyone.

*Emotional Abuse and Girl Child Neglect*

- Every second child reported facing emotional abuse.
- Equal percentage of both girls and boys reported facing emotional abuse.
- In 83% of the cases parents were the abusers.
- 48.4% of girls wished they were boys.

## Crime Against Children

The crime against children is a world wide concern. But in India where 19 per cent of the total children of the world reside and where one third of its population is below 18 years old, the problem of crime against children has acquired a severe gravity. Every day there are crimes, brutalities taking place against the children in the country. The children are supposed to go to school, get clean and healthy environment, decent care of parents, nutrient diet, and overall conducive environment for their all-round development. But unfortunately in India, the children have been murdered, kidnapped, sexually harassed, raped, sold and bought for flesh trade, girls forcefully indulged into prostitution, and the male children are indulged into begging or smuggling of drugs. The problem of crime against children in India is very complex and complicated. It is almost impossible to estimate the number, rate or ratio of crime against children in India. Because majority of the crimes against children remain unreported.

The statistical data of the NCRB of 10 years since 1999 to 2008 has been observed and analyzed to be acquainted with the number and intensity of crimes against children. As per data, the number of cases reported in India regarding crime against children was 4957 in 1999. There were total 5023 reported cases of crime against children in 2000. The number had increased to more than double in the next year with 10814 cases in 2001. The increase continued in the successive years and there were 10469 cases of crime against children in 2002, total 11633 cases in 2004, and 14423 cases in 2004. The NCRB had reported 14975 cases in 2005, well increased number of 18967 cases in 2006, and 20410 cases in 2007. In 2008, there were total 22500 reported cases of crime against children.

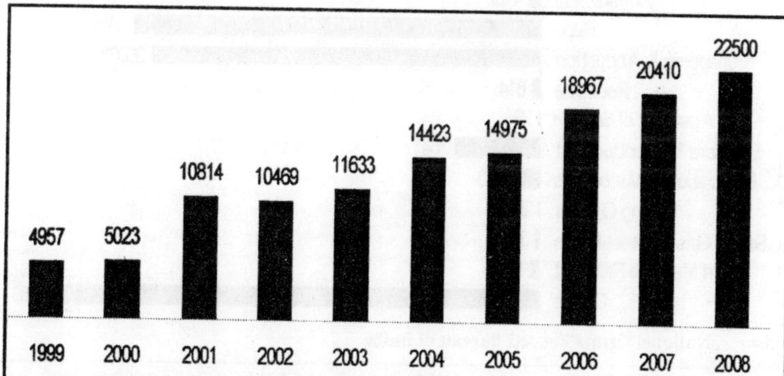


*Source:* National Crime Record Bureau of India.

**Figure 1: Crime Against Children in India (1999-2008)**

The data divulges that total 134171 cases of 'crime against children' are reported in India in 10 years since 1999 to 2008. It means that average 13417 cases are reported regarding crime against children in India. The data further confirms that average 37 cases of crime against children are reported in India every day. It establishes that average 1 case o f crime against children is reported in India after every 39 minutes. The number of total reported cases of the crime against children has been increasing year after year. The number of cases has increased to 17543 (353.90 per cent) in 10 years, from 4957 cases in 1999 to 22500 cases in 2008. It means there is an average increase of 35.39 per cent in the total number of reported cases of crime against children in India every year.

### *Major Categories of Crime against Children*

There are several types and forms of crimes against children. Major categories of crime against children include murder of children, infanticide, rape of children, kidnapping and abduction, foeticde, abetment of suicide,, Exposure and abandonment, procuration of minor girls, buying and selling of girls for prostitution, child marriage etc.

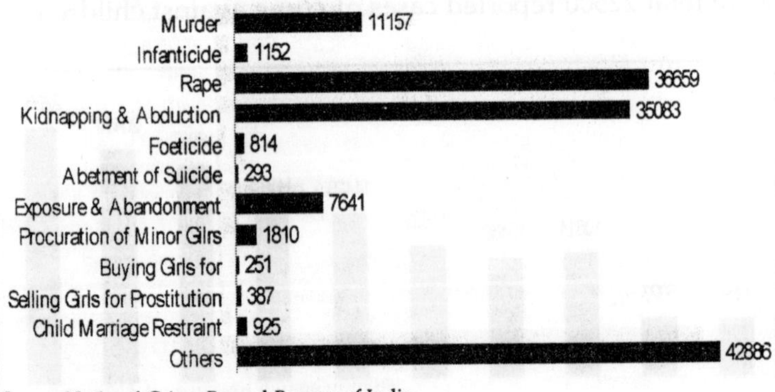


*Source:* National Crime Record Bureau of India.

**Figure 2: Major Categories of Crime Against Children from 1999 to 2008**

As per statistical data of 10 years of the NCRB since 1999 to 2008, there were as many as 11157 cases of murder of children in 2000. Noticeably the number of reported cases since 1999 to 2008 regarding infanticide was 1152, while worryingly there had been 36659 cases of the rape of children. Furthermore in such a short span of time of 10 years since 1999 to 2008, there were 35083 reported cases of kidnapping and abduction of children through out India. In these years 814 cases of foeticide, 293 cases of abetment of suicide, and total 7641 cases of exposure and abandonment of children were reported by the NCRB. Total 1810 minor girls were procured unlawfully; while 251 girls were reported to be bought and 387 girls were sold in India since 1999 to 2008 in India as per the data of NCRB. Besides that, there were 925 cases of the violation of Child Marriage Restraint Act during these 8 years.

The data asserts that there are total 134171 cases of crime against children are reported in India in 10 years since 1999 to 2008. The data further reveals that rape of the children occurs as the largest crime against children in India, as 27.32 per cent of the total number of reported cases of crime against children in India is regarding rape of children. Kidnapping and abduction of children has been confirmed as the second largest crime against children occupying 26.14 per cent of the total number of reported cases of crime against children. The murder of children (8.31 per cent cases) stands as the third largest crime against children; while exposure and abandonment of children (5.69 per cent cases) occurs as the fourth largest crime against children in India. The crime of the procurement of minor girls (1.34 per cent cases) arrears as the fifth largest crime against children and the crime of infanticide (0.85 per cent cases) establishes as the sixth major crime against children. The crimes of child marriage (0.68 per cent cases) and of foeticide (0.60 per cent cases) emerge as respectively seventh and eighth major crimes against children in India. Furthermore, the crime of selling the girls for prostitution comes in to view as the ninth major crime against children; while the 'abetment of suicide' emerges as the tenth largest crime against children in India. The buying of girls for prostitution comes out as the eleventh major crime against children in India.

### *Murder of Children*

The murder of children has been emerging as a severe problem for the whole Indian society generally and for the children in India particularly. There are innumerous reports of the killing of the children, especially the female children. Now the incidence of child murder is among the highest in India.[36] Formal legislations are executed in India against the murders of children, which establish the provisions of severe punishments in case of the occurrence of any violation. But the dearth of exact reporting and appropriate investigation makes the execution of these laws ineffective and the crime of the murder of children has been increasing day by day in spite of decreasing.

According to the statistical data of the NCRB not even single case of murder of children was reported throughout India in 1999; while there were total 1177 reported cases of murder in India in 2000. The number was 1175 in 2001. The NCRB had reported total 1073 cases in 2002 and 1212 cases in 2003. The NCRB had further reported 1304 cases of murder of children in 2004, total 1219 cases in 2005 and 1324 cases in 2006. In the number of the cases regarding murder of children reported by NCRB was 1377 in 2007, and 1296 in 2008.

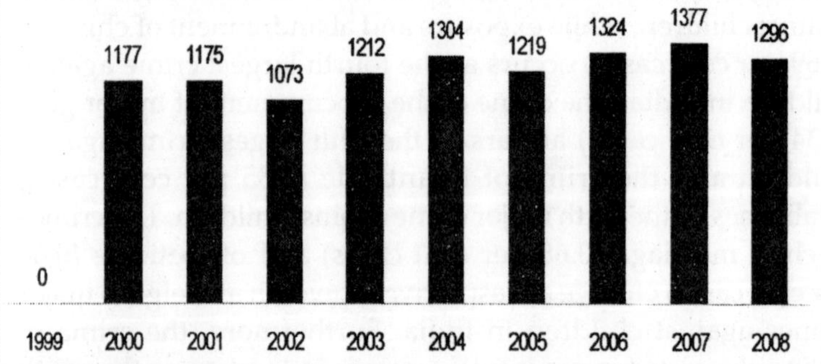


*Source:* National Crime Record Bureau of India.

**Figure 3: Total Reported Cases of Murder of Children in India (1999-2008)**

The data states that there occurred total 11157 reported cases of murder of children reported in India in 10 years since 1999 to 2008. It means that average 1116 cases of the murder of children are reported in India every year. The in depth analysis of the data asserts that average at least three cases of the murder of the children are reported in India every day; and average 1 case of murder of children occurs in India after every 8 hours. Moreover, there are ascendances and decadences in the number of cases year after year. In 1999, there was not even single case reported by the NCRB. The number of cases had declined in 2001 and 2002 by respectively 0.16 per cent and 8.83 per cent cases in comparison with 2000. In 2003 there was an increase of 12.95 per cent, and in 2004 increase of 21.52 per cent in comparison with 2002. The year 2005 witnessed a decrease of 6.51 per cent in comparison with 2004. In 2007, after two years, an increase of 12.96 per cent was noticed in comparison with 2005. However, the number of cases declined to 5.88 per cent in 2008 in contrast with 2007.

### *Infanticide*

Another form of eliminating the girl child has been the practice of female infanticide. It is a deliberate and intentional act of killing a female child within one year of its birth either directly by using poisonous organic and inorganic chemicals or indirectly by deliberate neglect to feed the infant by either one of the parents or other family members or neighbours or by the midwife. Infanticide is defines as, "Killing of an entirely dependent child under "one year of age" who is killed by mother, parents or others in whose care the child is entrusted".[37] It is unfortunate that the parents also view her as a liability. This attitude is rooted in a complex set of social, cultural, and economic factors. It is the dowry system, lack of economic independence, social customs and traditions that have relegated the female to a secondary status. The degree may vary but the neglect of the girl child and discrimination goes hand-in- hand.[38]

Total 87 cases of Infanticide were reported by the NCRB in 1999. The NCRB had reported 104 cases of infanticide in 2000. In 2001, it had reported 133 cases, while 115 cases were reported in 2002. The NCRB, in 2003 had reported total 103 cases of infanticide. In 2004, however, the number was 102. Total 108 cases of infanticide were reported by the NCRB through out India in the year 2005, while the number was followed by 126 cases in 2006. Afterwards, the NCRB had reported respectively 134 and 140 cases of infanticide in 2007 and 2008.

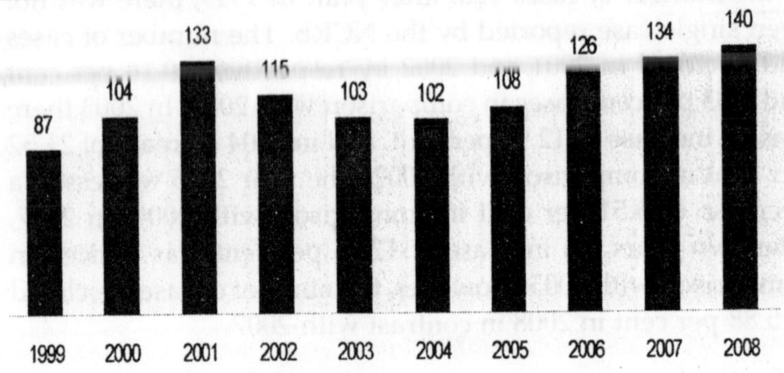


*Source:* National Crime Record Bureau of India.

**Figure 4: Total Number of Reported Cases of Infanticide in India (1999-2008)**

The data asserts that total 1152 are reported in India in 10 years (1999 to 2008) regarding infanticide. It means that average 115 cases of infanticide are reported in India every year. It further confirms that average 10 cases of infanticide are reported in India in one month. It further establishes that average 1 case of infanticide is reported in India after every 3 days. There are a few ups and downs in the number of cases in these ten years. The number increased from 1999 to 2001, and there was an increase of 52.87 per cent in 2001 in comparison with 1999. Since 2002 to 2004, a decrease was noticed in the number of reported cases and the number decreased to 23.30 per cent n 2004 n comparison with 2001. Again there was a constant increase in the number of reported cases since 2005 to 2008. The number had increased to 37.25 in comparison with 2004.

### *Rape of Female Children*

There is no safe place for children. Children have been becoming the soft targets of sex abuse particularly rapes. Moreover, the rapists are allowed to go free or are acquitted. Prevention and control of child rape must involve severe and rigorous punishment of rapists. Though, rape is one of the cruelest crimes against children. Children, the innocents, immature and consecrated creatures on the earth, after becoming the victims of the rape, suffer from psychological effects of embarrassment, disgust, depression, guilt, and even suicidal tendencies. There is police and prosecution indifference as well as social stigma and social ostracism of the victim and her family. Many cases go unreported. The case studies illustrate the difficulties for the victim of experiencing the rape and the social responses: police harassment, shame and fear, and occasionally public outrage. The case studies illustrate rape in familiar settings, such as schools, family homes, and neighbors and friends' homes; rape by policemen; and rape by political influential. Most offenders are young, married, and socioeconomically poor.[39]

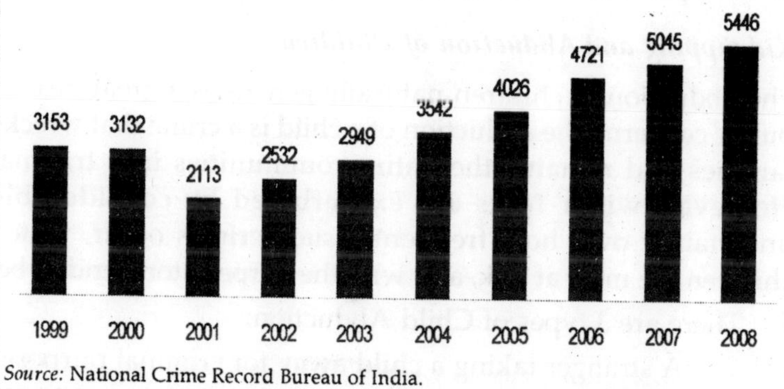


*Source:* National Crime Record Bureau of India.

**Figure 5: Rape of Children in India (1999-2008)**

The statistical data of the NCRB asserts that total 3153 cases were reported in 1999 regarding the rape of children in India. While 3132 cases of rape of children were reported in 2000 throughout India. The number of cases had declined to 2113 in the year 2001. In 2002, as many as 2532 cases were reported. In 2003 and 2004, the number of cases had increased and respectively 2949 and 3542 cases were reported by the NCRB in these two years. The increase in the number disturbingly continued with 4026 cases in 2005, total 4721 cases in 2006 and 5045 cases in 2007. In 2008, the NCRB had reported a noticeably huge number of 5446 cases regarding the rape of children throughout India.

The data asserts that there are total 36659 reported cases of rape of children in ten years since 1999 to 2000. That much massive number of cases confirms the crime of rape of children as the largest crime against children. The data further confirms that average 3666 cases in India are reported in a year regarding rape of children. It means average 10 cases are reported daily and average 1 case after every 2.5 hours in India regarding rape of the children. The number of cases had decreased to 0.66 per cent and 32.98 per cent in respectively 2000 and 2001 in comparison with 1999. But there was a consistent increase in the number of cases since 2002. The number increased to 115.08 per cent in 2008 in contrast with 2003. Overall increase of 72.72 per cent was noticed in ten years since 1999 to 2008.

### *Kidnapping and Abduction of Children*

The abduction of children naturally generates a great deal of public concern. The abduction of a child is a crime that wrecks families and remains the entire communities in a trauma. However, wider fears are exacerbated by considerable uncertainty over how frequently such crimes occur, which children are most at risk, and who the perpetrators tend to be.

There are 3 types of Child Abduction:

- A stranger taking a child away for criminal purposes (such as sexual assault or ransom.
- Child is stolen to be brought up by the abductor;
- It occurs when a parent removes a child from the other parent's care.

Most of the times, child abductions are assumed as the acts of children being taken out of a shopping mall or other crowded place by a stranger. While this kind of thing does happen, it is not the only kind of child abduction. In fact, children are in more danger from people known to them. Parental abductions account for the highest number of abductions of children. Parental child abduction, while difficult to understand, is a very serious crime, and it can have very serious effects on the child, as well as the parent from which the child was taken.

Child abduction, as described through the sensationalized news headlines, often misses or misrepresents a problem of national concern. Politicians rush to develop strong rhetoric about predators with subsequent policies that speak to so-called rampant crimes while overlooking the data on parent abduction of children and the posttraumatic stress disorder that can result in survivors of family and non-family abductions. These need as much attention as we give to the criminal aspects of the stories.

**Effect on Children**

Children who have been psychologically violated and maltreated through the act of abduction are more likely to exhibit a variety of psychological and social problems and difficulties. Some of the deleterious effects of parental child abduction on the child victim include:

- Depression;
- Loss of community;
- Loss of stability, security and trust;
- Excessive fearfulness, even of ordinary occurrences;
- Loneliness;
- Anger;
- Helplessness;
- Disruption in identify formation; and
- Fear of abandonment.

According to most statistics, the 'stereotypical' abductions, such as those involving a stranger who kidnaps a child with malicious intent are far lower than we might be lead to believe. According to the Justice Department, in the past 20 years the per-capita child abduction by non-family members has not increased appreciably. Almost 80% of child abductions are not by strangers. Over 200,000 children are kidnapped each year by family members seeking to interfere with parental visitation rights, while 58,000 are taken by non-family members and returned unharmed. By comparison, only 115 cases of kidnappings for the purpose of ransom or harm occurred, and although each and every single case is unfathomable, the proportion of stranger abduction is actually small.[40]

Total 791 cases of kidnapping and abduction of children were reported in India in 1999. The NCRB, in 2000 had reported 711 cases of kidnapping and abduction of children in India. In 2001, it had reported 2845 cases. In 2002, the number of cases reported by NCRB regarding kidnapping and abduction of children was 2322. The NCRB had reported 2571 cases in 2003 and 3196 cases in 2004. The number of cases had increased to 3518 in 2005. The increase proceeded rapidly in the time span of one year and the NCRB reported 5102 cases of kidnapping and abduction of children in the year 2006. The increase further continued in the succeeding years with 6377 reported cases in 2007 and 7650 cases in 2008.

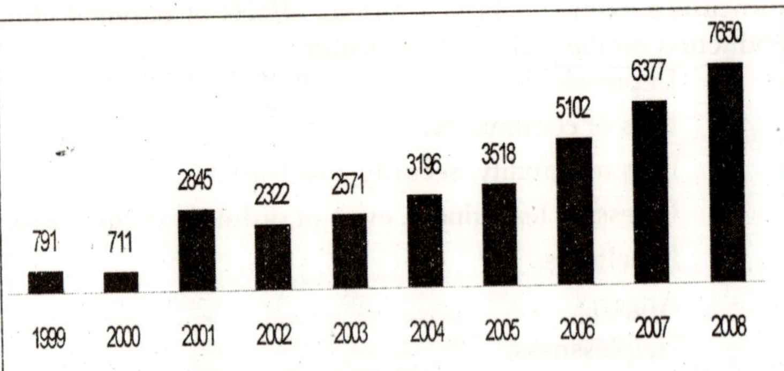


*Source:* National Crime Record Bureau of India.

**Figure 6: Cases of Kidnapping and Abduction of Children in India (1999-2008)**

The data affirms total 35083 reported case of kidnapping and abduction of children in India in 10 years (1999 to 2008). It constitutes 26.14 per cent of the total number of reported crime against children. The percentage establishes the crime of 'kidnapping and abduction of children' as the second largest crime against children in India. The data confirms that average 3508 cases of kidnapping and abduction of children are reported in India every year, while average 10 cases are reported every day in India. It means that average 1 case of kidnapping and abduction of children is reported in India after every 2 hours and 40 minutes. The number of the cases has been increasing enormously except an ambiguous nature of ups and downs since 1999 to 2001. The data had decreased to 10.11 per cent in 2000 in contrast with 1999, and then drastically increased to 300 per cent in 2001 in comparison with 2000. Again a decrease of 18.38 per cent was noticed in 2002 in comparison with 2001. There was a consistent increase of the number of reported cases since 2003 to 2008. An increase of 197.54 per cent was in 2008 in comparison with the number of cases in 2003.

### *Foeticide*

The statistical data of the NCRB asserts that there were 61 cases of foeticide reported in India in 1999. Total 91 cases of foeticide in India were reported in the year 2000. In 2001, the NCRB had reported 55 cases. The number of cases was 84 in 2002. Total 57 cases were reported by the NCRB n 2003. The NCRB, in 2004 and 2005, had reported 86 each cases of foeticide in India. There were total 125 cases reported by the NCRB in 2006. In 2007 the number of cases was 96, and in 2008 total 73 cases were reported by the NCRB regarding foeticide.

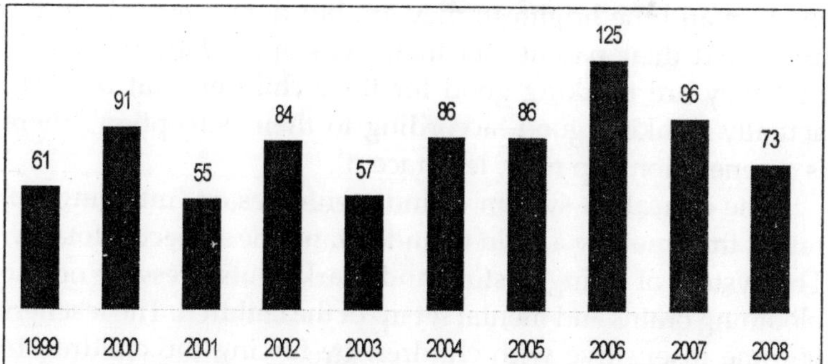


*Source:* National Crime Record Bureau of India.

**Figure 7: Foeticide in India (1999-2008)**

The data reveals that total 814 of foeticide were reported in India in 10 years (1999 to 2008). It means average 81 cases of foeticide are reported in India every year. There are several ups and downs in the number of cases since 1999 to 2008. It is an obvious fact that the number of reported cases is much less than the actual number of cases happening in India. Numerous cases of foeticide remain unreported and even untraced in the country, which results in the reporting of less number of cases.

### *Abetment to Suicide*

India is the suicide capital of the world. According to medical proof, suicidal tendencies have been present in 1/3 of people with mild cases of depression and in nearly three quarters of people who are severely depressed. No age, group, or social or professional class is exempt from suicide. Particularly shocking and by no means rare, is the suicide among child. Out of every three cases of suicide reported every 15 minutes in India, one is committed by a youth in the age group of 15 to 29. Unfortunately, the children below 18 years of age are also committing suicides. For every student who commits suicide, there are 13 who attempt it.

Undoubtedly, parents are responsible for giving children lives and in some odd ways, even taking their lives. No parent wants to kill her kids, but they do so by setting unrealistic goals in front of them. Every parent wants her children to be the best and the brightest; they are but not necessarily in the areas that their parents set their eyes upon. Parents believe that they are thinking good for their children, but they are actually thinking good 'according to their perception' 'there is a generation gap now, let's face it'.

The education system of India enforces on 'mugging up' rather than making a child to understand the subject in totality. The system of rating, testing and marks puts pressure on the blooming brains and mental set up of the children. The teachers become insensitive with children by forcing the children to study and learn beyond their capacities.

Section 306 of IPC states that if any person commits suicide, whoever abets the commission of such suicide shall be punished with imprisonment of either description for a term which may extend to 10 years, and shall also be liable to a fine. Under section 107 of IPC, a person is guilty of abetment of suicide only if instigates someone to do the thing, engages with one or more persons to do the thing, intentionally aids its commitment or facilitates the act.

The NCRB had reported 24 cases of abetting the children to suicide in 1999. Total 18 cases of abetment of suicide to children were reported in 2000. It further reported 26 cases in 2001 and 24 cases in 2002. In 2003, the NCRB had reported total 25 cases of abetment to suicide. As many as 33 cases were reported in 2004 by the NCRB. In the year 2005, 43 cases were reported, and in 2006, the number of reported cases by NCRB was 45. The NCRB, in 2007 had reported 26 cases; while in 2008 total 29 cases of abetment to suicide to the children were reported.

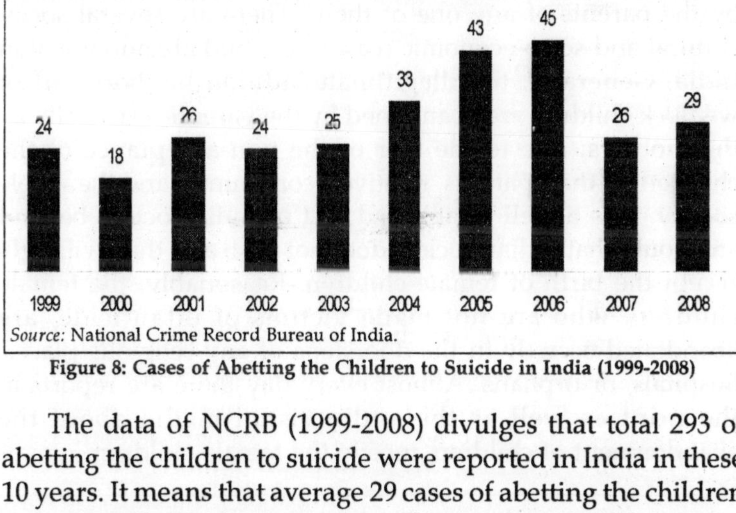


*Source:* National Crime Record Bureau of India.

**Figure 8: Cases of Abetting the Children to Suicide in India (1999-2008)**

The data of NCRB (1999-2008) divulges that total 293 of abetting the children to suicide were reported in India in these 10 years. It means that average 29 cases of abetting the children are reported in India every year. The number of total reported cases was comparatively less since 1999 to 2003. But a consistent increase in the number of cases was noticed since 2004 to 2006. Contrarily, there was a decrease in the number in 2007 and 2008, in comparison with 2006. Furthermore, a reduced amount of number of cases regarding abetting the children to suicide cannot be considered as the less severe nature of the problem. Like other crimes against children, that crime is also unreported most of the times, because, most of the times, the accused of this crime against children are parents, teachers, or relatives.

### *Exposure and Abandonment of Children*

In legal terms, the word abandonment means the voluntary leaving of a person to whom one is bound by a special relation, as a wife, husband, or child. Especially in Family Law, Exposure or Abandonment of children is often recognized as a crime, in which case the child is usually not physically harmed directly as part of the abandonment. Child abandonment, also called Child Exposure or Child Exposition, is a crime occurs by leaving an infant in the open, most probably by the parents or one of the parents.

In India, thousands of children are exposed or abandoned by the parents of any one of them. There are several socio-cultural and socio-economic reasons of child abandonment in India. Generally, the illegitimate/adulterine/born out of wedlock children are abandoned by the parents, especially by the mothers, due to the fear of the non-acceptance of the children by their parents, relatives, community and the whole society. It is a well established fact of India society beyond any doubt that Indian society does not wish and then willingly accept the birth of female children. Reasonably, the female children, who are not made victims of infanticide, are abandoned secretly in the doorsteps of any religious places, hospitals, or orphans. Almost every day there are reports in the print as well as the audio-visual media about the abandonment of children, mostly the female children.

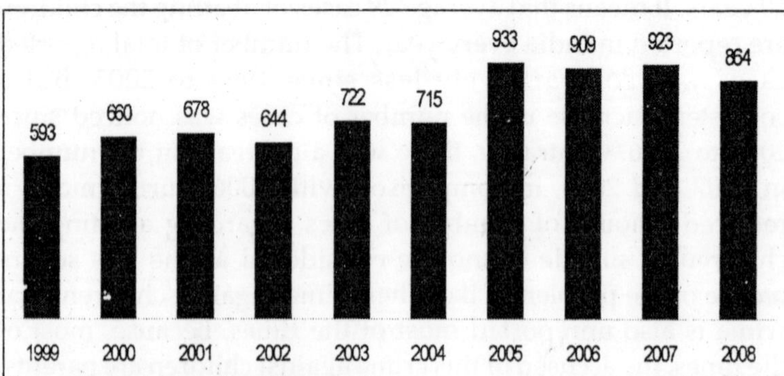


*Source:* National Crime Record Bureau of India.

**Figure 9: Exposure and Abandonment of Children in India (1999-2008)**

According to the data of NCRB, 593 cases of the exposure and abandonment of girls were reported in 1999. In 2000, total 660 cases of exposure and abandonment of children were reported. In 2001, the number of cases regarding that crime against children was 678 in 2001 and 644 in 2002. The NCRB, in 2003, had reported 722 cases in 2004. In the year 2005 and 2006, the NCRB had reported 715 and 933 cases respectively. The number of cases regarding exposure and abandonment of children had reached to 923 in 2007, which had just declined to 864 cases in 2008.

The data divulges that there are total 7641 reported cases of abandonment and exposure of children in India in ten years (1999 to 2008). It means that average 764 cases of abandonment of children are reported in India every year. The in depth analysis of the data exposes that average 2 cases of abandonment of the children are reported in India every day. The number of cases has a noticeable increase year after year. In the year 2000, there was an increase of 11.29 per cent in comparison with 1999. Further increase of 2.72 per cent was noticed in 2001 in contrast with 2000. The number of cases had decreased to 5.01 per cent in 2002 in comparison with 2001. An increase of 12.11 per cent was noticed in 2003 over the year 2002. The number had decreased to 0.96 per cent in 2004 in contrast with 2003. In 2005, an increase of 30.4 per cent was witnessed over the year 2004. There was a decrease of 2.57 per cent in the number of cases in 2006 in comparison with 2005. The year 2007 had witnessed an increase of 1.54 per cent cases in contrast with 2006. A decrease of 6.39 per cent was noticed in the year 2008 in comparison with 2007.

### *Procuration of Minor Girls*

Trafficking and procuration in human beings, especially in women, and female children has become a matter of serious national and international concern. Children, both boys and girls, have been exposed to unprecedented vulnerabilities commercial exploitation of these vulnerabilities has become a massive organized crime and a multimillion dollar business. Nations are attempting to combat this trade in human misery through legislative, executive, judicial and social action. Trafficking and procuration of children is a worldwide phenomenon affecting large numbers of children, especially the girls everyday. Teen aged girls and their families are often lured by the promise of better employment and a more prosperous life far from their homes. The minors are kidnapped and sold. Trafficking and procuration violates a child's right to grow up in a family environment and exposes him or her to a range of dangers, including violence and sexual abuse.

In India too, over the last decade, the volume of human trafficking has increased though the exact numbers are not known, it is one of the most lucrative criminal trades, next to arms and drug smuggling undertaken by highly organized criminals. In India, a large number of children are trafficked not only for the sex 'trade' but also for other forms of non-sex based exploitation that includes servitude of various kinds, as domestic labour, industrial labour, agricultural labour, begging, organ trade and false marriage.[41] The minor girls procured from different parts of the country are indulged into forced prostitution, socially and religiously sanctified forms of prostitutions, sex tourism and pornography.

According to NHRC Report on Trafficking in Women and Children, in India the population of women and children in sex work in India is stated to be between 70,000 and 1 million of these, 30% are 20 years of age. Nearly 15% began sex work when they were below 15 and 25% entered between 15 and 18 years. A rough estimate prepared by an NGO called End children's prostitution in Asian Tourism reveals that there are around 2 million prostitutes in India. 20% among them are minors. A study conducted in 1992 estimates that any one time 20,000 girls are being transported from one part of the country to any other.[42]

As per statistical data of NCRB, 172 cases of procuration of minor girls in 1999 and 147 cases in 2000 were reported in India. The number of cases regarding the same crime against children was 138 in 2001 and 124 in 2002. In 2003, there was a noticeable increase in the number of cases with total 171 cases in that year. The increase in the number continued in the next year and the NCRB reported 205 cases of procuration of minor girls in India in the year2004. In 2005, the number of cases had slightly declined to 145 cases, which were worryingly remunerated off by the huge number of cases in next two years with 231 and 253 cases respectively in 2006 and 2007. The NCRB reported 224 cases of procurement of minor girls in India in 2008.

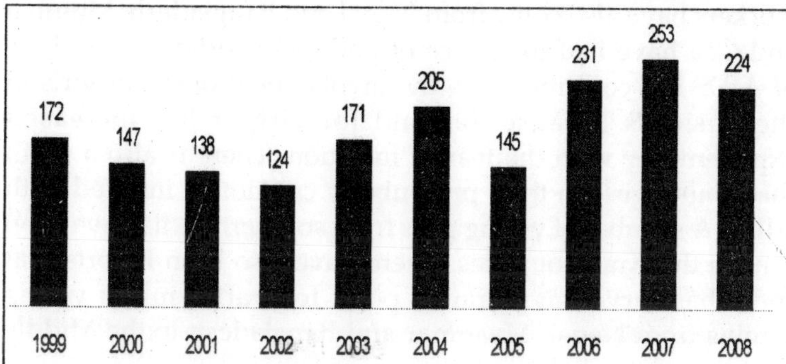


*Source:* National Crime Record Bureau of India.

**Figure 10: Procurement of Minor Girls in India (2000-2008)**

The data exposes that total 1810 cases of procuration of minor girls are reported in India in ten years (1999 to 2008). It confirms that average 181 cases are reported in India in a year; while average 1 case of procuration of minor girls is reported in India after every 48 hours. The number of cases decreased to 14.53 per cent in 2000 in comparison to 1999. Again there was a decrease of 6.12 per cent in 2001 as compared to the number of cases in 2000. The number of cases had declined to 10.14 per cent in 2002 as compared to 2001. In 2003 there was increase of 37.90 per cent in contrast with 2002. The year 2004 had witnessed a further increase of 19.88 per cent over the year 2003. In the year 2005, there was a steep decline of 29.26 per cent as compared with 2004. An increase of 59.31 per cent was witnessed in 2006 over 2005; while an increase of 9.52 per cent was noticed in the number of cases in 2007 in comparison with 2006. However, the year 2008 had reported decrease of 11.46 per cent as compared to 2007.

### *Buying and Selling of Girls for Prostitution*

Commercial sex in India is a 400000 million Rupees annual business. Thirty percent of the sex workers are children who earn about Rupees 110000 million every year. There could be about 0.3 million child sex workers in India of which 0.1 million could be less than 18 years of age. 15% of the sex workers have been residing in the six metropolitan cities of Mumbai, Calcutta, Delhi, Chennai, Bangalore and Hyderabad. Some sex workers have also come from Nepal and Bangladesh. Mumbai and Goa have had incidence of pedophilic offences too. Fear of AIDS has contributed to the involvement of minor girls in the business because demand for virgins has increased exponentially with the fear of infection. There is also a myth that young girls in their pre-puberty can not be infested with AIDS. A number of young girls from southern India have been sent to the Arab countries. There have also been reports that India has served as a transit point for trafficking of young virgins from Nepal, Myanmar and Bangladesh to the Middle East, mostly Dubai.[43]

Suppression of Immoral Traffic in Women and Girls Act, 1956 was the main Act to deal with these offences. This Act was amended in 1978 and was reenacted under the name of 'Immoral Traffic (Prevention) Act in 1986' to rectify some lacunae in the older Act. Punishment could be imprisonment for a period of 7-10 years or for life. Indian Penal Code stipulates that sexual intercourse with or without her consent with a girl less than 16 years of age amounts to rape punishable with imprisonment for life.[44]

As per data of NCRB, 5 cases of buying of girls in India for prostitution were reported in 1999. The NCRB had reported 53 cases of buying of girls for prostitution in India in 2000. In 2001, there were 6 reported cases of such crime. 9 cases were reported by NCBR in 2002, while 24 cases were reported in 2003. Total 21 case in 2004 and 28 cases in 2005 were reported by the NCRB regarding buying of girls for prostitution. The NCRB, in 2006 reported 35 cases, and in 2007, it reported 40 cases. In 2008, total 30 cases of buying of girls for prostitution in India were reported by the NCRB.

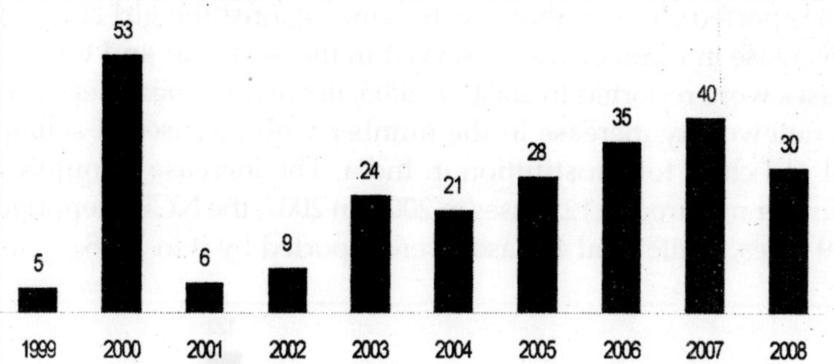


*Source:* National Crime Record Bureau of India.

**Figure 11: Buying of Girls in India for Prostitution (1999-2008)**

The data asserts that there are total 251 cases of buying the girls in India in 10 years (1999 to 2008). It means that average 1 cases of buying the girls is reported in India after every 42 hours. There are several increases and decreases in the number of reported cases regarding the buying of girls in India. The number of cases had increased to 960 per cent in 2000 as compared to 1999, but drastically declined to 883.33 per cent per cent in 2001. There was an increase of 50 per cent as compared to 2001. The increase continued and was noticed as 166 per cent in 2003 over 2002. In 2004, the number of cases declined to 12.5 per cent in comparison with 2003. In 2005, the number of cases increased to 33.33 per cent over the year 2004. The increase continued consistently and the year 2006 noticed an increase of 25 per cent than the year 2005. Similarly an increase of 14.28 per cent was witnessed in the year 2007 in contrast with 2006. In 2008, a decrease of 25 per cent was noticed in the number of cases in comparison to 2007.

### *Selling of Girls for Prostitution*

According to the statistical data of the NCRB, 13 cases of the selling of girls for prostitution were reported in India; while 15 cases of selling of girls for prostitution were reported in 2000. The number was quite bearable in 2001 and 2002, and the NCRB had reported respectively 8 and 5 cases of selling of girls for prostitution. The number increased rapidly in 2003 to

36 reported cases of that severe crime against the girl child. A decrease in number was observed in the next year and total 19 cases were reported in 2004. In 2005, however, again there was a noteworthy increase in the number with 50 cases of selling of girl child for prostitution in India. The increase in number further matured to 123 cases in 2006. In 2007, the NCRB reported 69 cases, while total 49 cases were reported by it in 2008.

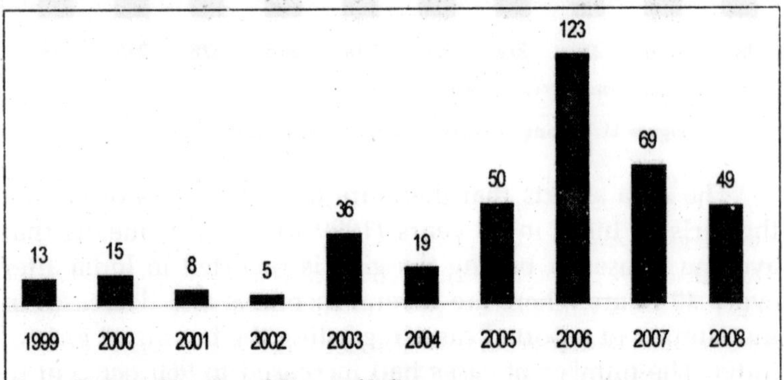


*Source:* National Crime Record Bureau of India.

**Figure 12: Selling of Girls in India for Prostitution (1999-2008)**

The data divulges that total 387 cases of the selling of the girls for prostitution are reported in India in 10 years (1999-2000). It means that average 39 cases of such crime against children are reported in a year in India. The number of cases has noticeably varied year after year. There was 15.38 per cent increase in the number of cases in 2000 than the year 1999. Afterwards there followed a decrease in the number and the number of cases had decreased to 66.66 per cent in 2002 in comparison to 2000. In 2003, the number of cases had increased to 620 per cent in contrast with 2002. A decrease of 47.22 per cent had followed in the year 2004 over 2003. Afterwards, there was a consistent increase of respectively 163.15 per cent and 146 per cent in the number of cases for two consecutive years 2005 and 2006 from their previous years respectively. In 2007, a decrease of 43.90 per cent was noticed than 2006, while decease of 28.98 per cent was witnessed in 2008 in comparison to 2007.

In a shocking revelation by a leading newspaper from Europe, a 13 year old virgin girl called *Suli* near the town of Bharatpur of Rajasthan is up for sale on a highway. The highest bidder is expected to fetch the family Rs.20, 000. *Suli* is being displayed as a commodity - sitting on a stool with heavy make-up in a bright pink sari to attract attention of passing vehicles. She belongs to the *Bedia* community that is well known for its caste-based prostitution. The normal going rate for a night starts from Rs.100 rate, however virgins are valued "commodities" and a pretty face can fetch as much as Rs.40,000 ($1000). *Suli* is likely to fetch about $500 and is awaiting the highest bidder.[45]

### *Child Marriage*

Child marriage, also known as early marriage, is defined as "any marriage carried out below the age of 18 years, before the girl is physically, physiologically, and psychologically ready to shoulder the responsibilities of marriage and childbearing."[46] Child marriage, on the other hand, involves either one or both spouses being children and may take place with or without formal registration, and under civil, religious or customary laws. In many societies in developing countries, child marriages are used to build or strengthen alliances between families. Sometimes this may even include the betrothals of young children or babies.

The persistent neglect of the plight of child marriages in Rajasthan, Andhra Pradesh, Assam, Bihar, and Madhya Pradesh is a direct reflection of the failure of our collective responsibility to protect the human rights of vulnerable young people. The silenced voices of the many thousands of young boys and girls forced into marriage before their eighteenth birthday signify complacency and discrimination. The country has laws on the minimum age of marriage, but they are largely ineffective, not enforced or operate alongside customary and religious laws. Traditions and cultural norms which rule the social lives of many practicing communities in the country should not be used as an excuse to neglect the duty to protect, respect and fulfill the rights of children.[47]

Child marriage remains a widely ignored violation of the health and development rights of girls and boys in India. Governments are often either unable to enforce existing laws, or rectify discrepancies between national laws on marriage age and entrenched customary and religious laws. This is because of the "official tolerance of cultural, societal and customary norms that shape and govern the institution of marriage and family life."[48] In general, there is seldom political will to act when it comes to boys' and girls' human rights. Additionally, the international development community has largely failed to target development assistance to address this gross rights violation in India. Child marriage is culturally packaged in several parts of the country as a social necessity, but in many cases this amounts to "socially licensed sexual abuse and exploitation of a child."[49]

Child marriage results in psychosocial disadvantage, adolescent health and reproduction, the denial of education, violence and abandonment, lost of childhood etc. One thing is clear: the impact of early marriage on girls - and to a lesser extent on boys - is wide-ranging. Within a rights perspective, three key concerns are the denial of childhood and adolescence, the curtailment of personal freedom and the lack of opportunity to develop a full sense of selfhood as well as the denial of psychosocial and emotional well-being, reproductive health and educational opportunity. Early marriage also has implications for the well-being of families, and for society as a whole. Where girls are uneducated and ill-prepared for their roles as mothers and contributors to society, there are costs to be borne at every level, from the individual household to the nation as a whole.[50]

It is very difficult to get accurate data on the true extent of child marriages in the country. This is because most marriages are not officially registered, and many parents resort to falsifying girls' ages. Such acts are made easier in rural areas where birth certificates are often non-existent or not properly recorded. There is also very little data on girls married before the age of 15. Available data are often outdated and fail to provide adequate information to support meaningful policy and programme development. The data published by the NCRB in its annual publications, somehow is the only official and formal source to provide the exact number of the total reported cases of child marriages in India every year.

The NCRB of India had reported 58 cases of the violation of Child Marriage Restraint Act in 1999. In 2000, it reported 92 cases of the violation of Child Marriage Restraint Act. In 2001, it reported 85 cases and in 2002, 113 cases of such violation. The NCRB reported total 63 cases of the violation of Child Marriage Restraint Act in 2003. In 2004, the number of cases reported by the NCRB reached to 93, which further increased to 122 cases in 2005. In 2006, the NCRB had reported 99 cases of the violation of Child Marriage Restraint Act. In 2007, the number of the total cases for the violation of above said Act was 96, while total 104 cases were reported by the NCRB in 2008.

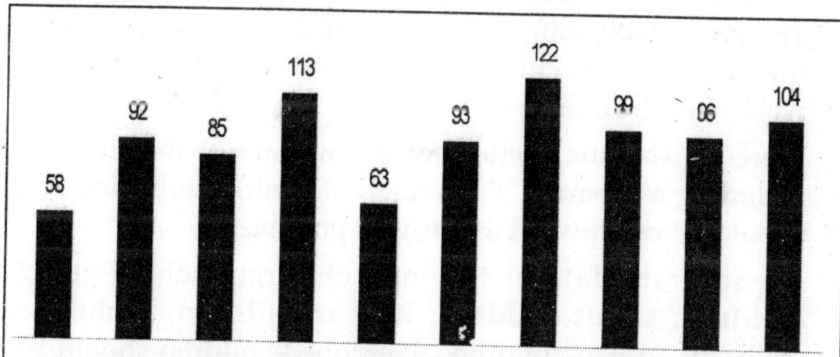


*Source:* National Crime Record Bureau of India.

**Figure 13: Violation of Child Marriage Restraint Act (1999-2008)**

The data asserts that there are total 925 cases of the violation of the Child Marriage Restraint Act reported by NCRB in 10 years (1999 to 2008). It exposes that average 93 cases of the violation of the aforesaid Act are reported in India in a year. It further confirms that average 1 case of violating the Act has been reported in India after every 4 days.

Thus it establishes as an explicit reality that the rights of children in India are in misery. Majority among them die after a few days, weeks or months of their birth. Those who survive, majority among them live their life while roaming in the streets in the day and sleeping on foot-paths at night. Innumerous among them are not able to get proper food to satisfy their appetite, hygienic and nutritional diet is a joke on them. Millions of them are working at the factories, mills, *dhabas*, restaurants, and tea-stalls in the hazardous conditions proving the 'Right to Education Act' dead combating their most fundamental need to work for survival.

Some suggestions are advised underneath which can facilitate in improving the physical, social, economic and mental conditions of the children in India.

## Suggestions and Recommendations

- All constitutional provisions and legislations passed in India imparting various rights, liberties, facilities and amentias to the children should be properly implemented. The law establishing agencies should be strengthened for the adequate execution of the laws constituted for the welfare of the children.
- More legislations needed for the welfare of the children including a separate 'Prevention of Child Trafficking Act should be constituted as early as possible.
- An accurate data of the total children, school-going children, street-children, beggar-children, homeless children, orphan-children, abandoned-children should be carried out to chalk out appropriate programmes and policies for them according to their separate problems and needs.
- The legislation passed by the Indian Parliament regarding making the Primary Education a fundamental right, should be strictly and sincerely implemented.
- It should be made possible to report all crime against the children and prosecute the guilty as per law. Separate and more effective laws can be constituted to alleviate rape, sexual harassment, molestation of children.

- It is sturdily required to aware the common masses regarding the legislations, programmes, schemes, policies constituted and executed for the welfare of the children.
- The civil society and the NGOs should be encouraged and even provided more financial and logistic support to take more concrete and fruitful initiatives for the welfare of the children and to combat the increasing graph of crimes against children.
- The governmental organizations, including the National and State Human Rights Commission, National Commission for the Protection of Child Rights and other nodal agencies, should be given some additional and effective powers to protect the child rights in an appropriate and expected manner.

The violation of the child rights is a serious concern and a complex issue. The protection of child rights needs a launch of a nation-wide campaign at the grass-root level. The common masses should be awakened, the civil society is to be trained, and the governmental agencies are required to be more vigilant to make the ideal of child rights a reality in India. In reality, the legislations should be brought out in the streets from the chambers, the governmental schemes need to appear out among the rural folk and the campaigns of the civil society are required to centralize in the slums and distinct places, if the children of India are to be developed in an multifaceted manner.

## References

1. Savita Bhakhrey, *Children in India and their Rights*, National Human Rights Commission, 2006, p. 9.
2. Pairvi (NGO), State of Child Rights in India, 2007, p. 1.
3. UNICEF, *Child Rights in India*, 2008, p. 1.
4. Deepa Jain Singh, "Foreword", in Loveleen Kacker, et al., *Study on Child Abuse: India 2007*, Ministry of Women and Child Development, Government of India, 2007, p. iii.
5. UNICEF, *State of the World's Children*, 2006, p17.
6. SAVE THE CHILDREN (NGO), *Corporate Social Responsibility and Children's Rights in South Asia*, Published by Regional Office of Save the Child, Kathmandu, 2007, p. 11.

7. Global Union, *International Conference for Child Rights Organizers and Campaigners*, Conference Report, 20-21 February, 2008, p.6.
8. United Nations Children Fund (UNCEF), *Child Labour: Child Protection Information Sheet*, UNICEF, New York, 2006, p. 1.
9. International Labour Conference, *Accelerating Action against Child Labour* (A Report for the Director General) 99th Session, International Labour Office, Geneva, 2010, p. 2.
10. Work has been defined in the Census 2001 as 'participation in any economically productive activity with or without compensation, wages or profit.' Such participation could be physical and/or mental in nature. This work includes supervisory work as well as direct participation in the work. For the first time, the Census includes part-time help or unpaid work on the farm, family enterprise or in any other economic activity such as cultivation and milk production for domestic consumption as work. All persons engaged in 'work' as defined in the Census are considered workers. Main workers are defined as those who have worked for the major part of the reference period that is 6 months or more. And marginal workers are those who have not worked for the major part of the reference period. All those workers who are not cultivators or agricultural labourers or engaged in household industry are categorized as 'Other Workers'.
11. National Commission for the Protection of Child Rights (NCPCR), Abolition of Child Labour in India: Strategies for the XI Five Year Plan (Executive Summary), September 2007, pp. 1-2.
12. Asha Bajpai, *Child Rights in India, Law, Policy and Practice*, Oxford University Press, New Delhi, 2003, p. 213.
13. United States Department of State, *Country Reports on Human Rights Practices for 1995*, Department of State, United States, 1996, p. 771.
14. U.S. Department of State, *India - Country Report on Human Rights Practices for 1998*, Bureau of Democracy, Human Rights and Labour, , Feb. 26, 1999.
15. Kamayani Singh, Dial 1098 to Report Child Labour, The Times of India,timesofindia.indiatimes.com/articleshow
16. U.S. Department of State, *India - Country Report on Human Rights Practices 1997*, p. 19.
17. L. M. Mittal, "No End in Sight", *Social Welfare*, June, 1997, p.17.
18. Global March Against Child Labour & International Centre for Child Labour and Education (ICCLE), *Review of Child Labour, Education and Poverty Agenda: India Country Report, 2006*,p. 9-10.
19. NCPCR, 2007, *op.cit.*, p. 2.
20. P.D. Singh Bhagwan and Mahanty Shukla, "Children at Work: Problems and Policy Options", *The Indian journal of LabourEeconomics*, Indian Society of Labour Economics, Volume 40, 1997, p. 97.
21. Gopal Bhargava, *Child labour in India: A politico-Legal Study*, Gyan Publishing House, 2003, p. 78.

22. Sibnath Deb, *Children in Agony: A Source Book*, Concept Publishing Company, New Delhi, 2006, p. 262.
23. Rabinder Nath Pati, *Rehabilitation of Child Labourers in India*, Ashish Publishing House, New Delhi, 1991, p. 121.
24. D. Sarada, Child Rights and Young Lives: Theoretical Issues and Empirical Studies, Discovery Publishing House, New Delhi, 2009, p. 69.
25. Rabindra Nath Pati, 1991, *op.cit.*, 122.
26. C. K. Shukla, S. Ali, *Child Labour and the Law*, Sarup & Sons Publishers, 2006, pp. 51-52. Also see, R.N. Misra, *Child Labour in Hazardous Sectors*, Discovery Publishing House, 2003, pp. 4-8.
27. Santosh K. Mehrotra, *The Economics of Elementary Education in India: The Challenge of Public Finance, Private Provision, and Household Costs*, SAGE Publications, California, 2006, p. 14.
28. S. Wall, *Combating Child Labour Legal Approach*, (Volume 4), Sarup & Sons, New Delhi, 2006, p. 17.
29. D. Sarada, *Child Rights and Youung Lives: Theoretical Issues and Empirical Studies*, Discovery Publishing House, 2009, p. 67.
30. Mahavir Jain, *Insights on Child Labour*, Manak Publications, Delhi, 2006, p. 117-118.
31. S.N. Mishra & Sweta Mishra, *Tiny Hands in Unorganised Sector*, Shipra Publiations, Delhi, 2004, p. 61.
32. Human Rights Watch, *World Report 2007: India*, p.5.
33. World Health Organization, *Report of the Consultation on Child Abuse Prevention*, Geneva, 1999, retrieved from, http://www.who.int/violence_injury_prevention/violence/neglect/en/
34. Loveleen Kacker, *op. cit.*, p. 3.
35. Loveleen Kacker, *op.cit.*, pp. vi-vii.
36. Chris King, Daughters, *Wives and Widows*, Retrieved from http://ebcache.googleusercontent.com/search?q=cache:HIHVpiYvCR0J:www.dhushara.com/paradoxhtm/girlchild.
37. T.M Kolloor, "Female Infanticide: A Psychological Analysis, *Grass Roots Action*, special issue on Girl Child, April 3, 1990, p. 73.
38. Sneh Lata Tondon & Renu Sharma, "Female Foeticide and Infanticide in India: An Analysis of Crimes against Girl Children", *International Journal of Criminal Justice Sciences*, Vol. 1, Issue 1, January 2006, 121-122.
39. K.D. Gangrade, et al., *Facets of a Heinous Crime*, National Library of Medicine, National Institute for Health, Retrieved from http://www.ncbi.nlm.nih.gov/pubmed/12158004.
40. Child Abduction in India, Retrieved from, http://www. awareindia online.com/2010/07/23/child-abduction-in-india/
41. Intezar Khan, *Child Trafficking in India: A Concern*, Retrieved from, http://india.gov.in/allimpfrms/alldocs/12262.pdf
42. *Ibid.*

43. Sanjiv Kumar Upadhyay, *Crime in India,* 116th International Training Course Participants' Papers, Resource Material Series No. 58, United Nations Asia and Far East Institute for the prevention of Crime and the Treatment of the Offenders, 2004, pp. 201-202.
44. *Ibid.*, p. 202.
45. 13 Year Old Virgin on Sale in India, retrieved from, http://www.medindia.net/news/indiaspecial/13
46. The Inter-African Committee (IAC) on Traditional Practices Affecting the Health of Women and Children, (1993), *Newsletter*, December, 2003, p. 77.
47. International Planned Parenthood Federation and the Forum on Marriage and the Rights of Women and Girls, *Ending Child Marriage: A Guide for Global Policy Action*, 2005, p. 3.
48. Centre for Reproductive Rights. (2000) *Reproductive Rights 2000: Moving Forward.* New York: Centre for Reproductive Rights, p52
49. Forum on Marriage and the Rights of Women and Girls, *Early Marriage: Sexual Exploitation and the Human Rights of Girls*, London, 2001, p. 2.
50. UNICEF, "Early Marriage: Child Spouses", *Innocenti Digest*, No. 7, March United Nations, 2001, p. 9.

# 10

## Violation of the Human Rights of SCs and STs in India

India's caste system is perhaps the world's longest surviving social hierarchy. A defining feature of Hinduism, caste encompasses a complex ordering of social groups on the basis of ritual purity. A person is considered as a member of the caste into which he or she is born and remains within that caste until death, although the particular ranking of that caste may vary among regions and over time. Differences in status are traditionally justified by the religious doctrine of *karma*, a belief that one's place in life is determined by one's deeds in previous lifetimes.[1] Traditional scholarship has described this more than 2,000-year-old system within the context of the four principal V*arnas*, or large caste categories. In order of precedence these are the *Brahmins* (priests and teachers), the *Kshyatriyas* (rulers and soldiers), the *Vaishyas* (merchants and traders), and the *Shudras* (labourers and artisans). The fourth category belonging to *Shudras* falls lowest in the *Varna* system and consists of those known as "untouchables" or *Dalits;* they are often assigned tasks too ritually polluting to merit inclusion within the traditional *Varna* system.

Within the four principal castes, there are thousands of sub-castes, also called *jatis,* endogamous groups that are further divided along occupational, sectarian, regional and linguistic lines. Collectively all of these are sometimes referred to as 'Hindu Castes' or those falling within the caste system. The *Dalits* are even described as *Varna-Sankara.*[2] They are so inferior to other castes that they are deemed polluting and therefore 'untouchables'. Even as outcasts, they themselves are divided into further sub-castes.[3] Although untouchability was abolished under Article 17 of the Indian constitution, the practice continues to determine the socio-economic and religious standing of those at the bottom of the caste hierarchy.

The Scheduled Castes (SCs), also known as Untouchables, *Harijans,* or Dalits, have historically been poor, deprived of basic human rights, and treated as social inferiors in India. They still face economic, social, cultural, and political discrimination in the name of caste. Centuries of this 'hidden apartheid' that has perpetuated discrimination and denial of their human rights, has resulted not only in Dalits representing a disproportionate amount of the poor in India, but also in the creation of numerous other obstacles that hinder Dalits' ability to change their situation.[4] According to Minority Rights Group International's report of 2006, Dalits make up approximately 170 million of India's billion people. Many are agricultural laborers. They have a limited share in India's agricultural holdings and an even more limited share in its irrigated land holdings.

Discriminatory and cruel, inhuman and degrading treatment of over 165 million people in India has been justified on the basis of caste.[5] Caste divisions in India dominate in housing, marriage, employment and general social interaction-divisions that are reinforced through the practice and threat of social ostracism, economic boycotts, and physical violence. India has consistently cited its numerous legislations and government policies as a measure of compliance with its obligations to end caste-based discrimination, choosing to ignore its failure to implement these measures which has resulted in continued and sometimes enhanced, brutalities against Dalits. Dalits who have contested political office in village councils and municipalities through seats that have been constitutionally 'reserved' for them have been threatened with physical abuse and even death in order to get them to withdraw from the campaign. In the village of *Melavalavu,* Madurai district Tamil Nadu, following the election of a Dalit to the village council presidency, members of a higher-caste group murdered six Dalits in June 1997, including the elected council president, whom they beheaded.[6] Dalits' political rights, especially the right to vote freely and right to stand for election, have repeatedly been denied by upper caste community members by booth-rigging and both capturing, denial of access to polls, intimidation and violence. In Madhya Pradesh, woman was raped because she contested and won the election to a panchayat defeating an upper caste rival.[7]

Despite the fact that untouchability was abolished under India's constitution in 1955,[8] the practice of untouchability-the imposition of social disabilities on persons by reason of their birth in certain castes- remains very much a part of rural India. Untouchables, in several parts of the country, may not cross the line dividing their part of the village from that occupied by higher castes. They may not use the same wells, visit the same temples, drink from the same cups in tea stalls, or lay claim to land that is legally theirs.[9] There are several cases where the Dalit children are frequently made to sit in the back of classrooms in the schools,[10] and communities as a whole are made to perform degrading rituals in the name of caste. Dalits throughout the country also suffer in many instances from de facto disenfranchisement. During elections, those unpersuaded by typical electioneering are routinely threatened and beaten by political party strongmen in order to compel them to vote for certain candidates.[11] Most Dalits continue to live in extreme poverty, without land or opportunities for better employment or education. With the exception of a minority who have benefited from India's policy of quotas in education and government jobs, Dalits are relegated to the most menial of tasks, as manual scavengers, removers of human waste and dead animals, leather workers, street sweepers, and cobblers.[12] Dalit children make up the majority of those sold into bondage to pay off debts to upper-caste creditors.

The Scheduled Castes and Scheduled Tribes (Prevention of Atrocities) Act, enacted in 1989, provides a means to address many of the problems Dalits face in India. The act is designed to prevent abuses and punish those responsible, establish special courts for the trial of such offenses, and provide for victim relief and rehabilitation. A look at the offenses made punishable by the act provides a glimpse into the retaliatory or customarily degrading treatment Dalits may receive. The offenses include forcing members of a scheduled caste or scheduled tribe to drink or eat any inedible or obnoxious substance; dumping excreta, waste matter, carcasses or any other obnoxious substance in their premises or neighborhood; forcibly removing their clothes and parading them naked or with painted face or body; interfering with their rights to land; compelling a member of a scheduled caste or scheduled tribe into forms of forced or bonded labor; corrupting or fouling the water of any spring, reservoir or any other source ordinarily used by scheduled castes or scheduled tribes; denying right of passage to a place of public resort; and using a position of dominance to exploit a scheduled caste or scheduled tribe woman sexually.[13] Although constitutional provisions and legal texts exist to abolish untouchability and to protect the members of the scheduled castes and tribes, and social and educational policies have been adopted to improve the situation of members of the scheduled castes and tribes and to protect them from abuses, widespread discrimination against those people, and the relative impunity of those who abuse them, points to the limited effect of these measures. Most Dalits in rural areas live in segregated colonies, away from the higher castes.[14]

India's failure to ensure that all public authorities and public institutions do not engage in caste-based discrimination is widespread. Two examples exemplify this failure: treatment of Dalits by the police and discrimination in the provision of disaster relief. National Human Rights Commission has commented that the law enforcement machinery is the greatest violator of Dalits' human rights. According to the NHRC, widespread custodial torture and killings of Dalits, rape and sexual assault of Dalit women and looting Dalit property by the police are condoned or at best ignored.[15]

Dalits are particularly vulnerable to arrest under draconian security laws under a theory of collective punishment, the police often target entire Dalit communities in search of one individual and subject the community to violent search and seizure operations. Dalit women are particularly vulnerable to sexual violence by the police, which is used as a tool to punish Dalit communities. According to separate investigations by the National Campaign on Dalit Human Rights(NCDHR) and Human Rights Watch, India has failed to protect Dalits from discrimination in the distribution of aid in the wake of two's of India's largest natural disaster movements in the recent years- the Gujarat earthquake in January 2001 and the Indian Ocean Tsunami in December 2004. India has also failed to encourage integrationist movements or eliminate barriers between castes. It has allowed segregation in schools and housing. India has also failed to faithfully implement constitutional and legislative abolitions of untouchability practices. In its 1999 Annual Report, the Special Rapporteur on Contemporary Forms of Racism, Racial Discrimination, Xenophobia and Related Intolerance found untouchability to be very alive in rural area, as reflected in caste-based segregation in housing, schools, public services, public places and in the prohibition against Dalits' use of shared water sources. A survey investigating the extent of untouchability practices in 565 villages in 11 India State found that the constitutionally abolished crime of untouchability continues to profoundly affect the lives and psyches of millions of Dalits.[16]

India grants Dalits a certain number of privileges, including reservations in education, government jobs and government bodies. Like many of the protective measures adopted, the reservation policy has not been successfully implemented for Dalits. According to government estimates in 2000, the unemployment rate for Dalits and tribal groups was double that of non-Dalits and tribal people.[17] Additionally, public sector divestment to private owners is estimated to have left 200,000 Dalit employees jobless.[18] An estimated forty million people in India, among them fifteen million children, are bonded labourers, working in slave-like conditions in order to pay off debts.[19] The majority of them are Dalits.

Physical attacks on Dalits have risen. This is reflected in the rising graph of physical crimes including assault, murder and rapes committed against Dalits across the country. Not a day goes by when a newspaper or television channel does not report an incident. The increase of physical attacks against Dalits is to counter their resistance to the traditional role assigned to them by the Hindu caste system. Dalits' right to freedom of residence is severely curtailed by the practice of untouchability which often dictates where Dalits must live. Strict prohibitions on marriage and other social interaction between Dalits and the upper-caste routinely violate the rights of Dalits to marry and choose their spouse. In Bihar, Dalits are stripped naked and paraded on the streets by the upper caste people if they dare to try to establish matrimonial relations or try to get home next to the upper caste community.[20]

Dalits in India face a number of restrictions on their right to freedom of thought, conscience and religion. Dalits are, for instance, routinely denied entry into Hindu temples. Besides that, upper-castes usually violate the right to religion of Dalits by disrespecting, plundering or pulling down the temples constructed by Dalits. In Bibipur, a small village in Haryana's Karnal district, the Dalit struggle to build a temple to Sant Ravidas had come up against severe forward caste and official resistance. The temple had been razed ostensibly because it was sought to be built on village school land.[21] Dalits continue to face violence and discrimination in nearly every sphere of their lives. Abuses against Dalits range from harassment and use of excessive force by security forces in routine matters, to mutilations and killings by members of other castes for attempting to cross caste barriers.[22] Abuses against Dalits include harassment, mutilations and killings by members of other castes. For instance, in January 2006, Bant Singh, a Dalit man who had led a campaign to protect the rights of agricultural workers, was so brutally assaulted by members of the feudal upper caste that his limbs had to be amputated.[23]

**Crimes and Atrocities against SCs in India**

Caste based discrimination and atrocity against Dalit community is alarmingly increased all over India that lead to bloody and brutal killing of Dalits everyday. The severity of violence's against Dalits is beyond any human comprehension as Dalits are lynched, murdered and mutilated. This kind of violence is not seen even in animal world. There is hardly any day goes by when Dalits are not killed, harassed, socially boycotted by the upper castes. Dalits houses are burnt, physical violence against dalit woman like rape, terrorizing the dalit woman by parading naked on streets, cutting genitals of dalit children's, beating elderly Dalits are rampant and it is like an epidemic in rural areas and villages across India. Any social activities of Dalits such as marriages, temple festivals, and funeral proceedings of Dalits cannot go smoothly without violence and dalit killings.

The violence and attack on Dalits are so horrendous that dalit people live in constant fear, insecurity and torturous life. It is a gross human rights violation. Murder of entire dalit family members, dalits being lynched like animals in a day light under the blessings of law and enforcement (the local police), raping of minors as young as 5 year old dalit girl, parading dalit woman's naked in broad day light in the presence of entire village people are few of the thousands of examples of organized and well planned caste brutality against Dalits.

The statistical data of National Crime Record Bureau of India (NCRB), which reports, records and publishes the total number of crime of different categories that takes place in India in a year, reveals a severe, constant and intense violation of human rights of SCs. The statistical date of NCRB regarding crime against SCs since 2000 to 2008 has been analyzed to get the accurate information regarding crimes against SCs in different spheres of their life. According the NCRB, total 25093 cases of crime against SCs were reported in India in 1999. There were total 25455 reported cases of crime against SCs in 2000. In 2001, the number of crime against SCs was 33501. The number was almost same in 2002 with total 33507 cases, and had decreased slightly in 2003 with 26252 cases in that year. There were 26887 cases of crime against SCs reported by NCRB in 2004. The number of reported cases of crime against SCs was 26127 in 2005 and 27070 in 2006. In 2007, the NCRB had reported 30031 cases and in 2008 total 33615 cases of crime against SCs.

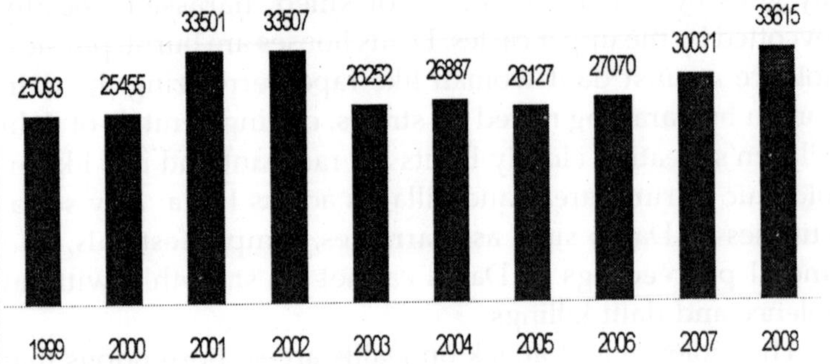


*Source:* National Crime Record Bureau of India.

**Figure 1: Cases of Crime Against SCs (1999-2008)**

The data divulges that total 287538 cases of 'crime against the SCs' are registered in 10 years (1999 to 2008). It means that average 28754 cases of crimes committed against the SCs are reported in India in a year. Average 2396 cases of crime against SCs are reported every month; while 599 cases of crime against SCs are reported every week. The data further confirms that average 86 cases of the crimes committed against the SCs are reported every day. It establishes that average approximately 4 cases of the crimes committed against the SCs are reported in India every hour; while average 1 crime against SCs is reported in India after every 19 minutes. A few variations are noticed in the number of cases in different years. The number of cases was approximately similar in 1999 and 2000, with a minimal increase of 1.44 per cent in 2000. But the number of cases drastically increased in 2002 to 31.60 per cent in comparison to 2000. That increase remained unchanged in the year 2002 also. In 2003, the number of cases had decreased to

21.65 per cent in contrast with the year 2002. A consistent increase had been noticed every year than the previous year in the number of cases since 2004 to 2008. The number of cases had increased to 25.02 per cent in 2008 after 5 years, in comparison to the year 2004.

## Major Categories of Crime against SCs

Undoubtedly, the rights of the SCs are violated in every sphere of their life and there are several types of the crimes committed against them which make their life miserable. Some major categories of crime against SCs include murder of SCs, rape of SC women, kidnapping and abduction, incidents of arson, hurt and deliberate atrocities against SCs. The SCs living in urban areas, particularly who are literate and/or working as government employees due to privileged reservation to them, are the least targets of these type of inhuman and lethal crimes. But the SCs living in rural, backward or distinct areas are the soft targets of these crimes. Every year thousands of SCs become the victims of these crimes which make their condition most of the times physically handicapped, socially more deprived, economically shoddier, and mentally stressed.

According to the year-wise statistical data of NCRB since 2000 to 2008, total 5905 SCs had been murdered in those 8 years. On the other side, 11171 SC women were raped since 2000 to

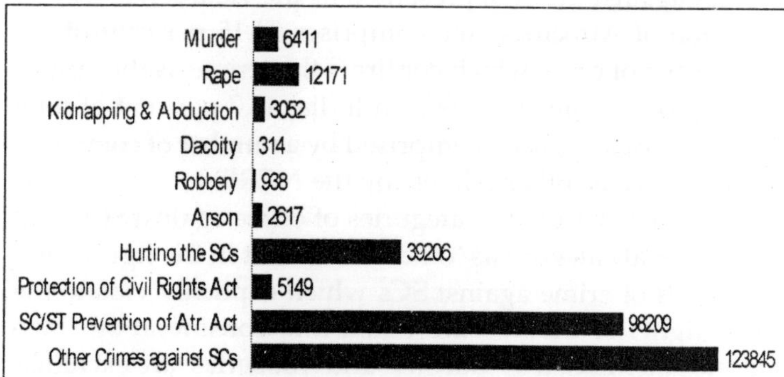


*Source:* National Crime Record Bureau of India.

**Figure 2: Major Categories of Crime Against SCs (1999-2008)**

2008. Furthermore, according to NCRB, there occurred total 2824 cases of kidnapping and abduction of SCs in those 8 years. The NCRB had reported 2280 cases of arson against SCs and 35965 cases of hurting the SCs since 2000 to 2008. Moreover, total 4471 regarding the violation of the Protection of Civil Rights Act against SCs were reported by the NCRB since 2000 to 2008. As many as 90908 SC had suffered due to the violation of SC/ST Prevention of Atrocities Act since 2000 to 2008.

Among total 287538 cases reported by the NCRB in 10 years since 1999 to 2008, 6411 cases in these 10 years are regarding murder of SCs which constitutes 2.22 per cent of the total number of cases. Furthermore 12171 cases of the rape of SC women are reported which comprises 4.23 per cent of total number of cases. 3052 cases reported regarding kidnapping and abduction of SCs contains 1.06 per cent of the total number of cases. 314 cases of dacoity and 938 cases of robbery compose 0.10 per cent and 0.32 per cent of total number of cases respectively. There were total 2617 cases of arson which comprise 0.91 per cent of total number of cases. The crime of hurt establishes as the second largest crime against SCs by constituting 13.63 per cent of the total number of cases. 1.79 per cent of total number of cases was constituted by the crime of violating Protection of Civil Rights Act by practicing untouchability against the SCs. The crime of committing atrocities against the SCs, presented as the violation of SC/ST Prevention of Atrocities Act, comprises 34.15 per cent of the total number of cases which confirms that crime as the largest reported crime against the SCs in India. 43.7 per cent of total number of cases has been comprised by a number of combined crimes labeled as 'other crimes' by the NCRB.

The NCRB displays 9 categories of crime against SCs, and one additional category as 'other cases'. But in the figure only 7 categories of crime against SCs which explicitly violate the human rights of the SCs are taken into consideration. Two categories mentioned as 'dacoity' and 'robberies' are excluded from the categories of those crimes against SCs which violate their human rights.

*Murder of SCs*

The SCs are frequently murdered in almost every part of the country. They are murdered if they unknowingly or deliberately, attempt to cross the strict lines drawn by the upper castes between SC communities by daring to marry an upper caste girl, while performing the religious rituals in temples, or even while entering in the localities of the upper castes. They are brutally killed if they try to contest election against any upper caste politicians. SCs are murdered for not performing the unjustified economic, social, political duties assigned to them by the upper castes.

According to the NCRB, total 506 cases of the murder of SCs were reported throughout India in 1999. There were 526 reported cases of murder of SCs in 2000. In 2001, the NCRB had reported the murder of 763 SCs, while according to the data of NCRB, 739 SCs were murdered in 2002. The NCRB of India had reported 581 cases in 2003 and 654 cases in 2004 regarding the murder of SCs throughout India. The number of cases of murder of SCs was 669 in 2005 and 673 in 2006. The NCRB reported 674 cases of murder of SCs in 2007. In 2008 the NCRB reported total 626 cases of murder of SCs in India.

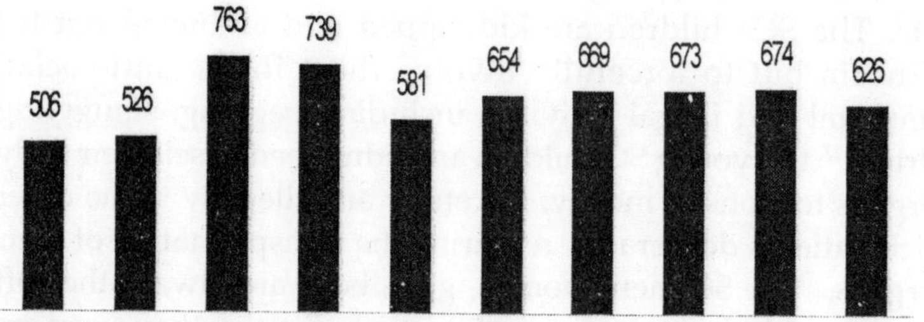


*Source:* National Crime Record Bureau of India.

**Figure 3: Murder of SCs in India (1999-2008)**

The data asserts that there are total 6411 reported cases of the murder of the SCs in 10 years since 1999 to 2008. It confirms that average 641 cases of the murder of the SCs are reported by the NCRB every year. The data further confirms that average 1 SC has been reported to be killed in India after every 15 hours. Unfortunately, the number of cases regarding the murder of the SCs has been consistently increasing year after year. The number of cases was approximately same in 2000 as compared to 1999, noticing a minor increase of 3.95 per cent. But there was a drastic increase of 45.05 per cent in 2001 in contrast with 2000.

### *Kidnapping and Abduction of SCs*

Another brutal crime against SCs is their kidnapping and abduction. The SCs are abducted in indulge them in forced or bonded labour, a contemporary form of slavery. During their abduction the economically downtrodden, socially deprived, politically marginalized SCs are left with only one option, to work as bonded labourers, without demanding any wages.[24] The SC women, especially young girls are kidnapped or abducted to sell them to the procurators or the brothels for prostitution.[25] The SC young girls are kidnapped and then trafficked to the other countries for prostitution[26] or stay permanently with the known men to satisfy their sexual instincts. The SC women are also abducted and then sold in the urban areas to perform household duties as, servants, mates etc. The SC children are kidnapped and abducted not for ransom but to forcefully involve them in the anti-social, immoral and illegal activities including begging, smuggling drugs.[27] The young SC children are kidnapped to sell their body organs for tons of money, forcefully and illegally to the other rich patients desperately requiring the transplantation of their organs. The SC men, women, girls, boys are always the soft targets of kidnapping and abduction. Firstly, they keep on roaming to the distinct places in search of work, shelter or food. A massive number of SCs are homeless in India. Reasonably, they are easily available to the abductors or kidnappers. Particularly, in case of SC boys and girls, they always become vulnerable victims of kidnapping and abduction, due to their separation from their parent during most hours of the day. Their parents are supposed to leave them behind at least for whole day while going at the work, which results in making the SC children more insecure. The SC children, most among them are street children, keep on roaming in the streets, markets, or on the roads, in search of food etc. These circumstances make them more susceptible targets of kidnapping and abduction.

According to the NCRB, there occurred total 228 cases of kidnapping and abduction of SCs in 1999. The number of total reported cases of kidnapping and abduction of SCs was 268 in 2000. While In 2001, total 400 cases were reported by the NCRB. The Bureau reported 319 cases in 2002 and 232 cases in 2003 regarding the kidnapping and abduction of SCs throughout India. In 2004, the NCRB reported 253 cases; while in 2005 it reported 258 cases of kidnapping and abduction of SCs. The number of cases reported by the NCRB regarding the kidnapping and abduction of SCs was 332 in 2007 and 482 in 2008.

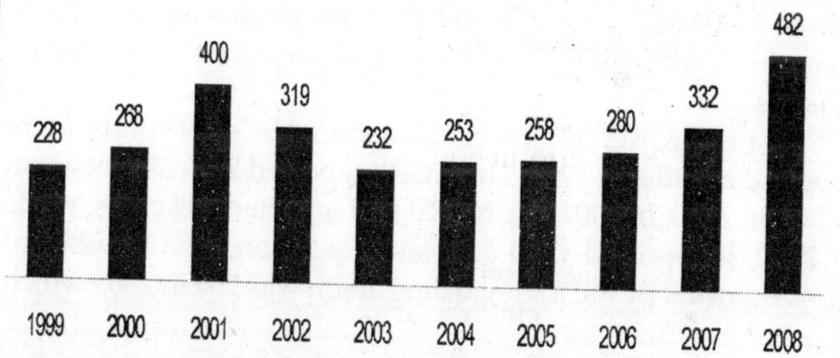


*Source:* National Crime Record Bureau of India.

**Figure 4: Kidnapping and Abduction of SCs (1999-2008)**

As per data, there were 3052 cases of kidnapping and abduction of the SCs reported throughout India in ten years (1999 to 2008). It confirms that average 305 cases of such crime against SCs are reported in India every year. The data further establishes that average 25 cases of the kidnapping and abduction of the SCs are reported in India in a month; while average 6 cases of aforesaid crime are reported in India every week. There is an aggregate increase in the data of that crime against SCs year after year. The number of cases had increased to 17.54 per cent in 2000 in contrast with 1999. A further increase of 49.25 per cent was witnessed in 2001 over 2000. Afterwards, a decrease of 20.25 per cent and 27.27 per cent was noticed in 2002 and 2003 respectively. Since 2004 to 2008, a consistent increase was witnessed in the number of cases. After five years, there was a drastic increase of 90.51 per cent in 2008 in comparison to 2004.

### *Arson*

Every now and then, there are reports of the arson of the property of the SCs in India. Sometimes the *Rajputs* set a fire to the houses of the SCs in Rajasthan and sometimes, the *jats* of Haryana emblaze the houses of the SCs along with a number of alive SCs. There are some reports from Punjab and Utter Pradesh also regarding arson of the SCs' property. [28] The arson of the property of the SCs or even the alive SCs is the most brutal, vicious crime not only against the SCs but against the whole mankind. The SCs and their properties are set on fire sometimes for negligible reasons and sometimes even for no reasons.

As per NCRB, 337 cases of arson of SCs' property were reported in India in 1999. The NCRB reported 290 cases of arson of SCs in 2000. In 2001, the NCRB had reported 354 cases; while in 2002, it reported total 322 cases of arson. The number of cases reported by NCRB regarding arson was 204 in 2003 which

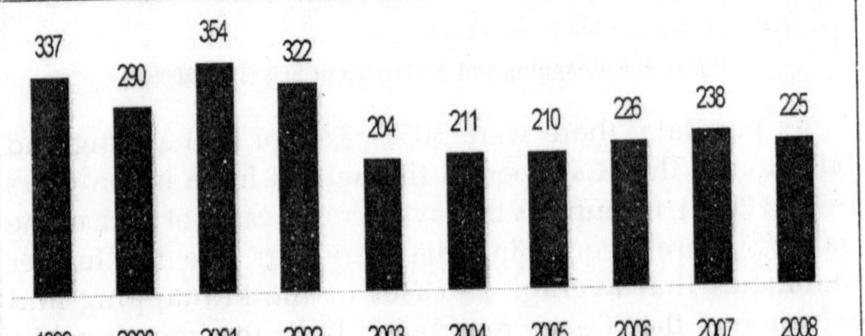


*Source:* National Crime Record Bureau of India.

**Figure 5: Arson of the Property of SCs (1999-2008)**

decreased to 211 in 2004 and 210 in 2005. In 2006 and 2007, the NCRB reported 226 and 238 cases respectively. In 2008 the NCRB reported total 225 cases of arson.

The date reveals that total 2617 cases of arson of SCs' property were reported in India in ten years since 1999 to 2008. It confirms that average 262 cases of such crime are reported in India every year. The data further establishes that average 22 cases of the arson of SC property are reported in India every month; while average 5 cases of such crime are reported in India every week. Providentially, the year-wise number of cases depicts a decrease which confirms that the crime of arson of SCs' property has been declining in the country year after year. 1303 cases (approximately 50 per cent) of the total number of 2617 cases were reported in first 4 years (1999 to 2002), while other 50 per cent cases were noticed in the last 6 years.

**Hurting the SCs**

It has been an undoubted reality that the upper caste people hurt the SCs physically, emotionally or morally. The SCs are abused vulgarly, beaten up, called by undignified names and titles, like *Neech, Chandals, Ashoot*; SC women are also physically assaulted, sexually harassed, paraded naked in an open. These miserable conditions further aggravate the social deprivation, cultural backwardness, economic insufficiency, and political unconsciousness of the SCs.

The NCRB had reported 3241 cases of the hurt of SCs in 1999. Respectively 3497 and 4547 cases were reported in 2000 and 2001. In 2002, the number of cases was 4491; while 3969 cases were reported n 2003. As per NCRB, total 3824 cases of hurting the SCs were reported throughout India in the year 2004. In 2005, the number of reported cases was 3847, and in 2006, total 3760 cases were reported. The NCRB had reported 3814 cases in 2007 and 4216 in 2008, of hurting the SCs throughout India.

The data depicts that total 39206 crimes are reported in India in ten years since 1999 to 2008. It corroborates that average 3921 cases of hurting the SCs are reported in India every year. The data further confirms that average 327 cases

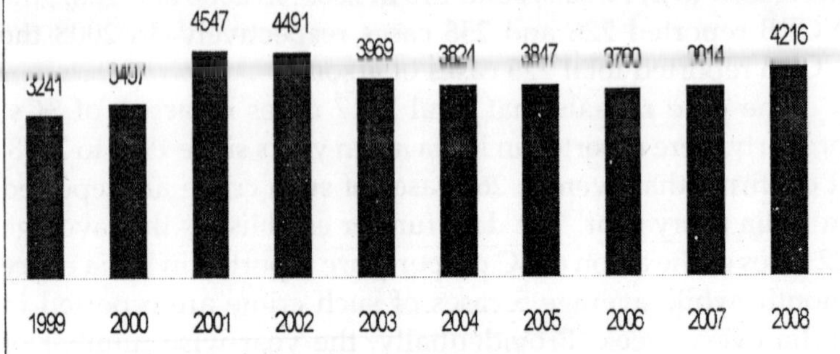


*Source:* National Crime Record Bureau of India.

**Figure 6: Crime of Hurting the SCs (1999-2008)**

of hurting of SCs are reported in India in a month; average 82 cases are reported in a week; while average 12 cases of hurting the SCs are reported in India every day. The data confirms an overall increase in the number of cases since 1999 to 2008, however, with variations in different years. There was 40.49 per cent increase in the number of cases in 2001 over number of cases in 1999. A constant decrease in the number of cases was witnessed since 2002 which continued till 2006. The number of cases had decreased to 17.52 per cent in 2006 in comparison to 2002. Afterwards, the years 2007 and 2008 had noticed an increase of respectively 1.43 per cent and 10.54 per cent in contrast with their previous years.

### *Violation of Protection of Civil Rights Act Against SCs*

The Constitution of India not only guarantees equality, liberty, fraternity, justice and basic human rights as Fundamental Rights but also prohibits the practice of Untouchability in any form. Article 17 of the Constitution abolished Untouchability and its practice in any form is forbidden. Article 25(2b) of the Constitution provides that Hindu religious institutions of a public character shall be open to all classes and sections of Hindus. This provision is contrary to the traditions of some sects of Hinduism that prohibits Scheduled Caste members from entering temples. Two important legislations were enacted to give effect to these articles. The Protection of Civil Rights Act, 1955 punishes the preaching and practice of

Untouchability. The Protection of Civil Rights Act prescribes punishment for the preaching and practice of Untouchability. A recent study on Untouchability in rural India,[29] covering five hundred sixty five villages in eleven States, found that public health workers refused to visit Dalit homes in 33% of villages, and Dalit children sat separately while eating in 37.8% of government schools. Dalits were prevented from entering police stations in 27.6% of villages, did not get mail delivered to their homes in 23.5% of villages, and were denied access to water sources in 48.4% of villages.[30] Thus, it establishes as an explicit reality that despite the constitutional provisions and

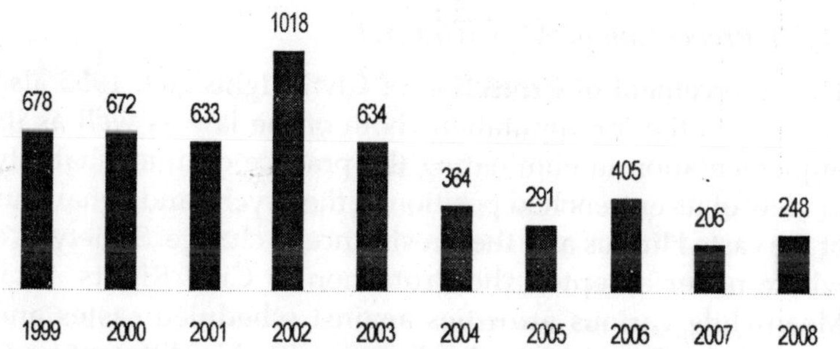


*Source:* National Crime Record Bureau of India.

**Figure 7: Violation of the Protection of Civil Rights Act Against SCs (1999-2008)**

existence of appropriate legislation, the practice of untouchablity has been practiced in India, though all cases of such an inhuman practice against more than SC 78 per cent of India's population are not highlighted.

As per NCRB Total 678 cases of the violation of the aforesaid Act were reported in India in 1999. The NCRB, in 2000, had reported 672 cases of the violation of the above said Act. The number of cases was 633 in 2001 and had increased to 1018 in 2002. In 2003, the NCRB reported 634 cases of the violation of the Act, while it reported 364 cases in the year 2004. Total 291 cases were reported by the NCRB in 2005, while 405 cases were reported by it in 2006. In 2007, the number declined to 206 cases. The NCRB had further reported 248 cases of the violation of the Protection of Civil Rights Act in 2008.

The data asserts that total 5149 cases of the violation of the Protection of Civil Rights Act victimizing the SCs are reported in India in ten years (1999 to 2008). It establishes that average 515 cases of the violation of the aforesaid Act are reported in India every year. Average 43 cases are reported in India every month; average 11 cases are reported in a week; while average 1 case of the violation of the Protection of Civil Rights Act victimizing the SCs is reported in India after every 15 hours. Positively, there is overall decrease in the number of cases regarding such crime year after year, which is a positive sign as far as the implementation of the above mentioned Act as well as the dignity of SCs is concerned.

### *SC/ST Prevention of Atrocities Act*

The enforcement of Protection of Civil Rights Act, 1955 also brought to the fore limitations both of the law as well as its implementation in eliminating the practice of untouchability in view of its entrenched position in the psyche and behaviour of the caste Hindus and their resistance to change. Society as a whole never accepted the Protection of Civil Rights Act3. Meanwhile various atrocities against scheduled castes and scheduled tribes continued to be committed in different parts of the country. It was realized that even the amended Protection of Civil Rights Act, 1955 and normal provisions of IPC did not provide deterrence in preventing violence on scheduled castes and scheduled tribes especially offences committed on caste grounds4. Accordingly, Parliament passed another law called 'Scheduled Castes and Scheduled Tribes (Prevention of Atrocities) Act, 1989'. The Rules under the Act were framed in 1995 to prevent commission of atrocities against members of the Schedules Castes and Tribes, to provide for special courts for the trial of such offences and for the relief and rehabilitation of the victims of such offences and for matters connected there with or incidental thereto.[31]

The SCs are denied a number of civil rights and are subjected to various offences, indignities, humiliation and harassment. They have been, in several brutal instances, deprived of their life and property. Serious atrocities are committed against them for various historical, social and economic reasons.[32] The Act, for the first time, lays down the contours of 'atrocity' so as to cover all multiple ways through which members of scheduled castes and scheduled tribes have been for centuries humiliated, brutally oppressed, degraded, denied their economic and social rights and relegated to perform the most menial jobs.[33]

As per the data of the NCRB, 11657 cases of the violation SC/ST Prevention Act were reported in India in 1999 victimizing the SCs. There were 11587 reported cases of the violation of SC/ST Prevention of Atrocities Act in 20001. In 2001, there were 12201 reported cases, and in 2002, there were 14383 reported cases of the violation of the aforesaid Act. The NCRB reported 11401 cases in 2003 and total 11435 cases in 2004 regarding the infringement of the Act. In 2005, the NCRB had reported 11077 cases. The number of cases was 11808 in 2006 and 13490 in 2007. The NCRB reported total 14623 cases of the violation of the SC/ST Prevention of Atrocities Act in 2008.

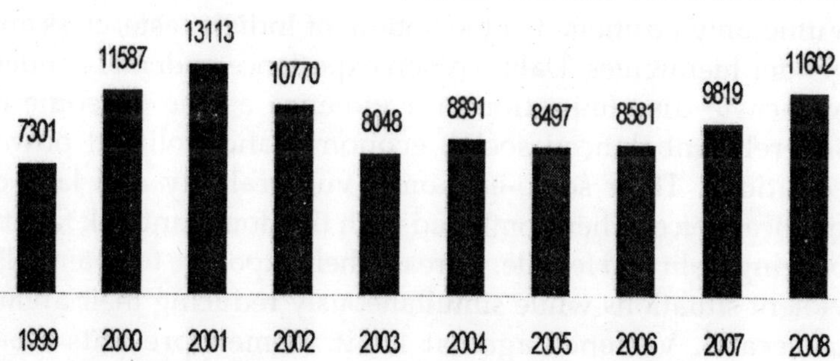


*Source:* National Crime Record Bureau of India.

**Figure 8: Violation of SC/ST Prevention of Atrocities Act Victimizing SCs (1999-2008)**

The data divulges that there are total 98209 cases of the violation of the SC/ST Prevention of Atrocities Act victimizing the SCs reported throughout India in ten years (1999 to 2008). It confirms that average 9821 cases of such crime are reported in India in a year. The date further establishes that average per cent 818 cases of the violation of the aforesaid Act are reported in India every month; while average 205 cases are reported in a week. The data further corroborates that average 29 cases of the violation of the SC/ST Prevention of Atrocities Act are reported in India every day. It further verifies that average 1 crime is reported in India after every 45 minutes. The year-wise data depicts noticeable variations as far as the increase and decrease in the number of cases is concerned. A consistent increase in the number of reported cases has been observed since 1999 to 2001. The number of cases had increased to 79.60 per cent in 2001 over 1999. Contrarily, a consistent decrease of respectively 17.86 per cent and 26.27 per cent was witnessed in 2002 and 2003 in comparison to their previous years respectively. In 2004 an increase of 10.48 per cent was noticed in contrast with the year 2003. In 2005, there was a decrease of 4.49 per cent than the year 2004. In 2006 there was an increase of 0.98 per cent over the year 2005. The number of cases further increased to 14.42 per cent in 2007 in contrast with 2006, 18.15 per cent in 2008, in comparison to 2007.

**Dalit Women**

Vulnerably positioned at the bottom of India's caste, class and gender hierarchies, Dalit women experience endemic gender-and-caste discrimination and violence as the outcome of severely imbalanced social, economic and political power equations. Their socio-economic vulnerability and lack of political voice, when combined with the dominant risk factors of being Dalit and female, increase their exposure to potentially violent situations while simultaneously reducing their ability to escape. Violence against Dalit women presents clear evidence of widespread exploitation and discrimination against these women subordinated in terms of power relations to men in a patriarchal society, as also against their communities based on caste. As the National Commission for Women has commented, "in the commission of offences against... scheduled caste [Dalit] women the offenders try to establish their authority and humiliate the community by subjecting their women to indecent and inhuman treatment, including sexual assault, parading naked, using filthy language, etc.[34]Hence, violence, which serves as a crucial social mechanism to maintain Dalit women's subordinate position in society, is the core outcome of gender-based inequalities shaped and intensified by the caste system.[35]

Dalit women face the triple burden of caste, class, and gender. Dalit girls, in some parts of India have been forced to become prostitutes for upper-caste patrons and village priests.[36] Sexual abuse and other forms of violence against women are used by landlords and the police to inflict 'political lessons' and crush dissent within the community. According to a Tamil Nadu state government official, the raping of Dalit women exposes the hypocrisy of the caste system as "no one practices untouchability when it comes to sex."[37] Like other Indian women whose relatives are sought by the police, Dalit women have also been arrested and tortured in custody as a means of punishing their male relatives who are hiding from the authorities.[38]

Additionally, India has failed to address the multiple axes of discrimination faced by Dalit women. It includes their unequal access to services, employment opportunities and justice mechanisms as compared to Dalit men. Largely uneducated and consistently paid less, they bear the brunt of exploitation, discrimination and physical attacks.[39] There are threats to their personal security, including through brutal acts of sexual violence and through the system of *devdasi*, practiced in the southern States, in which a girl, usually before reaching the age of puberty, is ceremoniously dedicated or married to a deity or to a temple. These girls are forced to become prostitutes for the priests of temples and upper caste patrons.[40]

### *Rape of Dalit Women*

Rape is a common phenomenon in rural areas. Women are raped as part of caste custom or village tradition. Dalit girls have been forced to have sex with the village landlord.[41] In rural areas, women are induced into prostitution through reportedly *Devadasi* system which is forced on them in the name of religion.[42] The prevalence of rape in villages contributes to the greater incidence of child marriage in those areas. Early marriage between the ages of ten years and sixteen years persists in large part because of Dalit girls' vulnerability to sexual assault by upper-caste men.[43] Once a girl is raped, she becomes unmarriageable. An early marriage also gives parents greater control over the caste into which their children are married. Dalit women are also raped as a form of retaliation. Women of scheduled castes are raped as part of an effort by upper-caste leaders to suppress movements to demand payment of minimum wages, to settle sharecropping disputes, or to reclaim lost land.[44]

According to the data of the NCRB, there were total 1000 cases of the rape of the SC women reported in India in 1999. The NCRB had reported 1083 cases of rape of SC women in 2000. There were total 1316 cases in 2001 and 1331 cases in 2002 regarding the rape of Dalit women in India. There occurred 1089 cases in 2003 of such crime against women. The NCRB, in 2004, reported 1157 cases, in 2005, total 1172 cases, and in 2006, 1217 cases of rape of SC women. In 2007, the number of cases reported by NCRB was 1349. The NCRB reported total 1457 cases of rape of SC women in 2008.

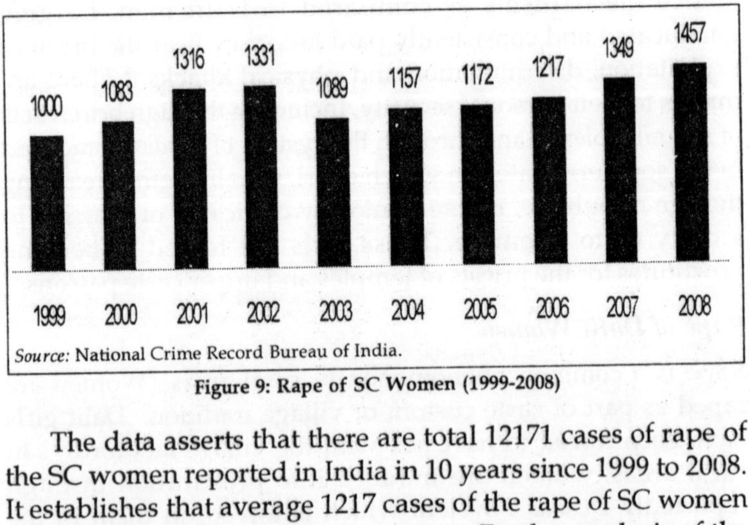


*Source:* National Crime Record Bureau of India.

**Figure 9: Rape of SC Women (1999-2008)**

The data asserts that there are total 12171 cases of rape of the SC women reported in India in 10 years since 1999 to 2008. It establishes that average 1217 cases of the rape of SC women are reported in the country every year. Further analysis of the data confirms that average 101 cases of the rape of SC women are reported in India in a month; while average 25 cases of such crime against SC women are reported in a week. The data corroborates that average 3 to 4 cases of the rape of SC women are reported in India every, which depicts that average 1 case of the rape of SC women is reported in India after every 7 hours.

## Violation of the Human Rights of STs in India

The northeast states of India including Tripura, Assam, Meghalaya, Manipur, Nagaland, Arunachal Pradesh, Mizoram and Sikkim are the habitats of the ST people in India. This region is located in the extreme northeast corner of India bordering China to the north, Myanmar to the east and southeast, and Bangladesh to the southwest. According to the 2001 Census, the total population of these seven states is 38,495,089 persons. The northeast states are home to around 270 indigenous peoples, including the Bodo, Karbi, Dimasha, Ahomia, Adi, Khasi, Garo, Naga, Kuki, and Meitei. Some of have a population in the millions while some number as few as two thousand persons. The vast majority practice a subsistence economy based on sustainable use of their natural resources, particularly in the remaining forested areas of the region.

Human right applies universally to all. The process of identifying vulnerable groups within the health and human right generated from the pressing reality on the ground that stemmed from the fact that there are certain groups who are vulnerable and marginalized lacking full enjoyment of a wide range of human rights, including rights to political participation, health and education. Certain groups in the society often encounter discriminatory treatment and need special attention to avoid potential exploitation.

### Crime against STs

The Schedule Tribes also called *Adivasi* in India, like the Scheduled Castes are among those vulnerable groups of Indian society who face discrimination, humiliation, inequality, torture, atrocities. Unlike the Scheduled Castes, the Scheduled

Tribes are a product of marginalization based on ethnicity. In India, the Scheduled Tribes population is around 84.3 million and is considered to be socially and economically disadvantaged. Their percentages in the population and numbers however vary from State to State. They are mainly landless with little control over resources such as land, forest and water. They constitute a large proportion of agricultural labourers, casual labourers, plantation labourers, industrial labourers etc. This has resulted in poverty among them, low levels of education, poor health and reduced access to healthcare services. They belong to the poorest strata of the society and have severe health problems. They are less likely to afford and get access to healthcare services when required. 9 The health outcomes among the Scheduled Tribes are very poor even as compared to the Scheduled Castes. The Infant Mortality Rate among Scheduled Castes is 83 per 1000 live births while it is 84.2 per 1000 per live births among the Scheduled Tribes.[45]

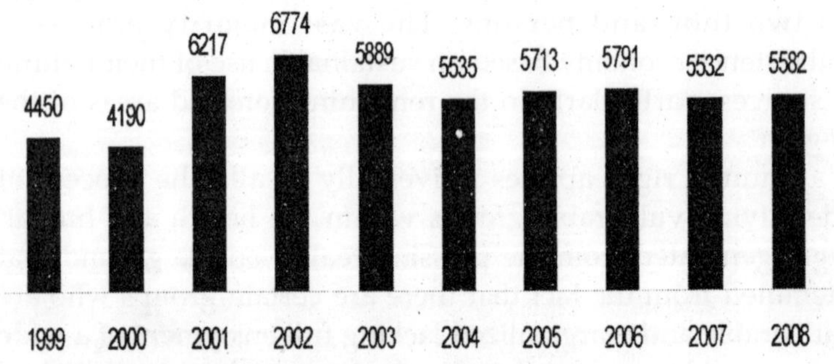


*Source:* National Crime Record Bureau of India.

**Figure 10: Crime Against STs in India (1999-2003)**

According to the statistical data of 10 years regarding 'crime in India' reported by the NCRB since 1999 to 2008, there is huge and severe violation of rights and liberties of STs in India. The ratio of crime against STs has been constantly increasing every year which has resulted in a brutal violation of their human rights. There were total 4450 cases of crime against STs reported by the NCRB in 1999. The NCRB had reported total 4190 cases of crime against STs in the year 2000. In 2001, the number of cases was 6217 which had further increased to 6774 cases in 2002. There was a slight decrease in the number of cases regarding crime against STs in the successive years, and the NCRB reported respectively 5889 and 5535 cases of such type in 2003 and 2004. The number started increasing to some extent afterwards with the reporting of 5717 cases in 2005 and 5791 cases in 2006. The NCRB further reported 5532 cases in 2007 and 5582 cases in 2008 regarding crime against STs in India.

The data divulges that total 55673 cases of the crime against STs are reported in India in ten years (1999 to 2008). It means that an average 5567 cases of crime against STs are reported in India every year; average 464 cases are reported in a month; while average 116 cases are reported in a week. The in depth analysis of the data further establishes that average 17 cases of crime against STs are reported in India every day.

## Major Categories of Crime against STs

The STs in India are one of the most vulnerable targets of crimes and violation of human rights due to their geographical distinctions, economic insufficiency and social deprivation. They bear several types of discriminations, torture and brutalities in their day to day life. They are indiscriminately murdered, their women are raped, and their houses are

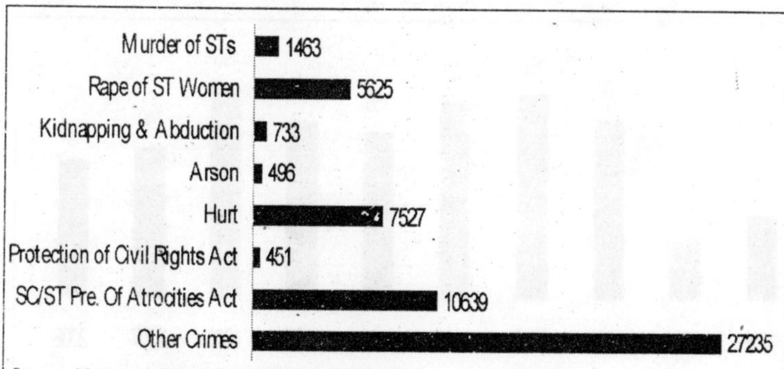


*Source:* National Crime Record Bureau of India.

**Figure 11: Major Categories of Crimes Against STs (2000-2008)**

emblazed. Moreover there is an explicit violation of SC/ST Prevention of Atrocities Act and several types of brutalities and atrocities are faced by the STs in spite of the presence of the legislations to protect their basic rights. Some major crimes and brutalities against STs are mentioned below in brief.

### *Murder of STs*

The STs have been indiscriminately murdered in India consistently and unfortunately neither the government nor the non-governmental organizations and associations seem to be worried or ever sincerely concerned to the genocide of the STs in India. The STs residing in the conflicted area, especially the Naxalite-effected areas of Chhattisgarh, Manipur, and West Bengal are bearing double jeopardy to their lives. The common Naxalites are indiscriminately killed by the alleged Naxalites to disseminate terror in the region or to fulfill their demands. The STs or the Adivasi who possess any sympathy towards the Naxalite ideology or Naxalite persons, those Adivasi who provide any material or manual support to the Naxals are murdered by the security forces extra-judicially.[46]

As per data of the NCRB, 80 cases of the murder of the SCs were reported in the year 1999. There were 59 reported cases of murder of STs in India in the year 2000. The number increased to 167 in 2001 and further increased to 189 in the year 2002. In 2003, the NCRB reported 185 cases of the murder of STs. The number slightly decreased to 156 cases in 2004. In

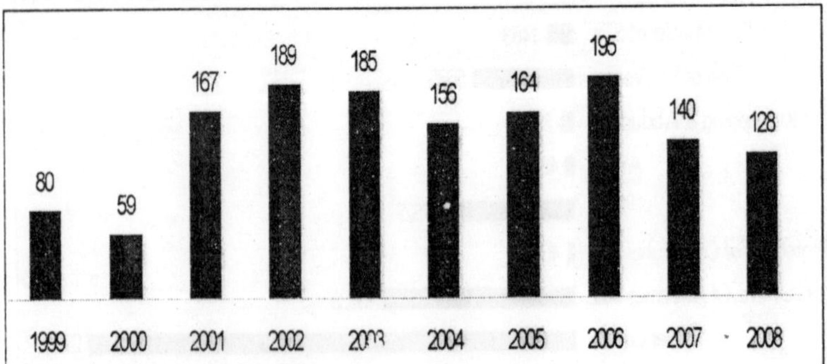


*Source:* National Crime Record Bureau of India.

**Figure 12: Murders of STs in India (1999-2008)**

2004, the NCRB had reported 164 cases. There was again an increase in the number and the NCRB reported total 195 cases of murder of STs in India in 2006. The number of total reported cases of murder of STs was 140 in 2007; and 128 in 2008.

The analysis of the data confirms that 1463 cases of the murders of the STs have been reported throughout India during the span of ten years (1999-2008). 72.18 per cent of the total number of cases of crimes against SCs had been reported from 2001 to 2006. The cases of the murder of the SCs were reported at large scale during the time period from 2001 to 2006. However since 2007, a decrease has been noticed in the cases of the murder of the SCs reported throughout India.

### *Kidnapping and Abduction of STs*

The incidents of the kidnapping and abduction of the STs have been on the increase. The *adivasis* of the Naxal-effected areas are kidnapped and abducted by the alleged Naxalites. The *adivasis* are abducted by the Naxalite to forcefully indulge them into the movement of Naxalite. The young males as well as the females belonging to the adivasi families are always the soft targets of kidnapping and abduction for the Naxalites. Moreover, the police informers, *adivasi* government employees, and the *adivasi* not favouring the Naxalite ideology are also abducted by the alleged Naxalites. Several times the STs are kidnapped by the Naxalite for putting the pressure on the government for fulfilling their demands. Besides that, the ST people are kidnapped or adducted by other anti-social elements. The young ST girls are abducted to sell them or traffic them to the other parts for prostitution. The ST minor boys and girls are abducted to forcefully involve them in begging and working as household servants. The ST boys and girls are abducted to forcefully and illegally sell and transplant their body organs.

There were 59 cases of the kidnapping and abduction of STs reported in India in 1999. The NCRB had reported 48 cases of kidnapping and abduction of STs throughout India in 2000. It further reported 67 cases in 2001. The NCRB reported each 69 cases in 2002 and 2003 regarding the same crime against the STs. In 2004, the number of cases of the kidnapping of STs had increased to 79 cases. The NCRB, in 2005 and 2006, reported respectively 72 and 88 cases. In 2007, the number of cases reported by NCRB was 89. Total 93 cases were reported by the NCRB in the year 2008.

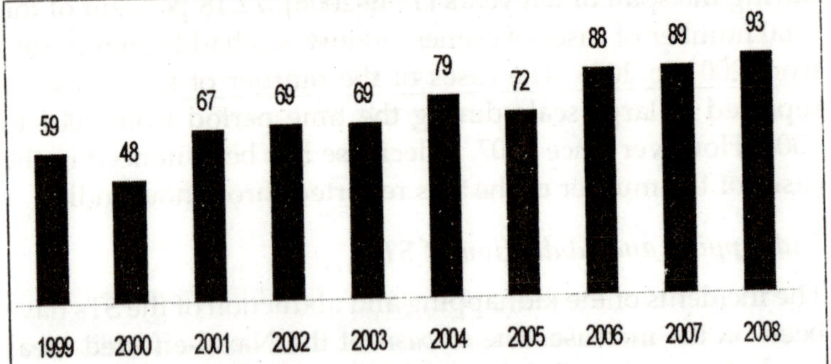


*Source:* National Crime Record Bureau of India.

**Figure 13: Kidnapping and Abduction of STs (1999-2008)**

The data divulges that total 733 cases of the kidnapping and abduction of the STs are reported in India in ten years since 1999 to 2008). It means that average 73 cases of the kidnapping and abduction of the STs are reported in India every year. The data further establishes that average 6 cases regarding such crime against STs are reported in India every month; while average 1 case of kidnapping and abduction of the STs is reported n India after 2 months. The year-wise analysis of the data depicts a consistent increase in the number of cases, though the variations do exist in a number of years.

### *Hurting the STs*

The dams, industries and mining developments have been taking place in the tribal areas o India, with the consent of the governmental authorities, without even consulting the local indigenous people who are going to suffer a huge economic, geographical, cultural loss and mental agony due to these illegal, unconstitutional and unethical projects.[47] The persons who agitate for the rights of the indigenous people are illegally arrested, detained and tortured by the police.[48]

The harassment, physical torment and mental anguish of the tribal people confirm India's failure to recognize and protect indigenous peoples' property and other rights. India's disregard for its international obligations and the rights of indigenous peoples in the northeast goes beyond a failure. There are innumerous incidents mentioning the state police firing rubber buliets and teargas shells on the peaceful protestors. Almost every day thatre are reports of the police lathi-charging the adivasi villagers and setting on fire many shops and houses, injuring the people. It appears that, in blatant disregard of Constitutional values, several platoons of police are involved in this well-planned and brutal operation against the villagers who launch any peaceful protest against the proposed unethical and unconstitutional mining developments or proposed industries.[49]

As per NCRB, total 646 cases of hurting the STs were reported throughout India in 1999. In 2000, the NCRB had reported 447 cases of hurting the STs. The number f cases increased to 756 cases in 2001. The increases in the number continued with 788 cases in 2002 and 790 cases in the year 2003. The NCRB reported 767 each cases of hurting the STs in 2004 and 2005. Again a nationwide increase in the number of cases regarding hurting the STs was noticed and the NCRB had reported 838 cases in 2006 and 855 cases in 2007. The number of cases further increased to 873 cases in 2008.

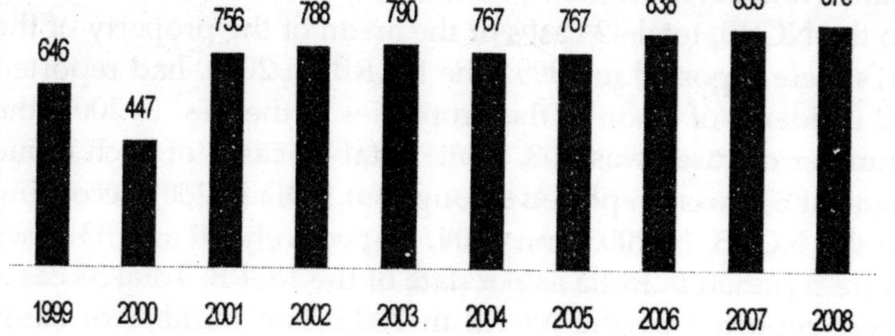


*Source:* National Crime Record Bureau of India.

**Figure 14: Cases of Hurling the STs in India (1999-2008)**

The data of the NCRB asserts that in 10 years, total 7527 cases are reported in India regarding hurting the STs. It confirms that average 752 cases of hurting the STs are reported in India every year. The data further corroborates that average 63 cases of hurting the STs are reported in India every month; average 16 cases are reported every week; while average 2 cases of hurting the STs are reported in India every day. Except a few disparities, there is overall a huge increase in the number of cases in 10 years.

### *Crime of Arson against STs*

As discussed above, there are continuous, deliberate and brutal attempts to displace the STs from their native and natural habitats, the possession of which they are justifiably claiming on the constitutional, legal and ethical grounds. To create a threat among the STs and to deteriorate their agitations for their fair and justified claims over their lands and properties, the business firms, with the help of the anti-social elements, mercilessly arson the houses, shops, community places and other property of the STs. Moreover, the governmental agencies including the local police have a hand in glove with the elements provoking and funding these activities of arson.[50] In recent times the incidents of the arson of the houses and other property have drastically risen in the North-Eastern parts of India.

There are continuous reports of the crimes of maliciously, voluntarily, and willfully setting fire to the houses, community places and even religious places of the STs in India. According to the NCRB, total 43 cases of the arson of the property of the STs were reported in 1999. The NCRB, in 2000, had reported 32 incidents of arson of the properties of the STs. In 2001, the number of cases was 108, while total 55 cases of such crime against STs were reported throughout India in 2002 according to the NCRB. In 2003 and 2004, respectively 38 and 33 cases were reported in India as per data of the NCRB. Total 38 cases were reported by the NCRB in 2005. The number of cases regarding arson of the property of STs throughout India was 46 in 2006 and 54 in 2007 according to the data of NCRB. In the year 2008, total 49 cases of the arson of the property of the STs were reported throughout India.

The analysis of the data of the NCRB of 10 years (1999-2008) asserts that total 496 cases of arson of the property of STs are reported in India in these years. It means that average 50 cases of the arson of STs' property are reported in India every year; average 4 cases are reported in a month and average 1 case of arson the property of the STs is reported in India every week. The year-wise analysis of the data depicts noticeable variations in the number of cases in different years. However, the crime of arson has been consistently committed against the STs of India.

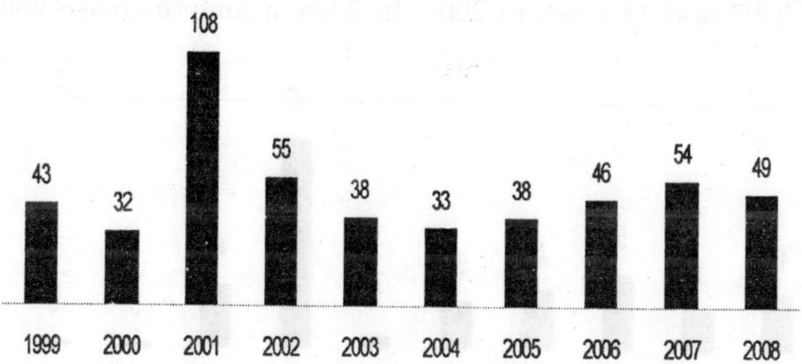


*Source:* National Crime Record Bureau of India.

**Figure 15: Arson of the Property of STs (1999-2008)**

## *Violation of the Protection of Civil Rights Act Against STs*

The Protection of the Civil Rights Act 1955 strictly prohibits any form of untouchability against the SCs and STs in India, and considers the preaching and practice of untouchability as a punishable crime. But the STs in India have been facing several forms of untouchability in their routine life. The practice of untouchability against the STs has been increasing day by day and year after year in spite of the existence of the legislations since 55 years. In north-eastern parts of the country, the indigenous people are not allowed by the reportedly urban or more civilized community to mix up in their culture, religion and society. Even today the tribal or the indigenous people are not allowed to enter in the temples to perform religious rituals, in community places. The indigenous children are not commended to enter in the schools. Establishing matrimonial relations with the tribal people is strictly forbidden in the country. There are innumerous cases of the practice of untouchability against the STs, however majority of then remain unreported and even unrevealed.

According to the data of the NCRB, 45 cases regarding the violation of the Protection of Civil Rights Act victimizing the STs were reported in 1999. There were 31 reported cases of the violation of the Act against the STs. The number of total reported cases had increased to 58 in 2001 which had slightly decreased to 47 in 2002. The number further decreased to 37 in 2003 and 11 cases in 2004. In 2005, a huge increase was

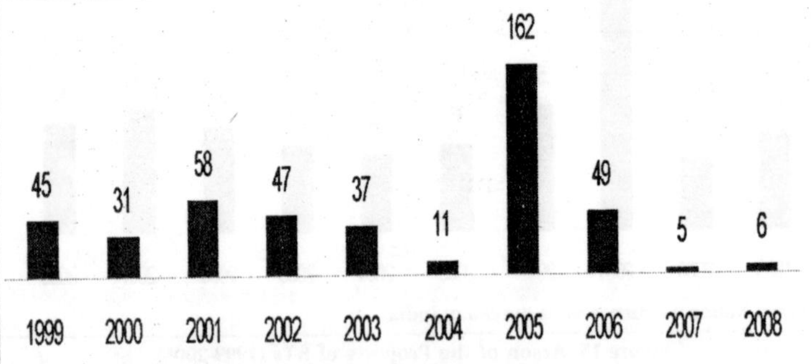


*Source:* National Crime Record Bureau of India.

**Figure 16: Violation of Protection of Civil Rights Act Against STs (1999-2008)**

noticed and the NCRB reported 162 cases in that year. The decrease was again there in the number of cases and the Bureau reported 49 cases in the year 2006. However, there was noticeable decrease in the number in the successive years and the NCRB had reported respectively 5 and 6 cases in the years 2007 and 2008.

The data divulges that total 451 cases of the violation of the Protection of Civil Rights Act, particularly regarding the practice of untouchability against the STs, are reported in 10 years (1999 to 2008). It confirms that average 45 cases of the practice of untouchability against the STs are reported in India every year; average 4 cases are reported every month; while average 1 case regarding the practice of untouchability is reported in India every week. Providentially, the year-wise analysis of the data of the number of cases depicts a huge decrease in the number of cases in last three years in comparison to the previous years. A minimal number of cases do mean that the practice of untouchability has been found rarely and exceptionally. In fact, the indigenous people have been facing that untouchability since centuries. Hence, they take it as a part of their life and do not seriously bother it as a severe crime against them. Moreover, the ignorance to law also forbade the tribal people to complain against the practice of untouchability.

### *Atrocities against STs*

The SC/ST Prevention of Atrocities Act legally prohibits to all to commit any atrocities to the SC and STs and considers it as a severely punitive offence. The objectives of the Act very clearly emphasize the intention of the Government to deliver justice to these communities through affirmative action to enable them to live. Unfortunately, the poor implementation of the legislation has resulted in the huge atrocities to the STs. Scheduled Castes and Scheduled Tribes (Prevention of Atrocities) Act 1989 criminalizes certain acts against members of the Scheduled Castes and Scheduled Tribes such as traffic in human beings, *'begar (free labor)'* and forced labor in any form.

The adversity of the STs seems further aggravated because in many parts of the Country, the state supported/sponsored repression and outright violence and atrocities are frequently occurring. The incidents of brutality such as the suppression of Adivasi uprising in *Kalinganar* in 2005 when 14 local activists were killed; the recent attempts to evict peasants and Adivasis by force so as to enable corporations to invade and make profits from their lands; the massacres in *Nandigram*, West Bengal in March and November, 2007 and the deadly attacks in late November, 2007 in Orissa. All these brutal incidents against the STs prove the atrocious state of ST communities in India. All these illustrate a lack of interest by the National and local State governments to prevent such attacks, which are forcing tribal people off their land to create Special Economic Zones (SEZs) and the like for a few, such as the Salim Petrochemical Plant SEZ and the Posco iron and steel project in West Bengal and Orissa respectively. The horrific situation of Adivasis in Jharkhand is another case in point. Projects of resource extraction for wealth accumulation by and for the few have entailed massive forced migrations and impoverishment for Adivasis. It is astonishing that such projects are being promoted by the State and Union governments.

Correspondingly, atrocities against tribal people to suppress local protests against the above mentioned injustice against tribal people are getting high handed both by the state and by corporate bodies. Brutal attacks on adivasis have increased where women and children are also being beaten, killed, put in false custody or harassed into submission. Such atrocities on adivasi children was witnessed in several places in the recent past - in Nagarnar (Chattisgarh), in Koel Karo (Jharkhand), in Kasipur (Orissa), in Muthanga (Kerala) and there is no record or repentence from the authorities regarding these crimes.[51]

The NCRB of India had reported 574 cases of atrocities of the STs in the year 1999. In 2000, the number of total reported cases was 502. A huge number of 1667 cases were reported by the NCRB in 2001. The number of cases regarding atrocities to the STs had further increased to 1800 cases in 2002. Total 1340 cases were reported by the Bureau in the year 2003. In 2004, total 1175 cases were reported by the NCRB regarding the violation of the Prevention of Atrocities Act. The number of cases was respectively 1283 and 1232 in the years 2005 and 2006. The NCRB reported 1104 cases in 2007 and 1022 cases in 2008 regarding the violation Prevention of Atrocities Act.

As per data, total 10639 cases of the violation of the SC/ST Prevention of Atrocities Act 1989 are reported in India in 10 years (1999 to 2008). It establishes that average 1064 cases of the atrocities of the STs are reported in India every year. The

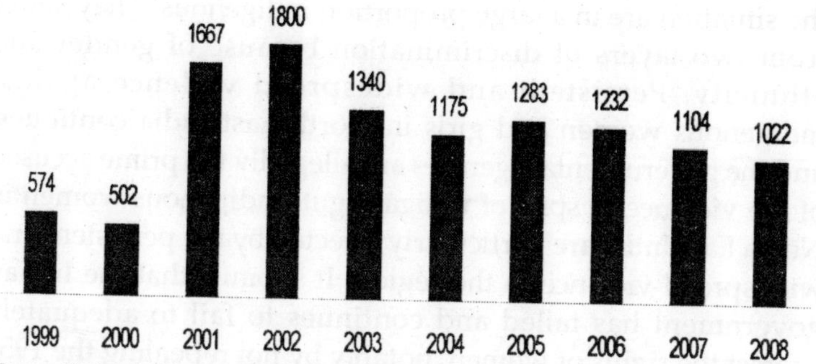


*Source:* National Crime Record Bureau of India.

**Figure 17: Violation of SC/ST Prevention of Atrocities Act (1999-2008)**

in-depth analysis of the data further confirms that average 89 cases against the atrocities of the STs are reported every month; average 22 cases of such crime against STs are reported every week; while average 3 cases of the atrocities of the STs are reported in India every day. The data further discloses that average 1 case of atrocities of STs is reported in India after every 8 hours. In 1999 and 2000, the number of cases was very less in comparison to the successive years. The number of cases rapidly increased to 232 per cent in 2001in contrast to 2000. It further increased to 7.97 per cent in 2002 in comparison to 2001. The year 2003 had witnessed a decrease of 25.55 per cent in contrast with 2002. Further a decrease of 12.31 per cent was noticed in 2004 over 2003. The number had increased to9.19 per cent in 2005 than the year 2004. Since 2006 to 2008, there was a constant decrease in the number of cases. The number decreased to 3.97 per cent, 10.38 per cent and 7.42 per cent respectively in 2006, 2007 and 2008, in comparison to their previous years respectively.

## State of the Human Rights of ST Women

Though women in tribal areas of India, particularly in North East India are perceived as having a high social status in society, they are increasingly vulnerable to the numerous conflicts involving both Indian State and non-State actors in the region. North East India's population is primarily comprised of indigenous peoples, thus the women affected by the situation are in a large proportion indigenous. They suffer from two layers of discrimination because of gender and ethnicity. Persistent and widespread violence against indigenous women and girls in North East India continues, and the governmental agencies are allegedly the prime accused of the violence in spite of mitigating it. Indigenous women in North East India are particularly affected by the persistent and widespread violence in the region. It submits that the Indian government has failed and continues to fail to adequately protect the rights of women, notably by not repealing the 1958 *Armed Forces (Special Powers) Act* ("AFSPA") and by not implementing the *Domestic Violence Act*. It also submits that India routinely fails to adequately prevent, investigate and punish cases of rape and other types of violence against women in the North East. Moreover, the indigenous women in North East India are disproportionately subject to trafficking.[52]

### *Widespread Violence and its Impact on ST Women*

Women in North East India are affected by the frequent and heavy bombings and fighting taking place in the region, which involve both Indian State forces and their paramilitary clients, and non-State actors such as underground armed groups. Many women and girls are injured or killed as a direct result of these frequent acts of violence. Women victims of violence also suffer from the lack of health care. The rate of domestic violence is growing in North East India. A specific *Domestic Violence Act* was enacted in India in 2005, but is not being implemented in the region as there are no officials to provide protection and other services, such as shelters for women victims of domestic violence. Sensitization and services to address domestic violence issues are still very much needed.[53]

Trafficking is also a significant and ongoing problem for indigenous women in North East India. In 2001, the former *Special Rapporteur on Violence against Women, Its Causes and Consequences*, Ms. Radhika Coomaraswamy, submitted a report in which important concerns were raised regarding the issue of trafficking of women and girls in India.[54] In some cases, victims of trafficking escape their oppressors and after transiting through refugee camps or shelters, they return home. The returned women are then often in need of psychological and physical health services and require help for social reintegration. For example, in October 2008, two of the submitting organizations transmitted a communication to the United Nations Special Rapporteur on trafficking in persons, especially women and children regarding the case of five indigenous women between the ages of 18 and 26. These women had escaped from the traffickers after a period of severe physical abuse and were living in a shelter for victims of trafficking in Kuala Lumpur, Malaysia. The women have recently returned home, but are in need for health and social services, services that are not currently provided by the Indian State.[55]

### *Rape of ST Women*

The government of India routinely fails to prevent, investigate and punish rape and violence against women in the North East. In the few instances where prosecutions have gone forward, the reported set of cases shows patterns of gender discrimination in the prosecution or sentencing. The Manipur Women's Commission reports that most of the cases of rape and violence against women which come before it involve individuals serving in the security forces such as the Indian army, Central Reserve Police Force (CRPF), Indian Reserved Battalion (IRB), and the police.[56]

As per NCRB, 384 cases of the rape of ST women were reported in 1999 throughout India. The NCRB had reported 403 cases of rape of ST women in 2000. In 2001, the number of cases increased to 573 which further increased to 597 cases in 2002. The NCRB had reported 551 cases of the rape of ST women in 2003. In the year 2004 and 2005, the NCRB reported 566 and 640 cases of rape of ST women. The number further increased to 699 cases in 2006. The NCRB, in 2007, had reported 627 cases of such crime against ST women. In the year 2008, the NCRB reported total 585 cases of rape of ST women in India.

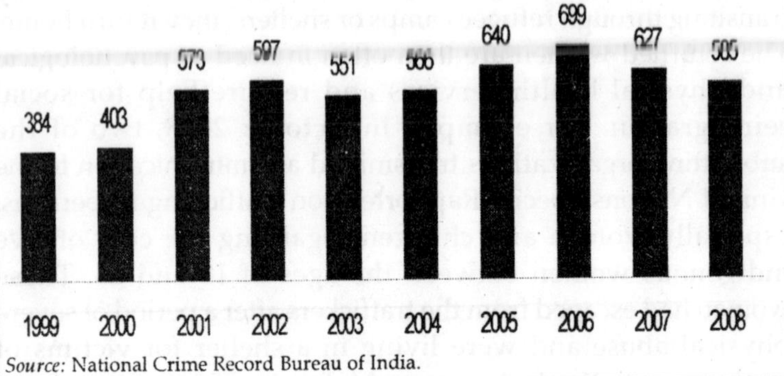


*Source:* National Crime Record Bureau of India.

**Figure 18: Rape of ST Women in India (2000-2008)**

The data asserts that total 5625 cases of the rape of the ST women are reported in India in ten years (1999 to 2008). It confirms that average 562 cases of rape of the ST women are reported in a year. It further establishes that average 47 cases are reported in a month; average 12 cases of the rape of the ST women are reported in a week; approximately 2 cases of the rape of the ST women are reported in a week, or in other words, average 1 case of the rape of the ST woman is reported in India after every 14 hours. The aggregate analysis of the number of cases in 10 years depicts an overall increase, though there are a number of deprivations in some particular years. 6.82 per cent cases of the total number of cases of rape of ST women were reported in 1999, while 7.16 per cent of the total number of cases was reported in 2000. 10.18 per cent in 2001, 10.61 in 2002 and 9.79 per cent of the total number of cases of rape of the ST women were reported in 2003. In 2004, 10.06 of the total number of cases were reported, while in 2005, 11.37 per cent of the total number of cases regarding the rape of ST women was reported. 12.42 per cent cases were reported in 2006; and 11.14 per cent cases were reported in 2007. In the year 2008, 10.4 per cent of the total number of cases of rape of ST women were reported. The data corroborates that in 2006 (12.42 per cent) most number of cases were reported, while the year 1999 (6.82 per cent) emerges as the year with least number of reported cases. These statistics further warn that the number of cases regarding the rape of the ST women have been swiftly and consistently on a rise year after year.

The social, cultural, economic and political conditions of the SCs and STs are in a miserable state. They are ferociously discriminated in several parts of the world, and moreover untouchability still prevails against them in spite of the existence of the Protection of Civil Rights Act which prohibits untouchability and the SC/ST Prevention of Atrocities Act. Socially the SCs and the STs are sidelined, their economic condition is also downtrodden, and their political rights are frequently violated. A huge majority of the SCs as well as the STs have been not able to earn satisfactory meals for their families, although they have been provided reservations in all governmental jobs. A vast majority of them are totally illiterate, though there are free provisions of free or almost free education for them There political participation is minimal in Sate and Central legislations in spite of reserved representations for them in the State as well as Central legislation elections.

The STs who are living in the tribal and distinct areas seldom get benefit of the constitutional and legislative privileges especially arranged for their social, economic and political upliftment, due to their total unawareness or their overall incapacity to be benefitted of these privileges. The STs in India have been facing the crisis for their survival and existence. Because, they are forcefully displaced and dispossessed from their natural habitats they own since the time immemorial. For the sake of so-called development, modernization and industrialization, the STs are expected even by 'the centre and State governments to sacrifice their native land, identity and eventually the existence.

Similarly, the facilities initiated for the downtrodden and sidelined SCs are in fact enjoyed by a nominal number of SC crème-layer. Hence, it is strongly and immediately required to commence a grass-root mass movement to awaken the SCs to uplift themselves by getting education, and other Constitutional and legal privileges provisioned especially for their all-around development. The other castes, especially the so-called upper castes should also be enlightened to abandon any form of discrimination, hate, untouchability against the SCs. There are some suggestions for the government, civil society, and for the SCs themselves, which if acknowledged, can help in the upliftment and development of SCs in every aspect of their lives including social, economic and political.

**Suggestions and Recommendations**

- The Central Government and the State Governments should ensure wide publicity of the Protection of Civil Rights Act so as to improve the awareness about the provisions of the Act among the Scheduled Castes as also non-Scheduled Castes.
- As is evident from the name of the Act itself, the focus of the SCs & STs (Prevention of Atrocities) Act 1989 is on prevention; a number of steps and measures have been provided for in the Act and the Rules, which include setting up of Committees at various levels268 Atrocities Against Scheduled Castes for monitoring and review of cases, identification of atrocity prone areas, formal recognition of potential criminals and better policing and vigilance in atrocity prone areas. It is, however, observed that in most of the States, either the Committees have not been formed or wherever such committees have been formed, its meetings are not held on regular basis. Such meetings, which have SC/ST elected representatives and the officers concerned with implementation of these Acts, provide the forum and opportunity to work out the preventive strategies and to discuss specific issues relating to effective implementation of the provisions of these Acts. All the State/UT governments should be instructed to constitute Vigilance and Monitoring Committees at the State and District levels and to take urgent measures to ensure their effective functioning.
- Publicity and related activities both of the Central and State Governments should be carefully reviewed, to make them impact-oriented and capable of reaching effectively the far-flung and remote habitations.

- The Central Government should review the kind of facilities, including legal aid being provided by the State Governments to the SC/ST victims of Untouchability, discrimination and atrocities and issue guidelines to ensure proper implementation of this provision of the Protection of Civil Rights Act.
- Training programme may be conducted by every State Government for police personnel to sensitize them regarding implementation of the provisions of SCs & STs (Prevention of Atrocities) Act, 1989 and the Protection of Civil Rights Act, 1955 either through its Police Training Institutions or otherwise.
- Ensure that States constitute and oversee State and District level Vigilance and Monitoring Committees, as required by Rules 16 and 17 of the Scheduled Castes and Scheduled Tribes (Prevention of Atrocities) Rules, 1995, for the purpose of properly implementing the Scheduled Castes and Scheduled Tribes (Prevention of Atrocities) Act, 1989 [hereinafter the Atrocities Rules and the Atrocities Act].
- This effort should ensure that a sufficient number of investigators (including appropriate representation of Dalit men and women) are included in the committees to guarantee full implementation of the act.
- An Awareness Programme should be conducted through Non-governmental Organizations about the provisions of SCs & STs (Prevention of Atrocities) Act, 1989, Protection of Civil Rights Act, 1955 and the economic relief to be provided to the victims of torture, harassment and atrocities as per scale laid down in the SCs & STs (Prevention of Atrocities) Rules, 1995. The Government should consider organizing seminars of the NGOs for eliciting their help in Awareness Programme.
- The police officials of every State should be trained and then strictly ordered to report every case of crime against the SCs and STs immediately. There should be an immediate, in depth and impartial investigation of every

complaint filed by the SCs/STs regarding any type of atrocity, discrimination or crime against them.

- In all cases of crime and atrocities against SCs/STs, immediate relief, rehabilitation and compensation should be provided keeping in view the mandate of the Parliament.
- The National Commission for Scheduled Castes and Scheduled Tribes should be empowered to oversee all complaints and grievances regarding torture, harassment, cruelty and discrimination against the SCs and STs in all States. The capacity of the National Commission for Scheduled Castes and Scheduled Tribes should be strengthen to operate legal cells and open branch offices in all States with enough financial resources and powers to initiate prosecution of cases.
- The capacity of the National and State Human Rights Commissions and the National and State Commissions for Women should be strengthened with more powers and enough manual and financial resources to initiate prosecution of cases. For the purpose, the Protection of Human Rights Act, 1993 needs to be amended so that National and State Human Rights Commissions are not automatically exempted from enquiring into matters related to human rights violation of SCs/STs already pending before a State Commission or any other Commission duly constituted under any law.
- A nationwide public awareness campaign should be launched regarding the prohibition of untouchability, atrocities, crime and other forms discrimination and violence against the SCs and STs.
- The SCs and STS, especially residing in the remote and distant areas, who are more vulnerable to the human rights violations, should be provided education, mobilization and social awareness particularly regarding their prerequisite Constitutional and legal rights. The SCs and STs should be made aware about from where and how to get police support and legal aid in case of the infringement of their human rights.

Undoubtedly, the human rights of the SCs and STs are in jeopardy. The reason of all above mentioned deprivations of the SCs/STs is the lack a mass movement for their upliftment at grass-root level. Until or unless the people who are victims or are vulnerable to the violation of human rights, get proper awareness regarding their rights and the constitutional and legal mechanism to protect their rights, their rights and liberties will be at the risk every now and then. As far as the promotion and protection of the human rights of the SCs and the STs in India is concerned, the government authorities and the civil society can supplement a lot, but primarily and eventually the SC and ST communities themselves have to awaken, demand and protect their rights.

## References

1. William A. Haviland, et al., *The Essence of Anthropology*, Cengage Learning, Stamford, 2009, p. 263.
2. Peniel Rajkumar, *Dalit Theology and Dalit Liberation: Problems, Paradigms and Possibilities*, Ashgate Publishing Ltd. Aldershot, UK, p. 16.
3. Prem Kumar Shinde, *Dalits and Human Rights: Dalits and Racial Justice*, Gyan Publishing House, New Delhi, 2005, p. 81.
4. Sesha Kethineni, Gail Diane Humiston, "Dalits, the 'Oppressed People' of India: How are Their Social, Economic, and Human Rights Addressed", *War Crimes, Genocide, & Crimes against Humanity*, Volume 4, 2010, p. 100.
5. Human Rights Watch, *Hidden Apartheid: Discrimination Against India's Untouchables*, February, 2007, p. 2.
6. Samita Narula, *Broken People: Caste Violence Against India's Untouchables*, Human Rights Watch, 1999, p. 7.
7. Namrita Shukla, *Their Tomorrow Never Comes*, The Hindu, December 29, 2002.
8. The abolishment of "untouchability" has been made enforceable through the Protection of Civil Rights Act 1955.
9. Amnesty International, *India's Unfinished Agenda: Equality and Justice for Million Victims of the Caste System*, A Report Prepared to Present for the Hearing Before the Subcommittee on Africa, Global Human Rights International Operations of the Committee on International Relations, House of Representatives, U.K., One Hundred Ninth Congress, First Session, October 6, 2005, Diane Publishing, p. 6.
10. Ramesh Chandra, *Liberation and Social Articulation of Dalits*, Gyan Publishing House, New Delhi, 2004, p. 2.
11. Prem Kumar Shinde, 2005, *op.cit.*, p. 44.

12. Prem Kumar Shinde, *Dalits and Human Rights: Dalits-The Broken Future*, Gyan Publishing House, New Delhi, 2005, p. 40.
13. Scheduled Castes and The Scheduled Tribes (Prevention of Atrocities) Act, 1989 [Act No. 33 of 1989 dated 11th September, 1989]
14. Jaganath R. Shinde, *Organisations of Schedule Castes and Social Change*, Gyan Publishing House, New Delhi, 2005, p. 79.
15. Human Rights Watch, *India-Hidden Apartheid- Caste Discrimination against India's Untouchables*, a report produced to the UN Committee on the Elimination of Racial Discrimination (CERD) by Centre for Human Rights and Global Justice, Human Rights Watch, Vol. 19 No. 3(c) Feb. 2007, pp. 2-4.
16. *Ibid.*, pp. 4-5.
17. Human Rights Watch Report, "Growing Violence Against Untouchables in India", in *PUCL Bulletin*, October 1999, p. 37.
18. Himanshu Charan Sadangi, *Dalit: The Downtrodden of India*, Gyan Publishing House, New Delhi, 2008, p. 210.
19. Raka Ray & Mary Fainsod Katzenstien, *Social Movements in India: Poverty, Power and Politics*, Rowman and Littlefield, Boston, p. 135.
20. "Their Tomorrow Never Comes: An Opinion", News Analysis, *The Hindu*, Sunday, December 29, 2002.
21. Vidya Subramaniam, *A Dalit temple's Encounter with Official India*, The Hindu, Thursday, March15, 2007.
22. Human Rights Watch, *World Report 2006: India*, 2007, p. 7.
23. *Ibid.*, p. 2.
24. Dipankar Gupta, *Caste in Question: Identity or Hierarchy*, SAGE Publications, 2004, p. 2013.
25. Onkar C. Sharma, *Crime against Women*, Ashish Publishing House, New Delhi, 1994, p. 147.
26. Amy Risley, "Trafficking and the International Market in Women and Girls", in Joyce Gelb & Marian Lief Palley, *Women and Politics around the World: A Comparative History and Survey*, ABC-CLIO, Oxford, 2009, p. 179.
27. P.M. Nayyar, Sankar Sen, *Trafficking in Women and Children in India*, Oriental Blackswan, 2005, p. 190.
28. K. Samu, *Dalit Atrocities: 2007*, Human Rights Documentation, Indian Social Institute, New Delhi, 2008, p.13-15.
29. Shah, Mander, Thorat, Deshpande and Baviskar, *Untouchability in Rural India*. Sage Publications, Delhi, 2006, p. 17.
30. N. Paul Divakar, *Untouchability and Violence against Dalits*, Retrieved from, http://www.hurights.or.jp/asia-pacific/048/02.html
31. K.B. Saxsena, *Report on Prevention of Atrocities Against SCs and STs*, National Human Rights Commission of India (NHRC), 1999, p. 14.
32. T.R. Naval, *Legally Combating Atrocities on Scheduled Castes and Scheduled Tribes*, 2004, Concept Publcatons, New Delhi, p. 17.

33. K.B Saxsena, *op.cit*, p. 14.
34. National Commission for Women (NCW), *Women of Weaker Sections: Socio-Economic Development of Scheduled Caste Women*, New Delhi, 1996, p.33.
35. Jayshree P. Mangubhai, *Dalit Women Speak Out: Violence Against Dalit Women in India*, (Overview Report), National Campaign on Dalit Human Rights, New Delhi, March 2006, p. 2.
36. Samita Narula, *op.cit.*, 1999, p. 2.
37. Meena Anand, *Dalit Women: Fear and Discrimination*, Gyan Publishing House, New Delhi, 2005, p. 19.
38. Human Rights Watch, *Caste Discrimination: A Global Concern*, 2001, p. 17.
39. Meena Anand, 2005, *op.cit.*, p. 157.
40. Human Rights Watch Report, *op. cit.*, 1999, p. 37.
41. Human Rights Watch, 2008, *op.cit.*, p. 19.
42. M.P. Nair & Sankar Sen, Trafficking in Women and Children in India, Orient Blackswan Publications New Delhi, 2005, p. 157.
43. Prem Kumar Shinde, *op.cit.*, 2005, p. 108.
44. Samita Narula, 1999, *op.cit.*, p. 31.
45. Chandrima Chatterjee & Gunjan Sheoran, *Vulnerable Groups in India*, Centre of Enquiry into Health and Allied Themes (CEHAT), Mumbai, 2007, p. 9.
46. Asian Centre for Human Rights (ACHR), *The Adivasis of Chhattisgarh: Victims of the Naxalite and Salwa Judum Campaign*, Asian Centre for Human Rights Publications, New Delhi, 2006, pp. 14-25.
47. Fatimata-Binta Victoire (Chairperson of the Committee on the Elimination of Discrimination), *Letter to the United Nations High Commissioner for Human Rights*, September 28, 2009.
48. Amnesty International, *India: Revoke Preventive Detention of Human Rights Defender in Manipur*, A Public Statement, 15 October 2009, p. 1.
49. Forest Peoples Programme (FPP), *An Open Letter to Mr. Manmohan Singh, the Prime Minister of India, Regarding Unprovoked Shooting, Atrocities and Arson by Police against Indigenous People, Farmers and Fisher Folk in Jagatsinghpur District, Orissa*, FPP, Morton-in-Marsh, U.K., May 18, 2010.
50. *Ibid.*
51. K.Bhanumathi, *Globalization in the Fifth Schedule Areas: Alienation of Lands and Resources of Tribals in India*, http://www. samata india.org/documents/Globalisation%20in%20the%20Fifth%20 Schedule%20 Areas-cry.pdf
52. Forest Peoples Programme (FPP), *Special Rapporteur on Violence against Women, Its Causes and Consequences*, FPP, Morton-in-Marsh, UK, March 18, 2009, p. 1.
53. *Ibid.*, p. 5.

54. A Report Submitted by Radhika Coomaraswamy, *Special Rapporteur on Violence against Women, Its Causes and Consequences*, in Accordance with Commission on Human Rights Resolution, February 6, 2001.
55. Forest Peoples Programme (FPP), March 81, 2009, *op.cit.*, p. 6.
56. *Ibid.*, p. 5.

# 11

## Concluding Remarks

Human Rights are dynamic, inalienable and indivisible rights and are fundamental to the dignified existence of all individuals. They allow the human beings to fully use their human qualities, their intelligence, talent, their conscience and to satisfy their social, political, economic, and spiritual needs. They are based on mankind's increasing demand for life in which the inherent dignity and worth of each individual receives respect and protection. These rights are essential for full development of human personality and for human happiness. Human rights are basic civil, political, economic, social and cultural conditions to which every individual is entitled as a human being, equally by virtue of their humanity, irrespective of race, nationality, or membership of any particular social group. Human rights are as old as the human civilization.

Human rights are innate in individuals and are an inherent factor in the human persons. In western world, the root of the concern for human rights may be traced to religion, humanitarian traditions and to the unleashing struggle for freedom and equality in all parts of the world. The Western perspective thus develops liberal theory of rights which believes that man by nature possesses certain inherent and inalienable rights. So, it is the duty of the State to protect these natural rights of the individuals, without which the individuals cannot grow and express and elaborate all their abilities and capabilities.

Most of the Third World countries, freed from the cluster of colonial rule, have the common goals to achieve. All Third World countries desperately need to accelerate the economic development through industrialization. These countries possess the characteristics of multi-ethnicity and multi-religious societies. So the nation-building is another goal which these countries want to achieve. In due course of time, one of the most important as well as pertinent question that has made the process of development all the more difficult is the question of the rights and freedoms of the man vis-à-vis State in these countries. The Third World countries are characterized by their traditional cultural patterns and ethnic social set up. They do not fully share either the intellectual heritage of the West or that of the socialist interpretation of the rights. Heterogeneous character of their societies has compelled them to give emphasis on the group rights or the rights the minorities. They realize that the enjoyment of the individual rights is vested in providing all rights and privileges to all groups of the society and especially the minority or marginal groups.

India possesses its own different and unique perception of human rights that emanates from its ancient culture and civilization. It has its own experience and overview regarding human rights which develops from its culture and civilization, which is oldest, greatest and unique of the whole world. It is a matter of great national pride for all Indians that the concept of human rights prevailed in its highest stage in our Indian scriptures and religious books. In the long history of the Indian civilization, the freedom of thought and speech, freedom of one's own life in the light of one's beliefs, freedom of association and freedom of public debate between the contending philosophical schools were taken to be natural foundations of human relationships. The scriptures of ancient religion and society, the Sufi movement, Bhakti movement and other religious reform movements of medieval period, the social reform movements of modern era and ultimately, the nationalist movement for freedom struggle are the milestones of the great movement of human rights development in India.

During post-independence era, India has fulfilled all obligation of a mature and responsible democracy and is dedicated to provide all reasonable rights and liberties to the people. India has established different ways of protecting human rights. Promulgation of the constitution by the People of India in January 1950 is a watershed in the history of the development of the concept of human rights in India. The Preamble, Fundamental Rights and the Directive Principles of State Policy together provide the basic human rights for the people of India. Democratic socialism spelt out in the Preamble and the Directive Principles is meant to provide the context in which the fulfillment of Fundamental Rights has to be achieved. While Fundamental Rights stress on individual and the existing rights, Directive Principles provide the dynamic movement towards the goal of providing collective human rights for all.

Undoubtedly, India has made honest efforts for the protection and promotion of human rights the world over and is a great champion of human rights in the third world. However, the fact remains that there is huge gap between theory and practice. All that is preached is not always put into practice and India is no exception. Despite the existence of Constitution remedies, Violation of human rights now has been taking place in almost every part of the country. Police atrocities are a common feature of Indian scenario. Some of the common features of human rights violations are the torture of the arrested persons, the disappearances of the suspects allegedly in the police custody, deaths in fake encounters and at police stations, and under-trials detained in jails for years without trials.

Among all these worst forms of human rights violations, custodial torture has become a serious and alarming problem in India. Brutal atrocities perpetuated by the police, jail authorities, and other law enforcing agencies on the suspects/ accused persons are menacingly on the increase day by day. The State and the police remain in worrying denial. Torture in police custody remains a widespread and systematic practice in India. The methods as well as the equipments used by the

Police to torture the accused are brutally violent. The inhuman and lethal custodial torture, most of the times, result in custodial deaths, where the accused dies in the police lock up, while reaching to the hospital or even after reaching the hospital.

The political and Extra-judicial killings by government forces have certain common features. They are committed outside the judicial procedure and in violation of national laws and international standards forbidding the arbitrary deprivation of life. They are unlawful and deliberate. This distinguishes them from accidental killings and from deaths resulting from the use of reasonable force in law enforcement. Indian security forces have been responsible for a number of custodial killings that they later claimed occurred during an "armed encounter." Enforced disappearances in India have often begun with illegal detention. In the majority of cases, security forces abduct the victims in front of witnesses, often family members. Security forces do not officially acknowledge detentions. The family members are not provided any information regarding the causes of illegal detention and whereabouts of the victims. The persons arrested and detained are not presented before magistrate within 24 hours, as required by the law. In many cases, security forces extra-judicially execute victims and dispose off their bodies without acknowledging the deaths or informing family members of the whereabouts of the remains and residues of the deceased.

The prisons in India have proved to be the places where irregularities, inequality, harassment and torture are common and part of the routine happenings. Prison conditions in India are harsh, life-threatening and do not meet with international standards. Prisons are severely overcrowded and the basic requirements such as hygienic food and medical care, bedding, sanitation are inadequate. The Indian prisons do not even depict the encouraging picture in the way of developing a healthy atmosphere for the human rights. The prisons are over crowded; often have dirt floors, no furnishings and offer poor quality food. The use of handcuffs and fetters is common. The required basic infrastructure is not available in the prisons.

Today, the reported crime against women indicates that cruelty to women, molestation, rape, abetment to suicide, all are increasing year after year. India has an elaborate system of laws to protect the rights of women, including the Equal Remuneration Act, the Prevention of Immoral Traffic Act, the Sati prevention Act, Dowry Prohibition Act. However, the Government often is unable to enforce these laws, especially in rural areas where traditions and rituals are deeply rooted. Female bondage and forced prostitution are widespread in parts Indian society. Crimes against women- including molestation, rape, kidnapping, sexual harassment and killing of brides for dowry- has been increasing, in spite of declining. Female Foeticide has been a common practice in India since centuries. Indian census has always shown a gendered imbalance. This marked gap between boys and girls which has nationwide implications is the result of decisions made at the most local level- the family. It is a matter to be anxious that Sex selective abortion cases have become a significant social phenomenon in several parts of India. It transcends all castes, class and communities and even in the North South dichotomy. The girl children become target of attack even before they are born.

Child labour is socially condemned and legally prohibited in most parts of the world. India has the largest child labour force in the world. The Government does not provide compulsory, free and universal education to the children in India. Approximately, only 59 percent children between the ages of 5 and 14 attend school. India has earned the dubious distinction of having the world's largest child labour population with 5.5 per cent share of the world's total child population as child labour. According to U.N. estimates, of every five working children, one is from India. The largest number of child labourers in the country was found to be in Andhra Pradesh, Madhya Pradesh, Uttar Pradesh, Maharashtra, Karnataka, Bihar and Tamil Nadu followed by other states. Karnataka is a state where child labour prevails to a considerably large extent. Child abuse is another vicious reality which ruins the rights and liberties of the children.

Physical abuse, emotional abuse, sexual abuse, neglect are major forms of child abuse which are prevalent in India also. Crime against children, which include murder of children, infanticide, rape of children, kidnapping and abduction, foeticde, abetment of suicide, Exposure and abandonment, procuration of minor girls, buying and selling of girls for prostitution, child marriage, have been constantly increasing throughout country.

India's caste system is perhaps the world's longest surviving social hierarchy. Caste divisions in India dominate in housing, marriage, employment and general social interaction-divisions that are reinforced through the practice and threat of social ostracism, economic boycotts, and physical violence. India has consistently cited its numerous legislations and government policies as a measure of compliance with its obligations to end caste-based discrimination, choosing to ignore its failure to implement these measures which has resulted in continued and sometimes enhanced, brutalities against Dalits. Despite the fact that "untouchability" was abolished under India's constitution in 1950, the practice of "untouchability"-the imposition of social disabilities on persons by reason of their birth in certain castes- remains very much a part of rural India. Most Dalits continue to live in extreme poverty, without land or opportunities for better employment or education. Dalits throughout the country also suffer in many instances from de facto disenfranchisement. Human rights violations and crimes against Dalits have been increasing day by day. Undoubtedly, the rights of the SCs are violated in every sphere of their life and there are several types of the crimes committed against them which make their life miserable. Some major categories of crime against SCs include murder of SCs, rape of SC women, kidnapping and abduction, incidents of arson, hurt and deliberate atrocities against SCs. The SCs living in urban areas, particularly who are literate and/or working as government employees due to privileged reservation to them, are the least targets of these type of inhuman and lethal crimes. But the SCs living in rural, backward or distinct areas are the soft targets of these crimes. Every year thousands of SCs become the victims of these crimes which make their condition most of the times physically handicapped, socially more deprived, economically shoddier, and mentally stressed.

In recent decades, communal tensions and religion based politics have become prominent. Although India is generally known for religious pluralism, the Hindutva ideology propagates that India belongs to be Hindus and the Christians and Muslims are 'aliens', and not the natives of India. Some rigid and bigot groups belonging to that orthodox Hindu ideology portray violence against Muslim and Christians as a form of self-defense against invaders. In recent years, there has been a sharp increase in violent attacks on Christians in India. In the past several years, however, Christians have become the soft target of a campaign of violence and propaganda orchestrated by Hindu nationalist groups attempting to stem the tide of defecting low-caste and tribal voters. The intolerance of orthodox and bigot Hindu communal groups for the Muslims has led to several major incidences of religious violence such as Bombay riots, 1993 Bombay bombings, Ghodhra Train Burning and 2002 Gujarat violence. Hindus occupy more than 82 percent of the total population in India. It does not mean that Hindus are only accused of the violations against the religious minorities, but they usually become the victims of the atrocities and violence by other religious communities, in the regions where they are in minority.

To sum up, it can be said that India presents an ideal, holistic, and a universally acknowledged theory of human rights. The movement for the promotion and protection of human rights in India has been found to be existing since ancient times. After Independence, the constitution formulated by India has guaranteed all civil, legal, political, social, economic, cultural and religious rights of all its citizens. But while observing the actual practice of human rights, a distressing and miserable state of human rights appears to be restraining the ideals of the theory of human rights. There are abundant of causes, of the remorseful practice of human rights. But primarily, the lack of the required awareness among common masses about their human rights is the root cause of the despondent status of human rights. Unfortunately the civil society in India has not yet succeeded to launch a nation-wide human rights movement initiating from the grass-root level to make the common Indians know about their human rights and make them mobilized for the protection of their human rights. Secondly the colonial mind set of the common masses as well as the administrative authorities is also responsible for the severe violation of human rights in India. The people still acknowledge the police authorities and other administrative officials as those supreme powers which are beyond the law and their illegitimate acts, causing a ruthless violation of human rights cannot be challenged. Moreover, the administrative authorities themselves have not abandoned their colonial attitude and are not acknowledging their legitimate obligations to serve for the welfare of the people.

# Index

## M

T